utsa
memorial
fund

in memory
of

Tommy Maurer

from a gift
to utsa
by

*Nelda and Jim
Walls*

First American edition published in 1984 by
Peter Bedrick Books
125 East 23 Street
New York, NY 10010

Published by agreement with Muller, Blond & White Ltd, London

Library of Congress Cataloging in Publication Data
Main entry under title:

The Biographical dictionary of scientists, biologists.

Includes index.
1. Biologists — Biography. I. Abbott, David, 1937-
QH26.B54   1984   574'.092'2   [B]   84-10972
ISBN 0-911745-82-3

Manufactured in the United States of America
Distributed in the USA by Harper & Row
and in Canada by Book Center, Montreal

THE BIOGRAPHICAL DICTIONARY OF SCIENTISTS

Biologists

General Editor
David Abbott PhD

PETER BEDRICK BOOKS
New York

First American edition published in 1984 by
Peter Bedrick Books
125 East 23 Street
New York, NY 10010

Published by agreement with Muller, Blond & White Ltd, London

Library of Congress Cataloging in Publication Data
Main entry under title:

The Biographical dictionary of scientists, biologists.

  Includes index.
  1. Biologists — Biography. I. Abbott, David, 1937-
QH26.B54   1984   574'.092'2   [B]   84-10972
ISBN 0-911745-82-3

Manufactured in the United States of America
Distributed in the USA by Harper & Row
and in Canada by Book Center, Montreal

Biologists

General Editor
David Abbott PhD

PETER BEDRICK BOOKS
New York

Contents

Acknowledgements

Many people are involved in the creation of a major new series of reference books. The General Editor and the publishers are grateful to all of them and wish to thank particularly the contributing authors: Jim Bailey; Mary Basham; Alan Bishop; William Cooksey; David Cowey; Richard Gulliver; Ian Harvey; Robert Mortimer; Valerie Neal; Jon and Lucia Osborne; Helen Rapson and Mary Sanders. Our thanks are also due to the contributing consultants: Lorraine Ferguson and Nicolas Law; to Bull Publishing Consultants Ltd, whose experience in the development of reference books has made a significant contribution to the series: John Clark; Martyn Page and Sandy Shepherd; and to Mick Saunders for his artwork.

Historical introduction

Like so much else, the systematic study of living things began with the Greeks. Earlier cultures such as those in Egypt and Babylon in the Near East, and the early Indian and Chinese civilizations in Asia, had their own approaches to the study of Nature and its products. But it was the Greeks who fostered the attitudes of mind and identified the basic biological problems and methods from which modern biology has grown. Enquiry begun by Greek philosophers such as Alcmaeon (*b. c.* 535 BC) and Empedocles (*c.* 492–*c.* 432 BC) culminated in the biological work of Aristotle (384–323 BC) and the medical writings of Hippocrates (*c.* 460–377 BC) and his followers.

Natural philosophy

Aristotle was an original thinker of enormous power and energy who wrote on physics, cosmology, logic, ethics, politics and many other branches of knowledge. He also wrote several biological works which laid the foundations for comparative anatomy, taxonomy (classification) and embryology. He was particularly fascinated by sea creatures, many of which he dissected as well as studying in their natural habitats. Aristotle's approach to anatomy was functional: he believed that questions about structure and function always go together and that each biological part has its own special uses. Nature, he insisted, does nothing in vain. He therefore thought it legitimate to enquire about the ultimate purposes of things. This teleological approach has persisted in biological work until the twentieth century. In addition, Aristotle studied reproduction and embryological development, and he established many criteria by which animals could be classified. He believed that animals could be placed on a vertical, hierarchical scale ("scale of being"), extending from man down through quadrupeds, birds, snakes and fishes to insects, molluscs and sponges. Hierarchical thinking (as reflected in the terms "higher" and "lower" organisms) is still present in biology. One of Aristotle's pupils, Theophrastus (*c.* 372–287 BC), founded for botany many of the fundamentals that Aristotle had established for zoology.

What Aristotle achieved for biology, Hippocrates and his followers contributed for medicine: they established a naturalistic framework for thinking about health and disease. Unlike earlier priests and doctors, they did not regard illness as the result of sin, or as a divine punishment for misdeeds. They were keen observers whose most influential explanatory framework saw disease as the result of an imbalance in one of the four physiologically active humours (blood, phlegm, black bile and yellow bile). The humours were schematically related to the four elements (earth, air, fire and water) of Greek natural philosophy. Each person was supposed to have his or her own dominant humour, although different humours tended to predominate at different times of life (such as youth and old age) or seasons of the year. The therapy of Hippocrates aimed at restoring the ideal balance, through diet, drugs, exercise, change or life style, and so on.

Galen's influence on medicine

After the classical period of Greek thought, the most important biomedical thinker was Galen (*c.* AD 129–*c.* 199), who combined Hippocratic humoralism with Aristotle's tendency to think about the ultimate purposes of the parts of the body. Galen should not be blamed for the fact that later doctors thought that he had discovered everything, so that they had no need to look at biology and medicine for themselves. In fact, Galen was a shrewd anatomist and the most brilliant experimental physiologist of antiquity. For most of that time, human dissection was prohibited and Galen learnt his anatomy from other animals such as pigs, elephants and apes. It took more than a thousand years before it was discovered that some of the structures which he had accurately described in animals (such as the five-lobed liver and the rete mirabile network of veins in the brain) were not present in the human body. Like that of Aristotle, Galen's anatomy was functional, and often his tendency to speculate went further than sound observation would have permitted, as when he postulated invisible pores in the septum of the heart which were supposed to allow some blood to seep from the right ventricle to the left.

Following Galen's death at the end of the second century and the collapse of the Roman Empire, biology and medicine remained stagnant for a thousand years. Most Classical writings

1

were lost to the European West, to be preserved and extended in Constantinople and other parts of the Islamic Empire. From the twelfth century these texts began to be rediscovered in southern Europe - particularly in Italy, where universities were also established. For a while scholars were content merely to translate and comment on the works of men such as Aristotle and Galen, but eventually an independent spirit of enquiry arose in European biology and medicine. Human dissections were routinely performed from the fourteenth century and anatomy emerged as a mature science from the fervent activity of Andreas Vesalius (1514-1564), whose *De humani corporis fabrica* (1543; *On the Fabric of the Human Body*) is one of the masterpieces of the Scientific Revolution. His achievement was to examine the body itself rather than relying simply on Galen; the illustrations in his work are simultaneously objects of scientific originality and of artistic beauty. The rediscovery of the beauty of the human body by Renaissance artists encouraged the study of anatomy by geniuses such as Leonardo da Vinci (1452-1519). Shortly afterwards, William Harvey (1578-1657) discovered the circulation of the blood and established physiology on a scientific footing. His little book *De Motu Cordis* (1628; *On the Motion of the Heart*) was the first great work on experimental physiology since the time of Galen. The eccentric wandering doctor Paracelsus (1493-1541) had also deliberately set aside the teachings of Galen and other Ancients in favour of a fresh approach to Nature and medicine and to the search for new remedies for disease.

The Age of Discovery

While these achievements were happening in medicine, anatomy and physiology, other areas of biology were not stagnating. Voyages of exploration alerted naturalists to the existence of many new kinds of plants and animals and encouraged them to establish sound principles of classification, to create order out of the apparently haphazard profusion of Nature. Zoological and botanical gardens began to be established so that the curious could view wonderful new creatures like the rhinoceros and the giraffe. And just as the Great World (Macrocosm) was revealing plants and animals unknown in Europe only a short time before, so the invention of the microscope in the seventeenth century gave scientists the opportunity of exploring the secrets of the Little World (Microcosm). The microscope permitted Anton van Leeuwenhoek (1632-1723) to see bacteria, protozoa and other tiny organisms; it enabled Robert Hooke (1635-1703) to observe in a thin slice of cork regular structures

which he called "cells". And it aided Marcello Malpighi (1628-1664) to complete the circle of Harvey's concept of the circulation of the blood by first seeing it flowing through capillaries, the tiny vessels that connect the arterial and venous systems. Many of these microscopical discoveries were communicated to the Royal Society of London, one of several scientific societies established during the mid-seventeenth century.

The full potential of the microscope as a biological tool had to wait for technical improvements effected in the early nineteenth century. But it also led scientists along some blind alleys of theory. Observations of sperm "swimming" in seminal fluid provided some presumed evidence for a theory that was much debated during the eighteenth century, concerning the nature of embryological development. Aristotle had thought that the body's organs (heart, liver, stomach and so on) only gradually appear once conception has initiated the growth of the embryo. Later scientists, including William Harvey, extended Aristotle's theory with new observations. But now the visualization of moving sperm suggested that some miniature, but fully formed organism was already present in the reproductive fluids of the male or female. The tiny "homunculi" were thought to be stimulated to growth by fertilization. If the homunculus was always there, it followed that its own reproductive parts contained all of its future offspring, which in turn contained its future offspring and so on, back to Adam and Eve (depending on whether the male or the female was postulated as the carrier). This doctrine, called preformationalism, was held by most eighteenth-century biologists, including Albrecht von Haller (1708-1777) and Lazzaro Spallanzani (1729-1799), two of the century's greatest scientists. Both men, like virtually all scientists of the period, were devout Christians, and preformationalism did not conflict with their belief that God established regular, uniform laws which governed the development and functions of living things. They did not believe that inert matter could join together by accident to make a living organism. They rejected, for instance, the possibility of spontaneous generation, and Spallanzani devised some ingenious experiments designed to show that maggots found in rotting meat or the teeming life discoverable after jars of water are left to stand did not spontaneously generate. Haller, Spallanzani, John Hunter (1728-1793) and most other great eighteenth-century experimentalists held that the actions of living things could not be understood simply in terms of the laws of physics and chemistry. They were Vitalists, who believed that unique characteristics separated living from non-living matter.

Man's special attributes were often ascribed to the soul, and lower animals and plants were thought to possess more primitive animal and vegetable souls which gave them basic biological capacities such as reproduction, digestion, movement and so on.

Taxonomy and classification

Experimental biology was well established in the eighteenth century; another great area of eighteenth-century activity was classification. Again inspired by Aristotle, and drawing on the work of previous biologists such as John Ray (1627-1705), the Swedish botanist Carolus Linnaeus (1707-1778) spent a lifetime trying to bring order to the ever increasing number of plants and animals uncovered by continued exploration of the earth and its oceans. His *Systema Naturae* (1735; *System of Nature*) was the first of many books in which he elaborated a philosophy of taxonomy and established the convention of binomial nomenclature still followed today. In this convention, all organisms are identified by their genus and species; thus man in the Linnean system is *Homo sapiens*. Depending on the nature of the characteristics examined, however, plants and animals could be placed in a variety of groups, ranging from the kingdom at the highest level through phyla, classes, orders and families and so on beyond the species to the variety and, finally, the individual. Naturalists had traditionally accepted that the species was the most significant taxonomic category, Christian doctrine generally holding that God had specially created each individual species. It was also assumed that the number of species existing was fixed during the Creation, as described in the Book of Genesis – no new species having been created and none becoming extinct. Linnaeus, however, believed that God had created genera and that it was possible that new species had emerged during the time since the original Creation.

Palaeontology and evolution

Some eighteenth-century naturalists such as Georges Buffon (1707-1788) began to suggest that the earth and its inhabitants were far older than the 6,000 or so years inferred from the Bible. General acceptance of a vastly increased age of the earth, and of the reality of biological extinction, awaited the work of early nineteenth-century scientists such as Georges Cuvier (1769-1832), whose reconstructions of the fossil remains of large vertebrates like the mastodon and dinosaurs found in the Paris basin and elsewhere so stirred both the popular and scientific imaginations of his day. Despite Cuvier's work on the existence of life on earth for perhaps millions of years, he firmly opposed the notion that these extinct creatures might be the ancestors of animals alive today. Rather he believed that the extent to which any species might change (variability) was fixed and that species themselves could not change much over time. His contemporary and scientific opponent, Jean Baptiste Lamarck (1744-1829), argued however that species do change over time. He insisted that species never become extinct; instead they are capable of change as new environmental conditions and new needs arise. According to this argument, the ancestors of the giraffe need not have had such a long neck, which instead might have slowly developed as earlier giraffe-like creatures stretched their necks to feed on higher leaves. Lamarck believed that physical characteristics and habits acquired after birth could – particularly if repeated from generation to generation – become inherited and thus inborn in the organism's offspring. We still call the doctrine of the inheritance of acquired characteristics "Lamarckianism", although most naturalists before Lamarck had already believed it. It continued to be generally accepted (for instance, by Charles Darwin) until late in the nineteenth century.

The debates between Cuvier and Lamarck were part of the new possibilities opened up by the revolution in thinking about the age of the earth and of life on it. During the same fertile period, the systematic use of improved microscopes revolutionized the way in which biologists conceived organisms. In the closing years of the eighteenth century a French pathologist named Xavier Bichat (1771-1802), aided only with a hand lens, developed the idea that organs such as the heart and liver are not the ultimate functional units of animals. He postulated that the body can be divided into different kinds of tissues (such as nervous, fibrous, serous and muscular tissue) which make up the organs. Increasingly, biologists and doctors began thinking in terms of smaller functional units, and microscopists such as Robert Brown (1773-1858) began noticing regular structures within these units, which we now recognize as cells. Brown called attention to the nucleus in the cells of plants in 1831 and by the end of the decade two German scientists, Matthias Schleiden (1804-1881) and Theodor Schwann (1810-1882) systematically developed the idea that all plants and animals are composed of cells. The cell theory was quickly established for adult organisms, but in certain situations – such as the earliest stages of embryological development or in the appearance of "pus" cells in tissues after inflammation or injury – it appeared that new cells were actually crystallized out of an amorphous fluid which Schwann called the "blastema". The notion of continuity of cells was enlarged upon by the pathologist Rudolf Virchow (1821–1902), who summarized it in his famous slogan "All cells from cells". The cell theory gave biologists and physicians a new insight into the architecture and functions of the body in health and disease.

Micro-organisms and disease

Concern with one-celled organisms also lay behind the work of Louis Pasteur (1822–1895), which helped to establish the germ theory of disease. Pasteur trained as a chemist, but his researches into everyday processes such as the souring of milk and the fermentation of beer and wine opened for him a new understanding of the importance of yeast, bacteria and other micro-organisms in our daily lives. It was Pasteur who finally convinced scientists that animals do not spontaneously generate on rotting meat or in infusions of straw; our skin, the air and everything we come into contact with can be a source of these tiny creatures. After reading about Pasteur's work Joseph Lister (1827–1912) first conceived the idea that by keeping away these germs (as they were eventually called) from the wounds made during surgical operations, healing would be much faster and post-operative infection would be much less common. When in 1867 Lister published the first results using his new technique, antiseptic surgery was born. He spent much time developing the methods, which were taken up by other surgeons who soon realized that it was better to prevent infection altogether (asepsis) by carefully sterilizing their hands, instruments and dressings. By the time Lister died, he was world famous and surgeons were performing operations that would have been impossible without his work.

After Lister drew attention to the importance of Pasteur's discoveries for medicine and surgery, Pasteur himself showed the way in which germs cause not only wound infections, but also many diseases. He first studied a disease of silkworms which was threatening the French silk industry; he then turned his attention to other diseases of farm animals and human beings. In the course of this research, he discovered that under certain conditions an organism could be grown which, instead of causing a disease, actually prevented it. He publicly demonstrated these discoveries for anthrax, then a common disease of sheep, goats and cattle which sometimes also affected human beings. He proposed to call this process of protection vaccination, in honour of Edward Jenner (1749–1823), who in 1796 had shown how inoculating a person with cowpox (vaccinia) can protect against the deadly smallpox. Pasteur's most dramatic success came with a vaccine against rabies, a much-dreaded disease occasionally contracted after a bite from an animal infected with rabies.

By the 1870s, other scientists were investigating the role played by germs in causing disease. Perhaps the most important of them was Robert Koch (1843–1910), who devised many key techniques for growing and studying bacteria, and who showed that tuberculosis and cholera – prevalent diseases of the time – were caused by bacteria. Immunology, the study of the body's natural defence mechanisms against invasion by foreign cells, was pioneered by another German, Paul Ehrlich (1854–1915), who also began looking for drugs that would kill disease-causing organisms without being too dangerous for the patient. His first success, a drug named Salvarsan, was effective in the treatment of syphilis. Ehrlich's hopes in this area were not fully realized immediately, and it was not until the 1930s that the synthetic sulfa drugs, also effective against some bacterial diseases, were developed by Gerhard Domagk (1895–1964) and others. Slightly earlier Alexander Fleming (1881–1955) had noticed that a mould called *Penicillium* inhibited the growth of bacteria on cultures. Fleming's observation was investigated during World War II by Howard Florey (1898–1968) and Ernst Chain (1906–1979), and since then many other antibiotics have been discovered or synthesized. But antibiotics are not effective against diseases caused by viruses; such infections can, however, often be prevented using vaccines. An example is poliomyelitis, vaccines against which were developed in the 1950s by Albert Sabin (1906–   ) and Jonas Salk (1914–   ).

Evolution and genetics

Many of these advances in modern medical science are a direct continuation of discoveries made in the nineteenth century, although of course we now know much more about bacteria and other pathogenic micro-organisms than did Pasteur and Koch. Another nineteenth-century discovery which is still being intensively investigated is evolution. Charles Darwin (1809–1882 was not the first to suggest that biological species can change over time, but his book *The Origin of Species* (1859) first presented the idea in a scientifically plausible form. As a young man, Darwin spent five years (1831–1836) on HMS *Beagle*, during which he studied fossils, animals and geology in many parts of the world, particularly in South America. By 1837 he had come to believe the fact of evolution; in 1838 he hit upon its mechanism: natural selection. This principle makes use of the fact that organisms produce more offspring than can survive to maturity. In this struggle for existence, those offspring with characteristics best suited to their particular environment will tend to survive. In this way, Nature can work on the normal variation which plants and animals show and, under changing environmental conditions, significant change can occur through selective survival.

Darwin knew that his ideas would be controversial so he initially imparted them to only a few close friends, such as the geologist Charles Lyell (1797-1875) and the botanist Joseph Hooker (1817-1911). For 20 years he continued quietly to collect evidence favouring the notion of evolution by natural selection, until in 1858 he was surprised to receive a short essay from Alfred Russel Wallace (1823-1913), then in Malaya, perfectly describing natural selection. Friends arranged a joint Darwin-Wallace publication, and then Darwin abandoned a larger book he was writing on the subject to prepare instead *The Origin of Species*. In it he marshalled evidence from many sources, including palaeontology, embryology, geographical distribution, ecology (a word coined only later) and hereditary variation. Darwin did not have a very clear idea of how variations occur, but his work convinced a number of scientists, including Thomas Huxley (1825-1895), Ernst Haeckel (1834-1919) and Francis Galton (1822-1911), Darwin's cousin. Huxley became Darwin's chief publicist in Britain, Haeckel championed Darwin's ideas in Germany, and Galton quietly absorbed the evolutionary perspective into his own work in psychology, physical anthropology and the use of statistics and other forms of mathematics in the life sciences.

Meanwhile, unknown to Darwin (and largely unrecognized during his lifetime), a monk named Gregor Mendel (1822-1884) was elucidating the laws of modern genetics through his studies of inheritance patterns in pea plants and other common organisms. Mendel studied characteristics that were inherited as a unit; this enabled scientists to understand such phenomena as dominance and recessiveness in these units, called genes in 1909 by the Danish biologist W.L. Johannsen (1859-1927). By 1900, when Hugo de Vries (1848-1935), William Bateson (1861-1926) and others were recognizing the importance of Mendel's pioneering work, much more was known about the microscopic appearances of cells both during adult division (mitosis) and reduction division (meiosis). In addition, August Weismann (1834-1914) had developed notions of the continuity of the inherited material (which he called the "germ plasm") from generation to generation, thus suggesting that acquired characteristics are not inherited. Only a few scientists in the twentieth century, such as the Soviet botanist Trofim Lysenko (1898-1976), have continued to believe in Lamarckianism, for modern genetics has accumulated overwhelming evidence that characteristics such as the loss of an arm or internal muscular development do not change the make-up of reproductive cells.

It is now believed that new inheritable variations occur when genes mutate. The study of this process and of the factors (such as X-rays and certain chemicals) that can make the occurrence of mutations likely was pioneered by geneticists such as Thomas Hunt Morgan (1866-1945) and Herman Muller (1890-1967). They did much of their work with fruit flies (*Drosophila*). While these and other scientists were showing that genes are located on chromosomes - strands of dark-staining material in the nuclei of cells - other researchers were trying to determine the exact nature of the hereditary substance itself. Originally it was thought to be a protein, but in 1953 Francis Crick (1916-   ) and James Watson (1928-   ) were able to show that it is dioxyribonucleic acid (DNA). Their work was an early triumph of molecular biology, a branch of the science that has grown enormously since the 1950s. Scientists now know a great deal about how DNA works. Among those who have contributed are George Beadle (1903-   ), Edward Tatum (1909-1975), Jacques Monod (1910-1976), Joshua Lederberg (1925-   ) and Maurice Wilkins (1916-   ). Molecular biologists and chemists have also been concerned with determining the structures of many other large biological molecules, such as the muscle protein myoglobin by John Kendrew (1917-   ) and Max Perutz (1914-   ). In their researches they often have to interpret the diffraction patterns produced when X-rays pass through these complex molecules, a technique pioneered by Dorothy Hodgkin (1910-   ), one of the many women who have contributed to modern science.

Modern biological sciences

Molecular biology is only one of several new biological disciplines to be developed during the past century. The oldest of these, biochemistry, was established in Britain by Frederick Gowland Hopkins (1861-1947) who, along with Casimir Funk (1884-1967) and Elmer McCollum (1879-1967), is remembered for his fundamental work in the discovery of vitamins, substances that help to regulate many complex bodily processes. Other biochemists such as Carl Cori (1896-   ) and his wife Gerty Cori (1896-1957) have studied the ways in which organisms make use of the energy gained when food is broken down. Many of these internal processes are also moderated by the action of hormones, one important example of which is insulin, discovered in the 1920s by Frederick Banting (1891-1941) and others.

Modern biologists also often use physics in their work, and biophysics is now an important discipline in its own right. Archibald Hill (1886-1977) and Otto Meyerhof (1884-1951) pioneered in this area with their work on the release of heat when muscles contract. More recently, Bernhard Katz (1911-   ) has used biophysical techniques in studying the events at the junctions between muscles and nerves, and at the junctions between pairs of nerves (synapses). The events at synapses are initiated by the release of chemical substances such as adrenaline and acetylcholine, as was demonstrated by Henry Dale (1875-1968) and Otto Loewi (1873-1961). The way in which nerve impulses move along the nerve axon has been investigated by Alan Hodgkin (1914-   ) and Andrew Huxley (1917-   ). For this work, they made use of the giant axon of the squid, an experimental preparation whose importance for biology was first shown by John Young (1907-   ). The complicated way in which the nervous system operates as a whole was first rigorously investigated by Charles Sherrington (1857-1952).

Another area of fundamental importance in modern biology and medicine is immunology. For instance, the discovery by Karl Landsteiner (1868-1943) of the major human blood group system (A, B and O) permitted safe blood transfusions. The development of the immune system – and the way in which the body recognizes foreign substances ("self" and "not-self") – has been investigated by such scientists as Peter Medawar (1915-   ) and Frank Burnet (1899-   ). Much of this knowledge has been important to transplant surgery, pioneered for kidneys by Roy Calne (1930-   ) and for hearts by Christiaan Barnard (1922-   ).

These are just some of the many areas of important biological research in the twentieth century. There are far more biologists at work today than ever before and, like other branches of science, biology is constantly expanding and changing. Increasingly, new developments result from a team effort, rather than from the work of an individual scientist. Some areas of research – such as biological warfare and genetic engineering – are controversial. Some biomedical achievements, such as pesticides, antibiotics, vaccines and a better knowledge of disease prevention, have contributed to the potential problems of over-population. Science is a human creation, and as such can be used for good or evil. As the philosopher Francis Bacon said: "Knowledge is power". A knowledge of biology is necessary for everyone, not only because it has much to teach us about ourselves, but also because biology and the other sciences are increasingly significant aspects of modern life.

A

Addison, Thomas (*1793-1860*), was a British physician and endocrinologist who was the first to correlate a collection of symptoms with pathological changes in an endocrine gland. He described a metabolic disorder caused by a deficiency in the secretion of hormones from the adrenal glands (caused, in turn, by atrophy of the adrenal cortex), a condition now called Addison's disease. He is also known for his discovery of what is now called pernicious (or Addison's) anaemia.

Addison was born in April 1793 in Longbenton, Northumberland, and studied medicine at Edinburgh University, graduating in 1815. He then moved to London, where he was appointed a surgeon at the Lock Hospital. He also studied dermatology under Thomas Bateman (1778-1821) during his first years in London. In about 1820 Addison entered Guy's Hospital as a student, despite being a fully qualified physician, and remained there in various positions for the rest of his life, becoming Assistant Physician in 1824, Lecturer in Materia Medica in 1827, and a full Physician in 1837. While at Guy's Hospital, Addison collaborated with Richard Bright, who also made important contributions to medicine. Addison's mental health deteriorated and he committed suicide on 29 June 1860 in Brighton, Sussex.

Addison gave a preliminary account of the condition now known as Addison's disease in 1849 in a paper entitled "On anaemia: Disease of the suprarenal capsules", which he read to the South London Medical Society. The paper went unnoticed, despite which Addison extended his original account in *On the Constitutional and Local Effects of Disease of the Suprarenal Capsules* (1855), in which he gave a full description of Addison's disease (characterized by abnormal darkening of the skin, progressive anaemia, weakness, intestinal disturbances and weight loss) and differentiated it from pernicious anaemia (characterized by anaemia, intestinal disturbances, weakness, and tingling and numbness in the extremities). He also pointed out that Addison's disease is caused by atrophy of the suprarenal capsules (later called the adrenal glands). (Pernicious anaemia is caused by failure of the stomach's secretion of intrinsic factor which, in turn, causes inadequate absorption of vitamin B_{12}.)

Addison also described xanthoma, (flat, soft spots that appear on the skin, usually on the eyelids) and wrote about other skin diseases, tuberculosis, pneumonia and the anatomy of the lung. In collaboration with John Morgan (1797-1847), he wrote *An Essay on the Operation of Poisonous Agents Upon the Living Body* (1829), the first book on this subject to be published in English. And in 1839 appeared the first volume of *Elements of the Practice of Medicine*, written by Addison and Richard Bright. In this volume - which was, in fact, written almost entirely by Addison, Bright was to have been the principal contributor to the second volume, which was never published - Addison gave the first full description of appendicitis.

Adler, Alfred (*1870-1937*), was an Austrian psychiatrist who broke away from the theories of Sigmund Freud, setting up the Individual Psychology Movement. He placed "inferiority feeling" at the centre of his theory of neuroses.

Adler was born in Vienna on 7 February 1870, the son of a corn merchant. He obtained his MD from the University of Vienna in 1895 and worked for two years as a physician at Vienna General Hospital. His interests soon turned towards mental disorders, and by 1902 he had made contact with Freud. He played a major part in the development of the psychoanalytical movement, and was President of the Vienna Psychoanalytical Society. But by 1907 he had shifted his theory away from Freud's emphasis on infantile sexuality towards power as the origin of neuroses; in 1911 Adler, and a number of others, left the Freudian circle and founded the Individual Psychology Movement. By the late 1920s Adler was making many trips to the United States, where he proved to be a popular lecturer; in 1927 he became a visiting professor at Columbia University. In 1935 he decided to make the United States his permanent home and he became Professor of Psychiatry at Long Island College of Medicine, New York. He died from a heart attack on 28 May 1937 in Aberdeen, Scotland, during a lecture tour.

The essence of Adler's theories differed from Freud's in that he thought that power not sex was the important factor in neurotic disorders. He popularized the term "inferiority feeling" - later changed to "complex" - and felt that much neurotic behaviour is a result of feelings of inadequacy or inferiority caused by, for instance, being the youngest in a family or being a child who is trying to compete in an adult world. In an attempt to overcome these inferiority feelings the patient overcompensates, often at the expense of normal social behaviour or, as Adler put it, "social interest". Thus, for example, a woman might feel inferior to men because of her sex and over-react by behaving in an aggressive, masculine way. Adler's belief led on to his idea that a person can realize this ambition alone, which has consequences on the way in which a psychiatrist helps a patient if help is needed. His impact was less forceful than those of Carl Jung or Freud, and even though his psychology made good sense it lacked adequate definition and rigour of method. Adler summarized his theories in *Practice and Theory of Individual Psychology* (1927).

Adler's more practical work included the setting up of a system of child guidance services in the schools in Vienna, which lasted until 1934, when they were closed by the Austrian Fascist government.

Adrian, Edgar Douglas, 1st Baron Adrian of Cambridge (*1889-1977*), was a British physiologist known for his experimental research in electrophysiology and, in particular, nerve impulses. He was one of the first scientists to study the variations in electrical potential of nerve impulses amplified by thermionic valve amplifiers, and was also one of the first to study the electrical activity of the brain. He shared the 1932 Nobel Prize in Physiology and Medicine with Charles Sherrington (1857-1952) for his work on neurons and their processes.

Adrian was born in London on 30 November 1889, the son of a lawyer. After attending Westminster School, he won a scholarship to Trinity College, Cambridge, where he studied natural sciences. During World War I he went to St Bartholomew's Hospital in London to study medicine, graduating in 1915 and then working on nerve injuries and shell shock (battle fatigue) at Queen's Square and later at the Connaught Military Hospital in Aldershot. Adrian was much in demand as a lecturer from 1919 - when he became a Cambridge University lecturer - especially on such subjects as sleep, dreams, hysteria and multiple sclerosis. From 1937 until 1951 he was Professor of Physiology at Cambridge. He was awarded the Order of Merit in 1942 and was President of the Royal Society from 1950 to 1955. In that same year he was raised to the peerage and took the barony of Cambridge. He was Master of Trinity College, Cambridge, from 1951 until he retired in 1965. He died in London on 4 August 1977.

In 1912 nothing was known about electrochemical transmission within the nervous system.

Adrian's most ambitious work in the pre-war years was to attempt to prove that the intensity of a nerve impulse at any point in a normal nerve is independent of the stimulus or of any change in intensity that may have occurred elsewhere.

The mechanism of muscular control was a subject of clinical interest in wartime, and Adrian studied and wrote on the electrical excitation of normal and denervated muscle. He showed that with normal muscle the time factor in excitation, known as the chronaxie, is very short and that it increases by a factor of one hundred in denervated muscle after the nerve endings have degenerated. With L.R. Yealland of Queen's Square he worked on the application of a method of treatment based on suggestion, re-education and discipline in cases of hysterical disorders such as mutism, deafness and paralysis of limbs.

Between 1925 and 1933 Adrian successfully recorded trains of nerve impulses travelling in single sensory or motor nerve fibres. This work was a turning point in the history of physiology. He began to use valve amplifiers and found that in a single nerve fibre the electrical impulse does not change with the nature or strength of the stimulus. He also discovered that some sense organs, such as those concerned with touch, rapidly adapt to a steady stimulus whereas others, such as muscle spindles, adapt slowly or not at all. His work at this time included the recording of optic nerve impulses in the conger eel, investigations of the action of light on frogs' eyes, and researching the problem of pain and the responses of animals to speech.

Between 1933 and 1946 he worked on the ways in which the nervous system generates rhythmic electrical activity. He was one of the first scientists to use extensively the recently devised electroencephalograph (EEG) - a system of recording brain waves - to study the electrical activity of the brain. This system has since proved an invaluable diagnostic aid - for example, in the diagnosis of epilepsy and the location of cerebral lesions. The last 20 years of his research life, from 1937 to 1959, were spent studying the sense of smell.

In 1932 Adrian published *The Mechanism of Nervous Action* and in 1947 *The Physical Background of Perception*, based on the Waynflete Lectures he gave in Oxford the preceding year.

Aristotle (*384-322* BC), was one of the most respected of learned men. He has structured Western thought more than any other philosopher and is regarded as the father of logic. He was a physician, and paved the way for empirical science with his ideas on the accumulation of knowledge.

He was born in 384 BC in Stagirus, a Greek

colony in Macedonia. The son of the court physician to the king of Macedonia, by tradition he inherited his father's medical knowledge. In 367 BC he was sent to the Academy of Plato in Athens, and became Plato's best pupil. In 348 BC, Aristotle left the Academy and travelled through the Greek empire for 12 years. It was on these travels that he began his research into natural history. In about 342 BC he was offered, and accepted, the position of tutor to the son of Philip II of Macedon, Alexander (later to become Alexander the Great). Three years later, Aristotle returned to Stagirus. In 335 BC he went back to Athens to resume his scientific studies and in the same year founded a rival university to the Academy of Plato - the Lyceum. When Alexander died in 323 BC, Aristotle left Athens because of anti-Macedonian feeling and went to Chalcis, where he died a year later of a stomach illness.

Aristotle was a painstaking observer, believing that Nature never created anything without a purpose. He examined more than 500 animals and arranged them like with like and in series of increasing complexity, foreshadowing modern schemes of classification. His investigations suggested to him that animals had increased in complexity throughout the ages, an idea of evolution such as that put forward by Darwin 2,200 years later. Aristotle's works suggest that he had first-hand knowledge of human anatomy in spite of the religious and ethical taboos of the time.

Although not an experimentalist, he believed that true knowledge could be obtained by observation and experience. His beliefs were not always right, however; for instance, he thought that the heart and not the brain was the centre of mental activity.

In the early years of the Roman Empire, Greek medical science was kept alive, but when Christianity gained popularity it was regarded as a heathen practice and Aristotle's teachings were forgotten. In the seventh century AD, however, as the Arab empire spread, the Arabs collected Aristotle's works and translated them into Arabic. In the tenth century, Constantine of Africa, a widely travelled doctor, translated the medical classics back from Arabic into Latin, and thus Aristotle's work returned to the West and was slowly revived in the following centuries. His books were revered as indisputable authority until the seventeenth century, when they became regarded as an obstacle to progress.

Aristotle's lectures were collected into 400 volumes which encompassed much of the knowledge of the time in science, politics, ethics and literature. Among his many scientific and philosophical treatises are the *Organon*, a collection of treatises on logic; the *Physica*, on natural science; the *Historia animalium*, a classification of animals; and *De incessu animalium*, on the progression of animals.

Attenborough, David Frederick (*1926-*), is a British naturalist, film-maker and author who is best known for his wildlife films, which have brought natural history to a wide general audience.

Attenborough was born on 8 May 1926. He was educated at Wyggeston Grammar School in Leicester and Clare College, Cambridge, where he read zoology. From 1947 to 1949 he did two years' military service in the Royal Navy, after which he became an editorial assistant in an educational publishers. In 1952 he joined the BBC Television Service as a trainee producer, then in 1954 he went on his first expedition, to West Africa. During the next 10 years he made annual trips to film and study wildlife and human cultures in remote parts of the world; these expeditions were recorded in the *Zoo Quest* series of television programmes and books. From 1965 to 1968 Attenborough was Controller of BBC2 and of the BBC Television Service, then from 1969 to 1972 he was Director of Television Programmes for the BBC and a member of its board of management. Despite the large amount of administrative work involved in these posts, he still managed to undertake several filming expeditions. His next major achievement was the television series *Life on Earth*, which was first shown in 1979. In this huge project, which took three years to complete, Attenborough attempted to outline the development of life on Earth - from its very beginnings to the present day - using plants and animals found today to illustrate this evolution. The series and its associated book (which also first appeared in 1979) met with great popular and critical acclaim and set new standards for the presentation of natural history to non-specialists.

Audubon, John James Laforest (*1785-1851*), was a French-born American ornithologist who painted intricately detailed studies of birds and animals. He was also an ardent conservationist.

Audubon was born at Les Cayes, Santo Domingo (now Haiti), on 26 April 1785. He was the illegitimate son of a French sea captain and a Creole woman who died soon after his birth. His father, who was also a planter, sent him back to France to his home near Nantes, where Audubon and his half-sister were taken in by the captain's wife who had no children of her own. The couple legally adopted him in 1794. The young Audubon acquired a deep interest for natural history, painting and music. He was educated locally and in Paris, where he had six months' tuition at the studio of the well-known painter Jacques Louis David. By 1803 young men in France were being conscripted for Napoleon's army, but the 18-year-old Audubon avoided the draft by making a timely emigration to the United States to take up the running of his father's properties near Philadelphia. In 1808 he married and opened a store in Louisville, Kentucky, but he was a casual and poor businessman, his time being so passionately absorbed by nature; he was even imprisoned for debt in 1819 and declared a bankrupt.

Despite his financial problems, Audubon maintained a successful marriage and travelled throughout the United States collecting and painting the wildlife around him, while his wife worked as a teacher and governess to help to support them. He also painted portraits and even street signs, and gave lessons in drawing and French. By 1825 he had compiled his beautiful set of bird paintings, but American publishers were not interested. The following year Audubon set sail for England, where the Havells engraved his plates which he published by subscription. His talent was lauded and he attracted much publicity by appearing in English society wearing the outlandish clothes so suitable for his travels in the wilds of America. Even so, he was elected a Fellow of the Royal Society in 1830. After 13 years in Britain he went back to the United States. He died in New York on 27 January 1851.

Before Audubon most painters of birds used stylized techniques; stuffed birds were often used as subjects. Audubon painted from life and his compositions were startling, his detail minute. *The Birds of America* was published in Britain in 87 parts between 1827 and 1838. On his return to the United States in 1839 he published a bound edition of the plates with additions. He illustrated *Viviparous Quadrupeds of North America* (1845–1848), compiling the text (1846–1854) with his sons and John Bachman. Audubon was one of the earliest naturalists to pioneer conservation, and the various Audubon societies of today are named in his honour.

Avery, Oswald Theodore (*1877-1955*), was a Canadian-born American bacteriologist whose work on transformation in bacteria established that DNA (deoxyribonucleic acid) is responsible for the transmission of heritable characteristics. He also did pioneering research in immunology – again working with bacteria – proving that carbohydrates play an important part in immunity. Avery's achievements gained him many honours, including election to the National Academy of Science in the United States and to the Royal Society of London.

Avery was born on 21 October 1877 in Halifax, Nova Scotia, the son of a clergyman, but spent most of his life in New York City, where he was taken by his father in 1887. After qualifying in medicine in 1904 at Columbia University, Avery spent a brief period as a clinical physician but soon moved to the Hoagland Laboratory in Brooklyn in order to research and lecture in bacteriology and immunology. In 1913 he transferred to the Rockefeller Institute Hospital in New York, where he remained until he retired in 1948. Avery died in Nashville, Tennessee, having moved there on his retirement.

Avery's work on transformation – a process by which heritable characteristics of one species are incorporated into another species – is generally considered to be his most important contribution and was stimulated by the research of F. Griffith, who in 1928 published the results of his studies on *Diplococcus pneumoniae*, a species of bacteria that causes pneumonia in mice. Griffith found that mice contracted pneumonia and died when they were injected with a mixture of an encapsulated strain of dead *Diplococcus pneumoniae* (living encapsulated bacteria are lethal to mice) and living, unencapsulated bacteria (which have no protective outer capsule to resist antibodies and therefore do not cause pneumonia), despite the fact that, separately, each of the mixture's components is harmless. From the corpses he then isolated virulent, living, encapsulated bacteria. These findings led Griffith to postulate that a transforming principle from the dead, encapsulated bacteria had caused capsule development in the living, unencapsulated bacteria, thereby making them virulent. Moreover, when these living bacteria reproduced, the offspring were encapsulated, suggesting that the transforming principle had become incorporated into their genetic constitution.

Initially, Avery dismissed Griffith's findings but when they were supported by later studies, Avery and his colleagues Colin MacLeod and Maclyn McCarthy began investigating the nature of the transforming principle. They started experimenting in the early 1940s, working on *Diplococcus pneumoniae*. They obtained a pure sample of the virulent, living, encapsulated bacteria which were killed by heat treatment. The bacteria's protein and polysaccharide (which makes up the capsule and is also found within the cells) were then removed and the remaining portion was added to living, unencapsulated pneumococcus. It was found that the progeny of these bacteria had capsules, so the active transforming principle still remained and was neither a protein nor a polysaccharide. Finally Avery extracted and purified the transforming principle and used various chemical, physical and biological techniques to identify it. His analysis proved conclusively that DNA was the transforming principle responsible for the development of polysaccharide capsules in the unencapsulated bacteria.

Avery's discovery (which he published in 1944) was extremely important because for the first time it had been proved that DNA controls the development of a cellular feature – in this case the polysaccharide capsule – and implicated DNA as the basic genetic material of the cell. Other researchers later confirmed that DNA controls the development of cellular features in different organisms, and also established that it is the fundamental molecule involved in heredity. Moreover, Avery's work stimulated interest in DNA, eventually leading to the determination of its structure and method of replication by Francis Crick and James Watson in the early 1950s.

Avery's early work also involved pneumococci, but was in the field of immunology. He demonstrated that pneumococci bacteria could be classified according to their immunological response to specific antibodies and that this immunological specificity is due to the particular polysaccharides that constitute the capsule of each bacterial type. This research established that polysaccharides play an important part in immunity and led to the development of sensitive diagnostic tests to identify the various types of pneumococcus bacteria.

B

Banks, Joseph (*1743–1820*), was a British naturalist who, although making relatively few direct contributions to scientific knowledge himself, did much to promote science, both in Britain and internationally.

Banks was born on 13 February 1743 in London, the son of William Banks of Revesby Abbey in Lincolnshire. Born into a wealthy family, Banks was educated at Harrow and Eton public schools and then at Oxford University. At that time the university curriculum was biased towards the classics, but Banks was more interested in botany so he employed Israel Lyons (1739–1775), a botanist from Cambridge University, as a personal tutor in the subject. After graduating in 1763, Banks moved to London in order to meet other scientists. Meanwhile his father had died in 1761, leaving Banks a large fortune, which he inherited when he came of age in 1764. In 1776 he made his first voyage, to Labrador and Newfoundland, as naturalist on a fishery protection ship. He collected many plant specimens during

the trip and, on his return to England, was elected to the Royal Society of London.

In 1768 preparations were being made for an expedition to the southern hemisphere to observe the transit of Venus in 1769. Banks obtained the position of naturalist on the voyage and accompanied by several artists and an assistant botanist, Daniel Solander (1736–1782), set sail in the *Endeavour* – commanded by Captain James Cook – in 1768; Banks paid for his assistants and all the equipment he needed out of his own pocket, at a cost of about £10,000. After the astronomical observations had been completed (the transit was observed from Tahiti), the expedition proceeded on its second objective, to search for the large southern continent that was then thought to exist. During this part of the voyage the expedition explored the coasts of New Zealand and Australia. Banks' plant-collecting activities at the first landing place in Australia (near present-day Sydney) gave rise to the name of the area – Botany Bay. He also studied the Australian fauna, discovering that almost all of the mammals are marsupials, which are less highly developed (in evolutionary terms) than are the placental mammals found on other continents. The expedition returned to England in 1771 and Banks brought back a vast number of plant specimens, more than 800 of which were previously unknown. (Banks kept a journal of the expedition, part of which was published, although not until long after his death, but he did not write an account of his scientific findings on the voyage.) On his return, Banks found himself a celebrity and was summoned to Windsor Castle to give a personal account of his travels to King George III; this visit was the start of a lifelong friendship with the King, which helped Banks to establish many influential contacts.

In 1772 Banks went on his last expedition, to Iceland, where he studied geysers. In 1778 he was elected President of the Royal Society (perhaps because of his influence in high places), an office he held until his death 42 years later. As President, Banks re-established good relations between the Royal Society and the King, who had previously quarrelled with the Society over the issue of the best shape for the ends of lightning conductors. He also brought several wealthy patrons into the Society and helped to develop its international reputation.

As a result of the friendship between Banks and George III, the Royal Botanic Gardens at Kew – of which Banks was the honorary director – became a focus of botanical research. Banks sent plant collectors to many countries in an attempt to establish at Kew as many different species as possible. He also conceived of Kew as a major centre for the practical use of plants, to which end he initiated several important projects, including the introduction of the tea plant into India from its native China, and the transport of the breadfruit tree from Tahiti to the West Indies. This latter project, however, was initially unsuccessful because of the famous mutiny on the *Bounty*, which was carrying the breadfruit trees. At George III's request, Banks also played an active part in importing merino sheep into Britain from Spain; after initial difficulties, the breed was later successfully introduced into Australia.

Banks' voyage to Australia on the *Endeavour* stimulated a lifelong interest in the country's affairs, and he was instrumental in establishing the first colony at Botany Bay in 1788. Thereafter he greatly assisted the growth of the colony and was in regular correspondence with its various governors.

Banks was a generous patron who gave financial assistance to several talented young scientists, notably Robert Brown (1773-1858), who later became an eminent botanist although he is better known today as the discoverer of Brownian motion. Banks also made his large home in Soho Square, London, a renowned meeting place for scientists and prominent figures from other fields. In addition, his international prestige did much to promote the exchange of ideas among scientists in many countries. He also obtained safe passages for many scientists during the American War of Independence and during the Napoleonic Wars, and petitioned on behalf of scientists who had been captured.

Banks received many honours during his life, including a baronetcy in 1781 and membership of the Privy Council in 1797. When he died on 19 June 1820 in Isleworth, near London, he left an extensive natural history library and a collection of plants regarded as one of the most important in existence, both of which are now housed in the British Museum.

Banting, Frederick Grant (*1891-1941*), was a Canadian physiologist who discovered insulin, the hormone responsible for the regulation of the sugar content of the blood and an insufficiency of which results in the disease diabetes mellitus. For this achievement he was awarded the Nobel Prize in Physiology and Medicine in 1923, which he shared with the Scottish physiologist John Macleod (1876-1935).

Banting was born in Alliston, Ontario, on 14 November 1891, the son of a farmer. He went to the University of Toronto in 1910 to study for the ministry, but changed to medicine and obtained his medical degree in 1916. He served overseas as an officer in the Canadian Medical Corps during World War I, and was awarded the Military Cross for gallantry in 1918. After the war he held an appointment at the University of Western Ontario, but in 1921 returned to the University of Toronto to carry out research into diabetes. In 1930 the Banting and Best Department of Medical Research was opened at the University of Toronto, of which Banting became Director. He was knighted in 1934. While serving as a major in the Canadian Army Medical Corps in 1941 he was killed in an air crash at Gander, Newfoundland.

At the University of Western Ontario, Banting became interested in diabetes, a disease (often fatal at that time) characterized by a high level of blood sugar (glucose) and the appearance of glucose in the urine. In 1889 Mehring and Minkowski had shown that the pancreas was somehow involved in diabetes because the removal of the pancreas from a dog resulted in its death from the disease within a few weeks. Other workers had investigated the effect of tying off the pancreatic duct in rabbits, which resulted in atrophy of the pancreas apart from small patches of cells – the islets of Langerhans. The rabbits did not, however, develop the diuretic condition of sugar in the urine.

It had therefore been suggested that a hormone, called insulin (from the Latin for "island"), might be concerned in glucose metabolism and that its source might be the islets of Langerhans. But efforts to isolate the hormone from the pancreas failed because the digestive enzymes produced by the pancreas broke down the insulin when the gland was processed. In 1921 Banting went to discuss his ideas on the matter with John Macleod, the Chairman of the Physiology Department (and an expert on the metabolism of carbohydrates) at the University of Toronto. Macleod was unenthusiastic but agreed to find Banting a place for research in his laboratories.

Banting reasoned that if the pancreas were destroyed but the islets of Langerhans retained, the absence of digestive enzymes would allow them to isolate insulin. With Charles Best (1899-1978), one of his undergraduate students, he experimented on dogs. They put several of the animals into two groups; each dog in one group had the pancreatic duct tied, and those in the other group were depancreatized. After several weeks, they removed the degenerated pancreases from the dogs of the first group, extracted the glands with saline and injected the extract into the dogs of the second group, which by then had diabetes and were in poor condition. They took regular blood samples from the diabetic dogs and found that the sugar content dropped steadily as the condition of the dogs improved.

These results encouraged Banting. He obtained foetal pancreas material from an abattoir, thinking that it might contain more islet tissue. With his assistants he set about extracting an active product, but purification proved to be very difficult. Eventually reasonably pure insulin was produced and commercial production of the hormone started. By January 1922 it was ready for use in the Toronto General Hospital. The first patient was a 14-year-old diabetic boy who showed rapid improvement after treatment. They also discovered that the dose of insulin could be reduced by regulating the amount of carbohydrate in the patient's diet.

When Banting and Macleod were awarded the Nobel Prize for this work Banting, feeling strongly that Best had made a valuable contribution, divided his share of the money with him. Banting's discovery of insulin and his attempts to purify the crude material led eventually to the commercial production of insulin, which has saved the lives of many diabetics.

Barnard, Christiaan Neethling (*1922–*), is the South African cardiothoracic surgeon who performed the first human heart transplant, on 3 December 1967 at Groote Schuur Hospital in Cape Town.

Barnard was born on 8 November 1922 in Beaufort West, South Africa. He attended the local High School and then in 1940 went to the University of Cape Town, where he received his medical degree in 1946. After working in private practice from 1948 to 1951, he became Senior Resident Medical Officer at the City Hospital in Cape Town for two years. In 1953 Barnard was elected Registrar at Groote Schuur Hospital, later to be the place of his most important work. In 1956 he was awarded a scholarship to the University of Minnesota, Minneapolis; he returned to South Africa two years later, taking with him a heart-lung machine. He became Director of Surgical Research at Groote Schuur and the University of Cape Town, and in 1961 was made Head of Cardiothoracic Surgery.

Barnard's early research involved experiments with heart transplants in dogs. His success convinced him that similar operations could be performed on human patients. In December 1967 Denise Duvall, a 25-year-old girl, was critically injured in a road accident in Cape Town, and after it was established that her brain was irreparably damaged, permission was obtained for her heart to be donated for transplant purposes. The recipient was a man in his fifties, Louis Washkansky, whose heart – in Barnard's words – was "shattered and ruined".

X-ray motion pictures (angiograms) were taken of Washkansky's heart by injecting radio-opaque dye into each side of it using catheters inserted into the veins and arteries. These films were taken to prepare the surgical team for the operation on Washkansky. Once the donor heart had been removed, Barnard cut away part of it so that it would fit what remained of the recipient's heart. Two holes were made in the donor heart, one through which the venae cavae could enter and one for the pulmonary veins. The edges of these holes were stitched onto the waiting part of Washkansky's heart. The difference in size of the hearts did not matter because the openings in the donor heart could be enlarged to match the recipient's heart.

Surgically this first transplant was a success, but Washkansky died 18 days after the operation from double pneumonia – probably contracted as a result of the immunosuppressive drugs administered to him to prevent his body rejecting the new heart. Barnard continued to perform heart transplants, improving his methods all the time. Unfortunately the number of operations performed by him decreased because of the worsening arthritis in his hands.

Open-heart surgery was first introduced in South Africa by Barnard, and he further developed cardiothoracic surgery by new designs for artificial heart valves. His other achievements have included the discovery that intestinal artresia – a congenital deformity in the form of a hole in the small intestine – is the result of an insufficient supply of blood to the foetus during pregnancy. It was a fatal defect before Barnard developed the corrective surgery.

Barnard's techniques for heart transplant surgery have been adopted and developed by many surgeons, and as the methods improve they can give a new lease of life to those suffering from fatal heart conditions.

Barr, Murray Llewellyn (*1908–*), is a Canadian anatomist and geneticist known for his research into defects of the human reproductive system, and particularly chromosomal defects.

Barr was born in Belmont, Ontario, on 20 June 1908, the son of a farmer (who was originally from Ireland). He attended the University of Western Ontario, where he gained his BA in 1930, his MD in 1933 and his MSc in 1938. Apart from serving as a medical officer with the Royal Canadian Air Force during World War II, he has spent his entire career at the University of Western Ontario, where he became Head of the Department of Anatomy in the Health Sciences Centre.

In 1949, working with Ewart Bertram, Barr noticed that the nuclei of nerve cells in females

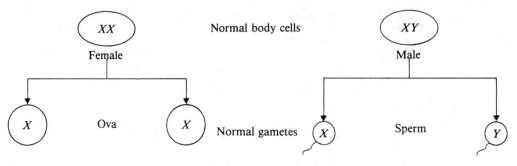

A Meiosis with the formation of normal gametes.

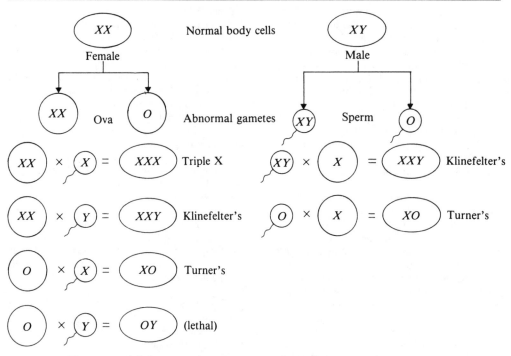

B Chromosomal defects arise from fertilization of abnormal gametes by normal gametes.

have a mass of chromatin (the nucleo-protein of chromosomes, which stains strongly with basic dyes) whereas those in males do not. He also found that this sex difference occurs in the cells of most mammals.

Improvements in cell culture methods made the closer examination of human chromosomes possible; for example, in 1954 it was discovered that the chromosome number in human beings is 46 and not 48, as was previously thought. From Barr's investigations, the sex chromatin (called the Barr body) is now known to be one of the two X-chromosomes in the cells of females; it is more condensed than the other chromosomes and is genetically inactive. The other X-chromosome in

females is attenuated and genetically active in resting cells.

Before the discovery of sex chromatin, the nature of the sex chromosome complex (XX female, or XY male) could be detected at cell level only by direct examination of chromosomes in dividing cells. The new comparative method using stained sex chromatin offered a much needed investigative and diagnostic procedure for patients with developmental anomalies of the reproductive system. Abnormalities of the sex chromosome complex often result in disorders such as Turner's syndrome (usually in females) and Klinefelter's syndrome. The former occurs when the gamete lacks a second sex chromosome so that the complex is XO. Klinefelter's syndrome, occurring in males only, results usually from a chromosomal complex of XXY.

Barr and his colleagues also devised a buccal smear test by rubbing the lining of the patient's mouth (the buccal cavity) and examining the cells obtained for chromosomal defects. This test is now used extensively to screen patients, including new-born babies and mental retardates, and has proved useful in the differential diagnosis of several kinds of hermaphroditism. Barr's research has thus been invaluable in simplifying diagnostic tests for chromosomal defects.

Bates, Henry Walter (*1825-1892*), was a British naturalist and explorer whose discovery of a type of mimicry (called Batesian mimicry) lent substantial support to Charles Darwin's theory of natural selection.

Bates was born on 8 February 1825 in Leicester, the son of a clothing manufacturer. He received little formal education, leaving school when he was 13 years old to work in his father's stocking factory, but he was interested in natural history and devoted much of his spare time to private study. In 1844 he met Alfred Wallace and aroused in him an interest in entomology, and they planned a joint venture to the Amazon region of South America to study and collect its flora and fauna, aiming to pay their expenses by selling the specimens they collected. In 1848 they arrived in Brazil at Para (also called Belem) near the mouth of the River Amazon, and for the next two years they worked together, thereafter separately. Wallace returned to England in 1852 but Bates remained in South America until 1859, during which time he explored much of the River Amazon. After returning to England, he spent several years organizing the specimens he had collected and writing about his observations, discoveries and explorations. In 1864 he was appointed Assistant Secretary to the Royal Geographical Society in London, a post he held until his death in London, on 16 February 1892.

During his Amazon exploration, Bates collected a vast number of specimens, including more than 14,000 species of insects, more than half of which were previously unknown. He travelled continually up and down the Amazon waterways, usually spending only a few days at each stopping-place to collect specimens. These had to be prepared and preserved – a difficult task in the hot, humid conditions of the Amazon rain forest – before being sent to his agent in England for sale. He also managed to find time to write to Charles Darwin, who used Bates' findings in the development of his theory of natural selection. After returning to England, Bates presented a paper to the Linnean Society in 1861 entitled "Contributions to an Insect Fauna of the Amazon Valley", in which he outlined his observations of mimicry in insects. He had discovered that several different species of butterflies have almost identical patterns of colours on their wings, and that some are distasteful to bird predators whereas others are not. Further, he suggested that the latter types, influenced by natural selection, mimic the distasteful species and thus increase their chances of survival. This form of mimicry is now called Batesian mimicry. (Subsequently Fritz Müller (1821-1897), a German-born Brazilian zoologist, discovered that, in some cases, all the species of similarly coloured butterflies are distasteful to predators, a phenomenon known as Müllerian mimicry.)

Bates' paper was well received and he was asked to write an account of his experiences in South America. The result was *The Naturalist on the River Amazon* (1863), a two-volume work (with an introduction by Charles Darwin) in which Bates described both his explorations and his scientific findings. The book quickly sold out and a second edition was published. But in this second edition, which has been reprinted many times, much of the scientific material was omitted, which has tended to diminish Bates' reputation as a scientist.

Bateson, William (*1861-1926*), was a British geneticist who was one of the founders of the science of genetics (a term he introduced), and a leading proponent of Mendelian views after the rediscovery in 1900 of Gregor Mendel's work on heredity. Bateson also made important contributions to embryology.

Bateson was born on 8 August 1861 in Whitby, Yorkshire. He was educated at Rugby School and St John's College, Cambridge, from which he graduated in natural sciences in 1883. He then travelled to the United States, remaining there for two years doing embryological research. During this period he met W.K. Brooks of Johns Hopkins University who interested Bateson in evolution, which he spent the rest of his life studying. On his return to Britain, Bateson spent several years investigating the fauna of salt lakes and undertaking other research into evolution and heredity. In 1908 he became the first Professor of Genetics at Cambridge University, but left this post in 1910 to be the Director of the newly established John Innes Horticultural Institution at Merton, Surrey, where he remained until his death on 8 February 1926 in Merton. In addition to his directorship, Bateson was Fullerian Professor of Physiology at the Royal Institution from

1912 to 1914 and a trustee of the British Museum from 1922.

Bateson's first important research was his embryological work in the United States. Studying the small, worm-like marine creature *Balanoglossus*, he discovered that although its larval stage is similar to that of the echinoderms, it also possesses a dorsal nerve cord and the beginnings of a notochord. Thus he demonstrated that *Balanoglossus* is a primitive chordate, which was the first indication that chordates had evolved from echinoderms – a theory now widely accepted.

His interest having turned to evolution while in the United States, Bateson spent the years immediately following his return to Britain investigating the fauna of the salt lakes of Europe, central Asia and northern Egypt. The result of these studies was his book, *Material for the Study for Variation* (1894), in which he put forward his theory of discontinuity to explain the long process of evolution. According to this theory, species do not develop in a predictable sequence of very gradual changes but instead evolve in a series of discontinuous "jumps". This theory was unacceptable to the traditional, biometrical evolutionists who maintained that there were no breaks in nature's pattern, and so Bateson began a series of breeding experiments to find corroborative evidence for his theory. When Mendel's work on heredity was rediscovered in 1900, Bateson translated Mendel's paper into English (as *Experiments on Hybrid Plants*), and found that Mendel's work provided him with the supportive evidence he was seeking for his discontinuity theory. Bateson also assumed the task of publicizing and defending the highly controversial discoveries of Mendel. The long debate finally culminated in 1904 when, as President of the Zoological Section of the British Association, Bateson succeeded in vindicating Mendel's findings at a meeting in Cambridge.

Thereafter Bateson continued with his breeding experiments, the results of which he described in his *Mendel's Principles of Heredity* (1908). In this book he showed that certain traits are consistently inherited together, an apparent contradiction to Mendel's findings; this phenomenon is now known to result from genes being situated close together on the same chromosome – a phenomenon called linkage. Towards the end of his life Bateson proposed his own vibratory theory of inheritance, based on the physical laws of force and motion, but this theory has met with little acceptance from other scientists.

Bayliss, William Maddock (*1860–1924*), was a British physiologist who discovered the digestive hormone secretin, the first hormone to be found,

and investigated the peristaltic movements of the intestine. He received many honours in recognition of his work, including the Royal Medal (1911) and Copley Medal of the Royal Society (1919), and in 1922 he was knighted.

Bayliss was born in Wolverhampton, Staffordshire, on 2 May 1860. He began studying medicine at University College, London, from 1881, but turned from medicine towards physiological research and entered Wadham College, Oxford, in 1885. After graduation he returned to University College where he began his main research. In 1893 he married the sister of Ernest Starling, the man with whom he worked during his major discoveries. In 1903 he became a Fellow of the Royal Society, and in 1912 a Professorship of General Physiology was created for him at University College. He was a longstanding member of the Physiological Society, first as its Secretary and then as its Treasurer. He died in Hampstead, London, on 27 August 1924.

Bayliss discovered the hormone secretin in 1902 when working with his brother-in-law Ernest Starling. He made an extract of a piece of the inner lining (mucosa) of the duodenum, which had already had hydrochloric acid introduced to it. When the extract was injected into the bloodstream the pancreas was stimulated to secrete digestive juices. Bayliss tried injecting hydrochloric acid intravenously, but no pancreatic secretion occurred. He then severed the nerves serving a loop of duodenum so that it was isolated from the pancreas except via the blood supply. Acid was introduced into the duodenum, and the pancreas produced secretions. Bayliss thus concluded that as hydrochloric acid (from the stomach's digestive juices) passes into the duodenum during the normal digestive process, the duodenal mucosa release a chemical (the hormone secretin) into the bloodstream which, in turn, makes the pancreas secrete its juices. The role of hormones in physiology is now commonly accepted, but at the time Bayliss' major discovery was a breakthrough. He then went on to study the activation of enzymes, particularly the pancreatic enzyme trypsin.

Bayliss and Starling also worked on the nerve supply to the intestines, and on pressures within the venous and arterial systems. Bayliss did independent research into vaso-motor reflexes. His method of treating patients suffering from surgical shock with saline to replace blood loss was widely used during World War I on injured troops. In 1915 he published *Principles of General Physiology*, which rapidly became a standard work.

Beadle, George Wells (*1903–*), **Tatum, Edward Lawrie** (*1909–1975*), and **Lederberg, Joshua** (*1925–*), three American scientists who shared the 1958 Nobel Prize in Physiology and Medicine for their pioneering work in the field of biochemical genetics.

Beadle was born on 22 October 1903 in Wahoo, Nebraska, and was educated at the University of Nebraska, graduating in 1926. After obtaining his doctorate in genetics at Cornell University, New York, in 1931, he went to the laboratory of Thomas Hunt Morgan at the California Institute of Technology, where he researched into the genetics of the fruit fly (*Drosophila melanogaster*). In 1935 he went to Paris, where he continued his work on *Drosophila* at the Institut de Biologie Physico-Chimique, collaborating with Boris Ephrussi. Beadle returned to the United States in 1936 and taught genetics for a year at Harvard University. From 1937 to 1946 he was Professor of Biology at Stanford University, California, and it was during this period that he collaborated with Tatum on the work that was to gain them the Nobel Prize. Beadle was appointed Professor and Chairman of the Division of Biology at the California Institute of Technology in 1946 and remained there until 1961, when he became Chancellor of the University of Chicago. In 1968 he retired from the university in order to direct the American Medical Association's Institute for Biomedical Research.

Tatum was born on 14 December 1909 in Boulder, Colorado, and was educated at the University of Wisconsin (where his father was head of the pharmacology department), from which he graduated in 1931 and gained his doctorate in 1934. From 1937 to 1941, after a period of post-doctoral study in the Netherlands, he was a research assistant at Stanford University, where he worked with Beadle. Tatum joined the faculty of Yale University in 1945 – as Associate Professor of Botany until 1946 then as Professor of Microbiology from 1946 to 1948. While at Yale he worked with Lederberg. Tatum returned to Stanford University in 1948 as Professor of Biology, becoming Professor of Biochemistry there in 1956. In 1957 he went to the Rockefeller Institute for Medical Research (now Rockefeller University), New York City. Tatum died on 5 November 1975 in New York City.

Lederberg was born on 23 May 1925 in Montclair, New Jersey. He studied at Columbia University, graduating in 1944, then did postgraduate work at Yale University, gaining his doctorate in 1947. It was while he was at Yale that Lederberg worked with Tatum. In 1947 Lederberg joined the University of Wisconsin, initially as Assistant Professor of Genetics then as Professor of Medi-

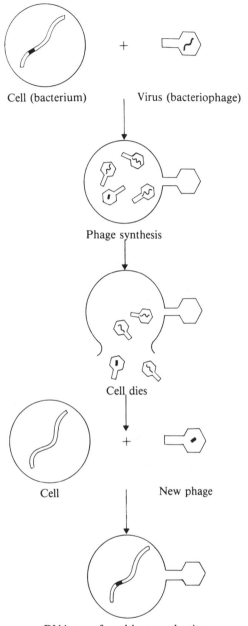

Cell (bacterium)   Virus (bacteriophage)

Phage synthesis

Cell dies

Cell   New phage

DNA transferred by transduction

Beadle demonstrated how a bacteriophage can bring about the transfer of DNA by transduction.

cine and Genetics and finally as Chairman of the Genetics Department. In 1959 he moved to Stanford University, where he was Professor of Genetics and Biology and Chairman of the Genetics Department and, from 1962, Director of the Kennedy Laboratories of Molecular Medicine.

The research that eventually led to the award

of a Nobel Prize had its origins in Beadle's early work on *Drosophila*. While at Morgan's laboratory, Beadle realized that genes influence heredity by chemical means. Later, working with Ephrussi in Paris, he showed that the eye colour of *Drosophila* is a result of a series of chemical reactions under genetic control. Because of the complexity of the relationship between genes and metabolic processes in *Drosophila* - itself a relatively simple organism - when Beadle returned to the United States and continued his research at Stanford, he used the red bread mould *Neurospora crassa*, which is even simpler than *Drosophila*. *Neurospora* can be cultured in a medium containing sugar and biotin as the only organic components, plus a few inorganic salts. Working with Tatum, Beadle subjected colonies of *Neurospora* to X-rays and studied the changes in the nutritional requirements of, and therefore enzymes formed by, the mutant *Neurospora* produced by the irradiation. By repeating the experiment with various mutant strains and culture mediums, Beadle and Tatum deduced that the formation of each individual enzyme is controlled by a single, specific gene. This one gene-one enzyme concept found wide applications in biology and virtually created the science of biochemical genetics.

After Tatum moved to Yale in 1945, he applied the mutation-inducing technique by Beadle and himself to bacteria. Using *Escherichia coli*, Tatum, working with Lederberg, showed that genetic information can be passed from one bacterium to another. The discovery that a form of sexual reproduction can occur in bacteria meant that these organisms could be used for research much more extensively than previously thought possible and, in fact, bacteria are now as important as *Drosophila* and *Neurospora* in genetic research.

Tatum's collaboration with Lederberg ended in 1947, when Lederberg went to the University of Wisconsin and continued to research into bacterial genetics. In 1952 he published a paper in which he revealed that bacteriophages can transfer genetic material from one bacterium to another, a phenomenon Lederberg termed transduction. This discovery further increased the usefulness of bacteria in genetic research. Later Lederberg diversified into other fields of investigation, devising means of identifying and classifying organic compounds by mathematical graph theory and developing statistical methods of studying human biology.

Beaumont, William (*1785–1853*), was an American surgeon who did important early work on the physiology of the human stomach by taking advantage of a bizarre surgical case that he treated early in his career. He established that digestion is a chemical process, and his work encouraged other researchers to study the physiology of digestion.

Beaumont was born in Lebanon, Connecticut, on 21 November 1785. He was the son of a farmer, and worked as a schoolteacher in Champlain, New York, before going to study medicine at St Albans, Vermont. He was granted a licence to practise, becoming an assistant surgeon in the army in 1812. He resigned his commission after three years and practised in Plattsburgh, resuming his army career in 1820 when he was sent to the frontier post of Fort Mackinac, Michigan. In 1834 he was transferred to St Louis, Missouri, and he worked there for the rest of his life, although he left the army in 1839. During this time (1837) he became Professor of Surgery at St Louis University. He died in St Louis on 25 April 1853.

On 6 June 1822 a young French Canadian trapper named Alexis St Martin was accidentally shot in the left side from the back at close range, causing severe injury where the shot passed right through his abdomen. Beaumont was at Fort Mackinac, and treated the trapper swiftly and skilfully. The young man survived although he retained a permanent traumatic fistula, or hole, between his stomach and the outside of his abdomen. Beaumont looked after St Martin for two years, and in 1825 began a series of experiments and observations on the behaviour of the human stomach under various circumstances. Through the fistula he was able to extract and analyse gastric juice and stomach contents at various stages of digestion, observe changes in secretions, and note the muscular movements of the stomach. But he so hounded the unfortunate St Martin that he left (and eventually outlived Beaumont by nearly 30 years). Beaumont published his findings in *Experiments and Observations on the Gastric Juice* (1833).

Beaumont's work predated by many years the use of endoscopic examinations of the stomach and was the first well-documented and accurate observation of the digestive processes of a living human being.

Beijerinck, Martinus Willem (*1851–1931*), was a Dutch botanist who in 1898 published his finding that an agent smaller than bacteria could cause diseases, an agent that he called a virus (the Latin word for poison).

Beijerinck was born in Amsterdam on 16 March 1851. His earliest scientific interest was botany, but he graduated in 1872 with a Diploma in chemical engineering from the Delft Polytechnic School, where one of his friends was Jacobus Van't Hoff (who later won the first Nobel Prize in Chemistry in 1901). After graduating, Beijerinck taught botany to provide himself with a living while he studied for his doctorate, which he gained in 1877. He then became interested in bacteriology and took a job as a bacteriologist with an industrial company. In order to learn more about the subject, he travelled extensively throughout Europe. In 1895 he returned to the Delft Polytechnic School, where he taught and carried out research for the rest of his career. He died on 1 January 1931 in Gorssel in the Netherlands.

In the early 1880s Beijerinck began studying the disease that stunts the growth of tobacco plants and mottles their leaves in a mosaic pattern (now called the tobacco mosaic virus disease). He tried to find a causative bacterium but was unsuccessful. This research stimulated his interest in bacteriology, however, and led to his taking a job as an industrial bacteriologist. While working in this capacity he discovered one of the types of nitrogen-fixing bacteria that live in the nodules on the roots of leguminous plants.

After he returned to academic life in 1895, Beijerinck resumed his study of the tobacco mosaic disease and again tried to isolate a causative agent. He pressed out the juice of infected tobacco leaves and found that the juice alone was able to infect healthy plants, but he could not detect a bacterial pathogen in the juice nor could he culture a micro-organism from it. Furthermore, he found that the juice remained infective after he had passed it through a filter that removed even the smallest bacteria. He was also certain that the causative agent was not a toxin because he could infect a healthy plant and from that plant infect another healthy plant, continuing this process indefinitely – therefore the infective agent had to be capable of reproduction.

Louis Pasteur had earlier postulated the existence of pathogens too small to be visible under the microscope; and Dimitri Ivanovski, a Russian bacteriologist, had in 1892 observed that tobacco mosaic disease could be transmitted by a filtered juice but he thought that there was a flaw in his filter and still believed the disease to be bacterial. It was Beijerinck who first published his findings and stated that the tobacco mosaic disease is caused by a non-bacterial pathogen. He believed that the filtered juice of the infected plants was itself alive, and he called the causative agent a filterable virus. Thus Beijerinck was the first to recognize the existence of a class of pathogens now known to cause a wide range of diseases in animals and plants, as well as in human beings. He was, however, mistaken in his belief that the

virus was a liquid; in 1935 the American biochemist Wendell Stanley (1904–1971) demonstrated that viruses are particulate.

Békésy, Georg von (*1899–1972*), was a Hungarian-born American scientist who resolved the long-standing controversy on how the inner ear functions. For his discovery concerning the mechanism of stimulation within the cochlea, he received the 1961 Nobel Prize in Medicine and Physiology (the first physicist to do so).

Békésy was born in Budapest on 3 June 1899, where his father was a member of the diplomatic service. He went to the University of Bern in 1916, graduated in 1920, and then enrolled at the University of Budapest where he took his PhD in physics in 1923. For the next 23 years he worked in the laboratories of the Hungarian Telephone System. During this time he was also employed at the central laboratories of Siemens and Halske AC in Berlin, and from 1932 to 1939 he was a lecturer at the University of Budapest. He was appointed Special Professor there from 1939 to 1940 and a full Professor from 1940 to 1946. In that year he emigrated to Sweden, disturbed by the Soviet occupation of Hungary, and worked at the Karolinska Institute in Stockholm. He held the title of Research Professor there, although he did not actually take up the post because, in 1947, he emigrated to the United States to become a research lecturer at the Psycho-Acoustic Laboratory at Harvard. From 1949 to 1966 he served as a Senior Research Fellow in Psychophysics. He then went to the University of Hawaii where he took up the appointment of Professor of Sensory Sciences, and remained there until his death in Honolulu on 13 June 1972.

While working as a telecommunications engineer for the Hungarian Telephone System, Békésy decided that to determine what frequency range a new cable should be able to carry, he would investigate how the human ear actually receives sound. He researched the functioning of the eardrum by glueing two mirrors to it and beaming light and sound into the ear. In this way he was able to observe reflections of the movements of the membrane when it was activated by sound waves.

In another series of experiments, Békésy observed how the auditory ossicles in the middle ear – the hammer, anvil and stirrup – pick up the vibrations transmitted to them by the eardrum, and how they relay these messages to the cochlea in the inner ear. It had long been known that nerves in the cochlea pick up sound signals and transmit them along the auditory nerve to the brain for interpretation. It was also known that the cochlea consists of a spiral-shaped channel

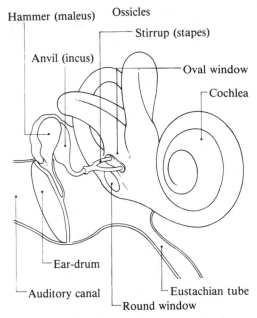

Hammer (maleus)
Ossicles
Stirrup (stapes)
Anvil (incus)
Oval window
Cochlea
Ear-drum
Auditory canal
Eustachian tube
Round window

Békésy's study of human hearing resulted in an analysis of the mechanism of the cochlea and the role of the basilar membrane within it.

through which runs a thin partition known as the basilar membrane, containing groups of fine fibres. Hermann von Helmholtz had postulated a theory, which was widely accepted at that time, that each fibre had a natural period of vibration and responded only to sounds that vibrated at that period. He claimed that each group of fibres stimulated different nerve endings, which thus enabled the brain to distinguish specific frequencies.

Békésy's painstaking and original work disproved the Helmholtz theory. He constructed models of the cochlea and also worked with cadavers whose auditory mechanisms he stimulated electrically. Békésy had to design new instruments and develop new techniques in order to experiment on the delicate cochlea. He devised extremely fine drills and probes, and the scissors he used had blades of only a few hundredths of a millimetre long. He reached the cochlea by grinding a small opening in the skull, and revealing part of the basilar membrane. By substituting a saline solution containing fine aluminium particles for the fluid in the cochlea and by using stroboscopic illumination, he was able to observe and measure for the first time a phenomenon he called the "travelling wave".

Békésy found that the innermost ossicle, the stirrup, acts as a lid on an opening in the cochlea, called the oval window. As sound vibrations

cause the stirrup to move it exerts pressure on the fluid within the cochlea, and these vibrations are transmitted to the basilar membrane in the form of travelling waves. He established that as the waves pass along the basilar membrane the entire membrane vibrates. Each wave causes maximum vibration at different sections of the membrane according to its frequency. High-frequency waves produced by high-pitched sounds reach their peak on that part of the basilar membrane nearest the stirrup. Low-frequency waves, from low sounds, attain a maximum amplitude farther along the membrane.

Later, Békésy extended his interests to visual and tactile sensations, which he measured and recorded. He developed an audiometer which determines whether deafness is caused by damage to the brain or to the ear, so that the appropriate treatment could be determined at an earlier stage.

Békésy also devised a means by which he enabled the skin to "hear". His apparatus consisted of a greatly enlarged version of a cochlea – a long tube filled with fluid and with a membrane running along its length. If the forearm of a person were pressed against the membrane, the skin of the arm felt the high and low sounds sent through the tube at distinctly different positions along the arm. Békésy's experiments pointed the way to methods which could enable the totally deaf to hear through tactile sensations, and improved modern interpretations of deafness.

Bell, Charles (*1774–1842*), was a British anatomist and surgeon who carried out pioneering research on the human nervous system. He gave his name to Bell's palsy, an extracranial paralysis of the facial nerve (the VIIth cranial nerve) – not the same as the long thoracic nerve of Bell which he also named, and which supplies a muscle in the chest wall.

Bell was born in Edinburgh in November 1774. His brother, John Bell, was a renowned surgeon who taught him anatomy. After qualifying in 1799 Bell became a surgeon at the Edinburgh Royal Infirmary. He went to London in 1804 as a lecturer, and in 1812 was appointed surgeon at the Middlesex Hospital, London. He became Professor of Anatomy and Surgery at the Royal College of Surgeons in 1824 and four years later was invited to become the first Principal of the Medical School at University College, London. He was knighted in 1831. In 1836 he became Professor of Surgery at the University of Edinburgh. He died at Hallow, Worcestershire, on 28 April 1842.

Bell carried out meticulous dissections and made the important discovery that nerves are composite structures, each with separate fibres for sensory and motor functions. His findings first appeared in a short essay *Idea of a New Anatomy of the Brain* (1811); his main written work was *The Nervous System of the Human Body* (1830). The chief significance of Bell's discovery was the impetus it gave to other researchers in neurology.

Berg, Paul (*1926–*), is an American molecular biologist who shared (with Walter Gilbert and Frederick Sanger) the 1980 Nobel Prize in Chemistry for his work in genetic engineering, particularly for developing DNA recombinant techniques that enable genes from simple organisms to be inserted into the genetic material of other simple organisms. He is also well known for advocating restrictions on genetic engineering research because of the unpredictable, even dangerous, consequences that might result from uncontrolled DNA recombinant experiments.

Berg was born on 30 June 1926 in New York City. He was educated at Pennsylvania State University, from which he graduated in 1948, and at the Western Reserve University, from which he obtained his doctorate in 1952. From 1952 to 1954 he was an American Cancer Society Research Fellow at the Institute of Cytophysiology in Copenhagen and at the School of Medicine at Washington University, St Louis. Between 1955 and 1974 he held several positions at Washington University: from 1955 to 1959 he was an assistant then Associate Professor in the Microbiology Department of the School of Medicine; from 1959 to 1969 he was Professor of Microbiology; and from 1969 to 1974 he was Chairman of the Microbiology Department. In 1970 he was also appointed Willson Professor of Biochemistry at the Medical Center of Stanford University, California.

Berg's early work, concerned the mechanisms involved in intracellular protein synthesis. In 1956 he identified an RNA molecule (later known as a transfer RNA) that is specific to the amino acid methionine. He then began his Nobel prize-winning work in which he perfected a method for making bacteria accept genes from other bacteria. This genetic engineering technique for DNA recombination can be extremely useful for creating strains of bacteria to manufacture specific substances, such as interferon. But there are also considerable dangers in the controlled use of these methods – a new, highly virulent pathogenic micro-organism might accidentally be created, for example. Berg became aware of this danger and campaigned for strict controls on certain types of genetic engineering experiments. As a result, an international conference was held in California, followed by the publication in 1976 of

guidelines to restrict genetic engineering research.

Berg has also studied how viral and cellular genes interact to regulate growth and reproduction, and has investigated the mechanisms of gene expression in higher organisms.

Binet, Alfred (*1857–1911*), was a French psychologist who is best known for his pioneering work on the development of mental testing, particularly the testing of intelligence.

Binet was born on 8 July 1857 in Nice. He went to Paris in 1871 to study law, but became interested in the work of the neurologist Jean-Martin Charcot on hypnosis and abandoned law in 1878 to study first neurology and later psychology at the Salpêtrière Hospital in Paris. He remained there until 1891, when he went to work in the physiological psychology laboratory at the Sorbonne in Paris. He became Director of the laboratory in 1895 and held this post until his death on 18 October 1911.

Binet was principally interested in applying experimental techniques to the measurement of intellectual abilities and, after joining the Sorbonne, began to devise various tests in an attempt to gain an objective measure of mental ability. After experimenting with various combinations of different tests Binet, with Théodore Simon, published in 1905 the Binet-Simon intelligence test. This test, which was designed to measure intellectual ability in children, required the subject to perform such tasks as naming objects, copying designs and rearranging disordered patterns. The subject was then given a mental-age score according to how well he or she had performed in the tests compared with previously established norms for various age groups. This was one of the first attempts at objectively measuring intelligence and, because of its usefulness, quickly became adopted in France and other countries. The original Binet-Simon test subsequently underwent many revisions, probably the most notable of which was the scoring of intelligence as an intelligence quotient (IQ) - calculated as the ratio of mental age to chronological age, multiplied by 100 - introduced in 1916 by Lewis Terman (1877–1956), an American psychologist working at Stanford University, in the adaptation known as the Stanford-Binet test. (The Stanford-Binet test was later revised several times and, in its latest form, is still used today.)

Binet wrote several books on mental processes and reasoning ability, notably *L'Étude expérimentale de l'intelligence* (1903; *Experimental Study of Intelligence*), a study of the mental abilities of his two daughters and, with Simon, *Les enfants anormaux* (1907; translated in 1914 as *Mentally Defective Children*). In addition he devised several tests that involved interpreting a subject's response to various visual stimuli (such as inkblots and pictures), the forerunners of some types of modern personality tests. Binet also studied and wrote about hypnosis and hysteria.

Blakemore, Colin (*1944-*), is an English physiologist who has made advanced studies of how the brain works, especially in connection with memory and the senses.

Blakemore was born in Stratford-on-Avon on 1 June 1944 and educated at King Henry VIII School in Coventry. In 1962 he won a scholarship to Corpus Christi College, Cambridge, to study natural sciences and in particular, medicine; he graduated in 1965. Blakemore then declined a scholarship to St Thomas's Hospital, London, and went instead to study physiological optics at the Neurosensory Laboratory at the University of California in Berkeley; he obtained his PhD in 1968. He was a demonstrator at Cambridge University from 1967 until 1972, when he was appointed Lecturer in Physiology, a position he held until 1979. He then went to work at Oxford University.

In his experimental work, Blakemore has shown that cells in the visual cortex of the brain of a new-born kitten are able to detect visual outlines. But if the kitten is kept at a critical period in an environment with only, say, vertical lines, it will later prove to have in the cortex only cells that can "recognize" these patterns and not others. Blakemore suggests that it is possible that the inherited DNA of genes already contains the capacity to synthesize RNA, the protein that is involved in the storage of any new remembrance.

Blakemore is known for his ability to explain complex science to the layman. This talent was demonstrated, for example, by his award-winning educational film *The Visual Cortex of the Cat*, in his Reith lectures of 1976, and in his publication *Mechanics of the Mind* (1977). In this book he explains the mechanics of sensation, sleep, memory and thought, and discusses the philosophical questions of human consciousness, the evolution of thinking about body and mind, the relationship between art and perception, and the origin and function of language. He argues that an individual's system of knowledge, expertise and ethical standards has evolved gradually and that the resulting "collective mind" is a functional extension of all the human brains that have contributed to it.

Boerhaave, Hermann (*1668-1738*), was a Dutch physician and chemist of tremendous learning who dominated and greatly influenced various branches of science in Europe.

Boerhaave was born in Verhout, near Leiden (Leyden), on 31 December 1668, the son of a minister. He intended entering the Church, and in 1684 went to the University of Leiden to study theology. While there he also studied philosophy, botany, languages, chemistry and medicine. He qualified in natural philosophy in 1687 and gained his PhD two years later. Medicine and chemistry became his predominant interests and he entered the University of Haderwijk, from which he graduated in medicine in 1693. He went back to Leiden in 1701 as a physician, and also began teaching. In 1709 he took the Chair of Medicine and Botany at Leiden, was made also a Professor of Physic in 1714, as well as Professor of Chemistry in 1718. He was elected to the French Academy in 1728, and became a Fellow of the Royal Society in 1730. He died in Leiden on 23 September 1738.

For a man of such immense academic distinction and knowledge, Boerhaave made few original discoveries although he did describe the structure and function of the sweat glands, and was the first to realize that smallpox is spread by contact. He was, however, an excellent tutor and re-established the technique of clinical teaching, taking his students to the bedsides of his patients. During his time at Leiden it became a famous centre of medical knowledge, attracting students from throughout Europe.

Boerhaave's writings remained authoritative works for nearly a century. In 1708 he published a physiology textbook *Institutiones medicae* (a classification of diseases with their causes and treatment), followed by the *Book of Aphorisms* in the next year. In 1710 an *Index plantarum* was published, followed by *Historia plantarum* - a collection of his botanical lectures compiled by his ex-students. In 1724 his students published *Institutiones et experimenta chemiae*, a breakdown of Boerhaave's lectures on chemistry. He produced the official version of the lectures in 1732 called *Elementia chemiae*, which presented a clear and precise approach to the chemistry of the day and remains his most famous work.

Boveri, Theodor Heinrich (*1862-1915*), was a German biologist who performed valuable early work on chromosomes. Most of his life's work was devoted to investigating those processes by which an individual develops from the reproductive material of its parents.

Boveri was born in Bamberg on 12 October 1862, the second of four sons of a physician. He was educated at Bamberg from 1868 to 1875 and then for the next six years at the Realgymnasium in Nuremberg. He went to Munich University to study history and philosophy, but soon decided to change to natural sciences, and gained his doctorate in 1885. He then began a five-year fellowship at the Zoological Institute in Munich doing research into cytology under Richard Hertwig (1850-1937), and became a lecturer in zoology and comparative anatomy in 1887. He was appointed Professor of Zoology and Comparative Anatomy as well as Director of the Zoological-Zootomical Institute in Würzburg in 1893. Four years later he married Marcella O'Grady, an American biologist, and they had one child – Margret – who became a writer and journalist. Apart from visits to the zoological station at Naples, Boveri spent the rest of his working life at Würzburg. He declined the position offered to him in 1913 of Director of the Kaiser Wilhelm Institute for Biology in Berlin because of his failing health. He died in Würzburg on 15 October 1915, after successive physical breakdowns and recurrent depression.

Boveri's first piece of research was for his thesis in 1885, which had been on the structure of nerve fibres, but soon afterwards his interest was turned towards cell biology by Hertwig, when he worked as his assistant in Munich.

In the early 1880s the Belgian cytologist Edouard van Beneden was investigating eggs of the roundworm *Ascaris megalocephala*, which inhabits the intestine of horses. He discovered that the chromosomes of the offspring are derived in equal numbers from the nuclei of the ovum and spermatozoon, that is equally from the two parents. It was known that the fusion of the nuclei of the egg and the spermatozoon is the essential feature of fertilization, and that this fusion eventually leads to the creation of all the nuclei of the body. In 1884 it was concluded that the cell nucleus holds the fundamental elements of heredity. It was also shown that the chromosomes split into daughter cells and that the chromosome number is constant for each species.

Inspired by the experiments of Beneden, Boveri did some of his own and described some aspects of the development of eggs and the formation of polar bodies (minute bodies which are produced during the division of an unfertilized ovum). He then demonstrated that the nuclei of *Ascaris* eggs contain finger-shaped lobes which are chromosomes (each egg contains only two to four chromosomes), and also that chromosomes are separated into the daughter cells during division following fertilization by a central piece in the spermatozoon, which he termed the centrosome.

In 1889 Boveri experimented on sea-urchins' eggs, fertilizing nucleated and non-nucleated fragments, and found that both types could develop normally. He also discovered that those occasional non-fertilized fragments containing only a nucleus were also able to develop normally. He showed that at fertilization the egg and the spermatozoon incorporate the same number of chromosomes each in the creation of the new individual. He was eventually able to demonstrate that cytoplasm plays an important part in development and went on to show that it is not a specific number, but a specific assortment of chromosomes that is responsible for normal development, indicating that individual chromosomes possess different qualities.

Boveri's powers of observation as a microscopist were remarkable, but so were his theories. In 1914, he theorized that tumours may become malignant as the result of abnormal chromosome numbers, and was the first to view the tumour as a cell problem. He also tried to explain, on the basis of an irregular chromosome distribution, a condition in bees in which male and female characteristics are mosaically distributed in different parts of the body. He discovered segmental excretory organs in *Amphioxus* (an organism believed to be close to the type from which the vertebrates evolved).

Boveri enriched biological science with some fundamental discoveries and fruitful new conceptions. His theory of chromosomal individuality provided the working basis of nearly all cytological interpretations of genetic phenomena and is still true today.

Brenner, Sydney (*1927-*), is a South African-born British molecular biologist noted for his work in the field of genetics.

Brenner was born on 13 January 1927 at Germiston, South Africa, the son of an emigrant from Lithuania. He was educated there and studied at the University of the Witwatersrand, where he gained his MSc in 1947 and his MB and BCh in 1951. He then went to Britain and studied for a PhD at Oxford, which he received in 1954. In that year he also worked in the Virus Laboratory of the University of California in Berkeley, and from 1955 to 1957 was a lecturer in physiology at the Witwatersrand University. From 1957 he researched in the Molecular Biology Laboratory of the Medical Research Council, Cambridge, and in 1980 was appointed Director of that establishment.

Brenner's first research was on the molecular genetics of very simple organisms. Since then he has spent seven years on one of the most elaborate efforts in anatomy ever attempted, investigating the nervous system of nematode worms and comparing the nervous systems of different mutant forms of the animal. The nematode that lives in the soil and which feeds on or in roots can be as little as 0.5 mm in length. Brenner's experiments have included cutting a soil nematode into 20,000 extremely thin slices and, one at a time, projecting a long succession of electron micrographs onto a screen. The animal's nerves are traced in each picture by an electronic pen which automatically feeds information to a computer for storage. Brenner's reason for gathering and processing all this information is to compare the "wiring" of the nervous system of normal nematodes with that of mutant ones which show peculiarities in behaviour. About one hundred genes are involved in constructing the nervous system of a nematode and most of the mutations that occur affect the overall design of a section of the nervous system. These genes are therefore an organizational type and regulate the routing of the nervous system during the growth of the animal. The nematode is a simple animal although its make-up is extremely complicated. The amount of effort that has been put into this study indicates how much biologists still have to find out about the exact organization of living tissues.

Brenner is also interested in tumour biology and in the use of genetic engineering for purifying proteins, cloning genes and synthesizing amino acids. His experiments have given and still continue to give a great impetus to molecular biology.

Bright, Richard (*1789-1858*), was a British physician who was the first to describe the kidney disease known as Bright's disease, which is actually a rather vague term - now largely obsolete - sometimes used to denote any of several different kidney disorders that share a number of the same symptoms.

Bright was born on 28 September 1789 in Bristol and was privately educated in Exeter and Edinburgh. In 1809 he began studying medicine at Edinburgh University but interrupted his studies to travel to Iceland. On returning to Britain he resumed his medical training at Guy's Hospital and St Thomas's Hospital in London, receiving his medical degree from Edinburgh University in 1813. After spending several years touring Europe - during which time he worked in several European hospitals - Bright was appointed Assistant Physician at Guy's Hospital in 1820. Four years later he became a full Physician at Guy's, a post he held for the rest of his life. In 1837 he was also appointed Physician Extraordinary to Queen Victoria. Bright died in London on 16 December 1858.

Bright's principal interest was disorders of the kidneys, in which area he initiated the use of biochemical studies by working with chemists to demonstrate that urea is retained in the body in kidney failure. He also correlated symptoms in patients with the pathological changes he later found in post-mortem examinations of these same people. Using these methods he found that albuminuria (the presence of the protein albumin in the urine) and oedema (accumulation of fluid in the body) are associated with pathological changes in the kidneys - a condition that came to be called Bright's disease. Later, however, it was discovered that several different kidney disorders produce these symptoms (although the most common cause is glomerulonephritis - inflammation of the glomeruli) and the term Bright's disease is little used today. Bright first published his findings in *Reports of Medical Cases* (1827) and subsequently in the second volume of the *Reports* (1831) and in the first volume of *Guy's Hospital Reports* (1836), which he helped to establish.

In addition to his studies of kidney disorders, Bright investigated jaundice, nervous diseases and abdominal tumours. He also collaborated with Thomas Addison, a contemporary at Guy's Hospital, in writing *Elements of the Practice of Medicine* (1839); in fact Addison wrote most of this volume and the second volume - to which Bright was to have been the principal contributor - was never published.

Brown, Robert (*1773-1858*), was a distinguished British botanist whose discovery of the movement of suspended particles has proved fundamental in the study of physics.

Brown was born at Montrose, Scotland, on 21 December 1773, the son of an Episcopalian priest. He studied medicine at Edinburgh University but did not obtain his degree. He subsequently held the position of assistant-surgeon in a Scottish infantry regiment, but soon revealed that his true interest lay in botany. In the late 1790s he was introduced to the well-known English botanist Joseph Banks, who allowed him the free use of his library and collections. Shortly afterwards Brown resigned from the army in order to accept the post of naturalist on an expedition under Captain Matthew Flinders, on the *Investigator*, to survey the coast of the lately discovered Australian continent. He voyaged from 1801 to 1805 and on his return to England published, in 1810, the first part of his studies on the flora he had discovered on his Antipodean journey. The poor sales of the book discouraged him and he left the rest unpublished. In the same year, he was appointed Librarian to Joseph Banks, a post which he held until Banks' death in 1820. Banks bequeathed to Brown the full use of the library and its collections for life. In 1827, in compliance with the stipulations of Banks' will, he agreed to the transfer of the books and specimens to the

British Museum and was appointed Curator of the botanical collections there. He died in London on 10 June 1858.

In 1791 Brown submitted his first paper to the Natural History Society. It was a highly detailed classification of the plants he had collected in Scotland, with accompanying notes and observations. This list was to win him many introductions in the scientific world of his day. It was not until 1828, however, that he made one of his greatest contributions to science, published in the Edinburgh New Philosophical Journal. The paper was entitled *A brief account of Microscopical Observations made in the months of June, July and August 1827 on the particles contained in the pollen of plants, and on the general existence of active molecules in organic and inorganic bodies* and it was in this paper that Brown set out his observations on "Brownian movement", or "motion", which perpetuates his name. The concept arose from his observation that very fine pollen grains of the plant *Clarkia pulchella* when suspended in water move about in a continuously agitated manner. This phenomenon is true for any small solid particles suspended in a liquid or gas and can be viewed in a bright light through a microscope. Brown was able to establish that the constant movement was not purely biological in origin because inorganic materials such as carbon and various metals are equally subject to it, although he could not find the cause of the movement. During his lifetime there was no shortage of theories to explain his discovery, but it was not until the twentieth century that the question was answered.

Brown also published papers on *Asclepiadaceae* (1809) and on *Proteaceae* (1810), wrote on the propagatory process of the gulf-weed and on the anatomy of fossilized plants. He also described the organs and mode of reproduction in orchids. In 1831, while investigating the fertilization of both *Orchidaceae* and *Asclepiadaceae*, he discovered that a small body which is fundamental in the creation of plant tissues, occurs regularly in plant cells – he called it a "nucleus", a name which is still used. Another significant revelation Brown made was the identification of the difference between gymnosperms and angiosperms.

Brown's various papers on his findings and opinions in every division of botanical science made him the outstanding authority on plant physiology of his day, and he did much to improve the system of plant classification by describing new genera and families. His observation of Brownian movement was important in showing how molecular motion forms the basis of kinetic theory.

Buffon, Georges-Louis Leclerc, Comte de (*1707-1788*), was a French naturalist who compiled the vast encyclopaedic work *Histoire naturelle générale et particulière*.

Buffon was born in Montbard in France on 7 September 1707 and was educated at the Jesuit's College in Dijon. He graduated in law in 1726 and took the opportunity to study mathematics and astronomy. He travelled a great deal, and spent some time in England where science was undergoing a renaissance. Buffon set himself the task of translating works of Newton and Hales into French. In 1732 Buffon's mother died and left him a handsome legacy, so the young man was financially stable enough to devote himself entirely to his scientific interests. Buffon was elected Associate of the French Academy of Sciences in 1739 and took up the appointment of Keeper of the Botanical Gardens (Jardin du Roi), a post that stimulated his interest in natural history. He was a prolific writer, and he turned his skills towards compiling what would eventually be a 44-volume work on natural history encompassing both the plant and the animal kingdoms. He became a member of the French Academy in 1753, was made a Count in 1771 and a Fellow of the Royal Society in 1739. He died in Paris on 16 April 1788 after a long and painful illness.

Buffon's encyclopaedia was the first work to cover the whole of natural history and it was extremely popular. He wrote in a clear and interesting style – which he regarded as more important than originality – and did not personally originate a great deal of the material. He was aided by several eminent naturalists of the time, and organized the sometimes confusing wealth of material into a coherent form.

Although Buffon's work was inclined to generalizations, he proposed some innovatory and stimulating theories. He suggested that a cosmic catastrophe initiated the Earth's beginnings, and that its existence was far older than the 6,000 years suggested by the Book of Genesis. He observed that some animals retain parts that are vestigial and no longer useful, suggesting that they have evolved rather than having been spontaneously generated. Theories such as these could have caused a furore at a time when it was strongly believed that the creation of the world and mankind occurred as defined in the Bible, and even though Buffon wrote with political care he did upset the authorities and had to recant. It was not until the theories of Charles Lyell and Charles Darwin that people began to take such ideas seriously.

Buffon's encyclopaedia did, however, arouse a great interest in natural science which carried through to the early part of the nineteenth century.

Burkitt, Denis Parsons (*1911–*   ), is a British surgeon who is best known for his description of the childhood tumour named after him, Burkitt's lymphoma. He is also known for stressing the importance of roughage in the diet.

Burkitt was born on 28 February 1911 at Enniskillen, near Lough Erne in Northern Ireland. He was educated at the local school and later at schools in Anglesey and Cheltenham. When he was 18 years old he entered Dublin University to study engineering, but later turned his interests to medicine. He worked as a surgeon in the Armed Forces and became FRCS in 1938 in Edinburgh. In 1946 he was accepted into the Colonial Service and eventually became Senior Consultant to the Ministry of Health in Kampala, in 1961. He returned to England in 1966 and now lives in Gloucestershire.

In 1957 Burkitt examined a child in Kampala. This was his first case of the lymphoma that typically affects the face and jaw, presenting several swellings. Subsequent observations convinced him that these diversely distributed lumps were of a single tumour type. This has now been histologically confirmed by the presence of "starry sky" cells within the tumours. Burkitt undertook a 15,000-km safari with two other doctors, Edward Williams and Clifford Nelson, to discover if there is a geographical correlation with the incidence of Burkitt's disease. Their research eventually showed that the lymphoma is commonest in areas of certain temperature and rainfall, in fact, where malaria is endemic. It is also associated with the presence of antibodies to the Epstein-Barr virus. Burkitt's work in the comparatively new field of geographical pathology was acknowledged in 1972 when he was elected a Fellow of the Royal Society.

He also became well known for his theories that a high-fibre diet prevents many of the common ailments of the Western world, such as appendicitis, diverticular disease and carcinoma of the bowel, all of which are rarely encountered among the African peoples, for example. Burkitt pioneered the popular trend of high-roughage diets.

Burnet, Frank Macfarlane (*1899–*   ), is an Australian immunologist whose research into viruses inspired his theory that antibodies could be produced artificially in the body in order to develop a specific type of immunity, which led to the concept of acquired immunological tolerance, particularly important in tissue transplant surgery. For this work he was awarded the 1960 Nobel Prize in Physiology and Medicine, which he shared with Peter Medawar.

Burnet was born in Australia on 3 February 1899 at Traralgon, Victoria. After graduating in biology from Geelong College, Victoria, he obtained his medical degree at Melbourne University in 1923 and for the following year was Resident Pathologist at Melbourne Hospital. He studied at the Lister Institute, London, from 1926 to 1927 and in that year gained his PhD from the University of London. He then returned to Australia as Assistant Director of the Walter and Eliza Hall Institute for Medical Research, Melbourne, and held this position until 1944, when he became the Institute's Director. Burnet was knighted in 1951. He was appointed Emeritus Professor of Melbourne University in 1965 and made an Honorary Fellow of the Royal College of Surgeons in 1969.

Early in his career Burnet did extensive virus research. He was the first to investigate the multiplication mechanism of bacteriophages (viruses that attack bacteria) and devised a method for identifying bacteria by the bacteriophages that attack them. This work was of immense importance, particularly 20 years later, when bacteriophages were first used as research tools in genetics and molecular biology.

In 1932 Burnet developed a technique for growing and isolating viruses in chick embryos, a technique that was to be used as a standard laboratory procedure for more than 20 years. Burnet's work on the chick embryo increased interest in the specific character of an embryo by which it seemed to be unable to resist virus infection or to produce any antibodies against viruses. Early attempts were made in Burnet's laboratory to use the chick embryo to show that tolerance could be produced artificially.

As a result of his virus research, Burnet became interested in immunology and in 1949 he predicted that an individual's ability to produce a particular antibody to a particular antigen was not innate, but was something that developed during the individual's life. In 1951 Medawar carried out the experiments that confirmed this theory.

Burnet's second major contribution to immunology was made in 1957 – his highly controversial "clonal selection" theory of antibody formation, which explains why a particular antigen stimulates the production of its own specific antibody. According to Burnet, there is a region in the genes of the cells that produce antibodies that is continually mutating, such that each mutation leads to a new variant of antibody being produced. Normally the cells that produce a particular variant are few, but if the antibody they produce suddenly finds a target, then they multiply rapidly to meet this demand, and the other, useless, variants die out.

In recent years there has been a large amount of research on the immune response and on the many ways of imitating nature's way of reacting without inoculating the embryo. In particular, work has been carried out on the production of tolerance by drugs such as 6-mercaptopurine, in the hope that it will prove effective in surgical organ transplants. Burnet's investigations have stimulated research into the way viruses cause infection. His own research has helped to eradicate diseases such as myxomatosis and isolate organisms such as *Rickettsia burneti*, which causes Q fever.

Burnet's publications include *Viruses and Man*, published in 1953, and *The Clonal Selection Theory of Acquired Immunity* (1959).

C

Cairns, Hugh John Forster (*1922–*), is a British virologist known for his research into cancer.

Cairns was born on 21 November 1922, the son of Professor Sir Hugh Cairns, a physician and Fellow of Balliol College, Oxford. He attended Edinburgh Academy from 1933 to 1940, when he went to Balliol and gained his medical degree in 1943. His first appointment was in 1945 as Surgical Resident at the Radcliffe Infirmary, Oxford, and the next five years were spent in various appointments in London, Newcastle and Oxford. From 1950 to 1951 Cairns was a virologist at the Hall Institute in Melbourne, Australia, and he then went to the Viruses Research Institute, Entebbe, Uganda. In 1963 he became Director of the Cold Spring Harbor Laboratory of Quantitative Biology in New York, a position he held until 1968. He then took professorships at the State University of New York and with the American Cancer Society. From 1973 to 1981 he was in charge of the Mill Hill laboratories of the Imperial Cancer Research Fund, London. Since 1982 he has been in the United States at the Department of Microbiology of the Harvard School of Public Health, Boston.

One of Cairns' first pieces of research in the early 1950s was into penicillin-resistant staphylococci, and their incidence in relation to the length of a patient's stay in hospital. He found that the rapid rise in their incidence was caused by continuous cross-infection with a few strains of the bacteria rather than repeated instances of fresh mutations. These findings are now generally accepted, although they were not at the time.

Cairns has also done much research on the influenza virus and in 1952 discovered that the virus is not released from the infected cell in a burst – as is a bacteriophage – but in a slow trickle. This evidence has since been found also to be true for the polio virus. In the following year he showed that the influenza virus particle is completed as it is released through the cell surface (also unlike a phage). This discovery has since been confirmed by electron microscopy and isotope incorporation techniques. In 1959 Cairns succeeded in carrying out genetic mapping of an animal virus for the first time. In 1960 he showed that the DNA of the vaccinia virus is replicated in the cytoplasm or protoplasm of the cell (excluding the nucleus) and that each infecting virus particle creates a separate DNA "factory".

Cairns' investigations into DNA have also led him to look at the way that DNA replicates itself and to compare the rates of replication of DNA in mammals with those in *E. coli* (a bacterium). He has found that mammalian DNA is replicated more slowly than that of *E. coli*, but is replicated simultaneously at many points of replication.

His later work studied the link between DNA and cancer, some forms of which may be caused by the alkylation of bases in the DNA. He showed that bacteria are able to inhibit the alkylation mechanism in their own cells, and later demonstrated this ability in mammalian cells. A similar mechanism probably prevents a high incidence of DNA mutations in human beings despite the presence of alkylating agents in the environment. Cairns made many important advances in the study of cancer and its relation to society. He has also spent much time in fund-raising for cancer research.

Calne, Roy Yorke (*1930–*), is a British surgeon who has developed the technique of organ transplants in human patients, and pioneered kidney transplant surgery in the United Kingdom.

Calne was born on 30 December 1930 and educated at Lancing College and later at Guy's Hospital Medical School, London, where he qualified with distinction in 1953. He held a junior post at Guy's Hospital for one year before serving with the Royal Army Medical Corps from 1954 to 1956. After military service Calne spent two years at the Nuffield Orthopaedic Centre, Oxford, as a Senior House Surgeon, and then became Surgical Registrar at the Royal Free Hospital, London, until 1960. From 1960 to 1961 he went to the Peter Bent Brigham Hospital, Harvard Medical School, and on his return to Britain was appointed Lecturer in Surgery at St Mary's Hospital, London. In 1962 he became Senior Lecturer at the Westminster Hospital, where he remained until accepting the appointment of Professor of Surgery at Cambridge University in 1965.

The idea of removing a diseased organ and grafting on a healthy one is ancient. This concept was not finally realized, however, until the middle of the present century; Peter Medawar demonstrated in 1957 how the rejection of tissue grafts could be prevented, and Joseph Murray and his team working in Boston, USA, successfully transplanted a kidney from one identical twin to the other whose kidneys were afflicted with an incurable disease. Calne further developed the technique of kidney transplants, decreasing the possibility of rejection.

He has also carried out liver transplants. The liver is a complicated organ with many vital functions, and liver transplants presented serious technical problems. These have now been overcome, although liver transplants are still not carried out to the same extent as kidney transplants. One reason is that the patient cannot be kept in reasonable health while waiting for a suitable transplant – unlike a kidney patient who can be treated by dialysis (using a kidney machine).

Once the surgical techniques for tissue transplants were perfected, research centred around the development of specific immunosuppressive drugs to prevent the donor organs being rejected by the antigens produced by the recipient. Calne has persevered with his operations, despite the ethical arguments surrounding this type of surgery, and has encouraged many developments in transplant techniques.

Chain, Ernst Boris (*1906–1979*), was a German-born British biochemist who, in collaboration with Howard Florey, first isolated and purified penicillin and demonstrated its therapeutic properties. Chain, Florey and Alexander Fleming shared the 1945 Nobel Prize in Physiology and Medicine, Chain and Florey for their joint work in isolating penicillin and demonstrating its clinical use against infection, and Fleming for his initial discovery of the *Penicillium notatum* mould. Chain also received many other honours for his work, including a knighthood in 1969.

Chain was born on 19 June 1906 in Berlin, the son of a chemist. He was educated at the Luisengymnasium then at the Friedrich Wilhelm University in Berlin, from which he graduated in chemistry and physiology in 1930. After graduation he did research in the Chemistry Department of the Pathological Institute at the Charité Hospital in Berlin, but with the rise to power of Adolf Hitler in 1933, Chain emigrated to Britain. Initially he worked for a short time at University College, London, and then, on the recommendation of J.B.S. Haldane, he worked under Freder-

ick Gowland Hopkins at the Sir William Dunn School of Biochemistry at Cambridge University from 1933 to 1935. In that year Florey invited Chain to work with him at the Sir William Dunn School of Pathology at Oxford University as University Demonstrator and Lecturer in Chemical Pathology. In 1949 Chain was invited to be Guest Professor of Biochemistry at the Istituto Superiore di Sanita in Rome; in the following year he accepted a permanent position as Professor there and was also appointed Scientific Director of the International Research Centre for Chemical Microbiology. In 1961 he returned to Britain as Professor of Biochemistry at Imperial College, London, where he did much to ensure that the laboratories were equipped with modern facilities. On his retirement in 1973, Chain was made Emeritus Professor and Senior Research Fellow of Imperial College. He died on 12 August 1979 in Ireland.

At Oxford University, Chain initially investigated the observation first made by Fleming in 1924 that tears, nasal secretion and egg white destroyed bacteria. Chain showed that these substances contain an enzyme, lysozyme, which digests the outer cell wall of bacteria. In 1937, while preparing this discovery for publication, Chain found another observation of Fleming's, that the mould *Penicillium notatum* inhibits bacterial growth. In the following year, Chain, in collaboration with Florey, started research to try to isolate and identify the antibacterial factor in the mould. Chain first developed a method for determining the relative strength of a penicillin-containing broth by comparing its antibacterial effect (as shown on culture plates) with that of a standard penicillin solution, $1 \, cm^3$ of which is defined as containing 1 Oxford Unit of penicillin. Then he developed a method of purifying penicillin without destroying its antibacterial effect. He found that the optimum time for extraction of the penicillin is when the mould is one week old; he also found that free penicillin is acidic and is therefore more soluble in certain organic solvents than it is in water. He then agitated the penicillin broth with acidified ether or amyl acetate, reduced the acidity of the solution until it was almost neutral, removed impurities, and evaporated the purified solution at a low temperature to give a stable form of the active substance. Chain and his co-workers found that 1 mg of the active substance they had obtained contained between 40 and 50 Oxford Units of penicillin and that, in a concentration of only 1 part per million, it was still able to destroy staphylococcus bacteria. Furthermore, they also showed that their purified penicillin was only minimally toxic and that its antibacterial effect was not diminished by the presence of blood or pus. With E.P. Abraham, Chain then elucidated the chemical structure of crystalline penicillin, finding that there are four different types, each differing in their relative elemental constituents.

Chain also studied snake venoms and found that the neurotoxic effect of these venoms is caused by their destroying an essential intracellular respiratory co-enzyme.

Charnley, John (*1911-1982*), was a British orthopaedic surgeon who appreciated the importance of applying engineering principles to the practice of orthopaedics. He is best known for his work on degenerative hip disease and his new technique, the total hip replacement, or arthroplasty. He also successfully pioneered arthrodeses for the knee and hip. He was knighted in 1977 and awarded the Gold Medal of the British Medical Association in 1978.

Charnley was born on 29 August 1911 in Bury, Lancashire. He went to the local Grammar School and then to Manchester University. His academic achievements in medicine were impressive – he was the only student to pass primary FRCS before graduating MB (in 1935), and he obtained his FRCS in 1936, only a year after qualifying. At the outbreak of World War II Charnley became a major in the Royal Army Medical Corps and spent some time in the Middle East. At Heliopolis he ran the army splint factory, turning out the Thomas splint for treating leg fractures among the soldiers. When the war ended he went back to Manchester as a lecturer, and in 1947 he became Consultant Orthopaedic Surgeon at Manchester Royal Infirmary. He married in 1957 and had two children. In the mid-60s Charnley retired from the Infirmary in order to devote his time to hip arthroplasty at the Centre of Hip Surgery at Wrightington Hospital, Lancashire, where he became the Director. He built the centre up to become the primary unit for hip replacement in the world, and surgeons from many countries visited Wrightington to observe the latest techniques. The Royal Society acknowledged his contributions to surgery in 1975 when he was made a Fellow. He died suddenly on 5 August 1982.

The replacement of the femoral head and acetabulum (socket) in the hip had been researched and tried by McKee and others to treat the painful condition of degenerative hip disease, but Charnley realized that the fundamental problem was one of lubrication of the man-made joint. He carried out research on the joints of animals and tried using the low-friction substance polytetrafluoroethylene (PTFE or Teflon), with great success at first. Teflon was eventually abandoned,

but Charnley had learnt much – including the use of methyl methacrylate cement for holding the metal prosthesis or implant to the shaft of the femur. In 1962 the right high-density polythene was developed, and his results became increasingly successful.

For the treatment of rheumatoid arthritis Charnley devised a system for surgically fusing joint surfaces (arthrodesis) to immobilize the knee joint using an external compression device, which bears his name. A metal pin is passed through the lower femur and another through the upper tibia and these are clamped together externally to hold the bared joint surfaces together until the joint fuses, leaving it immobile but pain-free.

Throughout his career Charnley developed a series of highly practical and successful surgical instruments. In his fight against post-operative infection he used air "tents" which allowed the surgeon and the wound to be kept in a sterile atmosphere throughout the operation.

Cheyne, John (*1777-1836*), and **Stokes, William** (*1804-1878*), were two physicians who practised in Dublin and gave their name to Cheyne-Stokes breathing, or periodic respiration.

John Cheyne was born in Leith on 3 February 1777. He was educated at Edinburgh High School, and was formally apprenticed to his physician father at the age of 13. He qualified in 1795 and joined the British army as a surgeon. He returned four years later to take charge of an ordnance hospital at Leith and he began to take medicine seriously as a result of working for Charles Bell. He visited Dublin in 1809, and decided to settle there. In 1811 he became physician at Meath Hospital, where his practice flourished. He took the first professorial Chair in Medicine at the Royal College of Surgeons of Ireland in 1813, and was succeeded by Whitley Stokes, the father of William Stokes. Cheyne died in Newport Pagnell, Buckinghamshire, on 31 January 1836.

William Stokes studied clinical medicine at the Meath Hospital, then became a student in Edinburgh where he graduated in 1825. He went back to Dublin as physician to the Dublin General Dispensary, and later succeeded his father at the Meath Hospital. He died on 10 January 1878.

In 1818 Cheyne described the sign of periodic respiration which occurs in patients with intracranial disease or cardiac disease. His paper described the breathing that would cease entirely for a quarter of a minute or more, then would become perceptible and increase by degrees to quick, heaving breaths that gradually subside again. Stokes referred to Cheyne's paper in his famous book *The Diseases of the Heart and Aorta*, and thus their names became eponymous with the sign.

Stokes' name was also applied to Stokes-Adams attacks after his paper *Observations on Some Cases of Permanently Slow Pulse*, which was published in 1846.

Child, Charles Manning (*1869-1954*), was an American zoologist who tried to elucidate one of the central problems of biology – that of organization within living organisms.

Child was born on 2 February 1869 in Ypsilanti, Michigan, where his grandfather was a physician, then three weeks later was taken home to Higganum, a small village in Connecticut where his father was a farmer. The last-born and only surviving of five sons, Child was taught by his mother until he was nine years old, when he went to Higganum District School. He then attended High School in Middleton, Connecticut, from 1882 to 1886, after which he studied zoology at the Wesleyan University in Middletown, from which he graduated in 1890 and obtained his MSc in 1892. While studying at university he continued to live with his parents so that he could run the farm for his father, who had previously been incapacitated by a cerebral haemorrhage. His parents died in 1892, and two years later Child went to Leipzig University to research for his doctorate, which he gained in the same year. After returning to the United States, he went to the newly established University of Chicago in 1895 and remained there for almost all of his academic career – as Assistant (1895 to 1896), Associate (1896 to 1898), Instructor (1898 to 1905), Assistant Professor (1909 to 1916) and Professor (1916 to 1934). After his retirement in 1934, Child was appointed Professor Emeritus. The only interruptions to his association with the University of Chicago were two sabbaticals – to Duke University as Visiting Professor in 1930, and to Tohoku University in Japan as Visiting Professor of the Rockefeller Foundation from 1930 to 1931. On retiring, Child moved to Palo Alto in California and became a guest at Stanford University. He remained there until his death on 19 December 1954.

Child's early work concerned the functioning of the nervous system in various invertebrates, but his interest soon turned to embryology, in which field he did some important research into cell lineage – tracing the fate of each cell in the early embryo. In 1900, however, he began a long series of experiments on regeneration in coelenterates and flatworms, a topic that occupied him for most of his career. Child believed that the regeneration of a piece of an organism into a normal whole resulted from the piece functioning like the missing parts. In 1910 he perceived that there is a gradation in the rate of physiological processes along the longitudinal axis of organisms, and in the following year he developed his gradient theory. According to this theory, each part of an organism dominates the region behind and is dominated by that in front. In general, the region of the highest rate of activity in eggs, embryos and other reproductive regions becomes the apical end of the head of the larval form; in plants it becomes the growing tip of the shoot or of the primary root. Child also pointed out that regeneration is fundamentally the same as embryonic development, in that the dominant apical region is formed first then the other parts of the organism develop in relation to it. In 1915 Child demonstrated that the parts of an organism that have the highest metabolic rates are most susceptible to poisonous substances, but that these parts also have the greatest powers of recovery after damage.

Child's explanation of how the various cells and tissues in organisms are organized – by a gradation in the rate of physiological processes leading to relationships of dominance and subordination – may not be thought to be correct, but it was an important early contribution to the problem of functional organization within living organisms.

Clark, Wilfrid Edward Le Gros (*1895-1971*), was a British anatomist and surgeon who carried out important research that made a major contribution to the understanding of the structural anatomy of the brain.

Clark was born on 5 June 1895 in Hemel Hempstead, Hertfordshire. He went to Blundell's School in Tiverton and entered St Thomas's Hospital in 1912 on an entrance scholarship. He qualified in 1917 with a Conjoint Diploma, and joined the Royal Army Medical Corps without working his house appointments. He served in France until the end of World War I, after which he went back to St Thomas's as house surgeon to Sir Cuthbert Wallace. Clark became a Fellow of the Royal College of Surgeons in 1919. He took the post of Principal Medical Officer in Sarawak, Borneo, to gain experience in practical surgery, and began research into the evolution of primitive primates. After successfully treating several local people for yaws, he became highly venerated and was tattooed on the shoulders with the insignia of the Sea Dyaks as a mark of their esteem. Clark returned to England in 1923 as an anatomy demonstrator at St Thomas's until he moved to St Bartholomew's Hospital in 1924 as a reader, then Professor, of Anatomy. He returned to St

Thomas's as Professor of Anatomy in 1930, accepting the Professorship of Anatomy at Oxford in 1934, which he held until he retired in 1962. His work on primate evolution resulted in election to the Royal Society in 1935. During World War II his research was connected with the war effort despite his pacifist principles. After the war he created a new Department of Anatomy at Oxford which was finally opened in 1959. He was knighted in 1955, and was Arris and Gale lecturer (1932), Hunterian Professor (1934 and 1945), and editor of the *Journal of Anatomy*. He died suddenly in Burton Bradstock, Dorset, on 28 June 1971 on a visit to a friend from his student days.

Clark had a profound influence on the teaching of anatomy. He moved away from the popular topographical approach which encouraged students to learn repetitiously, and towards the importance of relating structure to function. His anatomy research was directed mainly towards the brain, and the relationship of the thalamus to the cerebral cortex. He also carried out further studies of the hypothalamus. His work on the sensory (largely visual) projections of the brain remains the basis of contemporary knowledge of this aspect of neuroanatomy.

His chief publications include: *Morphological Aspects of the Hypothalamus* (1938); *The Tissues of the Body* (1939); *History of the Primates* (1949); *Fossil Evidence of Human Evolution* (1955); and his autobiography *Chant of Pleasant Exploration* (1968).

Colles, Abraham (*1773-1843*), was an Irish surgeon who observed and described the fracture of the wrist which bears his name.

Colles was born on 23 July 1773 in County Kilkenny, Ireland; he was educated at Kilkenny Preparatory School and Kilkenny College. In 1790 he entered Trinity College, Dublin, as a student of arts, but swiftly began his clinical training as a resident surgeon at Steeven's Hospital. He was granted his diploma of the Royal College of Surgeons in Ireland in 1795. He then went to Edinburgh and graduated at Edinburgh University in 1797. He returned to Dublin that year to set up in practice and began to teach anatomy and surgery. In 1799 he was appointed Resident Surgeon at Steeven's Hospital (where he eventually became governor) and was elected a member of the Royal College of Surgeons in Ireland. At the age of 29 he became President of the College. In 1804 the Surgeons' School at the College made him Professor of Anatomy and Surgery (a position he held until 1836), and he gained his MA from the University of Dublin in 1832. He died at his home in Dublin on 16 November 1843.

In 1814 the paper on the Colles' fracture was published describing the fracture of the distal (carpel) end of the radius bone in the forearm. This common fracture causes deformity and swelling of the wrist, but can be easily and successfully treated once diagnosed. It must be remembered that the diagnosis of fractures in those days was made on purely clinical grounds because X-rays had not then been developed. Thus his accurate description of the fracture was that much more impressive. In his original paper he advocated the use of tin splints to stabilize the wrist after closed reduction of the fracture. Nowadays the reduction is followed by the use of plaster of Paris casts but exactly the same principles apply.

Although Colles is best remembered for the Colles' fracture, he was one of the greatest professors the Royal College of Surgeons in Ireland ever had. He was a brilliant anatomist and an excellent teacher who did much to make Dublin the leading medical centre it had become by the beginning of the nineteenth century.

Colles' other eponyms include Colles' fascia, Colles' space, the Colles' ligament (of inguinal hernia), and Colles' law of the communication of (congenital) syphilis.

Crick, Francis Harry Compton (*1916-*), **Watson, James Dewey** (*1928-*), and **Wilkins, Maurice Hugh Frederick** (*1916-*), shared the 1962 Nobel Prize in Physiology and Medicine for their work on determining the structure of DNA, generally considered to be the most important discovery in biology this century.

Crick was born on 8 June 1916 in Northampton and was educated at Hill School. After graduating in physics from University College, London, he worked from 1940 to 1947 for the British Admiralty on the development of radar and magnetic mines. He then chose to study biology and worked at the Strangeways Research Laboratory at Cambridge University from 1947 to 1949, after which he moved to the Medical Research Council's Laboratory of Molecular Biology (also at Cambridge University). It was while working there in 1951 that he met James Watson, an American student, and they performed their Nobel prize-winning research. Crick gained his PhD from Caius College, Cambridge, in 1953 and remained at the university - except for visiting lectureships to several American universities in 1959 and 1960 - until 1977, when he was appointed a Professor at the Salk Institute for Biological Studies in San Diego, California.

Watson was born on 6 April 1928 in Chicago and, when only 15 years old, entered the University of Chicago to study zoology. He graduated

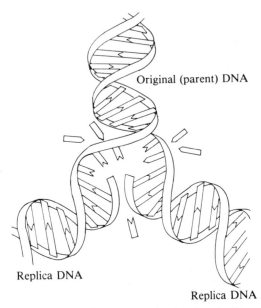

Original (parent) DNA

Replica DNA

Replica DNA

DNA replicates by a process that involves the "unzipping" of the parent double helix.

when he was 19, in 1947, and then did postgraduate research on viruses at the University of Indiana, from which he gained his PhD in 1950. In the same year he went to the University of Copenhagen to continue his work on viruses but his interest turned to molecular biology and in 1951 he went to the Cavendish Laboratory at Cambridge University, where he performed the famous work on DNA with Crick. In 1953 Watson returned to the United States, where he was Senior Research Fellow in Biology at the California Institute of Technology until 1955. He then held several positions in the Department of Biology at Harvard University: Assistant Professor from 1955 to 1958, Associate Professor from 1958 to 1961 and Professor from 1961. In 1968 he became Director of the Cold Spring Harbor Laboratory of Quantitative Biology.

Wilkins was born on 15 December 1916 in Pongaroa, New Zealand, the son of a physician. Taken to England at the age of six, he was educated at King Edward VI School, Birmingham, and St John's College, Cambridge, from which he graduated in physics in 1938. He gained his doctorate from the University of Birmingham in 1940 and then joined the Ministry of Home Security and Aircraft Production to work on radar, and later went to the University of California as part of the British team assigned to the Manhattan Project to develop the atomic bomb. Disillusioned with nuclear physics, he became interested in biophysics and in 1945 took up a position on

a biophysics project at St Andrews University in Scotland. In the following year he joined the Medical Research Council's Biophysics Research Unit at King's College, London, becoming its Assistant Director in 1950, Deputy Director in 1955 and Director in 1970 (until 1972). He was appointed Professor of Biophysics and Head of Department at King's College in 1970.

Following the discovery in 1946 that genes consist of DNA, Wilkins - working at King's College - began to investigate the structure of the DNA molecule. Studying the X-ray diffraction pattern of DNA, he discovered that the molecule has a double helical structure (one of his colleagues, Rosalind Franklin, also showed that DNA's phosphate groups are situated on the outside of the helix). Wilkins passed on his findings to Crick and Watson at Cambridge, who were trying to elucidate the detailed structure of DNA. Using Wilkins' results, Erwin Chargaff's discovery that nucleic acids contain only four different organic bases (with equal numbers of guanine and cytosine and equal numbers of adenine and thymine), and Alexander Todd's demonstration that nucleic acids contain sugar and phosphate groups, Crick and Watson postulated that DNA consists of a double helix consisting of two parallel chains of alternate sugar and phosphate groups linked by pairs of organic bases. They then built a series of accurate molecular models, eventually making one that incorporated all the known features of DNA and which gave the same diffraction pattern as that found by Wilkins. They envisaged replication occurring by a parting of the two strands of the double helix, each organic base thus exposed linking with a nucleotide (from the free nucleotides within a cell) bearing the complementary base. Thus two complete DNA molecules would eventually be formed by this step-by-step linking of nucleotides, with each of the new DNA molecules comprising one original strand and one new strand (so called semiconservative replication - as opposed to conservative replication, in which one DNA molecule would consist of both the original strands and the replicated molecule would consist of two new strands). Their model also explained how genetic information could be coded - in the sequence of organic bases. Crick and Watson published their work on the proposed structure of DNA in 1953, since when many other researchers have confirmed their hypothetical model and it is now generally accepted as correct.

Later Crick, this time working with Sydney Brenner, demonstrated that each group of three adjacent bases (he called a set of three bases a codon) on a single DNA strand codes for one specific amino acid. He also helped to determine the codons that code for each of the 20 main amino acids. Furthermore, he formulated the adaptor hypothesis, according to which adaptor molecules mediate between messenger RNA and amino acids. These adaptor molecules, now known as transfer RNAs, were later independently identified by Paul Berg and Robert Holley.

After working on the structure of DNA, Watson researched into the genetic code and, later, on cancer; and Wilkins applied his X-ray diffraction technique to RNA.

Cushing, Harvey Williams (*1869-1939*), was an American surgeon who pioneered several important neurosurgical techniques, made famous studies of the pituitary gland, and first described the chronic wasting disease now known as Cushing's syndrome (or disease).

Cushing was born on 8 April 1869 in Cleveland, Ohio, the fourth child in a family of physicians. He studied medicine at Yale College and at the Harvard Medical School, graduating from the latter in 1895. He then spent about four years in practical training at the Massachusetts General Hospital, Boston, and the Johns Hopkins Hospital, Baltimore, where he worked under William Halsted (1852-1922), a great innovator of surgical techniques. At about the turn of the century Cushing studied in Europe – under Emil Kocher (1841-1917) at Berne University and, briefly, under the famous neurophysiologist Charles Sherrington (1857-1952) in England – after which he returned to the Department of Surgery at the Johns Hopkins University. From 1912 to 1932 Cushing was Professor of Surgery at the Harvard Medical School and Surgeon-in-Chief at the Peter Bent Brigham Hospital in Boston. During this period he served in the Army Medical Corps in World War I and in 1918 was appointed Senior Consultant in Neurological Surgery to the American Expeditionary Force. In 1933 he became Sterling Professor of Neurology at Yale University, a post he held until his retirement in 1937. Cushing died on 7 October 1939 in New Haven, Connecticut. He bequeathed his large collection of books on the history of medicine and science to the Yale Medical Library.

Although Cushing is probably best known for his work on Cushing's syndrome, his major contribution was in the field of neurosurgery which, until he introduced his pioneering techniques, was seldom successful. As a result of experimenting on the effect of artificially increasing intercranial pressure in animals, Cushing developed new methods of controlling blood pressure and bleeding during surgery on human beings. Moreover, his whole approach to medicine was characterized by painstaking carefulness: before op-

erating he gave each of his patients an extremely thorough physical examination and took a detailed medical history. The operations themselves, which usually lasted for many hours, were performed with meticulous care and, over the years, were increasingly successful.

In addition to developing neurosurgical techniques, Cushing wrote a description – still valid today – of the stages in the development of different types of intercranial tumours, classified such tumours, and published (in 1917) a definitive account of acoustic nerve tumours.

In 1908 Cushing began studying the pituitary gland and, after experimenting on animals, discovered a way of gaining access to this gland which, being situated at the base of the brain and behind the nasal sinuses, is extremely difficult to approach surgically. As a result of this discovery it became possible to treat cases of blindness caused by tumours pressing on the optic nerve in the region of the pituitary gland. Cushing also investigated the effects of abnormal activity of the pituitary gland, establishing that hypopituitarism (undersecretion of pituitary hormones) in a growing person can cause a type of dwarfism and that hyperpituitarism (oversecretion of pituitary hormones) in fully grown adults can cause acromegaly (a form of giantism characterized by excessive growth of the bones of the hands, feet and face). As a result of his extensive studies of the pituitary gland, Cushing discovered the condition now called Cushing's syndrome, a rare chronic wasting disease with symptoms that include obesity of the face and trunk, combined with thin arms and legs; wasting of the muscles; atrophy of the skin, with the appearance of red lines on the skin; weakness; and accumulation of body fluids. Cushing attributed this disorder to a tumour of the basophilic cells of the anterior pituitary gland, but although this is one of the causes, the disorder is now known to be caused by any of several conditions that increase the secretion of glucocorticoids (particularly cortisol) by the adrenal glands, such as a tumour of the adrenal cortex itself.

Cushing was also interested in the history of medicine and in 1925 wrote a biography of William Osler (1849-1920) – one of the leading physicians of the time – which won him a Pulitzer Prize.

D

Dale, Henry Hallett (*1875-1968*), was a British physiologist who is best known for his work on the chemical transmission of nerve impulses (particularly for isolating acetylcholine), for which he was awarded – jointly with Otto Loewi, a German pharmacologist – the 1936 Nobel Prize in Physiology and Medicine. Dale also received numerous British honours, including the Copley Medal of the Royal Society in 1937, a knighthood in 1943, the Order of Merit in 1944 and, at various times during his career, the presidencies of the Royal Society, the British Association, the Royal Society of Medicine and the British Council. Furthermore, in 1959 the Society of Endocrinology struck the Dale Medal, an annual award, and in 1961 the Royal Society established the Henry Dale Professorship, bestowed by the Wellcome Trust, of which Dale had been the Chairman from 1938 to 1960.

Dale was born on 9 June 1875 in London, the son of a businessman, and was educated at Tollington Park College, London, then at Leys School, Cambridge. He read natural sciences at Trinity College, Cambridge, graduating in 1898, then succeeded Ernest Rutherford in the Coutts-Trotter Studentship at Trinity College. In 1900 Dale began his clinical training at St Bartholomew's Hospital, London, gaining a bachelor of surgery degree in 1903 and a medical degree in 1907. While undergoing his clinical training, Dale continued his physiological studies in London between 1902 and 1904 under Ernest Starling and William Bayliss, first as a George Henry Lewes Student and later as a Sharpey Student in the Department of Physiology at University College, London. He also studied under Paul Ehrlich in Frankfurt for several months. In 1904 Dale accepted a post at the Wellcome Physiological Research Laboratories, becoming Director there two years later. In 1914 he was appointed Head of the Department of Biochemistry and Pharmacology of the Medical Research Council, and from 1928 until his retirement in 1942 he was Director of the National Institute for Medical Research. He died in Cambridge on 23 July 1968.

Dale's earliest research, performed while he worked at the Wellcome Physiological Research Laboratories, concerned the chemical composition and effects of ergot (a fungus that infects cereals and other grasses). In 1910, working with G. Barger, he identified a substance in ergot extracts that produced dramatic effects, such as dilation of the arteries. Histamine, as this substance is now called, is found in all plant and animal cells and is one of the irritants in wasp venom, bee stings and stinging nettles.

In 1914 Dale isolated acetylcholine from biological material. Between 1921 and 1926 Otto Loewi and his co-workers showed that stimulation of the parasympathetic nerves in a perfused frog's heart (a heart which has an artificial passage of fluids through its blood vessels) resulted in the appearance of a substance that inhibited the action of a second heart that was receiving the perfused fluid from the first heart. This substance was later shown by Dale and Loewi to be acetylcholine, which is produced at the nerve endings of parasympathetic nerves. This finding provided the first definite proof that chemical substances are involved in the transmission of nerve impulses.

In addition to his research, Dale became concerned in his later years with the social effects of scientific developments. With Thorvald Madson of Copenhagen he was largely responsible for the adoption of an international scheme to standardize drugs and antitoxins. He was also concerned with preserving the apolitical nature of science and with the peaceful use of nuclear energy.

D'Arcy Thompson, Wentworth (*1860–1948*). See THOMPSON, D'ARCY WENTWORTH.

Darwin, Charles Robert (*1809–1882*), was a British naturalist famous for his theory of evolution and natural selection as put forward in 1859 in his book *The Origin of Species*.

Darwin was born in Shrewsbury on 12 February 1809. His father was a wealthy doctor, and his paternal grandfather was Erasmus Darwin, a well-known poet and physician; his mother's father was Josiah Wedgwood. Darwin was educated locally from 1818, and when he left school in 1825 he attended Edinburgh University to study medicine. But he abhorred medicine and the science taught to him there disgusted him, and two years later his father sent him to Christ's College, Cambridge, to study theology – which he did not enjoy either. Natural history was his main interest, which was very much increased by his acquaintance with John Stevens Henslow, who was Professor of Botany at Cambridge. Henslow recommended to the Admiralty that Darwin should accompany HMS *Beagle* as a naturalist on its survey voyage of the coasts of Patagonia, Tierra del Fuego, Chile, Peru and some Pacific islands. His father opposed this idea but, with the support of Wedgwood, Darwin sailed in the *Beagle* from Devonport on 27 December 1831 for a voyage of five years. On his return to England he found that some of his papers had been privately published during his absence and that he was regarded as one of the leading men of science. He published his findings on this epic voyage in the *Journal of Researches into the Geology and Natural History of the various countries visited by HMS Beagle (1832–1836)* in 1839. In 1838 he was appointed Secretary to the Geological Society, a position he retained until 1844. He married his cousin, Emma Wedgwood, in 1839, and the marriage produced ten children. He spent the rest of his life collating the findings made during the voyage and developing his theory for publication. He died on 19 April 1882 at Down, in Kent.

Before the voyage of the *Beagle* Darwin, like everyone else at that time, did not believe in the mutability of species. But in South America he saw fossil remains of giant sloths and other animals now extinct, and on the Galapagos Islands found a colony of finches that he could divide into at least 14 similar species, none of which existed on the mainland. It was obvious to him that one type must have evolved into many others, but how they did so eluded him. Two years after his return he read Malthus' *An Essay on the Principle of Population* (1798), which proposed that the human population is growing too fast for it to be adequately fed, and that something would have to happen to reduce it, such as war or natural disaster. This work inspired Darwin to see that the same principle could be applied to animal populations and he theorized that variations of a species which survive (while other members of the species do not) pass on the changed characteristic to their offspring. A new species is thereby developed which is fitter to survive in its environment than was the original species from which it evolved. Darwin did not make his ideas public at first, but put them into an essay in 1844 to which only his friend Joseph Hooker and a few others were privy.

In 1856 Darwin began writing fully about evolution and natural selection. Two years later he received a paper from a fellow naturalist, Alfred Wallace, explaining exactly the same theory of evolution and natural selection. At a loss for what to do, Darwin consulted his friends Charles Lyell and Hooker, who persuaded him to have the joint papers read in the absence of the authors before the Linnaean Society. The papers caused no stir, but Darwin was forced to speed up the completion of his work.

The abstract of Darwin's findings was published in 1859, and was called *The Origin of Species by means of Natural Selection or the Preservation of Favoured Races in the Struggle for Life*. It was very widely read, although many fellow scientists criticized it violently. Some considered that the book lacked a foundation of experimental evidence and was based purely on hypothesis; others were simply jealous. The Church was also shocked by Darwin's work because it implied that the Creation was not an actual occurrence, and if evolution worked automatically by natural selection then Divine intervention played no part in the lives of plants, animals, or man.

When Darwin wrote the book, he avoided the issue of the evolution of man and merely remarked at the end that "much light will be thrown on the origin of man and his history". He did not seek the controversy he caused but his ideas soon caught the public imagination. After the publication in 1871 of *The Descent of Man and Selection in Relation to Sex*, in which he argued that man evolved just like other organisms, the popular press soon published articles about the "missing link" between man and apes. In fact what Darwin believed was that man's ancestors, if alive today, would have been classified among the primates.

Darwin's name remains inseparably linked with the theory of evolution to this day. He never understood what actually caused newly formed advantageous characteristics to appear in animals and plants because he had no knowledge of heredity and mutations. The irony is that the key work on heredity by the Austrian monk Gregor Mendel was carried out during Darwin's own lifetime and published in 1865, but was neglected until 1900. Darwin's revolutionary publication, which is still widely read, marked a turning point in many of the sciences, including physical anthropology and palaeontology, and remains a source of strong controversy.

De Beer, Gavin Rylands (*1899–1972*), was a British zoologist known for his important contributions to embryology and evolution, notably disproving the germ layer theory and developing the concept of paedomorphism (the retention of juvenile characteristics of ancestors in mature adults). He received numerous honours for his work, including a knighthood in 1954.

De Beer was born on 1 November 1899 in London and, after military service in World War I, graduated from Oxford University. From 1926 to 1938 he was Jenkinson Memorial Lecturer in Embryology at Oxford University, after which he served in World War II. In 1945 he became Professor of Embryology at University College, London, then in 1950 was appointed Director of the British Museum (Natural History), a post he held until his retirement in 1960. De Beer died on 21 June 1972 in Alfriston, Sussex.

De Beer's first major work was his *Introduction to Experimental Embryology* (1926), in which he observed that some vertebrate structures, such as certain cartilage and bone cells, are derived from the outer ectodermal layer of the embryo. This finally disproved the germ layer theory, according to which cartilage and bone cells are formed from the mesoderm. Continuing his embryological investigations, de Beer described in *Embryos and Ancestors* (1940) his work which showed that certain adult animals retain some of the juvenile characteristics of their ancestors, a phenomenon called paedomorphism. This finding refuted Ernst Haeckel's theory of phylogenetic recapitulation, according to which the embryonic development of an organism repeats the adult stages of the organism's evolutionary ancestors.

Turning his attention to evolution, de Beer then suggested that gaps in the fossil records of early ancestral forms are due to the impermanence of the soft tissues in these early ancestors. Also in the field of evolution, his studies of the fossil *Archaeopteryx*, the earliest known bird, led him to propose mosaic evolution – whereby evolutionary changes occur piecemeal – to explain the presence of both reptilian and avian features in *Archaeopteryx*.

De Beer also researched into the functions of the pituitary gland, and applied scientific methods to various historical problems, such as the origin of the Etruscans (which he traced using blood group data) and establishing the route taken by Hannibal in his march across the Alps (for which de Beer used pollen analysis, glaciology and various other techniques).

De Duve, Christian René (*1917–*), is a British-born Belgian biochemist who discovered two organelles, the lysosome and the peroxisome. For this important contribution to cell biology he was awarded (jointly with Albert Claude and George Palade) the 1974 Nobel Prize in Physiology and Medicine.

De Duve was born on 2 October 1917 in Thames Ditton, Surrey, and was educated at the University of Louvain, Belgium, from which he graduated in medicine in 1941. He then held positions at the Nobel Institute, Stockholm, and Washington University before returning to Belgium in 1947. He now holds two positions: Professor of Biochemistry at the University of Louvain Medical School (since 1951) and Professor of Biochemistry at the Rockefeller Institute, New York City (since 1962).

De Duve discovered lysosomes in the cytoplasm of animal cells in 1955, since when a similar organelle has been found in plant and fungal cells. As seen under the electron microscope, lysosomes in animal cells are usually spherical, 0.2 to 0.4m in diameter, and are surrounded by a unit membrane. They are internally structureless but contain characteristic degradative enzymes, which can digest most known biopolymers, such as proteins, fats and carbohydrates. After his discovery of the lysosome, de Duve found that the main role of lysosomes in the normal functioning

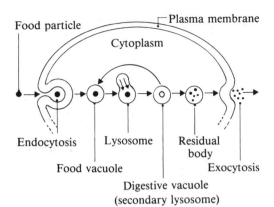

Intracellular digestion involving lysosomes.

of cells is intracellular digestion and he went on to describe the way in which this occurs. All cells require a supply of essential extracellular raw materials, some of which pass into the cell by diffusion. But with substances that are too large to diffuse into the cell, the cell membrane invaginates and surrounds the extracellular matter, forming a food vacuole; this process is called endocytosis. A lysosome then fuses with the food vacuole and releases its acid digestive enzymes into the vacuole (which at this stage is called a digestive vacuole or a secondary lysosome). The enzymes break down the material in the vacuole into molecules small enough to diffuse through the vacuole's wall into the cytoplasm. The undigested remnants contained within the residual body (as the vacuole is called at this stage) eventually pass out of the cell by exocytosis. In addition to intracellular digestion, lysosomes also play a part in the digestion and removal of dysfunctional organelles, a process known as autophagy.

Since the discovery of lysosomes and the elucidation of their role in intracellular processes, Hers – a collaborator of de Duve – found in 1964 that malfunctioning of the lysosomes (which often involves an absence or insufficiency of one or more of the lysosomal enzymes) is associated with several diseases, some of which are hereditary.

As a result of his research on lysosomes, de Duve suspected the existence of another organelle, and in the 1960s he discovered the peroxisome. Almost identical to the lysosome in structure, the peroxisome is characterized by the enzymes it contains. As yet, however, its function is unknown.

De Vries, Hugo Marie (*1848–1935*), was a Dutch botanist and geneticist who is best known for his rediscovery (simultaneously with Karl Correns and Erich Tschermak von Seysenegg) of Gregor

Mendel's laws of heredity and for his studies of mutation.

De Vries was born on 16 February 1848 in Haarlem, Holland. He studied medicine at the universities of Heidelberg and Leyden, graduating from the latter in 1870. He then taught at the University of Amsterdam from 1871 until 1875, when he went to work for the Prussian Ministry of Agriculture in Würzburg. In 1877 he taught at the universities of Halle and Amsterdam; he was appointed Assistant Professor of Botany at Amsterdam in the following year and became a full Professor there in 1881. De Vries remained at the University of Amsterdam - except for a visiting lectureship to the University of California in 1904 - until he retired in 1918. He died near Amsterdam on 21 May 1935.

De Vries began his work on genetics in 1886, when he noticed that some specimens of the evening primrose (*Oenothera lamarckiana*) differed markedly from others. He cultivated seeds of the various types in his experimental garden, and also undertook detailed research to discover the origin of the plants and the history of the species introduced into Europe. At the time it was believed that *Oenothera lamarckiana* had been introduced from Texas and was known by Jean Lamarck under the name *Oenothera grandiflora*. De Vries, however, discovered that the plant was unknown in the United States, from which he concluded that *Oenothera lamarckiana* was a pure species. Continuing his investigations, he began a programme of plant breeding experiments in 1892. Eight years later he formulated the same laws of heredity that - unknown to De Vries - Mendel had discovered 34 years previously; but while searching the scientific literature on the subject, De Vries came across Mendel's paper of 1866. De Vries' work went further than had Mendel's, however: he found that occasionally an entirely new variety of *Oenothera* appeared and that this variety reappeared in subsequent generations. De Vries first called these new varieties that appeared suddenly single variations but later called them mutations. He postulated that, in the course of evolution, a species produces mutants only during discrete, comparatively short periods (which he called mutation periods) in which the latent characters are formed. He also distinguished between mutants with useful characteristics (which he called progressive mutants) and those with useless or harmful traits (which he called retrogressive mutants), and proposed that only the progressive mutants contribute to the evolution of the species. Furthermore, he suggested that mutation was the means by which new species originated and that those mutations that were favourable for the survival of the individual per-

sisted unchanged until other, more favourable mutations occurred. He considered the slight variations caused by environmental factors to be insignificant in the evolutionary process, mutations being the most important factor involved. De Vries' work on heredity and mutations - which he summarized in *Die Mutationstheorie* (1901 to 1903; translated into English as *The Mutation Theory*, 1910 to 1911) was soon generally accepted and played an important role in helping to establish Darwin's theory of evolution.

Thomas Hunt Morgan, in his work on the fruit fly *Drosophila*, also encountered unexpected new variations that were capable of breeding true, and he assumed that this was the result of a change in their genes; using De Vries' terminology, Morgan applied the term mutation to this spontaneous change in a gene. It has since been discovered that the mutations found by De Vries resulted from changes in the number of chromosomes in the new species, not from changes to the genes themselves. Today the term mutation refers to any change in the genetic material and includes many additional types of changes not known to De Vries.

De Vries' other major contribution concerned the physiology of plant cells. Experimenting on the effects of salt solutions of various concentrations on plant cells, he demonstrated in 1877 how plasmolysis of the cells can be used to establish a series of isotonic solutions.

Dobzhansky, Theodosius (*1900-1975*), was a Russian-born American geneticist whose synthesis of Darwinian evolution and Mendelian genetics established evolutionary genetics as an independent discipline. He also wrote about human evolution and the philosophical aspects of evolution.

Dobzhansky was born on 25 January 1900 in Nemirov, Russia, the son of a mathematics teacher. His family moved to Kiev in 1910 and Dobzhansky first attended school there. In 1917 he went to Kiev University to study zoology and, after graduating in 1921, remained there to teach zoology until 1924, when he moved to Leningrad University as a teacher of genetics. Also in 1924 he married Natalia Sivertzev, whom he met while teaching at Kiev. In 1927 Dobzhansky went as a Rockefeller Fellow to Columbia University, New York City, where he worked with Thomas Hunt Morgan, one of the pioneers of modern genetics. Morgan moved to the California Institute of Technology in 1928 and, impressed with Dobzhansky's ability, offered him a post teaching genetics there when his fellowship ended in 1929. Dobzhansky, who had become an American citizen in 1937, remained at the California Institute of Technology until 1940, when he returned to Columbia University as Professor of Zoology. He then worked at the Rockefeller Institute (later the Rockefeller University) from 1962 until his official retirement in 1971, after which he moved to the University of California at Davis, where he remained until his death on 18 December 1975.

Dobzhansky's most important contribution to genetics was probably his *Genetics and the Origin of Species* (1937), which was the first significant synthesis of Darwinian evolutionary theory and Mendelian genetics - areas in which there had been much progress since about 1920. This book was highly influential and established the discipline of evolutionary genetics.

Dobzhansky's other major contribution was his demonstration in the 1930s that genetic variability within populations is greater than was then generally thought. Until this work the consensus of opinion was that, in the wild state, most members of a species had the same "wild-type" genotype and that each of the wild-type genes was homozygous in most individuals. Variant genes were usually deleterious mutants that rapidly vanished from the gene pool. Furthermore, when an advantageous mutation appeared, it gradually - over several generations - increased in frequency until it became the new, normal wild type. Working with wild populations of the vinegar fly *Drosophila pseudoobscura*, Dobzhansky found that, in fact, there is a large amount of genetic variation within a population and that some genes regularly changed in frequency with the different seasons. Continuing this line of research, he also showed that many of the variant genes are recessives and so are not commonly expressed in the phenotype - a finding that disproved the original assumption of a high level of homozygosis in wild populations. Furthermore, he found that heterozygotes are more fertile and better able to survive than are homozygotes and, therefore, tend to be maintained at a high level in the population.

Dobzhansky also investigated speciation and, using the fly *Drosophila paulistorum*, proved that there is a period when speciation is only partly complete and during which several races co-exist. In addition, he wrote on human evolution - in which area his *Mankind Evolving* (1962) had great influence among anthropologists - and on the philosophical aspects of evolution in *The Biological Basis of Human Freedom* (1956) and *The Biology of Ultimate Concern* (1967).

Domagk, Gerhard (1895-1964), was a German bacteriologist and a pioneer of chemotherapy who discovered the antibacterial effect of Prontosil, the first of the sulphonamide drugs. This important discovery led, in turn, to the development of a range of sulphonamide drugs effective against various bacterial diseases, such as pneumonia and puerperal fever, that previously had high mortality rates. For this outstanding achievement Domagk received many honours, including the 1939 Nobel Prize in Physiology and Medicine. At the time, however, Germans were forbidden by Adolf Hitler to accept such awards and Domagk did not receive his Nobel medal until 1947, by which time the prize money had reverted to the funds of the Nobel Foundation.

Domagk was born on 30 October 1895 in Lagow, Brandenburg (now in Poland), and studied medicine at Kiel University, graduating - after a period of military service during World War I - in 1921. In 1924 he became Reader in Pathology at the University of Griefswald then, in the following year, was appointed to a similar position at the University of Münster. In 1927 he accepted an invitation to direct research at the Laboratories for Experimental Pathology and Bacteriology of I.G. Farbenindustrie, Düsseldorf, a prominent German dye-making company. But he also remained on the staff of Münster University, which appointed him Extraordinary Professor of General Pathology and Pathological Anatomy in 1928 and a Professor in 1958. Domagk died on 24 April 1964 in Burgberg, West Germany.

Following Paul Ehrlich's discovery of anti-protozoon chemotherapeutic agents, considerable advances had been made in combating protozoon infections but bacterial infections still remained a major cause of death. While working for I.G. Farbenindustrie, Domagk began systematically to test the new azo dyes in an attempt to find an effective antibacterial agent. In 1932 his industrial colleagues synthesized a new azo dye called Prontosil red, which Domagk found was effective against streptococcal infections in mice. In 1935 he published his discovery, but it received little favourable response. In the following year, however, the British Medical Research Council confirmed his findings, and shortly afterwards the Pasteur Institute in Paris found that the sulphonilamide portion of the Prontosil molecule is responsible for its antibacterial action. (This latter was an important finding because sulphonilamide is much cheaper to produce than is Prontosil.) Meanwhile Domagk had demonstrated the effectiveness of Prontosil in combating bacterial infections in humans. His daughter had accidentally infected herself while working on the clinical trials of Prontosil and, after the failure of conventional treatments, Domagk had cured her with Prontosil.

From about 1938 other sulphonamide drugs

were produced that were effective against a number of hitherto serious bacterial diseases, but antibiotics were discovered shortly afterwards and they came to replace sulphonamides as the normal drugs used to treat bacterial infections. Nevertheless, sulphonamides and chemotherapy were - and still are - of great value, particularly in the treatment of antibiotic-resistant infections. In 1946 Domagk and his co-workers found two compounds (eventually produced under the names of Conteben and Tibione) which, although rather toxic, proved useful in treating tuberculosis caused by antibiotic-resistant bacteria. Subsequently Domagk attempted to find chemotherapeutic agents for treating cancer, but was unsuccessful.

Driesch, Hans Adolf Eduard (*1867-1941*), was a German embryologist and philosopher who is best known as one of the last advocates of vitalism, the theory that life is directed by a vital principle and cannot be explained solely in terms of chemical and physical processes. Nevertheless, he also made several important discoveries in embryology, although these have tended to be overlooked because of his mistaken belief in vitalism.

Driesch was born on 28 October 1867 in Bad Kreuznach (now in West Germany), the son of a prosperous gold merchant. He studied zoology, chemistry and physics at the universities of Hamburg, Freiburg, Munich and Jena, obtaining his doctorate from Jena - where he studied under Ernst Haeckel - in 1887. Coming from an affluent family, Driesch had no need of paid employment and he spent the next 22 years privately pursuing his embryological studies. After obtaining his doctorate, he travelled extensively in Europe and the Far East, spending nine years (1891 to 1900) working at the International Zoological Station in Naples. In 1899 he married Margarete Reifferscheidt; they later had two children, both of whom became musicians. Eventually Driesch settled in Heidelberg, and in 1909 he was appointed Privatdozent (unpaid lecturer) in Philosophy at the university there, becoming Professor of Philosophy in 1911. Subsequently he was Professor of Philosophy at Cologne University from 1920 to 1921 and at Leipzig University from 1921 to 1935, when he was forced to retire by the Nazi regime. Driesch died in Leipzig on 16 April 1941.

In 1891 Driesch, experimenting with sea-urchin eggs, discovered that when the two blastomeres of the two-cell stage of development are separated, each half is able to develop into a pluteus (a later larval stage) which is completely whole and normal, although of smaller than average size. Similarly he found that small, whole individuals can be obtained by separating the four cells of the four-cell stage of development. From these findings he concluded that the fate of a cell is not determined in the early developmental stages. Later, other workers discovered the same phenomenon in the early developmental stages of hydroids, most vertebrates and certain insects. (It should be noted, however, that not all animal eggs behave in this way; for example, separation of the early embryonic cells of annelids, molluscs and ascidians results in incomplete embryos.) Subsequently Driesch produced an oversized larva by fusing two normal embryos, and in 1896 he was the first to demonstrate embryonic induction when he displaced the skeleton-forming cells of sea-urchin larvae and observed that they returned to their original positions. These findings provided a great impetus to embryological research but Driesch himself - unable to explain his results in mechanistic terms (principally because at that time very little was known about biochemistry) - came to believe that living activities, especially development, were controlled by an indefinable vital principle, which he called entelechy. After his appointment as Privatdozent in 1909, Driesch abandoned scientific research and devoted the rest of his life to philosophy.

Dubois, Marie Eugène François Thomas (*1858-1940*), was the Dutch palaeontologist who in 1891 discovered the remains of *Pithecanthropus erectus*, known as Java Man.

Dubois was born in Eijsden, Holland, on 28 January 1858 and studied medicine and natural history at the University of Amsterdam. In 1886 he took the appointment of lecturer in anatomy there. A year later he joined the Dutch Army Medical Service and was posted to Java - then a Dutch possession - where he was commissioned by the Dutch government to search for fossils. The discoveries he made there brought him world-wide fame and he returned to Europe in 1895. Dubois took up a professorship in palaeontology, geology and mineralogy at the University of Amsterdam in 1899. He retired in 1928 and died at Halen in Belgium on 16 December 1940.

The excavations of Pompeii and Herculaneum in 1748, and later of Troy (1870) were the beginnings of archaeology and encouraged attempts to piece together the history of man's development. In 1857 Neanderthal Man was found and later Cro-Magnon Man was discovered in south-western France. After Darwin published his *Origin of Species* in 1859, many people thought that the evolutionary principles he had outlined could equally apply to the origin of the human species.

The skeletons already found were undoubtedly those of an early species of man, but there was still a large gap in evolutionary terms between modern man and the apes. Having first been involved in the comparative anatomy of vertebrates Dubois became fascinated with the problem of the "missing link" in the evolutionary chain and was convinced that somewhere there existed its remains. He reasoned that such a missing link could have lived in an area where apes were still numerous, such as Africa or south-eastern Asia. His posting to Java gave Dubois the opportunity to investigate this theory.

The remains of extinct animals had been found in the deposits of volcanic ash on the banks of the Solo River in East Java and it was in the bone beds near the village of Trinil that he concentrated his search. In 1891 Dubois found teeth, a skullcap and a femur. The skullcap was much larger than that of any living ape, and more primitive and ape-like than Neanderthal Man; the bones were heavily ridged and the vault of the braincase extremely low, indicating that the size of the brain was far smaller than that of modern man. The teeth were also intermediate between ape and man. The femur was definitely human, the ends of the bone and the straightness of the shaft suggesting that its owner had walked erect.

Dubois published a scientific description of the fragments he had found in 1894, and named them *Pithecanthropus erectus* (erect ape-man) after the name given to the intermediate man by the German zoologist Ernst Haeckel.

The femur Dubois had found was discovered some distance away from the skullcap and could therefore have been from some other form of man. Many people were not convinced that Dubois had discovered the missing link, especially when further excavations at Trinil produced no more traces of *Pithecanthropus erectus*. In response to the controversy aroused by his findings, Dubois withdrew his discovery from the public until 1923. But between 1936 and 1939 the German archaeologist, von Koenigswald, was working in the Solo River valley farther upstream from Dubois' original discoveries, and found more skullcaps, a lower and an upper jaw. Later, a child's skull was discovered at Modjokerto on Java and is now believed to be from a young *Pithecanthropus erectus*.

Detailed measurements of casts of the skull of *Pithecanthropus erectus* indicated that the brain cavity had a volume of about 940 cm³, whereas few apes have more than 600 cm³ and modern man has about 1,500 cm³. From these figures it was thought that *Pithecanthropus erectus* was almost exactly half-way between ape and man on the evolutionary scale, although it is now considered that he is definitely more human and is called *Homo erectus*. In contrast to this belief, in Dubois' later years he changed his ideas and stressed the ape-like similarities of his discovery rather than its hominid likenesses.

The history of man's descent has been further pieced together as archaeological techniques have been refined and more discoveries have been made. But it cannot be doubted that one of the most important of these contributions has been that of Dubois.

E

Edwards, Robert (*1925-*   ), is a British physiologist who, after many years of successful experimental work with embryos, became interested in the problem of human infertility. He and **Steptoe, Patrick** (*1913-*   ), a highly skilled and experienced British surgeon, devised a technique for fertilizing a human egg outside the body and transferring the fertilized embryo to the uterus of a woman. A child born following the use of this technique is popularly known as a "test-tube" baby.

Edwards was educated at the universities of Wales and Edinburgh and served in the British Army from 1944 to 1948. For the next three years he was at the University College of North Wales, Bangor, and from 1951 to 1957 at the University of Edinburgh. That year Edwards went to the California Institute of Technology but returned to England the following year to the National Institute of Medical Research at Mill Hill, remaining there until 1962 when he took up an appointment at Glasgow University. A year later he moved again to the Department of Physiology at Cambridge.

During his research in Edinburgh Edwards successfully replanted mouse embryos into the uterus of a mouse and he wondered if the same process could be used to replant a human embryo into the uterus of a woman.

One common cause of infertility in women is disease or damage to the Fallopian tubes, which prevents eggs from being fertilized. Normally these tubes allow the mature egg, when released from the ovary, to travel to the uterus and if spermatozoa are present the egg will become fertilized on the way. Gregory Pincus (1903-1967), the American biologist who developed the contraceptive pill, showed that human eggs could mature outside the body, when they would be ready for fertilization. Edwards, by then working in Cambridge, was able to obtain human eggs from pieces of ovarian tissue removed during surgery. He found that the ripening process was very slow, the first division beginning only after 24 hours.

During the following year he studied the maturation of eggs of different species of mammals, and in 1965 attempted the fertilization of human eggs. He left mature eggs with spermatozoa overnight and found just one where a sperm had passed through the outer membrane, but it had failed to fertilize the egg. In 1967 Edwards read a paper by Steptoe describing the use of a new instrument, known as the laparoscope, to view the internal organs, which he saw had a possible application to his own research. At about this time, Bavister, a research student at Cambridge, who had been trying to fertilize hamster eggs, devised a successful culture solution. Edwards used some of this solution with the one he used for the culture of human eggs and achieved fertilization.

Patrick Steptoe was educated at King's College and St George's Hospital Medical School, London, qualifying in 1939. During World War II he served in the Royal Naval Volunteer Reserve and was a prisoner of war in Italy from 1941 to 1943. He was appointed Chief Assistant Obstetrician and Gynaecologist at St George's Hospital, London, in 1947, and Senior Registrar at Whittington Hospital in 1949. From 1951 to 1978 he was Senior Obstetrician and Gynaecologist at Oldham General Hospital, and from 1969 Director of the Centre for Human Reproduction.

The paper which interested Edwards described laparoscopy, Steptoe's method of exploring the interior of the abdomen without a major operation. Steptoe inserted the laparoscope through a small incision near the navel and by means of this telescope-like instrument, with its object lens inside the body and its eyepiece outside, he was able to examine the ovaries and other internal organs.

Early in 1968 Edwards and Steptoe met and arranged to collaborate. During the next few months they repeated experiments on the fertilization of human eggs. Steptoe treated volunteer patients with a fertility drug to stimulate maturation of the eggs in the ovary, while Edwards devised a simple piece of apparatus to be used with the laparoscope for collecting mature eggs from human ovaries. The mature eggs were removed and Edwards then prepared them for fertilization using spermatozoa provided by the patient's husband. For a year they continued experiments of this kind until they were sure that the fertilized eggs were developing normally. The next step was to see if an eight-celled embryo would develop to the blastocyst stage (the last stage of growth before it implants itself into the wall of the uterus); success was achieved.

In 1971, Edwards and Steptoe were ready to introduce an eight-celled embryo into the uterus of a volunteer patient who hoped to become pregnant, but this and similar attempts over a period of three years were unsuccessful. In 1975 an embryo did implant, but in the stump of a Fallopian tube where it could not develop properly and was a danger to the mother. It was removed, but it did demonstrate the basic technique to be sound. In 1977 it was decided to abandon the use of the fertility drug and remove the egg at precisely the right natural stage of maturity; an egg was fertilized and then reimplanted (a process called *in vitro* fertilization) in the mother two days later. The patient became pregnant and 12 weeks later the position of the baby was found to be satisfactory and its heartbeat could be heard. The last eight weeks of the pregnancy were kept under close medical supervision and a healthy girl – Louise Brown – was delivered by Caesarean section on 25 July 1978.

Edwards and Steptoe have shown how one common cause of infertility may be overcome. In Britain, infertility due to non-functional Fallopian tubes affects several thousand newly married women every year, of which only a half can be helped by conventional methods. *In vitro* fertilization has also been used to overcome the infertility in men that is due to a low sperm count. Edwards' research has further added to knowledge of the development of the human egg and young embryo, and Steptoe's laparoscope is a valuable instrument capable of wider application.

Ehrlich, Paul (*1854-1915*), was a German bacteriologist who founded chemotherapy – the use of a chemical substance to destroy disease organisms in the body. He was also one of the earliest workers on immunology, and through his studies on blood samples the discipline of haematology was recognized. In 1908, together with the Russian-French bacteriologist Ilya Mechnikov (1845-1916), he was awarded the Nobel Prize in Physiology and Medicine for his work on serum therapy and immunity.

Ehrlich was born on 14 March 1854 in Silesia, which was then part of the Austro-Hungarian Empire, in a town called Strehlin (now Strzelin, in Poland). He studied in Breslau and Strasbourg, graduating in 1878 with a medical degree from the University of Leipzig. For the next six years he was a clinical assistant at the University of Berlin and then became Head Physician at the medical clinic in the Charité Hospital in Berlin; in 1884 he was promoted to Professor there. Ehrlich spent two years in Egypt, from 1886 to 1888, to cure himself of tuberculosis. Successful, he returned to Berlin in 1889 where he set up a small private laboratory. The following year, he took up a professorial appointment at the University of Berlin. In 1891 he joined the Institute of Infectious Diseases, Berlin, as a researcher and five years later became Director of the newly established Institute for the Investigation and Control of Sera, opened in Berlin by the German government which was impressed by his efforts. Ehrlich continued working in his laboratories until just before his death on 20 August 1915.

As a student, Ehrlich had shown unusual fascination with chemistry. Encouraged by his teachers he worked on the use of aniline dyes in microscopic techniques and discovered a few dyes for selectively staining, and therefore simplifying the study of, bacteria. He made histological preparations and stained them with various combinations of dyes to observe the different effects of basic and acidic stains. While at the Charité Hospital Ehrlich was able to distinguish between a number of blood disorders by examining blood cells in his stained preparations. In this way he discovered "mast cells" (connective tissue cells), and it was also while studying the staining of tubercle cells that he contracted a mild case of tuberculosis.

On his return from his curative stay in Egypt, Ehrlich teamed up with the German bacteriologist Emil von Behring (1854–1917) and the Japanese Shibasaburo Kitasato (1856–1931) to try to find a cure for diphtheria. Ehrlich had studied antigen-antibody reactions using toxic plant proteins on mice, gradually increasing the dose, and found that the mice developed specific antibodies in their blood. Litters bred from these immunized mice possessed a short-lived immunity, sustained by suckling from the immunized mothers. Behring and Ehrlich were able to produce antitoxins obtained from much larger mammals which had been immunized against the diphtheria organism; these antitoxins were concentrated and purified for use in clinical trials, and once Ehrlich had developed the correct dosage, in 1892, the antitoxin was ready for use. In 1894 it was tried on 220 children with diphtheria and achieved great success. Ehrlich then decided that antitoxins should be standardized, their potency described in terms of international units of antitoxin, and the distribution made in dried form in vacuum phials.

At the Institute for the Investigation and Control of Sera, the number of Ehrlich's staff allowed him to investigate his theory that chemical compounds could cure a disease and not merely alleviate the symptoms. This stage was the beginning of chemotherapy (Ehrlich's word). The search progressed for dyes that would stain only bacteria and not other cells, and from this research the team continued synthesizing and testing chemical substances that could seek out and destroy the bacteria without harming the human body. Ehrlich termed these compounds "magic bullets".

Ehrlich's first success developed from the use of trypan red to kill trypanosomes (parasitic protozoans which cause sleeping sickness) in infected mice. The results of the tests proved inconclusive, but Ehrlich decided that the active agents in trypan red were nitrogen compounds. Atoxyl – an arsenical organic compound, and therefore similar in chemical properties to its nitrogen analogues – had shown greater success in the treatment of sleeping sickness and Ehrlich believed that it should be possible to make more effective derivatives of the substance. The accepted formula for atoxyl was a benzene ring with one side chain; Ehrlich, however, believed it had two side chains. If the accepted formula was correct, any derivatives would be unstable; but if Ehrlich was correct, they would be stable. Ehrlich proved to be right. He and his staff prepared nearly a thousand derivatives of arsenic-containing compounds, testing each one on animals. In 1907, they reached Compound Number 606 (dihydroxy-diamino-arsenobenzene hydrochloride), which proved ineffective against trypanosomes and so was forgotten. But it was investigated again in 1909 and discovered to be effective, instead, against spirochaetes, the bacteria that cause syphilis. Ehrlich tried it on himself, without any harm, and in 1910 announced the discovery of the synthetic chemical, now called Salvarsan (arsphenamine), for treating syphilis.

Ehrlich devised scientific techniques for developing chemical cures that opened up new fields of research in twentieth-century medicine, particularly in chemotherapy, haematology and immunology. Innumerable lives have been saved and the economic and social effects of his work continue to be far-reaching.

Enders, John Franklin (*1897–*), is an American microbiologist who succeeded in culturing viruses in quantity outside the human body. Before this time, progress in research on viruses had been greatly hindered by the fact that viruses need living cells in which to grow. For his work on virus culture he was awarded the 1954 Nobel Prize in Physiology and Medicine, which he shared with Frederick Robbins (1916–) and Thomas Weller (1915–).

Enders was born on 10 February 1897 in West Hartford, Connecticut, the son of a banker. He was educated at Yale University but interrupted his studies to become a flying instructor during World War I and did not graduate until 1920. He then took up a business career but left it to study

English at Harvard. Enders changed to study medicine, and finally obtained a doctorate in bacteriology in 1930. He remained at Harvard Medical School, progressing from Instructor in 1930 to Professor in 1962 and Professor Emeritus in 1968. From 1947 to 1972 he was Chief of Research in the Division of Infectious Diseases at the Children's Hospital Medical Center, Boston. From 1972 he was Chief of the Virus Research Unit at the hospital.

Viruses cannot be grown, as bacteria can, in nutrient substances, and so a method had been developed for growing them in a living chick embryo. Enders believed that he could improve on this method and reasoned that it was unnecessary to use a whole organism, but that living cells might be sufficient. In 1948 Enders and his colleagues, Robbins and Weller, prepared a medium of homogenized chick embryo and blood and attempted to grow a mumps virus in it. This experiment had been tried before, unsuccessfully, but at that time penicillin had not been available and it was penicillin that they added to suppress the growth of bacteria in the mixture. The experiment worked and they turned to the growth of other viruses.

The disease poliomyelitis attacked and debilitated many children at that time and they decided to investigate the virus responsible. Previously the polio virus could be grown only in living nerve tissue of primates. But using their method, Enders managed to grow the virus successfully on tissue scraps obtained first from stillborn human embryos, and then on other tissue.

In the 1950s, the threesome produced a vaccine against the measles virus, which was improved and then produced commercially in 1963.

The virus culture technique developed by Enders and his co-workers enabled virus material to be produced in sufficient quantity for experimental work. The use of this technique meant that viruses could be more readily isolated and identified.

Erasistratus (*fl. c. 250* BC), was a Greek physician and anatomist regarded as the father of physiology. He came close to discovering the true function of several important systems of the body which were not fully understood until nearly a thousand years later when physiologists had access to far more advanced methods of experimentation and dissection.

Erasistratus was born on the island of Ceos (now the Aegean island of Khios). He learnt his skills in Athens and became court physician to Seleucus I, who governed western Asia. He then moved on to Alexandria where he taught and advanced some of the work of the Greek anatomist Herophilus. But the Egyptians, among whom he worked, were morally against the use of cadavers for dissection, so that after Erasistratus this type of anatomical research ceased until well into the thirteenth century.

Erasistratus dissected and examined the human brain noting the convolutions of the outer surface, and observed that the organ is divided into larger and smaller portions (the cerebrum and cerebellum). He compared the human brain with those of other animals and made the correct hypothesis that the surface area/volume complexity is directly related to the intelligence of the animal. He traced the network of veins, arteries and nerves and realized the topographical associations, but his conclusions ran too closely along the lines of popular opinion. He postulated that the nerves carry the "animal" spirit, the arteries the "vital" spirit, and the veins blood. He did, however, grasp a rudimentary principle of oxygen exchange, noting that air was taken from the lungs to the heart where it became vital spirit for distribution via the arteries (as vital spirit) to the brain and then via the nerves to the body as animal spirit. (If one reads vital spirit as haemoglobin, he was not far wrong.) He also put forward the idea of capillaries, explaining that the reason an artery bleeds when cut is because, as the vital spirit flows out, the blood rushes in from the veins through the capillaries to replace the vacuum created. He described the valves in the heart and condemned bloodletting as a form of treatment.

Erasistratus came near to discovering the principle of blood circulation (although he had it circulating in the wrong direction), but this mystery was not to be finally unravelled until Harvey's discoveries of the seventeenth century.

Eysenck, Hans Jurgen (*1916–*), is probably Britain's best-known psychologist, renowned for his controversial theories about a wide range of subjects, especially human intelligence.

Eysenck was born in Germany on 4 March 1916 and educated at various schools in Germany, France and Britain. With the rise to power of Adolf Hitler in the 1930s he left Germany and went to Britain. He studied psychology at London University, graduating in 1938 and gaining his doctorate in 1940. During the rest of World War II he was Senior Research Fellow Psychologist at the Mill Hill Emergency Hospital, London, and in 1946 he was appointed Director of the Psychology Department at the Maudsley Hospital, Surrey, a post he still holds. (Although he is head of this department, which treats more than 1,000 people every year for various neuroses, Eysenck does not involve himself directly in treatment; instead he produces theories for treatment.) He went to the United States in 1949 as Visiting Professor at the University of Pennsylvania, and on his return to Britain in 1950 became Reader in Psychology at London University's Institute of Psychiatry. In 1954 he again went to the United States, as Visiting Professor at the University of California. In the following year he was appointed Professor of Psychology at London University's Institute of Psychiatry, another position he still holds.

Eysenck has investigated many areas of psychology, often producing highly controversial theories as a result of his studies. But it is his theory that intelligence is almost entirely inherited and can be only slightly modified by education that has aroused the greatest opposition. The concept of intelligence is difficult to define and even more difficult to measure – the commonly used intelligence tests, for example, are often criticized for being culturally biased, favouring well educated white people and penalizing poorly educated black people. Eysenck has attempted to devise a fairer, culture-free method for assessing intelligence. It involves neither problem-solving nor even conscious thought and therefore, Eysenck argues, it cannot be criticized for being culturally biased. Basically his method involves subjecting a person to stroboscopic light flashes and buzzing sounds while simultaneously recording the electrical activity of the person's brain by means of an electroencephalograph. It has been known since the early 1970s that the pattern of brain waves is related to intelligence (as measured by conventional intelligence tests) but the correlation has been too approximate to be of practical use. Eysenck, however, claims to be able to measure the brain waves accurately enough to give a very high correlation with conventional intelligence tests which, if true, would mean that his method of measuring intelligence is as valid and useful as conventional tests. Using his method, Eysenck then did a cross-cultural comparison of intelligence and found that, on average, black people obtained significantly lower intelligence quotients than did whites. Combining this finding with his theory that intelligence is predominantly inherited, he claimed that black people are inherently less intelligent than are whites. This claim met with great – sometimes violent – opposition and was widely criticized by educationalists and other psychologists, who opined that, because Eysenck had validated the results obtained by electroencephalography with those from conventional intelligence tests the two methods must contain the same biases and therefore Eysenck's method could not be considered culturally unbiased.

Eysenck has also studied personality traits, anxiety and neurosis, the influence of violence shown on television on behaviour, and the psychology of smoking. In addition, he has written many popular psychology books, in which he presents his contentious ideas in relatively simple, non-technical language.

F

Fabre, Jean Henri (*1823–1915*), was a French entomologist whose studies of insects, particularly their anatomy and behaviour, have become classics.

Fabre was born on 22 December 1823 in Saint-Léons in southern France, the son of a farmer who had left the land and set up a small business. Fabre's family was poor and for much of his early childhood he lived with his grandmother in the country, which fostered his interest in natural history. When he was seven years old he returned to Saint-Léons to attend the village school. Later, after passing through senior school, he won a scholarship to Avignon, from which he gained his certificate of education in 1842. While at school Fabre had to take part-time jobs to help to pay for his education and contribute to his family's income and so, on obtaining his certificate he immediately took a teaching post at the lycée in Carpentras, a small town in northeastern Avignon. After further studies at Montpellier, he gained his teaching licence (which enabled him to teach in higher schools) in mathematics and physics and in 1851 was appointed a physics teacher at a lycée in Ajaccio, Corsica. But soon afterwards he contracted a fever, which forced him to resign and return to the mainland. After he had recovered, he went to Paris to gain a degree, then returned to Avignon where, in 1852, he became Professor of Physics and Chemistry at the lycée. He held this post for 20 years, eventually resigning because the authorities would not allow girls to attend his science classes. He then decided to abandon his teaching career and moved to the village of Orange, where he embarked on a serious study of entomology. He was very poor and had virtually no equipment to help him in his studies, but by writing articles for scientific journals he eventually managed in 1878 to buy a small plot of waste land in Serignan, Provence. He built a wall around the plot, treating it as an open-air laboratory, and remained there for the rest of his life, pursuing his entomological studies and writing about his findings. Towards the end of his life he became world famous as an authority on entomology, and in 1910 many leading scientific figures visited him in Serignan for a celebration given in his honour. Fabre died in Serignan five years later, on 11 October 1915. After his death, the French National Museum of Natural History purchased Fabre's plot of land as a memorial to the man and his work.

Although he had written several previous articles, Fabre's first important paper was published in 1855. It was a detailed account of the behaviour of a type of wasp that paralyses its prey (mainly beetles and weevils), which it then carries to its nest to feed to its young. In 1857 he wrote another important paper describing the life cycle of the Meloidae (oil beetles), hypermetamorphic beetles that begin life as larvae, then hatch into a second larval stage (called a triungulin) and climb onto particular types of flowers frequented by solitary bees of the genus *Anthophora*. When a bee visits the flower, the triungulin attaches itself to the bee and is carried to the bee's nest, where it passes through several other larval stages – feeding on honey – before finally developing into an adult beetle. The significance of this and other early work by Fabre was recognized by Charles Darwin, who quoted Fabre in *The Origin of Species*, but Fabre himself did not accept the idea of evolution.

Fabre began his most famous work after he settled at Serignan where, in addition to writing numerous entomological papers, he embarked on his 10-volume *Souvenirs Entomologiques*, which took him 30 years to complete. Based almost entirely on observations Fabre made in his small plot, this work is a model of meticulous attention to detail. It became a classic entomological work and also did much to revitalize interest in entomology.

Fabricius ab Aquapendente, Hieronymus (*1537-1619*), was an Italian anatomist and embryologist who gave the first accurate description of the semilunar valves in the veins and whose pioneering studies of embryonic development helped to establish embryology as an independent discipline.

Fabricius was born on 20 May 1537 in Aquapendente, near Orvieto in Italy, and studied first the humanities then medicine at the University of Padua, where he was taught anatomy and surgery by the eminent Italian anatomist Gabriel Fallopius (1523-1562). After graduating in 1559, Fabricius worked privately as an anatomy teacher and surgeon until 1565, when he succeeded Fallopius as Professor of Surgery and Anatomy at Padua University (the chair had been vacant since Fallopius's death in 1562). Fabricius remained at Padua University for the rest of his career, eventually retiring because of ill health in 1613. During his time at Padua, Fabricius built up an international reputation that attracted students from many countries, including William Harvey (who studied under him from 1597 to 1602). He also helped to establish a permanent anatomical theatre at the university, a structure that still exists today. About 1596 Fabricius started to acquire an estate at Bugazzi where, after retiring, he remained until his death on 21 May 1619.

Fabricius's principal anatomical work was his accurate and detailed description of the valves in the veins. Although they had previously been observed and crudely drawn by other scientists, Fabricius publicly demonstrated them in 1579 in the veins of the limbs and in 1603 published the first accurate description – with detailed illustrations – of these valves in *De Venarum Ostiolis* (*On the Valves of the Veins*). He mistakenly believed, however, that the valves' function was to retard the flow of blood to enable the tissues to absorb nutriment.

Fabricius's most important completely original work was in embryology. In his treatise *De Formato Foetu* (1600; *On the Formation of the Foetus*) – the first work of its kind – he compared the late foetal stages of different animals and gave the first detailed description of the placenta. Continuing his embryological studies, Fabricius published in 1612 *De Formatione Ovi et Pulli* (*On the Development of the Egg and the Chick*), in which he gave a detailed, excellently illustrated account of the developmental stages of chick embryos. Again, however, Fabricius made some erroneous assumptions. He believed that the sperm did not enter the ovum, but stimulated the generative process from a distance. He also believed that both the yolk and the albumen nourished the embryo and that the embryo itself was produced from the spiral threads (chalaza) that maintain the position of the yolk. Nevertheless, his embryological studies were extremely influential and helped to establish embryology as an independent science.

Fabricius also investigated the mechanics of respiration, the action of muscles, the anatomy of the larynx (about which he was the first to give a full description) and the eye (he was the first to correctly describe the location of the lens and the first to demonstrate that the pupil changes size).

Fisher, Ronald Aylmer (*1890-1962*), was a British geneticist and statistician who wrote a number of books on both subjects which have become indispensable to many students and research workers. He clarified the comparatively new science of statistics, and the Royal Society acknowledged the importance of his work by awarding him medals on three separate occasions. He was knighted in 1952.

Fisher was born in London on 17 February 1890. He attended Stanmore Park School and Harrow before going in 1909 to Gonville and Caius College, Cambridge, to study physics and mathematics. He graduated in 1912 and, after a year's extra study under James Jeans and F.J.M. Stratton, he took various jobs, continuing his work on statistics in his spare time. His poor eyesight made him unfit for military service during World War I and in 1919 he accepted a position at Rothamstead Experimental Station, where he turned his attention to biology and the opportunities to research in the field of genetics. He also analysed the accumulated data from more than 60 years' work on various field trials. He produced two important works which directly helped him towards beoming Galton Professor of Eugenics at University College, London, in 1933. During his ten years there he concentrated on studying the inheritance of blood groups, particularly the Rhesus factor; the department was evacuated to Rothamstead at the outbreak of World War II in 1939. In 1943 he was offered and accepted the Chair in Genetics at Cambridge University. He formally retired in 1957, but continued to work there for two years before going to Adelaide, Australia, to take up a research fellowship in the Division of Mathematical Statistics at the Commonwealth Scientific and Industrial Research Organization (CSIRO). He died in Adelaide on 29 July 1962.

Fisher's research at Rothamstead culminated in the publication of two books. *Statistical Methods for Research Workers* (1925) has a self-explanatory title, and soon became a standard text for statisticians. *The Genetical Theory of Natural Selection* (1930), which links the theories of Gregor Mendel with those of Charles Darwin and discusses the roles of dominant genes, has likewise become a classic among geneticists.

Although these were Fisher's best-known publications, he also produced texts on inbreeding and guides to working with variable materials.

Fleming, Alexander (*1881-1955*), was a British bacteriologist who discovered penicillin, a substance produced by the mould *Penicillium notatum* and found to be effective in killing various pathogenic bacteria without harming the cells of the human body. Penicillin was the first antibiotic to be used in medicine. For this discovery, he shared the 1945 Nobel Prize in Physiology and Medicine with Howard Florey and Ernst Chain, who developed a method of producing penicillin in quantity.

Fleming was born on 6 August 1881 in Lochfield, Ayrshire, Scotland, the son of a farmer. He was educated at Kilmarnock Academy and, after his father died in 1894, his poverty-stricken family sent him to London where he first studied at the London Polytechnic Institute and then got a job as a clerk in a shipping office. While working there, and encouraged by his brother who was a doctor, he won a scholarship to study medicine at St Mary's Hospital Medical School, London, in 1902. He graduated four years later and remained at St Mary's in the bacteriology department for the rest of his career.

In his early years Fleming assisted the bacteriologist Almroth Wright, an association that was continued when the two men were in the Royal Army Medical Corps and worked together in military hospitals during World War I. After the war, in 1918, Fleming returned to St Mary's as a lecturer, becoming Director of the Department of Systematic Bacteriology and Assistant Director of the Inoculation Department in 1920. He was appointed professor there and lecturer at the Royal College of Surgeons in 1928. He was knighted in 1944 and in 1946 became Director of the Wright-Fleming Institute, where he continued to work until he retired in 1954. He died in London on 11 March 1955.

In 1928 Fleming made his major discovery quite by accident. He was working on the bacterium *Staphylococcus aureus* and had put aside some Petri dishes that contained the cultures. He later noticed that specks of green mould had appeared on the nutrient agar and that the bacterial colonies around the specks had disappeared. The effect on the bacteria was "antibiosis" (against life). Fleming cultured the mould in nutrient broth and it formed a felt-like layer on the surface, which he filtered off. He tested the filtrate on a range of bacteria and found it killed some disease bacteria, but not all of them. He identified the mould as *Penicillium notatum*, a species related to that which grows on stale bread, and named the active substance it produced – the antibiotic element – "penicillin". Craddock, one of Fleming's assistants, grew some *Penicillium* in milk and ate the cheese-like product without any ill effects; no harm resulted, either, when mice and rabbits were injected with the material.

The purification and concentration of penicillin was, however, a chemical problem and Fleming was not a chemist. Two of his assistants made some progress but they left the matter unresolved until 1939, when Florey and Chain, in Oxford, isolated the substance and purified it. They published their results in 1940, and work began on the large-scale production of penicillin.

It was generally assumed that the original

phenomenon that Fleming had observed was a common event, but Fleming was never able to produce the effect again. It has since been shown that a similar result is achieved only under very precise conditions, which are unlikely to be met during the routine inoculation and incubation of a bacterial plate.

Fleming also developed methods, which are still in use, of staining spores and flagella of bacteria. He identified organisms that cause wound infections and showed how cross-infection by streptococci can occur among patients in hospital wards. He also studied the effects of different antiseptics on various kinds of bacteria and on living cells. His interest in chemotherapy led him to introduce Paul Ehrlich's Salvarsan into British medical practice.

In 1922 Fleming discovered the presence of the enzyme lysozyme in nasal mucus, tears and saliva, where it catalyses the breakdown of carbohydrates surrounding bacteria and kills them. Fleming later showed it to be present in most body fluids and tissues. The enzyme thus helps to prevent infections, and has become a useful research tool for dissolving bacteria for chemical examination.

Penicillin, the first of the antibiotics, has been used with outstanding success in the treatment of many bacterial diseases, including pneumonia, scarlet fever, gonorrhea, diphtheria and meningitis, and for infected wounds. Its discovery led to a scramble for further antibiotics in which streptomycin, chloromycetin and the tetracyclines were discovered. Most antibiotics can now be made synthetically, and penicillin can be modified by chemical means for specific purposes.

Florey, Howard Walter (*1898-1968*), was an Australian-born British bacteriologist who developed penicillin and made possible its commercial production. For this work he received the 1945 Nobel Prize in Physiology and Medicine, which he shared with Alexander Fleming (who discovered penicillin) and Ernst Chain.

Florey was born on 24 September 1898 in Adelaide. He was educated locally and read medicine at the University of Adelaide, qualifying in 1921 and winning a Rhodes scholarship to Oxford University to study physiology and pharmacology, where he worked under Charles Sherrington. He spent a brief period at Cambridge in 1924 before going to the United States to study. In 1926 he returned to Britain as a researcher at the London Hospital, moving back to Cambridge in the following year as a lecturer in Special Pathology and later Director of Medical Studies. Florey was appointed to the Chair of Pathology at Sheffield University in 1932 and became Pro-

fessor of Pathology at Oxford in 1935 and Head of the Sir William Dunn School of Pathology. He was knighted in 1944 and was President of the Royal Society from 1960 to 1965, the same year that he was made a life peer and member of the Order of Merit. He was elected Provost of Queen's College, Oxford, in 1962 and died in Oxford on 21 February 1968.

At Oxford, Florey conducted investigations on antibacterial substances and during these he successfully purified lysozyme, the bacteriolytic enzyme discovered by Fleming. In 1939, continuing his research, he decided to concentrate on Fleming's unresolved problem of the purification of penicillin. Florey's co-worker, Ernst Chain, an accomplished biochemist, set about growing Fleming's strain of *Penicillium* and extracting the active material from the liquid culture medium. Chain and Florey extracted a yellow powder from the medium, but the process proved to be an extraordinarily difficult task and 18 months later they had collected only 100 mg of it. Florey and his team began a series of carefully controlled experiments on mice infected with standard doses of streptococci. The team found that a dilution of one in a million inhibited the growth of streptococci but was harmless to mice, growing tissue cells and leucocytes. It was also discovered that the penicillin did not behave like an antiseptic or an enzyme, but blocked the normal process of cell division. The tests showed conclusively that penicillin could protect against infection but that the concentration of penicillin in the human body and the length of time of treatment were vital factors in the rate of success.

In 1940, during the early part of World War II, the German invasion of Britain seemed imminent; Florey and his colleagues smeared spores of the *Penicillium* culture on their coat linings so that, if necessary, any one of them could continue their research elsewhere. Further research was hindered by the great difficulty in producing enough penicillin for tests, and commercial firms were at that time too committed to vaccine production to participate. Florey's team persevered and improved their techniques which resulted in a purer product suitable for preliminary trials on human beings. Only desperately ill patients with little hope of recovery were selected. The first patient was a police constable with a rampant infection of the face, head and lungs. Within five days his improvement was miraculous, but he died one month later because it had been impossible to continue treatment long enough – the stock of penicillin was exhausted. The next five patients treated made complete recoveries.

The problem remained of producing penicillin in large quantities. Small-scale production continued in Florey's department supplemented by minimal contributions from two commercial firms. In 1943 he went to Tunisia and Sicily and used penicillin successfully on war casualties. By 1945 studies had progressed far enough to show that antibacterial activity could take place using a dilution of 1 part in 50 million and, with the war over, large-scale commercial production of penicillin could begin.

Florey and his co-workers resumed their researches on other antibiotics. They discovered cephalosporin C, which later became the basis of some derivatives, such as cephalothin, which can be used as an alternative antibiotic to penicillin.

Florey was a great scientist with abundant energy, experimental skill and a flair for choosing fruitful lines of research. He and his collaborators made penicillin available for therapeutic purposes, and were responsible for ushering in the era of antibiotic therapy.

Fraenkel-Conrat, Heinz (*1910-*), is a German-born American biochemist who showed that the infectivity of bacteriophages (viruses that infect bacteria) is a property of their inner nucleic acid component, not the outer protein case.

Fraenkel-Conrat was born on 29 July 1910 in Breslau, Germany (now Wroclaw, Poland), the son of a prominent gynaecologist. He studied medicine at the University of Breslau, graduated in 1933 and then, with the rise to power of Adolf Hitler, left Germany and went to Britain. He did postgraduate work at the University of Edinburgh and obtained his PhD in 1936 for a thesis on ergot alkaloids, after which he went to the United States. He settled there and became a naturalized citizen in 1941. He had been at the University of California since 1951, and a professor there since 1958.

In 1955 Fraenkel-Conrat developed a technique for separating the outer protein coat from the inner nucleic acid core of bacteriophages without seriously damaging either portion. He also succeeded in reassembling the components and showed that these reformed bacteriophages are still capable of infecting bacteria. This work raised fundamental questions about the molecular basis of life. He then showed that the protein component of bacteriophages is inert and that the nucleic acid component alone has the capacity to infect bacteria. Thus it seemed the fundamental properties of life resulted from the activity of nucleic acids.

Freud, Sigmund (*1856-1939*), was an Austrian psychiatrist and the father of modern psychoanalysis. He was best known for his use of the free-association method in analysis, and for his ideas on the interpretation of dreams. His theories on child and adult sexuality shocked Europe and greatly influenced later psychology.

Freud was born on 6 May 1856 at Freiberg, in Moravia (now Příbor, Czechoslovakia), the son of an unsuccessful Jewish wool merchant. The family moved to Vienna when he was four, and at the age of 17 he entered Vienna University to read medicine. He graduated in 1881 and continued neurological research in the university laboratories under Ernest Brücke (1819-92). In 1885 he went to Paris where he studied with Jean-Martin Charcot (1825-1893). The following year he returned to Vienna and set up private practice as a neurologist. He also married that year, and later had six children, one of whom was Anna Freud, a distinguished child psychoanalyst. Although derided by much of the medical profession, he gave psychoanalysis enough of an impetus to warrant the holding of the first psychoanalytic congress, in Salzburg in 1908. He was elected a member of the Royal Society in 1936. Two years later Nazi Germany invaded and occupied Austria and Freud had to leave. He moved to London and a year later, on 23 September 1939, he died of cancer of the jaw, from which he had suffered for 16 years.

While assisting the French neurologist, Charcot, Freud became influenced by his use of hypnosis in trying to find an organic basis for hysteria. Charcot had been investigating areas of the brain responsible for certain nervous functions, and encouraged Freud's interest in the psychological aspects of neurology, in particular hysteria. Freud set up his practice in Vienna to study the psychological basis of nervous disorders. The Viennese physician Josef Breuer (1842-1925) had told Freud of an occasion when he had cured symptoms of hysteria by encouraging a patient to recollect, under hypnosis, the circumstances of the hysteria and to express the emotions that accompanied them. Following the methods used by his colleague, Freud treated his patients with hypnosis and formulated his ideas about the conscious and the unconscious mind. He believed that repressed thoughts were stored in the unconscious mind and affected a person without the source of the effect being known.

Freud used this method until about 1895 when he replaced hypnosis by the technique of free-association (the "talking cure"), perhaps because he could not master the art of hypnosis. The free-association method allowed the patient to talk randomly and with little guidance. The patient relaxed to such an extent that thoughts came through that were previously hidden from the patient's conscious. The introduction of free-association marked the beginning of psychoanalysis in the sense used today. That is, that through a succession of periods of analysis, barriers that one puts up against knowledge of oneself are slowly broken down, with the help of the analyst.

Free-association led to the interpretation of dreams. Freud reasoned that dreams represented thoughts in the unconscious mind. He had noticed how often the train of thought in free-association included the recollection of a dream. By using free-association on the subjects of some of his own dreams he explained them as attempts to fulfil in fantasy some desire that he was repressing. The use of dream interpretation thus lay in revealing the contents of the unconscious which are repressed when one is awake.

Freud drew a comparison between the symbolism of dreams and of mythology and religion, stating that religion was infantile (God as the father image) and neurotic (projection of repressed wishes); he claimed that it was unnecessary and retarded social maturity by perpetuating the projection of these desires.

Around 1905 Freud was collecting about him a following of young men such as Alfred Adler and Carl Jung, whom he influenced deeply. It was at this time also that the most controversial part of his work was publicized, connected with his ideas on sex as a cause of some neurotic disorders. Freud maintained that sexual gratification in childhood could carry through to adulthood resulting in psychological problems. An example he gave was that the first sexual impulses are felt during the sucking phase of an infant's life, and if these impulses become fixated, the child may mature into an adult dependant on the mother. In Freud's terms, the sexual nature of a child's relationship with its parents could result in an Oedipus complex involving dormant sexual feelings towards the mother and jealousy towards the father, feelings which could last through adulthood.

Freud saw the mind as operating on two levels: the primary level, characterized by symbolic thinking, which he called the Id, and which was the source of all basic drives, and the secondary level, marked by logical thinking and characterized by a sense of reality, and critical faculties. The Id suppressed by social mores becomes the Superego, and eventually emerges as the Ego.

Freud produced several publications detailing his theories. The most well-known of these books are: *The Physical Mechanism of Hysterical Phenomena* (1893), *Studien über Hysterie* (*Studies in Hysteria*, 1895), *Die Traumdeutung* (*The Interpretation of Dreams*, 1900), and *Totem und Tabu* (*Totem and Taboo*, 1913).

In his early years Freud also carried out pioneer work on cocaine and advocated its use as a local anaesthetic for mild pain. Only later, however, was it accepted and introduced into the medical practice.

G

Galen (*c.* AD *129–c. 199*), was a Greek physician, anatomist and physiologist whose ideas – as conveyed in his many books, more than 130 of which have survived – had a profound influence on medicine for some 1,400 years.

Galen was born in about AD 129 in Pergamum (now Bergama in Turkey), the son of an architect. The city of his birth contained an important shrine to Asclepius, the god of medicine, and Galen received his early medical training at the medical school attached to the shrine; he also studied philosophy at Pergamum. From about 148 to 157 he continued his studies at Smyrna (now Izmir) on the west coast of present-day Turkey, Corinth in Greece and Alexandria in Egypt, after which he returned home to become chief physician to the gladiators at Pergamum. In 161 he went to Rome where he cured the eminent philosopher Eudemus, who introduced Galen to many influential people. Successful as a physician – and boastful of his successes – he soon became physician to Marcus Aurelius, then co-emperor with Lucius Verus. In about 166, however, Galen returned to Pergamum – because of the intolerable envy of his colleagues according to Galen himself, although it is also probable that he left Rome to escape the plague brought back by Verus' army after a foreign war. About two years later Marcus Aurelius recalled Galen to Rome, and when Lucius Verus died of the plague in 169, he was appointed physician to Commodus, the son of Marcus Aurelius. Little is known of Galen's life after this, although it is thought he remained in Rome until his death in about AD 199.

Galen was an expert dissector and his best work was in the area of descriptive anatomy. The dissection of human beings was then regarded as taboo and Galen made inferences about human anatomy from his many dissections of pigs, dogs, goats and especially Barbary apes – although there is some evidence that he did dissect humans as well. He was a meticulous observer and his detailed descriptions of bones and muscles, many of which he was the first to identify, are particularly good; he also noted that many muscles are arranged in antagonistic pairs. He described the heart valves, distinguished seven pairs of cranial nerves and noted the structural differences between arteries and veins. He also described the network of blood vessels under the brain, but although this network is present in many animals, it is not found in man, and Galen erroneously assigned it an important role in his tripartite scheme of circulation in the human body. In addition he performed several vivisection experiments: he tied off the recurrent laryngeal nerve to show that the brain controls the larynx; he demonstrated the effects of severing the spinal cord at different points; and he tied off the ureters to show that urine passes from the kidneys down the ureters to the bladder. More important, he demonstrated that arteries carry blood, not air, thus disproving Erasistratus's view, which had been taught for some 500 years.

In physiology, however, Galen was less successful. He thought that blood (the natural spirit) was formed in the liver and was then carried through the veins to nourish every part of the body, forming flesh in the body's periphery. Some of the blood, however, passed through the vena cava to the right-hand side of the heart, from where it then passed to the left-hand side through minute pores (the existence of which was pure conjecture on Galen's part) in the septum. In the left side the blood mixed with air brought from the lungs, and the resulting vital spirit was then carried around the body by the arteries. Some of this fluid went to the head where, in the hypothetical network of blood vessels beneath the brain, the fluid was infused with animal spirit (which was thought to produce consciousness) and distributed to the muscles and senses by the nerves (which Galen though were hollow). Thus Galen postulated a tripartite circulation system in which the liver produced the natural spirit, the heart the vital spirit, and the brain the animal spirit. Although this system is now known to be a complete misconception, it did provide a rational explanation of the facts known at the time and, because of the high esteem in which Galen was held until the Renaissance, persisted until William Harvey proposed his theory of blood circulation in 1628. Another of Galen's mistaken beliefs that inhibited the progress of medical knowledge was his subscription to Hippocrates' theory that human health relied upon a balance between the four humours (phlegm, black bile, yellow bile and blood).

Galen was a prolific author who, in addition to scientific works, also wrote about philosophy and literature. He believed that Nature expressed a divine purpose, a belief that was reflected in many of his books, including his scientific texts. Belief in divine purpose became increasingly popular with the rise of Christianity (Galen himself was not a Christian), which fact, combined with the eclipse of science until the Renaissance, probably ensured the survival of many of Galen's works and accounted for the enormous influence of his ideas.

Galton, Francis (*1822–1911*), was a British scientist, inventor and explorer who made contributions to several disciplines, including anthropology, meteorology, geography and statistics, but who is best known as the initiator of the study of eugenics (a term he coined).

Galton was born on 16 February 1822 near Sparkbrook, Birmingham, the youngest of nine children of a rich banker and a first cousin of Charles Darwin. Galton's exceptional intelligence was apparent at an early age – he could read before he was three years old and was studying Latin when he was four – but his achievements in higher education were unremarkable. Acceding to his father's wish, Galton studied medicine at Birmingham General Hospital and then King's College, London, but interrupted his medical studies to read mathematics at Trinity College, Cambridge. He returned to medicine, however, studying at St George's Hospital in London, but abandoned his studies on inheriting his father's fortune and spent the rest of his life pursuing his own interests.

Shortly after the death of his father, Galton set out in 1850 to explore various uncharted areas of Africa. He collected much valuable information, and on his return to England wrote two books describing his explorations. These writings won him the Royal Geographical Society's annual gold medal in 1853, and three years later he was elected a Fellow of the Royal Society.

Galton then turned his attention to meteorology. He designed several instruments to plot meteorological data, discovered and named anticyclones and made the first serious attempt to chart the weather over large areas – described in his book *Meteorographica* (1863). He also helped to establish the Meteorological Office and the National Physical Laboratory.

Stimulated by Darwin's *The Origin of Species* (1859), Galton then began his best-known work, that concerning heredity and eugenics, which occupied him for much of the rest of his life. Studying mental abilities, he analysed the histories of famous families and found that the probability of eminent men having eminent relatives was high, from which he concluded that intellectual ability is inherited. He tended, however, to underestimate the role of the environment in mental development, since intelligent parents tend to provide their children with a mentally stimulating environment as well as with genes for high intelligence. Galton described his study of mental abilities in eminent families in *Hereditary Genius* (1869), in which he used the term genius to define creative ability of an exceptionally high order, as shown by actual achievement. He formulated the theory that genius is an extreme degree of three traits, intellect, zeal and power of working. He also formulated the regression law, which states that parents who deviate from the average type of the race in a positive or negative direction have children who, on average, also deviate in the same direction but to a lesser extent.

Continuing his research, Galton devised instruments to measure various mental abilities and used them to obtain data from some 9,000 subjects. The results were summarized in *Inquiries into Human Faculty and its Development* (1883), which established Galton as a pioneer of British scientific psychology. He was the first to use twins to try to assess the influence of environment on development, but more important was his quantitative and analytical approach to his investigations. In order to interpret his results, Galton devised new statistical methods of analysis, including correlational calculus, which has since become an invaluable tool in many disciplines, especially the social sciences.

As a result of his research into human abilities, Galton became convinced that the human species could be improved, both physically and mentally, by selective breeding, and in 1885 he gave the name "eugenics" to the study of methods by which such improvements could be attained. He defined eugenics as "the study of the agencies under social control which may improve or impair the racial qualities of future generations, physically or mentally."

Galton also made a number of other contributions. He demonstrated the permanence and uniqueness of fingerprints and began to work out a system of fingerprint identification, now extensively used in police work. In 1879 he devised a word-association test which was later developed by Sigmund Freud and became a useful aid in psychoanalysis. Also, he invented a teletype printer and the ultrasonic dog whistle.

Galton was knighted in 1909, two years before his death on 17 January 1911 in Haslemere, Surrey. In his will he left a large bequest to endow a Chair in Eugenics at the University of London.

Galvani, Luigi (*1737-1798*), was an Italian anatomist whose discovery of "animal electricity" stimulated the work of Alessandro Volta and others to discover and develop current electricity.

Galvani was born in Bologna on 9 September 1737. He studied medicine at the University of Bologna, graduating in 1759 and gaining his doctorate three years later with a thesis on the de-

velopment of bones. In that same year (1762) he married Lucia Galeazzi, a professor's daughter, and was appointed Lecturer in Anatomy. In 1772 he became President of the Bologna Academy of Science and in 1775 he took up the appointment of Professor of Anatomy and Gynaecology at the university. The death of his wife in 1790 left him griefstricken. In 1797 he was required to swear allegiance to Napoleon as head of the new Cisalpine Republic, but Galvani refused and thereby lost his appointment at Bologna University. Saddened, he retired to the family home and died there on 4 December 1798.

Comparative anatomy formed the subject of Galvani's early research, during which he investigated such structures as the semicircular canals in the ear and the sinuses of the nose. He began studying electrophysiology in the late 1770s, using static electricity stored in a Leyden jar to stimulate muscular contractions in living and dead animals. The frog was already established as a convenient laboratory animal and in 1786 Galvani noticed that touching a frog with a metal instrument during a thunderstorm made the frog's muscles twitch. He later hung some dissected frogs from brass hooks on an iron railing to dry them, and noticed that their muscles contracted when the legs came into contact with the iron - even if there was no electrical storm. Galvani concluded that electricity was causing the contraction and postulated (incorrectly) that it came from the animal's muscle and nerve tissues. He summarized his findings in 1791 in a paper *De viribus electricitatis in motu musculari commentarius* which gained general acceptance except by Alessandro Volta (1745-1827), who by 1800 had constructed electric batteries consisting of plates (electrodes) of dissimilar metals in a salty electrolyte, thus proving that Galvani had been wrong and that the source of the electricity in his experiment had been the two different metals and the animal's body fluids. But for many years current electricity was called Galvanic electricity and Galvani's name is preserved in the word galvanometer, a current-measuring device developed in 1820 by André Ampère (1775-1836), and in galvanization, the process of covering steel with a layer of zinc (originally by electroplating). Galvani's original paper was translated into English and published in 1953 as *Commentary on the Effect of Electricity on Muscular Motion.*

Gilbert, Walter (1932   ), is an American molecular biologist who shared (with Paul Berg and Frederick Sanger) the 1980 Nobel Prize in Chemistry for his work in devising techniques for determining the sequence of bases in DNA. He also isolated the repressor substance postulated

E. coli extract ⌐ ⌐ Semi-permeable container

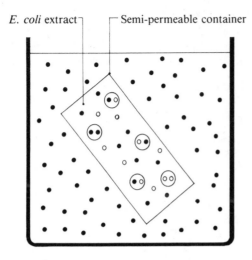

● = radioactive IPTG (inducer)
○ = non-radioactive IPTG
◯ = repressor molecules

In Gilbert's equilibrium dialysis experiment, IPTG diffuses through the membrane until its concentration is the same inside and outside. Repressor substance binds some radioactive IPTG, whose activity can be measured.

to exist by François Jacob, André Lwoff and Jacques Monod in their theory concerning the regulation of gene action.

Gilbert was born on 21 March 1932 in Boston, Massachusetts. He was educated at Harvard University, from which he graduated in physics in 1954, and at Cambridge University, England, from which he obtained his doctorate in mathematics in 1957. He then returned to Harvard, where he was a National Science Foundation Fellow in Physics from 1957 to 1958, and a Lecturer and Research Fellow from 1958 to 1959. In 1960, however, influenced by James Watson, Gilbert changed to biology, becoming Professor of Biophysics (1964 to 1968) then Professor of Molecular Biology (1969 to 1972) at Harvard. Since 1972 he has been American Cancer Society Professor of Molecular Biology at Harvard.

Gilbert began his first major biological project in 1965, when he attempted to isolate and identify repressor substances involved in the regulation of gene activity. Working with Benno Muller-Hill, he devised a special experimental technique called equilibrium dialysis that enabled him to produce relatively large quantities of the repressor substance, which he then isolated and purified, and by late 1966 he had identified it as a large protein molecule.

After his work on the repressor substance, Gilbert then developed a method of determining the sequence of bases in DNA, which involved using an enzyme that breaks the DNA molecule at specific known points, thereby effectively excising predetermined fragments of the DNA. It was for developing this important investigative technique that he shared the 1980 Nobel Prize in Chemistry.

Golgi, Camillo (*1843-1926*), was an Italian cytologist and histologist who pioneered the study of the detailed structure of the nervous system, made possible by his development of a new staining technique. For his outstanding work in this field, Golgi shared the 1906 Nobel Prize in Physiology and Medicine with Santiago Ramón y Cajal.

Golgi was born on 7 July 1843 in Corteno, near Brescia, the son of a physician. He studied medicine at the University of Pavia, graduating in 1865, then worked in a psychiatric clinic, before researching in histology. In 1872 he became principal physician at a hospital in Abbiategrasso near Milan, but managed to continue his histological research. In 1875 he was appointed Lecturer in Histology at the University of Pavia and Professor the following year, a post he held until 1879, when he became Professor of Anatomy at the University of Sienna. In the following year, however, he returned to Pavia University as Professor of Histology, subsequently becoming Professor of General Pathology, and remained there until his retirement in 1918. During his time at the university he took an active part in its administration, as Dean of the Faculty of Medicine and later as President of the university. He also played an important role outside the university, becoming a Senator in the Italian government in 1900. Golgi died on 21 January 1926 in Pavia.

At the time Golgi was studying medicine there were no techniques suitable for the study of nerve cells, with the result that very little was known about their structure and function. In 1873, however, Golgi invented a new technique of staining cells with silver salts, a method he found to be particularly suitable for studying nerve cells because it allowed controlled staining of certain features in the cells, thereby enabling them to be studied in great detail. From 1873 onwards he published many articles on the results of his systematic studies – using his new technique – of the fine anatomy of the nervous system. He verified Wilhelm von Waldeyer's view that nerve cells are separated by synaptic gaps, and he also discovered a type of nerve cell (later called the Golgi cell) that connects many other cells by means of dendrites. In 1896, while studying the brain of a barn owl, he detected flattened cavities near the nuclear membrane; the function of these structures – called Golgi bodies, the Golgi complex or the Golgi apparatus – is still largely unknown, although they are thought to be involved in intracellular secretion and transport.

From his examinations of different parts of the brain, Golgi put forward the theory that there are two types of nerve cells, sensory and motor cells, and that axons are concerned with the transmission of nerve impulses. He showed that there is a fine nerve network in the grey matter but could not say positively whether the filaments were joined or merely interwoven. Golgi made other contributions to the study of the nervous system, including the discovery of tension receptors in the tendons – now called the organs of Golgi.

Between 1885 and 1893 Golgi investigated malaria, the causative agent of which – the protozoon *Plasmodium* – had been discovered by the French physician Charles Laveran in 1880. (And by 1885 two Italian scientists had discovered the stages in the parasite's life cycle.)

Golgi's research verified a number of important facts about the disease and discovered that different species of *Plasmodium* are responsible for the two main types of intermittent fever – tertian fever, with attacks every three days, and quartan fever, with attacks every four days – and that the fever attacks coincide with the release into the bloodstream of a new generation of the parasites. He also put the results of his work to practical use by establishing a method of treatment that involved determining the type of malaria a person had contracted, and then giving the patient quinine (the only effective antimalarial drug then available) a few hours before the predicted onset of the fever.

Gray, Asa (*1810–1888*), was an American botanist who was the leading authority on botanical taxonomy in the United States in the nineteenth century and a pioneer of plant geography. He was also the chief American proponent of Charles Darwin's theory of natural selection.

Gray was born on 18 November 1810 in Sauquoit, New York, and studied medicine at Fairfield Medical School, Connecticut, teaching himself botany in his spare time. After graduating in 1831 he taught science at Bartlett's High School in Utica, New York, until 1834 when he became an assistant to John Torrey, a chemistry professor at the College of Physicians and Surgeons in New York. Also interested in botany Torrey became a lifelong friend of Gray and the two men collaborated on several botanical projects. In 1835 Gray accepted the post of Curator and Librarian of the New York Lyceum of Natural History, which gave him more time to devote to botany and provided greater financial security than did his previous position. Gray was made botanist to the United States Exploring Expedition in 1836, but he resigned in the following year because of delays in sailing. In 1838 he was appointed a professor at the newly established University of Michigan, but did not commence his duties because, in the same year, he travelled to Europe to acquire books for his library and to study specimens of American plants in European herbaria. On his return to the United States in 1839 he was occupied with writing and organizing the results of his studies. In 1842 Gray accepted the professorship of natural history at Harvard University, on the understanding that he could devote himself to botany. He held this position for 31 years, until he retired in 1873, during which time he made several journeys to Europe, meeting Charles Darwin in 1851, and donated his priceless collection of plants and books to Harvard University on condition that the university housed his collection in a special building; this led to the establishment of the botany department at Harvard University, and the botanical garden and herbarium were later named after him. Gray died on 30 January 1888 in Cambridge, Massachusetts.

Gray was a prolific author, writing more than 360 books, monographs and papers, but is probably best known for his *Manual of the Botany of the Northern United States, from New England to Wisconsin and South to Ohio and Pennsylvania Inclusive* (1848), often called *Gray's Manual*, which was an extremely comprehensive study of North American flora and which also helped to establish systematic botany in the United States. This work went through several editions and is still a standard text in its subject area. Before the publication of *Gray's Manual*, however, Gray had written several other important works, including the two-volume *Flora of North America* (1838–1843), which he co-authored with Torrey. This work was later expanded, under Gray's direction, and published in 1878 as the first volume of the *Synoptical Flora of North America*.

In addition to these contributions to botanical taxonomy, Gray also investigated the geographical distribution of plants, notably a comparison of the flora found in Japan, Europe, northern America and eastern America. This knowledge of plant distribution proved useful to Darwin, who asked Gray to analyse his plant-distribution data in order to provide him with evidence for his theory of natural selection. Darwin also told Gray about his ideas on natural selection as early as 1857, and after publication of *The Origin of Species* (1859) Gray became a leading advocate of Darwin's theory. In his own work, Gray reached conclusions about variations that foreshadowed the work of Gregor Mendel and Hugo De Vries.

Gray, Henry (*1827-1861*), was a British anatomist who compiled a book on his subject which, through its various editions and revisions, has remained the definitive work on anatomy for more than 100 years.

Little is known of Gray's early life and education. His father was a private messenger to King George IV and William IV. Gray became a "perpetual student" at St George's Hospital, London, on 6 May 1845. In 1848 he was awarded the Triennial Prize of the Royal College of Surgeons. When Gray was 25 years old, the Royal Society acknowledged his contribution to anatomy by electing him a Fellow, and the following year in 1853 he was awarded the Astley Cooper Prize of 300 guineas for a talk on the structure and function of the spleen. He was offered and accepted the post of Demonstrator of Anatomy at St George's Hospital. He became a Fellow of the Royal College of Surgeons, and was curator of the St George's Museum. He was also Lecturer in Anatomy and in line for the post of Assistant Surgeon. At this point his brilliant and promising career was cut short. He tended a nephew suffering from smallpox, and contracted a particularly virulent strain of the disease. He died in London in 1861 at the age of only 34.

The first edition of what is now known as *Gray's Anatomy* was published in 1858. He had painstakingly and methodically learnt all his anatomy on the merits of his own dissections, and had the good fortune to persuade his friend H. Vandyke Carter to do the drawings for him. Vandyke Carter was a demonstrator of anatomy as well as a draughtsman, and undoubtedly his beautiful illustrations were partly responsible for the success of the book. Gray prepared the second edition in 1860.

Gray's *Anatomy* was fundamentally different from other contemporary works of a similar nature because it was organized in terms of systems, rather than areas of the body. His layout and general philosophy remain in the current edition, although the book has been revised and updated nearly 50 times. Areas such as neuroanatomy have been greatly enlarged but the section that deals with, for example, the skeletal system is almost identical to Gray's original work. It remains a standard text for students and surgeons alike.

Guillemin, Roger Charles Louis (*1924-*), is a French-born American endocrinologist. His research has included the isolation and identification of various hormones, for which he received the 1977 Nobel Prize in Physiology and Medicine, together with his co-worker Andrew Schally (*1926-*) and the American physicist Rosalyn Yalow (*1921-*). Yalow developed radioimmunoassays of insulin, a technique that allows the analysis of minute amounts of substances such as hormones.

Guillemin was born in Dijon on 11 January 1924. In 1941 he obtained a BA from the University of Dijon, and the following year a BSc. He read medicine at the University of Lyons and gained his medical degree in 1949. During the following two years he was a resident intern at the University Hospital in Dijon, and then took up a professorial appointment at the Institute of Experimental Medicine and Surgery, Montreal, from which he gained his PhD in 1953. That year, Guillemin went to Baylor College of Medicine, Houston, Texas, and also became a naturalized American citizen. From 1960 to 1963 he was an Associate Director in the Department of Experimental Endocrinology at the Collège de France, Paris. He returned to Baylor College and worked there until 1970 when he joined the Salk Institute in La Jolla, California. He is now also Professor of Medicine at the University of California, San Diego.

While at the Baylor College, Guillemin attempted to prove the theory put forward by the British anatomist Geoffrey Harris that hormones secreted from the hypothalamus regulate those produced by the pituitary gland. Guillemin found that the brain controls the pituitary gland by means of hormones produced by central neurons – the neurosecretory cells of the hypothalamus.

Guillemin was joined in his studies by the Lithuanian refugee Andrew Schally, who went to Baylor College in 1957. They tried to isolate the substance that regulates the secretion of the adrenocorticotrophic hormone (ACTH), which is produced by the pituitary gland, but they were defeated.

Schally left Baylor College in 1962 and went to New Orleans but both he and Guillemin turned their attention to the isolation of other hormones. In parallel investigations between 1968 and 1973 they isolated and synthesized three hypothalamic hormones which regulate the secretion of the anterior pituitary gland. The first of these was the tripeptide TRH (thyrotropin-releasing hormone), isolated in 1968. This hormone in turn induces the pituitary gland to secrete TSH (thyroid-stimulating hormone). After months of hard work they finally extracted one milligram of the hormone, which they found to be a simple compound and easily synthesized. In 1971 Schally announced his discovery of LHRH (luteinizing hormone-releasing hormone) which regulates the release in the pituitary gland of the luteinizing and follicle-stimulating hormones that control ovulation in women. Two years later, working at the Salk Institute, Guillemin discovered somatostatin, which inhibits the secretion of the growth hormone somatotropin, and of insulin and gastrin.

Guillemin continued his work at the Salk Institute, and in 1979 investigated the possible presence in the pituitary gland of opiate-like peptides. The peptide structure discovered is called β-endorphin and represents the opiate-like effects of all pituitary extracts.

The discoveries of Guillemin and Schally are highly relevant to endocrinologists. Synthetic TRH is now used to treat conditions connected with deficiencies in the secretion of pituitary hormones; and somatostatin is under investigation for its possible use in treating diabetics, and for curing peptic ulcers.

Gurdon, John Bertrand (*1933-*), is a British molecular biologist who is probably best known for his work on nuclear transplantation.

Gurdon was born on 2 October 1933 in Dippenhall, Hampshire, and was educated at Eton College and then Christ Church College, Oxford, from which he graduated in zoology in 1956. From 1956 to 1960 he studied for his doctorate (in embryology) in the Zoology Department at Oxford University, then from 1960 to 1962 he worked at the California Institute of Technology as a Gosney Research Fellow. He then returned to Britain, and from 1963 to 1964 was a departmental demonstrator in Oxford University's Zoology Department. Also in 1963 he was appointed a Research Fellow of Christ Church College. He became a lecturer in Oxford's Zoology Department in 1965, remaining there until 1972, when he was made a staff member of the Laboratory of Molecular Biology at Cambridge; seven years later he was appointed Head of the Cell Biology Division.

Gurdon has worked mostly on the effects of transplanting nuclei and nuclear constituents, such as DNA, into enucleated eggs, mainly frogs' eggs. Using nuclei from somatic cells, he showed how the genetic activity changes in the recipient eggs; for example, after transplanting nuclei from differentiated somatic cells, Gurdon discovered that the somatic nuclei come to resemble the zygote nuclei of fertilized eggs in both structure and metabolism. From this and other research, he concluded that the changes in gene activity induced by nuclear transplantation are indistinguishable from those that occur in normal early development. He also demonstrated how nuclear transplantation and micro-injection techniques can be used to elucidate the intracellular movements of proteins, and has investigated the effects of known protein fractions on gene activity.

Haeckel, Ernst Heinrich (*1834-1919*), was a German zoologist well known for his genealogical trees of living organisms and for his early support of Darwin's ideas on evolution.

Haeckel was born in Potsdam, Prussia (now East Germany), on 16 February 1834. His father was a lawyer in Merseburg, where Ernst Haeckel was educated. He studied medicine (although his main interest was botany) at the University of Würzburg and obtained his degree from the University of Berlin in 1857. There he was taught by Johannes Müller (1801-1858), who interested him greatly in zoology; he also studied under Rudolph Virchow (1821-1902). He travelled through Italy and then, after practising medicine for a year, became a lecturer at the University of Jena in 1861. The following year he was appointed Extraordinary Professor of Comparative Anatomy at the Zoological Institute in Jena. He founded the Phyletic Museum in Jena and the Ernst Haeckel Haus, which contains his archives as well as many personal mementos. In 1865 he took up the full professorship at Jena, a position he retained until he retired in 1909. He died in Jena on 8 August 1919.

In 1866 Haeckel met Charles Darwin and was completely convinced by his theory of evolution. He went further and, using Darwin's research, developed Haeckel's law of recapitulation, which concerns resemblances between the ontogeny (the development from fertilized egg to adult) of different animals. According to the law of recapitulation, during its ontogeny an individual goes through a series of stages similar to the evolutionary stages of its adult ancestors, which show characteristics of less highly evolved animals. In this way ontogeny recapitulates phylogeny (the developmental history of a species). An example of the evidence on which Haeckel founded this view is the series of gill pouches found both in birds and mammals at the embryo stage. These gill pouches are not present in adult mammals, although the slits are present in full-grown birds and fish from which the embryo forms were descended. Haeckel's theory was thought to make ontogeny relevant to evolution simply because he believed that it should be possible to find out, by studying the development of an individual, what its adult ancestors were like. The concept that Haeckel revived had already been refuted by Karl von Baer, who had shown that embryos resemble the embryos only and not the adults of other species, but Haeckel's claims remained popular to the end of the nineteenth century.

In the same year that he met Darwin, Haeckel introduced a method of representing evolutionary history, or phylogeny, by means of tree-like diagrams. His method is still used today by animal systematists to show degrees of presumed relationship in the various groups and can be traced in present modified zoological classifications.

Haeckel also tried to apply Darwin's doctrine of evolution to philosophy and religion. He believed that just as the higher animals have evolved from the simpler forms of life, so the highest human faculties have evolved from the soul of animals. He denied the immortality of the soul, the freedom of the will and the existence of a personal God. He now occupies no serious place in the history of philosophy, although he was widely read in his own day.

Haeckel held some ideas that are still accepted, one of them being his view that the origin of life lies in the chemical and physical factors of the environment, such as sunlight, oxygen, water and methane. This theory has recently, as a result of laboratory experiments, been shown to be likely. He also believed that the simplest forms of life were developed by a form of crystallization. A further influence Haeckel had on science was the coining of the word "ecology", to mean the study of living organisms in relation to one another and to the inanimate environment. As a field naturalist Haeckel was a man of extraordinary energy, and he gave much of interest to biology, even if the theory was tenuous and was typical of the extreme evolutionists of his era.

Haldane, John Burdon Sanderson (*1892–1964*), was a British physiologist famous for his work in physiology and genetics.

Haldane was born in Oxford on 5 November 1892, the son of John Scott Haldane, himself a well-known physiologist. From the early age of eight he was introduced to medicine and assisted his father. He went to Eton and was later educated at New College, Oxford. After gaining a degree in mathematics he did equally well in classics and philosophy. During World War I he served on the Western Front and in Mesopotamia, where he was wounded twice; he returned to study physiology at New College in 1919. Two years later he moved to Cambridge to work under the English biochemist Frederick Garland Hopkins. In 1933 he took up the genetics chair at University College, London, and later the Chair in Biometry. Between 1927 and 1936 he also held a part-time appointment at the John Innes Horticultural Institution at Merton, where he carried

on the work of the previous director William Bateson (1861–1926). He was an outspoken Marxist during the 1930s and served for a time as chairman of the editorial board of the London *Daily Worker*. He worked for the Admiralty in World War II and left the Communist Party disappointed by the fame awarded to the Soviet biologist Trofim Lysenko. He emigrated to India in 1957 in protest at the Anglo-French invasion of Suez and was appointed Director of the Genetics and Biometry Laboratory in Orissa, which had excellent facilities. He became a naturalized Indian citizen in 1961, and died of cancer at Bhubaneshwar on 1 December 1964.

Haldane's interest in genetics was first aroused by a lecture in 1901 on the recently discovered work of Gregor Mendel, and in 1910 he began to study the laws of inheritance as shown by his sister's 300 guinea pigs. Some years later he published a paper on gene linkage in vertebrates. In 1922 he formulated Haldane's law and three years later investigated the variation of gene linkage with age, and published a paper on the mathematics of natural selection. He was convinced that natural selection and not mutation is the driving force behind evolution. In 1932 he estimated for the first time the rate of mutation of the human gene and worked out the effect of recurrent harmful mutations on a population. While he was at University College he continued his work on human genetics and in 1936 showed the genetic link between haemophilia and colour blindness.

While Haldane was still at school he helped his father with research on the physiology of breathing and aspects of respiration concerned with deep-sea diving and safety in mines. Haldane's interest in respiration led him, during World War I, to work with his father yet again, on the improvization of gas masks. After the war, at Oxford, he investigated how carbon dioxide in the bloodstream of human beings enables the muscles to regulate breathing under different conditions. He and his colleague, Peter Davies, consumed quantities of sodium bicarbonate and introduced hydrochloric acid into their blood by drinking ammonium chloride. They also experimented with changes in sugar and phosphate concentration in the blood and urine. During World War II, in 1942, Haldane and a friend spent two days in a submarine to test an air-purifying system. He also simulated conditions inside submarines and subjected himself to extremes of temperature and a concentration of carbon dioxide in the air.

In 1924, having been introduced to enzyme reactions by Hopkins, Haldane produced the first proof that they obey the laws of thermodynamics.

In 1930 Haldane published *Enzymes*, which gave an overall picture of how enzymes work.

Haldane is most remembered as a geneticist and a proponent of the unity of the sciences. His papers, lectures and broadcasts made him one of the world's best-known scientists.

Haldane, John Scott (*1860-1936*), was a British physiologist well known for his investigations into the safety measures necessary in stressful working conditions such as coal-mining and deep-sea diving, and for his studies on the exchange of gases during respiration.

Haldane was born in Edinburgh on 3 May 1860, the son of a lawyer and a member of the Cloan branch of the ancient Haldane family of Gleneagles. He was educated at the Edinburgh Academy, and graduated in medicine from Edinburgh University in 1884. He then spent short periods of time at the universities of Jena and Berlin, and was a demonstrator in physiology at the University of Dundee. In 1887 he became a demonstrator in physiology at Oxford University, and from 1907 until he resigned in 1913 was a reader there. He then became Director of the Mining Research Laboratory, Doncaster (which moved to Birmingham in 1921), a position he held until 1928. Haldane lectured at Yale in 1916, at Glasgow University from 1927 to 1929, and at Dublin University in the following year. He was elected to the Royal Society in 1897 and received its Royal Medal in 1916. He died in Oxford on 15 March 1936.

Haldane was concerned about the artificial differences that then existed between theoretical and applied science and strived to combine the two. His first piece of research was on the composition of the air in houses and schools in Dundee. Using the information he gained doing this research about the carbon dioxide content of inspired air and respiratory volume, he began investigating the health hazards to which coal miners were subjected, particularly suffocation. In a report in 1896 he laid stress on the lethal effects of carbon monoxide, which is usually present in mines after a mine explosion. Haldane then researched into the reasons for the toxicity of carbon monoxide and produced a significant paper in which he showed that this gas binds to the haemoglobin in the blood in preference to oxygen. The full clinical implications of this discovery were not appreciated, however, for another 50 years.

Between 1892 and 1900 Haldane devised methods for studying respiration and the blood. In 1898 he developed in principle the Haldane gas analyser and, a few years later, he invented an apparatus for determining the blood gas content from relatively small amounts of blood - the haemoglobinometer. Both methods are still used, although the blood gas apparatus has largely been superseded.

In 1905 Haldane published his idea that breathing is controlled by the effect of the concentration of carbon dioxide in arterial blood on the respiratory centre of the brain. He showed that, except under extreme conditions, the regulation of breathing depends more on the carbon dioxide content of the inspired air than on its oxygen content. Although this was his most influential work, it received little clinical attention until the late 1940s.

Haldane then attempted to unravel the basic problems of caisson disease (the bends), suffered by divers and other workers who have to breathe compressed air at high pressures. In 1907 he announced a technique of decompression by stages which allows a deep-sea diver to rise to the surface safely; it is still used today. In 1911 Haldane undertook an expedition to Pikes Peak, Colorado, with several American physiologists to study the physiological effects of low barometric pressures.

Haldane's studies of haemoglobin dissociation demonstrated the degree to which oxygenation of haemoglobin affects the uptake of carbon dioxide in the body tissues and its release in the lungs. He also researched the reaction of the kidneys to the water content of the blood, and the physiology of sweating.

The application of many of Haldane's findings contributed much to the safety and health of miners and divers. He also had a great interest in philosophical topics and wrote extensively on the relationship between science and philosophy. In the 25 years he was at Oxford he did more than anyone else to bring the Oxford school of physiology into international prominence. His concern was to show that there is a dynamic and constructive equilibrium between theoretical and applied science.

Hales, Stephen (*1677-1761*), was a British clergyman who devoted his life to the careful investigation of scientific matters. He researched the physiology and growth of plants, in particular transpiration.

Hales was born on 17 September 1677 at Bekesbourne in Kent. He spent 13 years at Cambridge, from 1696 to 1709, studying divinity at what is now Corpus Christi College. His long stay there allowed him to obtain a thorough grounding in all scientific disciplines, as well as to prepare for the priesthood. He was ordained in 1703 and in 1709 took up the post of Curate at Teddington, where he remained for the rest of his life. He died there on 4 January 1761.

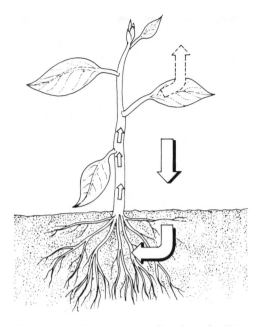

Transpirational stream-water flow through a living plant.

Hales' experiments on plants took place mainly between 1719 and 1725. In one experiment he cut off a vine at ground level in the spring, before the buds had burst. He attached a glass tube to the cut surface and showed that the sap rose up the tube to a height of 7.6 m, indicating that the sap was under considerable pressure (one unit of atmospheric pressure is equivalent to a column of 9.7 m).

It is now known that this high "root pressure" establishes a column of water between the roots and the buds in the spring. Once the leaves open, the column extends to the spongy tissues in the leaves, from which water evaporates. The transpirational stream is then set in motion, drawing water from the soil, through the plant and to the atmosphere via the leaves.

Hales also worked on vines in full leaf and was able to show that the pressure exerted by water in the transpiration stream is greatest when the plant is illuminated. He demonstrated this phenomenon by attaching his pressure-measuring apparatus to cut side-shoots (or roots) and taking measurements at various times of day. He further showed that water flows in a plant in one direction only, from root to stem to leaf. He used either a straight glass tube to measure the pressure of plant sap or a simple manometer filled with mercury. He calculated in this way the actual velocity of the sap and found that the rate of flow varies in different plants. In investigating the develop-

ment of plants, Hales was able to show that most of the growth in plant size is made by the younger shoots. On any one section of shoot, he found that it is usually the part of the shoot between the nodes that increases in size the most.

Hales was particularly interested in processes that are common to both plants and animals, such as the nature of growth, and the role of water and air in the maintenance of life. His animal studies involved inserting probes into the veins and arteries of domestic animals and recording the height to which their blood rose up a glass tube connected to the probe, which gave a measure of blood pressure.

He went on to make wax casts of the left ventricles of the hearts of several animals to measure the blood capacities. He also estimated the rate of blood flow through the capillaries by injecting chemicals into various body organs, and watching their movement and the dispersion of the chemicals. He showed that the presence of foreign chemicals can change the rate of flow of blood through an organ and therefore demonstrated (although indirectly) that capillaries are capable of dilation or contraction. As a result of these experiments Hales became convinced of the fallacy of the popular belief that the pressure of the blood itself was powerful enough to effect muscular movement in animals and human beings.

Hales also worked on gases, from both a biological and physical chemical point of view. He made several important discoveries about air but was unable to understand fully the significance of his results because, like his contemporaries, he believed that all gases were a single chemical substance. In his experiments, Hales heated up several materials and noted the change in the volume of air involved in the process, thereby confirming the findings of previous workers that some solids liberate "air" on heating whereas others absorb it. He devised an apparatus which allowed him to breath solely his own expelled air and found that he could continue to do this for about one minute. If, however, he introduced salt or tartar treated with an alkali, he could use the apparatus for eight-and-a-half minutes. (The alkali mixture absorbed carbon dioxide, thereby delaying for several minutes the response of his lungs to the high carbon dioxide levels.)

Hales' work on air revealed to him the dangers of breathing "spent" air in enclosed places, and he invented a ventilator for such situations which he had introduced on naval, merchant and slave ships, in hospitals, and in prisons. There was an immediate acknowledgement of the improvement in human health and survival following their introduction, although these favourable reactions foreshadowed an overemphasis on air quality as a factor in disease control in the eighteenth and nineteenth centuries.

Hales carried out many other investigations, such as examining stones taken from the bladder and kidney and suggesting possible chemical solvents for their non-surgical treatment. In the course of his investigations he also invented the surgical forceps.

Hales' research on plants together with his work on the nature and properties of air were published in his famous book *Vegetable Staticks* (1727). This book was subsequently republished in an enlarged form, containing an additional section on his findings on blood and circulation in mammals (in 1733). The enlarged work was entitled *Statical Essays, containing Haemastaticks, etc.* Hales' emphasis on the need for careful measurement of scientific phenomena may well have had as great an influence on his contemporaries as the results he obtained.

Haller, Albrecht von (*1708-1777*), was a Swiss physiologist, the father of neurology. By means of skilful investigations into the neuromuscular system he freed it from the remaining myths and superstitions of his day.

Haller was born in Bern on 16 October 1708. A sickly child, he spent most of his time indoors writing and studying. By the age of ten he had compiled a Greek dictionary and written on a number of scholarly topics. He was a medical student of the Dutch physician Hermann Boerhaave (1668-1738) at Leyden, graduating in 1727 and starting his own practice two years later. In 1736 he was appointed Professor of Medicine, Anatomy, Surgery and Botany at the new University of Göttingen, where he remained until he retired in 1753 to write. He died in Bern on 12 December 1777.

During the eighteenth century the idea prevailed that a mysterious force was associated with the nerves, which were believed to be liquid-filled hollow tubes in the body. Haller rejected these notions, especially as they could not be observed experimentally. His own experiments concerning the relationship between nerves and muscles demonstrated the irritability of muscle. He found that if he applied a stimulus to a muscle, the muscle contracted, and that if he stimulated the nerve attached to the muscle there was a stronger contraction. He therefore deduced that it is the stimulation of a nerve that brings about muscular movement.

Haller carried out further experiments to show that tissues are incapable of feeling, but that nerves collect and conduct away impulses produced by a stimulus. Tracing the pathways of nerves, he was able to demonstrate that they always lead to the spinal cord or the brain, suggesting that these regions might be where awareness of sensation and the initiation of answering responses are located. Haller also experimented on the brains of animals and observed the reactions resulting from the damage or stimulation of various parts of the brain.

While carrying out his experiments, Haller discovered several processes of the human body, such as the role of bile in digesting fats. He also wrote a report on his study of embryonic development.

In 1747 Haller published *De Respiratione Experimenta Anatomica* (*Experiments in the Anatomy of Respiration*) and between 1757 and 1766 his eight-volume encyclopaedia *Elementa Physiologiae Corporis Humani* (*The Physiological Elements of the Human Body*) was published.

Medicine was just one of Haller's many interests. Botany was another, and he was an avid collector of plants. He devised a botanical classification that equals that of Linnaeus, and wrote a work on the Swiss flora.

Hardy, Alistair Clavering (*1896-*), is the British marine biologist who designed the Hardy Plankton Continuous Recorder. His development of methods for ascertaining the numbers and types of minute sea organisms has helped to unravel the intricate web of life that exists in the sea.

Hardy was born in Nottingham on 10 February 1896 and was educated at Oundle School and then at Exeter College, Oxford. He served in World War I as a lieutenant and later as a captain, from 1915 to 1919. The following year he studied at the Stazione Zoologica in Naples and returned to Britain in 1921 to become Assistant Naturalist in the Fisheries Department of the Ministry of Agriculture and Fisheries. In 1924 he joined the *Discovery* expedition to the Antarctic as Chief Zoologist and on his return in 1928 he was appointed Professor of Zoology and Oceanography at Hull University, where he founded the Department of Oceanography. In 1942 he was made Professor of Natural History at the University of Aberdeen and, two years later, became Professor of Zoology at Oxford. He held this post for 15 years, from 1946 to 1961, when he served as Professor of Field Studies at Oxford. In recognition of his achievements in marine biology, he was knighted in 1957. He returned to Aberdeen in 1963 to take up a lectureship at the University.

Before Hardy's investigations, Johannes Müller, the German zoologist, had towed a conical net of fine-meshed cloth behind a ship and collected enough specimens from the sea to reveal an entirely new sphere for biological research. The really serious study of the sea began in the late nineteenth century with the voyage of HMS *Challenger*, the purpose of which was to investigate all kinds of sea life, and it returned to Britain with an enormous wealth of material. A German Plankton Expedition was led by Victor Hensen in 1899, who coined the word plankton to describe the minute sea creatures which, it has since been established, form the first link in the vital sea food-chain.

Hardy made his special study of plankton on the 1924 *Discovery* expedition. The aim of quantitative plankton studies is to estimate the numbers or weights of organisms beneath a unit area of sea surface or in a unit volume of water. Müller's original conical net of fine mesh is still the basic requirement in any instrument designed to collect specimens from the sea, but the drawback is that it can be used only from stationary vessels for collections at various depths, or from moving vessels whose speed must not exceed two knots. Faster speeds displace the small organisms by the turbulence created. Hardy developed a net that can be used behind faster moving vessels and which increases enormously the area in which accurate recordings can be made.

The first of these nets was the Hardy Plankton Recorder which, reduced to its simplest terms, is a high-speed net. It consists of a metal tube with a constricted opening, a fixed diving plane instead of a weight, and a stabilizing fin. The net itself is a disc of 60-mesh silk attached to a ring placed inside near the tail. It was designed for easy handling aboard herring fishing vessels to be towed when the skipper was near the grounds chosen for the night's fishing. If the disc showed plenty of herring food, the chances of a good catch were high. The indicator is no longer used for this purpose, having been superseded by more modern echo-sounding equipment, but it served as the basis for Hardy's second invention which is still used and through which it has been possible to map the sea life in the oceans of the world.

This improved instrument is known as the Hardy Continuous Plankton Recorder, and was first developed at the Oceanographic Department which Hardy himself founded at the University of Hull in 1931. The present Edinburgh Oceanographic Laboratory, which is the thriving continuation of Hardy's original Hull laboratory, still employs the improved version. The instrument can be used by unskilled personnel aboard ship after being suitably prepared by scientists ashore and is later returned to the laboratory where scientific observations can be made under more ideal conditions.

While the ship tows it along at normal cruising speed the instrument continuously samples the plankton. As the instrument is towed, the water flowing through it drives a small propeller which, acting through a gearbox, slowly winds a long length of plankton silk mesh and draws it across the path of the incoming water. As the mesh, which is graduated in numbered divisions, collects the plankton, it is slowly wound round a spool. This roll of silk mesh is then met by another roll and both are wound together in sandwich form, with the plankton collected by the first roll safely trapped between the two. The whole is stored in a small tank filled with a solution which preserves the plankton for later detailed study in the laboratory.

The recorder can be used at a depth of 10 m and at speeds ranging from eight to sixteen knots. Regular surveys, initiated at Hull and developed in Edinburgh, now annually cover many thousands of kilometres in the Atlantic, North Sea and Icelandic waters. The knowledge of plankton distribution, which is continuously being updated, is of major importance to the fishing industry because there is a vitally close relationship between the occurrence of plankton and the movements of plankton-feeding fish used for human consumption.

Hardy has suggested that if just 25 per cent of the pests that exist in the sea can be eliminated and fish can be allowed to have some 20 per cent of the potential food supply instead of the 2 per cent they have now, then any given area could support ten times the amount of fish it supports at present. Hardy's methods have therefore not only added to man's overall knowledge of sea life but have also indicated ways in which it could be put to better use.

Harvey, William (*1578–1657*), was an eminent English physician who discovered that blood is circulated around the body by pulsations of the heart, a landmark in medical investigations. His work did much to pave the way for modern physiology.

Harvey was born in Folkestone on 1 April 1578. He went to the King's School, Canterbury, and then attended Gonville and Caius College at Cambridge in 1593. He graduated with a BA from Caius College in 1597 and extended his studies under Fabricius of Aquapendente at the university medical school in Padua, Italy, gaining his medical degree in 1602. He returned to London, built up a successful practice, and in 1609 he was appointed Physician to St Bartholomew's Hospital, London, and served as a professor there from 1615 to 1643. In 1618 he became Physician Extraordinary to James I, and then Royal Physician, a position he retained until the death of Charles I in 1649. He was elected President of the

College of Physicians in 1654 but was too old to accept, and he died three years later in Roehampton on 3 June 1657.

Harvey was deeply involved in medical research and his spare time was devoted to his consuming interest, the investigation of the movement of blood in the body. He had developed this interest while studying in Padua under Fabricius, who had discovered the valves in the veins but had not appreciated their significance. The old idea about blood movement, established by Galen, was that food turned to blood in the liver, ebbed and flowed in vessels and, on reaching the heart, flowed through pores in the dividing wall (septum) from the right to the left side and was sent on its way by heart spasms. Andreas Vesalius (1514-1564), who secretly dissected corpses, failed to find the pores in the heart's dividing wall, and concluded that Galen could never have dissected a human body.

Harvey was not at all convinced by Galen's explanation either. Examining the heart and blood vessels of about 128 mammals, Harvey found that the valve separating the auricle from the ventricle, on each side of the heart, is a one-way structure, as are the valves in the veins discovered by his tutor, Fabricius. For this reason he decided that the blood in the veins must flow only towards the heart. Harvey tied off an artery and found that it bulged with blood on the heart side; he then tied a vein and discovered that it swelled on the side away from the heart. He also calculated the amount of blood that left the heart at each beat. He worked out that in human beings it was about 60 cm³ per beat, which meant that the heart pumped out 259 litres of blood an hour. This amount would weigh more than 200 kg – more than three times the weight of an average man. Clearly that was absurd, and therefore a much smaller quantity of the same blood must be circulating continuously around the body. Harvey demonstrated that no blood seeps through the septum and reasoned that it passes from the right side of the heart to the left through the lungs (pulmonary circulation).

The publication of these findings aroused the hostility Harvey had predicted, because to refute Galen was almost unthinkable in his time. His practice declined but he continued with his studies and, unlike many early scientists who made an outstanding discovery, he lived to see his work accepted.

The great classic Harvey published in 1628, *De Motu Cordis et Sanguinis in Animalibus* (*On the Motion of the Heart and Blood in Animals;* 1628), pointed the way for physicians who followed him. He also published *Exercitationes de Generatione Animalium* (1651) (*Anatomical Exercitations concerning the Generation of Living Creatures;* 1653).

Harvey was one of the first to study the development of a chick in the egg. He also carried out many dissections to find out how mammalian embryos are formed, and many of the animals he dissected were the royal deer put at his disposal by Charles I. Harvey suspected that semen might be involved in the making of an embryo, but did not have the microscopic apparatus, later developed by Leeuwenhoek, needed to study the tiny spermatozoa.

Harvey's discovery of the circulation of the blood marked the beginning of the end of medicine as taught by Galen, which had been accepted for 1,400 years. From then on, experimental physiology was to sweep away many old erroneous ideas and replace them with personal observations made by experiment and careful measurement.

Hill, Archibald Vivian (*1886-1977*), was a British physiologist who studied muscle action in great detail. For this work he received the 1922 Nobel Prize for Physiology and Medicine, which he shared with Otto Meyerhof (1884-1951).

Hill was born on 26 September 1886 in Bristol. He was educated at Blundell's School, Tiverton, and then went to Trinity College, Cambridge. There he excelled at mathematics and was greatly influenced by his tutor Morley Fletcher (1873-1933), who had collaborated with Frederick Hopkins in the discovery of the role of lactic acid in muscle contraction. Graduating with a medical degree in 1907 he remained at Trinity until 1914 when World War I broke out, in which he served with distinction. He became Professor of Physiology at Manchester University in 1920 after obtaining his doctorate from Trinity earlier that year. He joined the staff of University College, London, in 1923 and three years later took up a professorship at the Royal Society, a position he held until 1951. During that period he was Secretary to the Royal Society, from 1935 to 1946. He also served as Scientific Advisor to India from 1943 to 1944 and was active in various scientific organizations, including the Marine Biological Association, of which he was President from 1955. He was a member of the War Cabinet Scientific Advisory Committee during World War II. He died in Cambridge on 4 June 1977.

Influenced by his mentor Fletcher, at Cambridge, Hill researched into the workings of muscles as early as 1911. He was not concerned with the chemical details of muscle action, but wanted rather to ascertain the amount of heat produced during muscle activity. To do this he used delicate thermocouples, and discovered that contracting muscle fibres produce heat in two phases. Heat is first produced quickly as the muscle contracts. Then after the initial contraction, further heat is evolved more slowly but often in greater amounts. The thermocouples which Hill used recorded heat changes quickly and minutely in the form of tiny electric currents. He had to modify this apparatus for his particular purpose and was able to measure a rise in temperature of as little as 0.003°C over a few hundredths of a second.

By 1913 Hill was aware that heat is produced after the muscles have contracted and he showed that molecular oxygen is consumed after the work of the muscles is over and not during muscular contraction. This discovery was made by proving that if muscle fibre is made to contract in an atmosphere of pure nitrogen, the first phase of heat production is not affected but the second phase does not take place at all. He realized that oxygen is not necessary in the first phase - that is, the chemical reactions immediately involved in the contraction of muscles do not require oxygen. But in phase two, when muscle contraction has taken place, oxygen is needed to produce further energy for subsequent muscle contraction.

Mammals and birds maintain a constant body temperature which in human beings is 37°C (98.6F). The maintenance of such a constant temperature is under involuntary control, but can be partly attributed to muscular activity. When a warm-blooded animal such as man is cold, it is necessary for the body to produce heat. One of the ways in which it does so is by shivering, an involuntary contraction of muscles resulting in heat generation by the process elucidated by Hill.

Hill, Robert (*1899–*   ), is a British biochemist who has contributed greatly to modern knowledge of photosynthesis.

Hill was born on 2 April 1899. After serving in World War I in the Royal Engineers Pioneer Antigas Department, from 1917 to 1918, he studied at Emmanuel College, Cambridge. He remained researching there until 1938, by which time he had become a Senior Research Fellow. From 1943 to 1966 he was a member of the Scientific Staff of the Agricultural Research Council.

The process of photosynthesis has been shown to occur in two separate sets of reactions, those that require sunlight (the light reactions) and those that do not (the dark reactions). Both sets of reactions are dependent on one another. In the light reactions some of the energy of sunlight is trapped within the plant and in the dark reactions this energy is used to produce potentially energy-generating chemicals, such as sugar.

In 1894 Engelman first showed that the light reactions of photosynthesis occur within the chloroplasts of leaves. Hill's experiments in 1937 confirmed the localization of the light reactions within the chloroplast, as well as elucidating in part the mechanism of the light reactions. He isolated chloroplasts from leaves and then illuminated them in the presence of an artificial electron-acceptor. The electron-acceptor he used was a ferric salt (Fe^{3+}) which was reduced to the ferrous form (Fe^{2+}) during the reaction. He showed that during the reaction, oxygen is produced and that this derived oxygen comes from water. (He also demonstrated the evolution of oxygen in human blood cells by the conversion of haemoglobin to oxyhaemoglobin.) This process, known as the Hill Reaction, can be summed up by the following equation:

$$4\,Fe^{3+} + 2H_2O \xrightarrow[\text{Chloroplasts}]{\text{Light}} 4\,Fe^{2+} + 4\,H^+ + O_2 \uparrow$$

Much more is now known about the mechanism of the Hill Reaction in plants, and the equation has become more complicated:

$$2NADP + ADP + P_i + 2H_2O \xrightarrow[\text{Chloroplasts}]{\text{Light}}$$
$$2NADPH_2 + ATP + O_2 \uparrow$$

The electron-acceptor in the plant is now known to be NADP (nicotinamide adenine dinucleotide phosphate), and is reduced in the reaction to $NADPH_2$. ADP (adenosine diphosphate) is phosphorylated to ATP (adenosine triphosphate) in the reaction, a process known as photophosphorylation. In the plant the energy from sunlight is first stored as ATP and later as sugar, the final product of the dark reaction of photosynthesis which uses energy from ATP. Hill's findings were of great significance in further investigations into photosynthesis.

Hippocrates (*c. 460–c. 377* BC), is known as the father of medicine, and in ancient times was regarded as the greatest physician who had ever lived. In contrast to the general views of his time, which considered sickness to be brought about by the displeasure of the gods or by possession by demons, Hippocrates looked upon it as a purely physical phenomenon capable of rational explanation.

Hippocrates was born on the Greek island of Cos, the son of a physician (although the legends surrounding his feats ascribed him to being a member of a family of magicians). Not much is known for certain about his life as he is referred to little by his contemporaries. He travelled throughout Greece and Asia Minor where the cures he achieved, his great skill and humanity, together with his exemplary conduct, soon made him famous. Eventually, on his return to Greece, he founded a medical school on Cos, where he taught. This school was one of the first of its kind, and is one of the reasons for his title "father of medicine".

Hippocrates concerned himself with the whole patient, regarding the body as a whole organism and not just a series of parts. He used few medicines but considered rather that it was the duty of the doctor to find out by careful observation what Nature was trying to do and to meddle as little as possible with the process of healing, relying on good diet, fresh air, rest and cleanliness in both patient and doctor. Hippocrates did believe, however, that some diseases, such as those resulting from a poor diet, were caused by residues of undigested food which gave off vapours that seeped into the body.

The several generations of doctors who studied under Hippocrates are thought to have contributed to the 72 books known as the *Corpus Hippocraticus* (Hippocratic Collection), the library of the medical school at Cos which was later assembled in Alexandria, in the third century BC. These works comprise text books, research reports, lectures, essays and clinical notebooks. They contain few correct anatomical observations, although one book contains accurately observed symptoms with the likely outcome for the patient. Another book, *About the Nature of Man*, describes a theory of "humours", or body fluids. The theory

was based on the belief in the existence of four important fluids - blood, phlegm and yellow and black bile. If the normal levels of these fluids were unbalanced, illness ensued. This theory persisted among physicians in Europe right through the Middle Ages.

Hoagland, Mahlon Bush (*1921-*   ), is an American biochemist who was the first to isolate transfer RNA (tRNA), which plays an essential part in intracellular protein synthesis.

Hoagland was born on 5 October 1921 in Boston, Massachusetts. He studied medicine at Harvard University Medical School, obtaining his degree in 1948, after which he worked as a Research Fellow in Medicine in the Huntingdon Laboratory of Massachusetts General Hospital until 1951. He then spent a year at the Carlsberg Laboratory in Copenhagen as a Fellow of the American Cancer Society. From 1953 to 1967 he held several positions in the Huntingdon Laboratory at Harvard Medical School; he joined the laboratory as an Assistant in Medicine, progressed to Assistant Professor of Medicine, then in 1960 became Associate Professor of Bacteriology and Immunology. In 1967 he was appointed Professor of Biochemistry and Chairman of the Biochemistry Department at the Dartmouth Medical School. Since 1967 he has been President

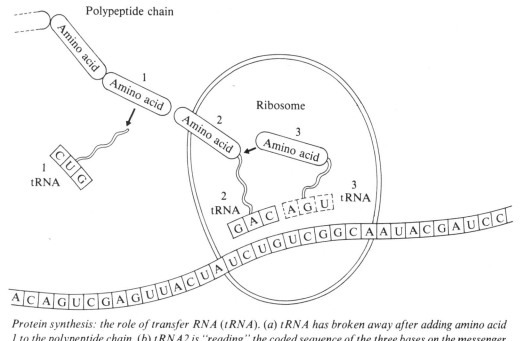

Protein synthesis: the role of transfer RNA (tRNA). (a) tRNA has broken away after adding amino acid 1 to the polypeptide chain. (b) tRNA2 is "reading" the coded sequence of the three bases on the messenger RNA strand and is marshalling amino acid 2 for the polypeptide. (c) tRNA3 is about to read the sequence for the next amino acid 3.

and Scientific Director of the Worcester Foundation for Experimental Biology in Shrewsbury, Massachusetts.

In the late 1950s Hoagland isolated various types of RNA molecules (now known as tRNA) from cytoplasm and demonstrated that each type of tRNA can combine with only one specific amino acid. Within the cytoplasm a tRNA molecule and its associated amino acid combine to form a complex - amino acyl tRNA. This complex then passes to the ribosome, where it combines with a messenger RNA (mRNA) molecule in a specific way: each tRNA molecule has as part of its structure a characteristic triplet of nitrogenous bases that links to a complementary triplet on the mRNA. A number of these reactions occur on the ribosome, building up a protein one amino acid at a time.

In addition to his research on tRNA and the biosynthesis of proteins, Hoagland has also investigated the carcinogenic effects of beryllium and the biosynthesis of co-enzyme A.

Hodgkin, Alan Lloyd (*1914-*   ), and **Huxley, Andrew Fielding** (*1917-*   ), are British physiologists who have contributed much to the understanding of how nerve impulses are transmitted. For their work concerning the movements of ions in the excitation of nerve membranes they shared the 1963 Nobel Prize in Physiology and Medicine with the Australian physiologist John Eccles (*1903-*   ).

Hodgkin was born on 15 February 1914, in Banbury, Oxfordshire. He was educated at Gresham School, Holt, and then at Trinity College, Cambridge, from which he graduated in 1936. In 1937 and 1938 he worked at the Rockefeller Institute and at Woods Hole Marine Biological laboratories in Massachusetts, where he began his research on the squid. On his return to Cambridge he began his collaboration with Huxley but their work was interrupted by the advent of World War II, during which Hodgkin researched airborne radar for the Air Ministry. After the war he went back to Cambridge and served as a lecturer and Assistant Research Director in the Department of Physiology from 1945 to 1952, when he became Foulerton Research Professor. In 1970 he accepted the biophysics professorship at Cambridge, and the following year took up the appointment of Chancellor of the University of Leicester. Hodgkin was awarded the Royal Medal of the Royal Society in 1958 and was President of the society from 1970 to 1975.

Andrew Huxley was born in London on 22 November 1917, the grandson of the distinguished nineteenth-century scientist Thomas Huxley. He was educated at University College

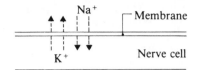

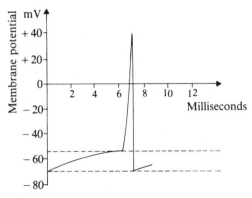

The potential inside an axon changes rapidly (and reverses) with the passage of a nerve impulse, accompanied by movement of sodium and potassium ions through the cell membrane.

and Westminster Schools and then at Trinity College, Cambridge, from which he graduated in 1938 and gained his MA in 1941. His researches were interrupted by World War II; he was involved in operational research for Anti-aircraft Command from 1940 to 1942, and then for the Admiralty until 1945. It was on his return to Cambridge after the war that Huxley collaborated with Hodgkin on their award-winning work. He became a demonstrator and then Assistant Director of Research at Cambridge from 1946 to 1960. He was appointed Director of Studies at Cambridge from 1952 to 1960, and was elected a Fellow of the Royal Society in 1955. In 1960 he moved to University College, London, and since 1969 has held a professorship there in the Department of Physiology. He succeeded Alexander Todd as President of the Royal Society in 1980.

The theory concerning the nervous system developed at the end of the nineteenth century stated that nerve cells have as their primary function the transmission of information in the form of changes in electric potential across the cell membrane. Hodgkin first became interested in the mechanics of nerve impulses in the late 1930s and devoted most of his research to the unknown quantities and qualities of the associated electric potentials.

In 1902 Julius Bernstein, an experimental neurophysiologist, had suggested that resting potential was due to the selective permeability of nerve membrane to potassium ions. He had also suggested that the action potential was brought about by a breakdown in this selectivity so that the membrane potential fell to zero. In 1945 at Cambridge, Hodgkin and Huxley attempted to measure the electrochemical behaviour of nerve membranes. They experimented on axons of the giant squid (*Loligo forbesi*) – each axon is about 0.7 mm in diameter. They inserted a glass capillary tube filled with sea water into the axon to test the composition of the ions in and surrounding the cell, which also had a microelectrode inserted into it. They succeeded in measuring the potential differences between the tip of the microelectrode and the sea water. Stimulating the axon with a pair of outside electrodes, it was shown that the inside of the cell was at first negative (the resting potential) and the outside positive, and that during the conduction of the nerve impulse the membrane potential reversed so the inside became positive and the outside negative. This was the first time that electrical changes across the cell membrane had been recorded and the discovery that the membrane potential exceeds the zero level during the action potential implied that some other process than that proposed by Bernstein must be involved. Hodgkin suggested that this process was a rapid and specific increase in the permeability of the membrane to sodium ions.

Working with Bernhard Katz, another cell physiologist, Hodgkin showed that when there was no current flowing through the membrane, the membrane potential could be given by a formula which acknowledges that sodium ions do play an important part in determining the membrane potential. The theory proposed that an excited membrane becomes permeable to sodium ions (which are positively charged), which on entry to a cell cause its contents also to become positively charged; it is known as the "sodium theory" and is now accepted to be of fairly general application.

In 1947 Hodgkin concluded that during the resting phase a nerve membrane allows only potassium ions to diffuse into the cell, but when the cell is excited it allows sodium ions to enter and potassium ions to move out. By 1952 Hodgkin had demonstrated that the inside of a cell has a great concentration of potassium ions, and the surrounding solution is rich in sodium ions. In that year, Hodgkin and Katz used a special technique now known as the "voltage clamp method" to measure the currents flowing across a nerve membrane. They found that during an action potential, the inside of the cell becomes electrically positive by 30 to 60 millivolts, and that the membrane recovers from an impulse within milliseconds. In 1953 Hodgkin investigated the role

played by potassium ions in nerve cells and showed that the internal potassium ions are free to move in an electric field. From this he concluded that almost all the potassium in the axoplasm is effectively in a free solution and that it contributes in some way to the production of the resting potential. Two years later Hodgkin devised an apparatus to measure the extrusion of radioactive sodium from the giant axons of a squid. It was shown that there is a relationship between the efflux of sodium and the time taken for it to diffuse out and, further, that when the axon was surrounded with DNP the amount of sodium efflux fell markedly but recovered when the DNP was washed away. This experiment implied that the extrusion of sodium is probably dependent on the metabolic energy supplied either directly or indirectly in the form of ATP (adenosine triphosphate). It was also discovered that the amount of sodium flowing in equals that of the potassium flowing out.

Hodgkin, with his associates, produced more conclusive evidence of this extrusion dependence in 1960 and also showed that the sodium efflux is dependent upon the external potassium ion concentration. The action potential would not be able to revert to the resting potential inside the cell if the influx of sodium ions were not balanced by the extrusion of another positively charged ion. The decrease from the peak is followed by the exit of potassium ions, so restoring the cell interior to a negative phase. In 1959 Hodgkin had found that the inward and outward flow of sodium in frog muscle was approximately equal, implying that the greater part of the sodium efflux must be dependent upon some active transport process. Keynes has since shown that there seems to be a "chloride pump" involved, but its function is still obscure.

Many scientists have used Hodgkin and Huxley's methods to study resting and action potentials in various excitable membranes. The "voltage clamp" method is used to obtain information on the elements affecting nerve conduction. Investigations are also being directed to discover the mechanism that possibly involves an enzyme, which is present in the peripheral cell membrane and breaks down ATP, thus releasing energy, but only if sodium and potassium ions are present.

Hodgkin, Thomas (*1798–1866*), was a British physician who described six cases of malignant reticulosis in his paper "On some morbid appearances of the absorbent glands and spleen" which was published in 1832. The disease is named after him.

Hodgkin was born in Tottenham, London, on 6 January 1798, and was tutored at home. Some of his education took place on the Continent, where he completed his medical training after a few years at Guy's Hospital, London. He gained his MD from Edinburgh University in 1821. In 1825 he was selected to become one of the first Fellows of the Royal College of Physicians, but he declined the honour. He became Curator of the new museum at Guy's and lectured in morbid anatomy; he was the first to give regular tuition in the subject. He was lauded at home and abroad by a number of societies for his work, but in 1837 he was passed over for the post of Assistant Physician at Guy's and was deeply disappointed. He resigned from the hospital and gradually devoted more and more of his time to philanthropic work. He was an excellent linguist, and an active crusader in the Aborigines Protection Society. He contracted dysentery and died at the age of 68 while on a mercy mission to the Jewish people in Jaffa. He is buried in Israel.

Hodgkin was the first to describe a particular type of lymphoma that usually affects young adults and causes malignant inflammation of the lymph glands. The spleen and liver may also become involved. Hodgkin's disease can now be definitely diagnosed by the histological presence of Reed Sternburg cells.

Hodgkin received little recognition of his observations until 1865, when Samuel Wilks of Guy's referred to Hodgkin's account in his paper "Cases of Enlargement of the Lymphatic Glands and Spleen (or Hodgkin's Disease)".

Hodgkin pioneered the use of the stethoscope in Britain after being favourably impressed in France by René Laënnec (1781-1826), who invented the instrument in 1816. He was also the first person to stress the importance of post-mortem examinations.

Hooker, Joseph Dalton (*1817-1911*), was a British botanist who made many important contributions to botanical taxonomy but who is probably best known for introducing into Britain a range of previously unknown Rhododendron species and for his improvements to the Royal Botanical Gardens at Kew.

Hooker was born on 30 June 1817 in Halesworth, Suffolk. He studied medicine at Glasgow University, where his father was Professor of Botany, graduating in 1839. In the same year he obtained the post of assistant surgeon and naturalist on an expedition to the southern hemisphere. The expedition, which was led by Captain James Clark Ross, set out in 1839 and returned in 1843; its main aims were to locate the magnetic South Pole and to explore the Great Ice Barrier, but other places were visited, including the Falkland Islands, Tasmania and New Zealand. On his

return to England, Hooker applied for the botany chair at Edinburgh University but was not accepted and so took a job identifying fossils for a geological survey. From 1847 to 1850 he took time off to undertake a botanical exploration of north-eastern India, mainly of the Himalayan state of Sikkim and eastern Nepal. In 1855 he became Assistant Director of Kew Gardens, where his father was by this time Director. On the death of his father in 1865 Hooker became the Director, a post he held until 1885, when he retired. He died on 10 December 1911 in Sunningdale, Berkshire.

While Hooker was on the expedition to the southern hemisphere he made extensive notes and sketches of the plants he saw and collected many specimens, which he pressed and mounted. On his return to Britain he produced a six-volume work (published between 1844 and 1860) of his observations and findings, with two volumes each on the flora of Antarctica, New Zealand and Tasmania. This work combined accurate and detailed descriptions of plants with perceptive essays on plant distribution and established Hooker's reputation as a botanist of the highest calibre. The importance of this work was quickly recognized by the Royal Society, which elected Hooker a Fellow in 1847.

In 1854 Hooker published a general account of his travels in the Indian subcontinent, entitled *Himalayan Journals*. He also wrote many scientific works based on his research on the Indian flora; the first of these was about rhododendrons and was published by Hooker's father while Hooker himself was still in India. In addition, Hooker sent back to England many previously unknown species of rhododendrons. His first general botanical work on Indian plants was the single volume *Flora Indica* (1855), written in conjunction with Thomas Thomson. This was superseded by Hooker's monumental seven-volume *Flora of British India* (1872 to 1897), written jointly with several other scientists. While in India, Hooker became interested in the genus *Impatiens* (a group that includes the Himalayan Balsam, which has since become naturalized in Britain), and gave descriptions of about 300 species of this genus. He supplemented his Indian work by writing volumes four and five of *A Handbook to the Flora of Ceylon* between 1898 and 1900, a work that had remained unfinished since the death in 1896 of its original author, H. Trimen.

As Director of Kew Gardens, Hooker introduced many improvements, with the introduction of the rock garden, the addition of new avenues and an extension of the arboretum. Several other important developments occurred during

Hooker's directorship. In 1876 T.J. Phillips Jodrell, a friend of the Hooker family, died and left a bequest for the foundation of a botanical laboratory at Kew. The Jodrell Laboratory is now world famous for the scientific work performed there on the structure and physiology of plants. Kew Gardens also became increasingly important as a repository for collections of pressed plants and as a centre for the propagation and distribution of many crop plants, including rubber, coffee and the oil palm. Furthermore, in 1883 the *Index Kewensis* was founded; this is a list of all scientific plant names, accompanied by descriptions which, since the publication of the first volume in 1892, has become an invaluable aid in preventing duplication and error in the naming of plants.

As well as establishing Kew Gardens as an international centre for botanical research, Hooker also continued his own botanical work. With the botanist George Bentham he published *Genera Plantarum* (1862 to 1883), a complete catalogue of all the known genera and families of flowering plants from all parts of the world. Nevertheless, Hooker did not neglect the British flora. In 1870 he published *Student's Flora of the British Isles*, and from 1887 to 1908 he edited various editions of Bentham's *Handbook of the British Flora*. He was also interested in aspects of botany other than taxonomy, such as the dispersal of plants over large areas and the evolution of new species. After much consideration he became an evolutionist, but his belief in the theory was founded on his own rather specialized knowledge of plants and regional floras and so he contributed little to the popular debate on the subject.

Hopkins, Frederick Gowland (*1861-1947*), was a British biochemist who was jointly awarded (with Christian Eijkman) the 1929 Nobel Prize in Physiology and Medicine for his work that showed the necessity of certain dietary components - now known as vitamins - for the maintenance of health. He received several other honours for his work, including a knighthood in 1925.

Hopkins was born on 20 June 1861 in Eastbourne, Sussex. He showed no remarkable distinction at school, except in chemistry, and after leaving school he was articled for three years to a consulting analyst in London. He then became an analytical assistant at Guy's Hospital in London, simultaneously studying for an external degree in chemistry at the University of London. In 1888 he became a medical student at Guy's Hospital Medical School, from which he graduated in 1894. He remained at Guy's Hospital until 1898, when he was invited by Michael Foster, Professor of Physiology at Cambridge University, to become a Lecturer in Chemical Physiology at Cambridge. This was an extremely taxing job, the strain of which adversely affected Hopkins' health, and it left little time for original research. In 1914, however, Hopkins was appointed Professor of Biochemistry at Cambridge and was able to devote more time to his own investigations; he held this position until he retired in 1943. He died in Cambridge on 16 May 1947.

Hopkins began his Nobel prize-winning work in 1906, when he realized that animals cannot survive on a diet containing only proteins, fats and carbohydrates. Experimenting on the growth rates of rats fed on diets of artificial milk, he noticed that they failed to grow unless a small quantity of cow's milk was added to the artificial milk. From this he concluded that the cow's milk contained accessory food factors that are required in only trace amounts but which are essential for normal growth. But he failed to isolate these substances (now called vitamins) and his hypothesis remained controversial for many years, although it had been proved correct by the time he was awarded a Nobel Prize in 1929.

Hopkins also made several other important contributions to biological knowledge. He discovered the amino acid tryptophan when one of his students - John Mellanby, who later became Professor of Physiology at Oxford University - failed to obtain the Adamkiewicz colour reaction for proteins (this involves adding acetic acid then strong sulphuric acid to the test solution). This led Hopkins, with the assistance of S.W. Cole, to investigate the reaction, which they found is the result of a reaction between glyoxylic acid - a common contaminant of acetic acid - and tryptophan. This discovery meant that tryptophan is an important constituent of proteins, which then led to the concept of essential amino acids. Hopkins also showed that tryptophan and certain other amino acids cannot be manufactured by the body and must therefore be supplied in the diet. In addition, he helped to lay the foundation for the modern understanding of muscle contraction with his demonstration (in collaboration with Morley Fletcher) that contracting muscle accumulates lactic acid. Hopkins also discovered the tripeptide glutathione, which is important as a hydrogen carrier in the intracellular utilization of oxygen.

Hunter, John (*1728-1793*), was a celebrated Scottish surgeon known for his occasional use of unorthodox methods. He built up a collection of 14,000 anatomical specimens and his memorial brass in Westminster Abbey records his "services to mankind as the Founder of Scientific Surgery".

Hunter was born in Long Calderwood, Lanarkshire, on 13 February 1728. He worked on the family farm after the death of his father and at the age of 20 went to London to join his brother, William, who was a distinguished surgeon and obstetrician. John Hunter had no formal university qualification; he assisted in the preparation of anatomical specimens for his brother's lectures and engaged in investigations of his own. He also attended surgical classes at various London hospitals. He was appointed a Master of Anatomy of the Surgeons' Corporation in 1753 and three years later served as house surgeon at St George's Hospital, London, (during which time he taught Edward Jenner). He joined the British army in 1759 and in 1760 worked in France and Portugal as an army surgeon. He returned to London in 1763 and set up a private practice, and continued with his research. During the late 1760s he took up a senior surgical post at St George's Hospital and was appointed physician extraordinary to George III. Ten years later he became Deputy Surgeon to the Army and in 1790 became Inspector General of Hospitals. Hunter collapsed and died at a meeting of the board of governors at St George's Hospital on 16 October 1793. He was buried at St Martin's-in-the-fields, but his remains were later taken to Westminster Abbey on 28 March 1859.

While Hunter was working with his brother, he made a detailed study of the structure and function of the lymphatic vessels, and the growth and structure of bone. He made these investigations by collecting a great deal of material from postmortem examinations. Many of the corpses that he dissected he obtained from "resurrectionists", who raided graveyards at night to sell newly buried corpses to surgeons for dissection.

Hunter also kept a number of animal specimens in his garden for dissection, that at one time included a bull and the carcass of a whale. The knowledge he gained performing these dissections allowed him to improve further the embalming technique by arterial injection, as developed by William Harvey. One of the most interesting of these experiments was the case of the late Mrs Martin van Butchell, whose husband took her body to Hunter for embalming in 1775. Mrs van Butchell had stated in her will that her wealth remained her husband's, as long as her body remained above the ground. Hunter embalmed the body, and Mr van Butchell clothed it and placed it in a glass case for visitors to view – and to meet the conditions of the will.

Hunter's keenness to collect specimens was well known. One of his most prized specimens was the skeleton of Charles Byrne, an Irishman who was 8 feet tall and who, determined not to fall into

Hunter's clutches, had arranged to be buried at sea. But Hunter, on hearing of his death, arranged for his body to be seized by the resurrectionists, for a fee of £500.

Surgical training was not easily available in Hunter's day, so when he moved nearer to central London he gave lectures from his own house. Later he had a lecture room and museum built in his garden where he held meetings of the Lyceum Medicum Londinense (London Medical Academy). He had helped to found this student society and encouraged each student to prepare a paper on a medical topic and read it to his fellow students.

Hunter's experiments were wide-ranging, including studies of lymph and blood circulation, the sense of smell, the structure of teeth and bone, tissue grafting and various diseases. He often carried out experiments on himself, such as the occasion when, trying to prove that syphilis and gonorrhoea are types of the same disease, he inoculated himself and later developed syphilis. When Hunter's health began to suffer, he took an army appointment on the surgical staff concerned with the Seven Years War. Whilst dealing with casualties, he gained the knowledge for his treatise on gunshot wounds.

During his lifetime Hunter published an impressive number of papers on a wide variety of medical and biological subjects such as his *Treatise on the Natural History of the Human Teeth* (1771) in which he describes his experiments on the transplantation of tissues – the best known of these being that of a human tooth fixed into a cock's comb. In 1786 he published his *Treatise on the Venereal Disease*, and his *Treatise on the Blood, Inflammation and Gun-shot Wounds* was published posthumously in 1794. Hunter's collection was handed to the Royal College of Surgeons in 1795 and later formed the basis of the Hunterian museum.

Huxley, Andrew Fielding (*1917–*   ). See HODGKIN, ALAN LLOYD.

Huxley, Hugh Esmor (*1924–*   ), is a British physiologist whose contribution to science has been concerned with the study of muscle cells.

Huxley was born in Birkenhead, Cheshire, on 25 February 1924 (he is not a member of the Huxley family descended from the nineteenth-century scientist Thomas Huxley). He was educated at Park High School, Birkenhead, and from 1914 at Christ's College, Cambridge. He read natural science there and graduated in 1943. He worked on radar research until the end of World War II and then returned to Cambridge in 1948, where he finally gained his PhD in 1952. He spent

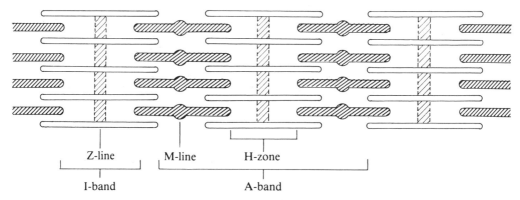

Z-line	M-line	H-zone
I-band		A-band

Banding in a fibril of striated muscle.

five years (1956–61) in the University of London Biophysics department and was a Fellow of King's College Cambridge from 1961 to 1967; from that time he has been a Fellow of Churchill College, Cambridge.

Prior to Huxley's research, the physiology of muscle structure had been under scientific scrutiny for a long time and it had been thought that muscular contraction involved a process of coiling and contraction, rather like the shortening of a helical spring. But investigations had been held up because adequate equipment, such as the electron microscope, was not available. Once this instrument was built in 1933, studies into the chemical reactions that produce muscle contraction progressed, but the real breakthrough came in the 1950s when Huxley, using the electron microscope and thin slicing techniques, established the detailed structural basis of muscle contraction. It had been ascertained that muscle fibres contain a large number of longitudinally arranged myofibrils, and that two main bands alternately cross the fibrils: the dark anisotropic (A) and the lighter isotropic (I) bands. Each A band is divided by a lighter region, the H zone (which in turn is bisected by an M line), and each I band by a dark line, the Z line.

Huxley demonstrated that the myofibrils are composed of interdigitating rows of thick and thin myosin and actin filaments. He found that the thin filaments are attached to the Z lines and extend through the I bands into the A bands, and that the M line is caused by a further thickening in the middle of the thick filaments. In addition he proved that the helical spring assumption was wrong. The A band does not change its length when the muscle is stretched or when it is shortened. Huxley suggested that contraction is brought about by sliding movements of the I filaments between the A filaments, and that the sliding is caused by a series of cyclic reactions between the myosin filaments and active sites on the actin filaments. This proposal is known as the sliding filament theory.

From previous research, Huxley knew that the contractile machinery of muscle cells consists of a small number of different proteins, and that actin and myosin are the two major ones involved. He proceeded to investigate the exact location of the actin and myosin. Using a solution of potassium chloride, pyrophosphate and magnesium chloride, he found that the A filaments are composed of myosin. He then discovered, using a solution of potassium iodide, that the I filaments are composed of actin. The Z lines were unaffected by the solutions which indicated that they are composed of some other substance. Huxley also noticed that the myosin-extracted fibres still retained their elasticity and he suggested that there is yet another set of filaments crossing the H zone. He called these hypothetical structures S filaments.

In 1953 Huxley had observed a series of projections which formed a repetitive pattern along the line of the A filament. The projections appeared to emerge in pairs from opposite sides of the myosin filaments at regular intervals, and he discovered that they are able to aggregate under suitable conditions to form "artificial" filaments of varying lengths. He proposed that the "tails" of the myosin molecules become attached to each other to form a filament with the heads projecting from the body of the filament, and that these projecting filaments play an important part in the sliding effect described in the sliding filament theory.

By coincidence, Andrew Huxley, working separately, came to the same conclusions at about the same time. Both Huxleys subscribe to the sliding filament theory although their interpretation of it is slightly different. H.E. Huxley suggests that the movement can be likened to that of a ratchet device or a cog-type operation, whereas A. Huxley proposes that each myosin filament has side pieces which can slide along the main backbone of the filament and that the slides can combine temporarily with sites on adjacent filaments. Many problems remain surrounding this discovery because although the sliding filament theory has been accepted by many scientists when applied to striated muscles, it has not yet been shown to apply to smooth muscles.

Huxley, Thomas Henry (*1825-1895*), was a distinguished British biologist who helped to break down the great barrier of traditional resistance to scientific advance during the mid-nineteenth century, and did a great deal to popularize science.

Huxley was born in Ealing, Middlesex, on 4 May 1825. He went to Ealing School in 1833, where his father taught mathematics, but his schooldays were limited to two years because his father was dismissed from his teacher post in 1835. Despite the lack of a formal education, he received some tuition in medicine from a brother-in-law, and obtained an apprenticeship in 1840 to a medical practitioner in London's East End. Huxley attended botany lectures in his spare time and in 1842, on entering a public competition, won a scholarship to study medicine at Charing Cross Hospital; he graduated in 1845. From 1846 to 1850 he was the assistant ship's surgeon on HMS *Rattlesnake* on its voyage around the South Seas. A year after his return, in 1851, he was elected to the Royal Society. Three years later he took up the appointment of Professor of Natural History at the Royal School of Mines (which in time became the Royal College of Science). From 1881 to 1885 he was President of the Royal Society. He then retired to continue his research and died in Eastbourne, of influenza and bronchitis, on 29 June 1895. His grandchildren include the Nobel prize-winning physiologist Andrew Huxley, the biologist Julian Huxley, and the author Aldous Huxley.

Huxley's original intention was to be a mechanical engineer but his success in the field of medicine dissuaded him. For instance, when he was 19 years old he discovered the structure at the base of the human hair known today as Huxley's layer.

Huxley established his reputation in the scientific world during the four-year voyage to the South Seas. Each day he dissected, drew and observed, with his microscope tied down against the lurching of the ship. Most naturalists of the time were interested only in collecting specimens which could be dried, stuffed and mounted, but Huxley concentrated on delicate creatures, such as the heteropods, which were difficult to preserve

and liable to disintegrate. He sent his detailed recordings back to England from each port the ship docked at, and these observations were published in various influential scientific journals. On his return to England in October 1850, Huxley was acclaimed by men such as Joseph Hooker and Charles Lyell. From being an unknown assistant surgeon, he found himself at the forefront of British science.

European zoology had long been under the shadow of the French anatomist Georges Cuvier (1769-1832). In 1817 Cuvier had formulated a system of classification which placed quadrupeds, birds, amphibians and fish into the class Vertebrata, and insects among the Articulata. Although he recognized the molluscs as a distinct group, he had lumped most other animals together as Radiata. While carrying out his examinations on the ship Huxley realized that Cuvier's classification was not good enough and that there was a vast range of distinctions in minute anatomy of which the great man had not been aware. Huxley therefore reclassified the animal kingdom into Annuloida, Annulosa, Infusoria, Coelenterata, Mollusca, Molluscoida, Protozoa and Vertebrata.

One of the illuminating suggestions Huxley was able to make from his detailed observations was that the inner and outer layers of the Medusae correspond with the two embryonic layers of higher animals. This suggestion provided the base to all later embryological thinking. Huxley also started a fundamental revision of the Mollusca. At that time a wide variety of non-segmented and non-radiate soft-bellied animals (sea squirts, sea-mats and lamp shells) were grouped together indiscriminately with the true molluscs. Although his intended project to produce a regular monograph of Mollusca never really materialized, he was able to "construct" an archetypal cephalous mollusc which was remarkably similar to the evolutionary ancestor of the molluscs deduced by zoologists more than 80 years later.

Huxley became very much embroiled in the great controversy that raged when Darwin published his *Origin of Species*, and he was one of Darwin's most outspoken champions. A famous example of his involvement in Darwinism is this extract from a public debate held in 1860 at Oxford University with Bishop Samuel Wilberforce. The bishop had questioned whether Huxley traced his descent to the apes through his mother or his father, to which Huxley replied: "If . . . the question is put to me, would I rather have a miserable ape for a grandfather or a man highly endowed by nature and possessed of great means of influence, and yet who employs these faculties and that influence for the mere purpose of introd-

ucing ridicule into a grave scientific discussion –
I unhesitatingly affirm my preference for the
ape."

Huxley is also credited with the founding of
craniology. In his investigations into the true origins of the newly discovered Neanderthal skull,
he devised a series of quantitive indices and the
first real rationale of the measurement of skulls.
He also produced a new system of classification
of birds based mainly on the palate and other
bony structures. Previously they had been classified according to their feeding habits, foot-web-
bing and beaks. Huxley raised bird classification
to a science and his own classification of birds is
the foundation of the modern system.

Although he was never a great experimenter,
Huxley's scientific work was distinguished by its
critical assessment of both pre-existing and newly
acquired knowledge. He produced more than 150
research papers on subjects as varied as the morphology of the heteropod molluscs, the hybridi-
zation of gentians, the taxonomy of crayfish and
the physical anthropology of the Patagonians.
His dissections and observations filled numerous
gaps in the knowledge of the animal kingdom,
and his attitudes did much to establish the idea
that science and the scientific method are the only
means by which the ultimate truths of the animal
world can be found.

I

Ingenhousz, Jan (*1730-1799*), was a Dutch biologist and physiologist who discovered photosynthesis and plant respiration.

Ingenhousz was born in Breda, in The Netherlands, on 8 December 1730, the son of a pharmacist. He was educated locally and received his
training in medicine and chemistry at the University of Louvain, graduating in 1753; he then studied at the University of Leyden during the following year. He went to universities in Paris and
Edinburgh for short periods, after which he set
up a private medical practice in Breda. On his
father's death in 1765, he left for England, encouraged by a physician from the British army
who had befriended his family during the war of
the Austrian Succession. In 1766 he worked at
the Foundling Hospital, London, where he was
responsible for inoculating patients against smallpox (using the hazardous live virus). His methods
were reasonably successful and in 1768 he was
sent to the Austrian court in Vienna, by George
III, to inoculate the royal family. He took up the
appointment of court physician there from 1772

to 1779. In that year he returned to England,
where he continued his research until he died on
7 September 1799, in Bowood, Wiltshire.

In 1771 Joseph Priestly had found that the
flame of a candle burning in a closed space
eventually goes out and that a small animal confined under similar conditions soon dies. He also
found that plants can restore the capacity of the
air to support life, or the burning of a candle.
Later Priestly discovered "dephlogisticated air"
(oxygen). It seems likely that Priestley's work inspired Ingenhousz to carry out similar experiments of his own.

Ingenhousz discovered in 1779 that the green
parts only of plants are able to "revitalize" the
air, and that they are capable of doing so only in
the sunlight. His investigations also showed that
the active part of the sun's radiation is not in the
heat generated, but rather in the visible light. He
found that plants, like animals, respire all the
time and that respiration occurs in all the parts of
plants.

In the following years Ingenhousz demonstrated that the amount of oxygen released by a
plant during photosynthesis is greater than that
absorbed in respiration. He suggested that green
plants take in carbon dioxide and produce
oxygen, whereas animals do the reverse, and
therefore that animals and plants are totally dependent on each other.

Ingenhousz believed that this discovery would
help to distinguish between animals and plants
among the lower orders of life. At that time a
controversy existed over the origin of carbon in
plants, some scientists believing that it is absorbed in some form by the roots – this belief was
termed the humus theory. Ingenhousz, however,
was of the opinion that carbon comes from the
carbon dioxide absorbed by a plant. This idea
explained the disappearance of the gas, and the
presence of carbon in plants. Whereas he was
right about the source of carbon, he was mistaken
about that of oxygen, and it is now known that
oxygen given off by plants comes from the water
they take in.

Apart from the life of plants, Ingenhousz had
various other interests, which led him in 1776 to
develop an improved apparatus for generating
large amounts of electricity; he also invented a
hydrogen-fuelled lighter to replace the tinderbox,
and investigated the use of an air and ether vapour mixture as a propellant for an electrically
fired pistol.

In 1779, Ingenhousz published his work *Experiments On Vegetables, Discovering their Great
Power of Purifying the Common Air in Sunshine,
and of Injuring it in the Shade or at Night*. His
discovery laid the foundations for the study of

photosynthesis, the process upon which most animals ultimately depend for their food.

Isaacs, Alick (*1921-1967*), was a British virologist who discovered interferon, an antibody produced by cells when infected by viruses.

Isaacs was born on 17 July 1921 in Glasgow, the first of four sons in a Jewish family of Russian origin (his grandparents were Russian Jews who had emigrated to Scotland in about 1880). He had a conventional Jewish upbringing and was educated at Pollockshields Secondary School in Glasgow, attending classes in Judaism every day after school. His family moved to Kilmarnock in 1939 but Isaacs stayed in Glasgow and enrolled at the university there to study medicine. He was an able student, graduating in 1944 and winning several prizes, but clinical medicine did not greatly interest him and in 1945 he became a McCann research scholar in the Department of Bacteriology at Glasgow University, where he came under the influence of Carl Browning, the professor there. In 1947 Isaacs was awarded a Medical Research Council studentship to research into influenza viruses under Stuart Harris at Sheffield University, and in the following year he went to Australia, having won a Rockefeller Travelling Fellowship to work under Frank Macfarlane Burnet at the Walter and Eliza Hall Institute for Medical Research in Melbourne. Isaacs returned to Britain in 1951 and went to work in the laboratory of the World Influenza Centre at Mill Hill, London, where he remained for the rest of his life. His work on influenza gained him his medical degree from Glasgow University and a Bellahousten Gold Medal. In 1958 to 1959 he suffered a three-month depression but seemed to recover, and in 1961 he took over the directorship of the World Influenza Centre. In 1964, however, he suffered a subarachnoid haemorrhage and died two years later, on 26 January, only 45 years old.

Although Isaacs began investigating influenza in 1947, it was not until 1956 that he discovered interferon. Working with a Swiss colleague, Jean Lindenmann, Isaacs found that chick embryos injected with influenza virus produce minute amounts of a protein that destroys the invading virus and also makes the embryos resistant to other viral infections. Isaacs and Lindenmann named this protein interferon. Further research demonstrated that most living creatures can make interferon, and that even plants react to viral infection in a similar way. When a virus invades a cell, the cell produces interferon, which then induces uninfected cells to make a protein that prevents the virus from multiplying. Almost any cell in the body can make interferon, which seems to act as the first line of defence against viral pathogens, because it is produced very quickly (interferon production starts within hours of infection whereas antibody production takes several days) and is thought to trigger other defence mechanisms.

In the 1950s there was no treatment or cure for viral infections (antibodies are effective only against bacteria and at that time anti-viral vaccines were in their early stages of development) and so the discovery of interferon was thought to be a major breakthrough. As a result, the Medical Research Council took out a patent on interferon and established a scientific committee to undertake further research into it. This initial enthusiasm waned, however, when it was found that interferon was species specific, and that it was very difficult and costly to produce. By the time Isaacs died, research into the substance had come to a virtual standstill.

Then in the late 1960s, after Isaacs' death, interest revived as a result of a chance discovery made by Ion Gresser, an American scientist then working in Paris. He found that interferon inhibits the growth of virus-induced tumours in mice and also that it stimulates the production of special cells that attack tumours. In addition, he later showed that interferon can be made in relatively large amounts from human blood cells. These findings stimulated further research, particularly into the use of interferon against cancer, leukaemia and certain viral diseases, such as hepatitis, rabies, measles and shingles. In early 1980 Charles Weissmann, a Swiss scientist, produced by genetic manipulation a strain of bacteria that can make human interferon, the effectiveness of which is still being investigated.

J

Jacob, François (*1920-   *), is a French cellular geneticist who was jointly awarded the 1965 Nobel Prize in Physiology and Medicine with André Lwoff and Jacques Monod for their collaborative work on the control of gene action in bacteria.

Jacob was born on 17 June 1920 in Nancy. He was educated at the Lycée Carnot and at the University of Paris, from which he gained his medical degree in 1947 - his studies having been interrupted by military service during World War II - and his doctor of science degree in 1954. In 1950 he joined the Pasteur Institute in Paris as a research assistant, becoming Head of Laboratory there in 1956. Since 1964 he has been Head of the Department of Cellular Genetics at the Pasteur

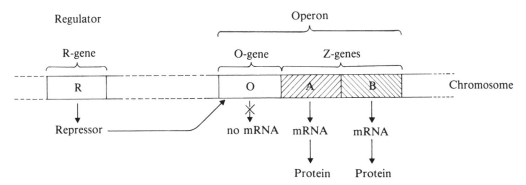

A regulator gene (R-gene) produces a repressor substance that prevents an operator (O-gene) from providing messenger RNA, blocking the production of protein.

Institute and also Professor of Cellular Genetics at the Collège de France.

Jacob began his Nobel prize-winning work on the control of gene action in 1958. Previous work by Francis Crick, James Watson and Maurice Wilkins had shown that the types of proteins produced in an organism are controlled by DNA, but it was Jacob – working with Lwoff and Monod – who demonstrated how an organism controls the amount of protein produced. Jacob performed a series of experiments in which he cultured the bacterium *Escherichia coli* in various mediums to discover the effect of the medium on enzyme production. He found that *E. coli* grown on a medium containing only glucose produced very little of the enzyme β-galactosidase, whereas *E. coli* grown on a lactose-only medium produced much greater amounts of this enzyme. This phenomenon, which is called enzyme induction, occurs because *E. coli* can metabolize glucose easily but requires β-galactosidase to metabolize lactose. From these findings, Jacob, Lwoff and Monod concluded that increased production of an enzyme (β-galactosidase in this case) occurs when an organism needs that particular enzyme, and they also proposed a theory to explain the mechanisms involved in this increased enzyme production. According to their theory there are three types of genes concerned with the production of each specific protein: a structural or Z-gene, which controls the type of protein produced, and a regulator or R-gene, which produces a repressor substance that binds to the third type of gene, the operator or O-gene. The binding of the repressor substance to the O-gene prevents the production of messenger RNA (mRNA) by the appropriate Z-gene and therefore also prevents the production of the specific protein coded for by that Z-gene. In Jacob's experiments, there was minimal production of β-galactinosidase in *E. coli* grown on glucose because the repressor substance pro-

duced by the R-gene was specifically bound to the O-gene, thereby preventing β-galactosidase production by the Z-gene. *E. coli* grown on lactose produced large amounts of β-galactosidase because lactose binds to the repressor substance produced by the R-gene, which alters the molecular conformation of the repressor substance so that it can no longer bind to the O-gene; as a result, the Z-gene can produce mRNA for β-galactosidase production. This theory has since been shown to be correct in the control of protein synthesis in *E. coli* and other bacteria.

Jenner, Edward (*1749-1823*), was a British biologist who was the first to prove by scientific experiment that cowpox gives immunity against smallpox. He was the founder of virology and was one of the pioneers of vaccination.

Jenner was born in Berkeley, Gloucestershire, on 17 May 1749, the son of a vicar. He was educated locally and in 1761 apprenticed to a surgeon in Sodbury. In 1770 he went to London to study anatomy and surgery under John Hunter, who took Jenner as his first boarding pupil at St George's Hospital in London. Returning to Gloucestershire in 1773, he set up in private practice and remained at Berkeley until he died there of a stroke on or about 26 January 1823.

In 1788, an epidemic of smallpox swept Gloucestershire and inoculations with live vaccine were used in spite of the tragedies that had previously accompanied this practice. The method used was well known in eastern countries and had been brought to England in 1721 by Lady Mary Wortley Montague, the wife of the British Ambassador to Turkey. It consisted of scratching a vein in the arm of a healthy person and working into it a small amount of matter from a smallpox pustule taken from a person with a mild attack of the disease. This treatment often resulted in the patient fatally contracting smallpox, despite the successes of Jan Ingenhousz.

In the course of his inoculations Jenner noticed that people who had suffered from cowpox, a disease affecting the teats of cows and later the hands of their milkers, remained quite unaffected by the smallpox inoculation, and did not even produce the symptoms of a mild attack of smallpox (as did other patients). Over the course of 25 years he observed that he was unable to infect previous cowpox victims with smallpox, and that where whole families succumbed to smallpox, a previous cowpox victim remained healthy. He also noticed that whereas inoculation with cowpox appeared to protect the patient from smallpox, it did not give immunity against cowpox itself. In his study of cowpox, Jenner was the first to coin the word "virus".

In 1796 Jenner carried out an experiment on one of his patients, James Phipps, a healthy eight-year-old boy. Jenner made two small cuts in the boy's arm and worked a speck of cowpox into them. A week later, the patient had a slight fever (the usual reaction) but quickly recovered. Some weeks later, Jenner repeated the inoculation, this time using smallpox matter. The boy remained healthy – vaccination was born (named after *vaccinia*, the medical name for cowpox).

Jenner continued with his experiments and reported his findings to the Royal Society but the Fellows considered that he should not risk his reputation by presenting anything "so much at variance with established knowledge", so in 1798 Jenner published his work privately. Within a few years vaccination was a widespread practice and Jenner not only improved his technique but also found a way of preserving active vaccine.

Jenner was also interested in natural history, one of his favourite hobbies being bird watching. He studied the habits of the cuckoo, which often lays its eggs in the nest of the hedge sparrow. It had been thought that the hen hedge sparrow threw out her young from the nest to make room for the developing cuckoo, but Jenner's patient observations revealed that it was the young cuckoo itself that heaved its competitors out of the nest. In 1788 he reported these findings to the Royal Society, who published them.

Jenner's work led to an immediate reduction in mortality from smallpox and, nearly 200 years later, the world-wide eradication of the disease. He may be considered to be one of the pioneers of immunology.

Jung, Carl Gustav (*1875–1961*), was a Swiss psychologist who founded analytical psychology as a deliberate alternative to the psychoanalysis of Sigmund Freud.

Jung was born in Kesswil, near Basel, on 26 July 1875, the son of a Protestant clergyman. Despite an early interest in archaeology – and a strong family background in religion and theology – he went to Basel University in 1895 to study medicine, graduating in 1900. He then attended Zurich University and obtained his MD in 1902, at the same time turning to psychiatry. For the next seven years he worked at the Burghölzi Psychiatric Clinic in Zurich under Eugen Bleuler, an expert on schizophrenia; also from 1905 to 1913 he lectured in psychiatry at the university. In 1907 he met Freud and for five years became his chief disciple, accepting the appointment as the first President of the International Psycho-Analytical Association on its foundation in 1911. But in 1913 following publication of his *Wandlungen und Symbole de Libido* (1912), translated as *The Psychology of the Unconscious* (1916), he broke with Freud, resigned from the Association, and set up his own practice in Zurich. In 1933 he became Professor of Psychology at the Zurich Federal Institute of Technology, a post he held for eight years. In 1943 he resigned almost immediately after being appointed Professor of Medical Psychology at Basel University (when he was 68 years old) because his health began to fail. But he continued to practise until he was over 80, and he died in Küsnacht, near Zurich, on 6 June 1961.

While Jung was at the Psychiatric Clinic in the early 1900s he devised the word-association test as a psychoanalytical technique for penetrating a subject's unconscious mind. He also developed his theory concerning emotional, partly repressed ideas which he termed "complexes". The chief reason for his split with Freud – like Alfred Adler's before him – was Freud's emphasis on infantile sexuality. Jung introduced the alternative idea of "collective unconscious" which is made up of many archetypes or "congenital conditions of intuition". Each person is born with access to these archetypes, which Jung tried to identify by studying cultures such as those of the North American Pueblo Indians and primitive peoples of Africa and India. Mythology and folklore, alchemical writings, religious texts and even dreams were also analysed for archetypes.

Jung also studied personality and its importance in human behaviour and in 1921 introduced the concept of "introverts" and "extroverts" in his book *Psychologische Typen*. This work also contained his theory that the mind has four basic functions: thinking, feeling, sensations and intuition. Any particular person's personality can be ascribed to the predominance of one of these functions.

K

Katz, Bernhard (*1911-*), is a German-born British physiologist who is renowned for his research into the physiology of the nervous system. He has received many honours for his work, including a knighthood in 1969 and the 1970 Nobel Prize in Physiology and Medicine (jointly with Ulf von Euler and Julius Axerod).

Katz was born on 26 March 1911 in Leipzig and studied medicine at the university there. After graduation in 1934 he did postgraduate work at University College, London, from which he obtained his PhD in 1938 and his doctor of science degree in 1943. He was a Beit Memorial Research Fellow at the Sydney Hospital from 1939 to 1942. He then served in the Royal Australian Air Force until the end of World War II, after which he returned to England. He spent the rest of his academic career at University College, London – as Assistant Director of Research at the Biophysics Research Unit and Henry Head Research Fellow from 1946 to 1950, Reader in Physiology from 1950 to 1951, and Professor and Head of Biophysics from 1952 until his retirement in 1978.

During the 1950s Katz found that minute amounts of acetylcholine (previously demonstrated to be a neurotransmitter by Henry Dale and Otto Loewi) were randomly released by nerve endings at the neuromuscular junction, giving rise to very small electrical potentials at the end plate; he also found that the size of the potential was always a multiple of a certain minimum value. These findings led him to suggest that acetylcholine was released in discrete "packets" (analogous to quanta) of a few thousand molecules each, and that these packets were released relatively infrequently while a nerve was at rest but very rapidly when an impulse arrived at the neuromuscular junction. Electron microscopy later revealed small vesicles in the nerve endings and these are thought to be the containers of the packets of acetylcholine suggested by Katz.

Kettlewell, Henry Bernard David (*1907-1979*), was a British geneticist and lepidopterist who carried out important research into the influence of industrial melanism on natural selection in moths.

Kettlewell was born in Howden, Yorkshire, on 24 February 1907 and was educated at Charterhouse School, at Godalming in Surrey, and in Paris. He studied medicine at Gonville and Caius College, Cambridge, and at St Bartholomew's Hospital, London, graduating in 1933. After graduation he held several appointments in various London hospitals, including St Bartholomew's, and was an anaesthetist at St Luke's Hospital in Guildford, Surrey. He served as an anaesthetist during World War II. From 1949 to 1952 he investigated methods of locust control at Cape Town University, South Africa, also going on expeditions to the Kalahari Desert, the Belgian Congo, Mozambique and the Knysna Forest. After his return to England, he was awarded in 1952 a Nuffield Research Fellowship in the Genetics Unit of the Zoology Department at Oxford University. In the following year he was appointed Senior Research Officer in Genetics at Oxford, a post he held until he retired in 1974, when he became an Emeritus Fellow of Wolfson College, Oxford. He died in Oxford on 11 May 1979.

Kettlewell's best-known research involved the influence of industrial melanism on the survival of the peppered moth (*Biston betularia*). Until 1845, all known specimens of this moth were light-coloured, but in that year one dark specimen was found in Manchester, then an expanding industrial centre. The proportion of dark-coloured peppered moths increased rapidly, until by 1895 they comprised about 99 per cent of Manchester's entire peppered moth population. This change from light to dark moths – a phenomenon called industrial melanism – corresponds with the increase in industry (and therefore pollution, especially of the atmosphere) since the Industrial Revolution, and today only a few populations of the original light-coloured variant exist in England, being found in unindustrialized rural areas. Kettlewell performed several experiments under natural conditions to demonstrate the significance of colour in protecting the peppered moths from birds, their only predators. He released a known number of light- and dark-coloured moths – specially marked so that they could be identified – in an industrial area of Birmingham (where 90 per cent of the indigenous peppered moths are dark-coloured) and in an unpolluted rural area of Dorset (where there are no dark-coloured moths). After an interval he collected the surviving moths and found that, in Birmingham, birds had eaten a high proportion of the light-coloured moths but a much lower proportion of the dark-coloured ones, whereas in Dorset the reverse had occurred. Thus Kettlewell demonstrated the efficiency of natural selection as an evolutionary force: the light-coloured moths are more conspicuous than the dark-coloured ones in industrial areas - where the vegetation is darkened by pollution - and are therefore easier prey for birds, but are less conspicuous in unpolluted rural areas - where the vegetation is lighter in colour - and therefore survive predation better.

In addition to his research into coloration and natural selection, Kettlewell co-founded the Rothschild-Cockayne-Kettlewell (RCK) Collection of British Lepidoptera, which is now called the National Collection (RCK) and is housed in the British Museum (Natural History) in London.

Kimura, Motoo (*1924–*), is a Japanese biologist who, as a result of his work on population genetics and molecular evolution, has developed a theory of neutral evolution which opposes the conventional neo-Darwinistic theory of evolution by natural selection. He has received many honours for his work, including Japan's highest cultural award, the Order of Culture.

Kimura was born on 13 November 1924 in Okazaki. He studied botany at Kyoto University, from which he gained his master of science degree in 1947, then worked as an assistant there from 1947 to 1949. He spent most of his subsequent career at the National Institute of Genetics in Mishima - as a Research Member from 1949 to 1957, as Laboratory Head of the Department of Population Genetics from 1957 to 1964, and as overall head of the same department from 1964. In 1953, however, he went to the United States as a graduate student; he spent nine months studying under Dr Lush at Iowa State College, then moved to the University of Wisconsin (where he worked under Dr Crow in the Genetics Department), from which Kimura gained his doctorate in 1956. Although he returned to Japan in that year, Kimura continued to collaborate with Crow, jointly writing a book on population genetics, for example.

While a student, Kimura became interested in genetics, particularly the mathematical aspects of genetics and evolution. Stimulated by the work of J.B.S. Haldane and Sewall Wright on population genetics, Kimura began original work in this field in 1949, teaching himself the necessary mathematics. He then began to investigate the fate of mutant genes, how the genetic constitution of living organisms adapts to environmental changes, and the role of sexual reproduction in evolution.

Extending this early research, Kimura then began the work that was to lead to his postulating the theory of neutral evolution in 1968. According to the neo-Darwinistic view, evolution results from the interaction between variation and natural selection; species evolve by accumulating adaptive mutant genes, but these mutant genes increase in the population only if they confer

advantageous traits on its individual members. With the advent of molecular genetics, it became possible to compare individual RNA molecules and proteins in related organisms and to assess the rate at which allelic genes (those that occupy the same relative positions on homologous chromosomes) are substituted in evolution. It also became possible to study the variability of genes within a species. Using these techniques, Kimura found that, for a given protein, the rate at which amino acids are substituted for each other is approximately the same in many diverse lineages, and that the substitutions seem to be random. Comparing the amino-acid compositions of the alpha and beta chains of the haemoglobin molecules in humans with those in carp, he found that the alpha chains have evolved in two distinct lineages, accumulating mutations independently at about the same rate over a period of some 400 million years. Moreover, the rate of amino-acid substitution observed in the carp-human comparison is very similar to the rates observed in comparisons of the alpha chains in various other animals. These findings led Kimura to his theory of neutral evolution. According to this theory, evolutionary rates are determined by the structure and function of molecules and, at the molecular level, most intra-specific variability and evolutionary change is caused by the random drift of mutant genes that are all selectively equivalent and selectively neutral. Thus Kimura's theory directly opposes the neo-Darwinistic theory of evolution by denying that the environment influences evolution and, as a concomitant of this, also denying that mutant genes confer either advantageous or disadvantageous traits.

Kitasato, Shibasaburo (*1852–1931*), was a Japanese bacteriologist who is generally credited with the discovery of the bacillus that causes bubonic plague. He also did much important work on other diseases, such as tetanus and anthrax. His work gained him many international honours, and in 1923 Japan made him a baron.

Kitasato was born on 20 December 1852 in a small mountain village on the island of Kyushu in Japan. Keenly interested in science, he studied medicine at the Kumamoto Medical School and later at Tokyo University, from which he graduated in 1883. After graduating he joined the Central Bureau of the Public Health Department, but in 1885 he was sent by the government to study new developments in bacteriology in Germany and went to work in the laboratory of Robert Koch in Berlin. Under Koch's guidance, Kitasato quickly mastered the new techniques and began his own research, which was so successful that he was made an honorary professor of Berlin University before he returned to Japan in 1891. On his return, Kitasato set up a small private institute of bacteriology, the first of its kind in Japan. Later the institute received financial assistance from the government, but in 1915 it was incorporated into Tokyo University against Kitasato's wishes and he resigned as its director. In the same year he founded another establishment, the Kitasato Institute, which he headed for the rest of his life. Kitasato died on 13 June 1931 in Nakanocho.

Kitasato did his first important work in Koch's laboratory in Germany where, in 1889, he became the first to obtain a pure culture of *Clostridium tetani*, the causative bacillus of tetanus. In the following year, working with Emil von Behring, Kitasato discovered that animals can be protected against tetanus by inoculating them with serum containing inactive tetanus toxin. This was the very important discovery of antitoxic immunity, and Kitasato and von Behring rapidly developed a serum for treating anthrax. In the same year they published a paper on their combined work, giving details of their success with tetanus and similar results with diphtheria, on which von Behring, helped by Paul Ehrlich, had concentrated.

After returning to Japan, Kitasato was sent by his government to Hong Kong in 1894 to investigate an epidemic of bubonic plague. France also sent a small research team led by Alexandre Yersin, a former pupil of Louis Pasteur. The two teams did not collaborate because of language difficulties and there is some doubt as to whether it was Kitasato or Yersin who first isolated *Pasteurella pestis*, the bacillus that causes bubonic plague. But Kitasato published his discovery of the bacillus several weeks before Yersin announced his findings and is therefore generally credited with the discovery.

Kitasato also isolated the causative organism of dysentery in 1898 and studied the method of infection in tuberculosis.

Koch, Robert (*1843-1910*), was a German bacteriologist who, with Louis Pasteur, is generally considered to be one of the two founders of modern bacteriology. He developed techniques for culturing, staining and observing micro-organisms and discovered the causative pathogens of several diseases - including tuberculosis, for which discovery he was awarded the 1905 Nobel Prize in Physiology and Medicine.

Koch was born on 11 December 1843 in Klausthal (now in West Germany), one of 13 children of a mining official. He studied natural sciences and then medicine at Göttingen University, where he was taught by Friedrich Wöhler and Friedrich Henle, obtaining his medical degree in 1866. After serving as an army surgeon (on the Prussian side) in the Franco-Prussian War, Koch became in 1872 District Medical Officer in Wollstein where, despite having few research facilities, he began important investigations into anthrax. For a brief period in 1879 he was Town Medical Officer in Breslau, before being appointed to the Imperial Health Office in Berlin to advise on hygiene and public health. By 1881 his work was becoming well known and he was invited to speak at the Seventh International Medical Congress in London. In 1882 he announced to the Berlin Physiological Society his discovery of the bacillus that causes tuberculosis, and in the following year, while investigating an outbreak of cholera in the Nile delta, he identified the cholera bacillus. In 1885 he was appointed Professor of Hygiene at Berlin University and Director of the Institute of Hygiene. The Tenth International Medical Congress was held in Berlin in 1890 and Koch was persuaded to announce the discovery of an antituberculosis vaccine; this proved to be premature, however, as the vaccine was ineffective. In 1891 he was appointed Director of the newly established Institute for Infectious Diseases, but he resigned his directorship in 1904 and spent much of the rest of his life advising foreign countries on ways to combat various diseases. Koch died on 27 May 1910 in Baden-Baden (now in West Germany).

Koch started his bacteriological research in the 1870s with the gift of a microscope from his wife, and built up a primitive laboratory in part of his consulting room. Out of necessity Koch devised simple and original methods for growing and examining bacteria. For three years he worked on anthrax in his spare time, developing techniques for culturing the bacteria in cattle blood and in aqueous humour from the eye. He trapped a small smear of blood from an anthrax victim with a drop of aqueous humour between two microscope slides and observed the bacteria grow and divide under the microscope, finding that the bacteria were short-lived but that they formed spores that were resistant to desiccation. He then inoculated animals with the spores and found that they developed anthrax, thus proving that the spores remained infective; this was the first time a bacterium cultured outside a living organism had been shown to cause disease. Koch published his findings, but only after Pasteur's demonstration of an anthrax vaccine in 1882 were Koch's findings accepted.

Koch experimented with various dyes and found some that stain bacteria and make them more visible under the microscope. He also devised an ingenious method of separating a mixture of bacteria, which involved inoculating an animal with the bacteria and passing the resulting infection from one animal to another until, at the end of the experimental chain, only one type of bacterium remained. Using this method he identified the bacteria responsible for several disorders, including septicaemia.

On joining the Imperial Health Office in 1879, Koch was provided with two assistants and for the first time had adequate laboratory facilities. Here he developed the technique of culturing bacteria on gelatin. Using this technique Koch and his assistants isolated several micro-organisms and showed that they cause disease. They also investigated the effects of various disinfectants on different bacteria and showed that steam is more effective than dry heat in killing bacteria, a discovery that revolutionized hospital operating theatre practice.

Koch then set out to discover the causative agent of tuberculosis, a common and frequently fatal disease at that time. Initially he was unable to find any micro-organisms that might cause the disease, but after developing a special staining technique he identified the bacterium responsible and, despite the difficulties caused by the bacterium's small size and slow rate of growth, managed to culture it in 1882.

In 1883 Koch went to the Nile delta to investigate a cholera epidemic. Finding bacteria in the intestinal walls of dead cholera victims and the same bacteria in the excreta of cholera patients, he succeeded in isolating the causative organism. On a later visit to Calcutta, where cholera was rife, he found similar bacteria in excreta and in supplies of drinking water. On returning to Berlin he advised regular checks on the water supply, made recommendations regarding sewage disposal, and organized courses in the recognition of cholera. And when the disease occurred in Hamburg in 1892, he recommended that the victims should be isolated, all excretory matter should be disinfected and that a special check should be made on the water supply.

Koch made several other important contributions. As a result of his investigations into a bubonic plague epidemic in Calcutta in 1897, he showed that rats are vectors of the disease (although there is no evidence that he knew that the rat flea was the actual vector). He also demonstrated that sleeping sickness is transmitted by the tsetse fly. His isolation of many disease-causing organisms eventually led to the development of vaccines and to the realization of the importance of the public health measures he recommended. Furthermore, many bacteriologists received their training as his assistants, including

Georg Gaffky, Friedrich Löffler, Shibasaburo Kitasato, and the Nobel Prize-winners Emil von Behring and Paul Ehrlich. Perhaps most important, however, Koch formulated a systematic method for bacteriological research, including various rules - still observed today - for identifying pathogens. According to these rules (called Koch's postulates), the suspected pathogen must be identified in all of the cases examined; the pathogen must then be cultured through several generations; these later generations must be capable of causing the disease in a healthy animal; and the newly infected animal must yield the same pathogen as found in the original victim.

Krebs, Hans Adolf (*1900-*), is a German-born British biochemist who is famous for his outstanding work in elucidating the cyclical pathway involved in the intracellular metabolism of foodstuffs - a pathway known as the tricarboxylic cycle, the citric acid cycle or the Krebs cycle. He received many honours for this work, including the 1953 Nobel Prize in Physiology and Medicine (which he shared with Fritz Lipmann, a German-born American biochemist), a knighthood in 1958, and several medals and honorary degrees.

Krebs was born on 25 August 1900 in Hildesheim (now in West Germany), the son of an ear, nose and throat specialist. He was educated at the universities of Göttingen, Freiburg, Munich, Berlin and Hamburg, gaining his medical degree from the last in 1925. From 1926 to 1930 he worked under Otto Warburg at the Kaiser Wilhelm Institute in Berlin, then taught at the University of Freiburg until 1933, when he moved to England because of the rise to power of Adolf Hitler and the Nazi movement in Germany. On his arrival in England, Krebs went to Cambridge University, as a Rockefeller Research Student from 1933 to 1934, then as a Demonstrator in Biochemistry until 1935. From 1935 to 1954 he worked at Sheffield University, as Lecturer in Pharmacology from 1935 to 1938, Lecturer in charge of the Department of Biochemistry from 1938 to 1945, and Professor of Biochemistry from 1945 to 1954. He then moved to Oxford University as Whitley Professor of Biochemistry and a Fellow of Trinity College, which positions he held until his retirement in 1967.

While working under Warburg, Krebs became interested in the process by which the body degrades amino acids. He discovered that, in amino-acid degradation, nitrogen atoms are the first to be removed (deamination) and are then excreted as urea in the urine. Continuing this line of research, Krebs then investigated the processes involved in the production of urea from the re-

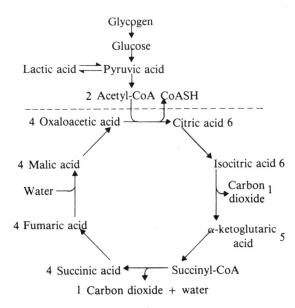

The Krebs cycle; the numbers indicate the number of carbon atoms in the principal compounds.

In this cycle, a 2-C molecule acetyl CoA condenses with a 4-C molecule oxaloacetic acid to form a 6-C molecule citric acid. The 6-C citric acid then undergoes a series of biochemical reactions to yield oxaloacetic acid again. Carbon dioxide (CO_2), water (H_2O) and hydrogen atoms are produced in the cycle. The hydrogen atoms ultimately combine with atmospheric oxygen in a complex set of biochemical reactions, to yield energy.

The role of the Tricarboxylic Acid Cycle in the degradation and biosynthesis of amino acids and fats is also shown. (For simplicity, not all the points of entry and exit from the Tricarboxylic Acid Cycle have been shown.)

N.B. All the compounds can be named on the IUPAC system e.g. citric acid becomes 2-hydroxypropan-1,2,3-tricarboxylic acid, malic acid becomes 2-hydroxybutan-1,4-dioic acid, succinic acid becomes butan-1,4-dioic acid, etc.

THE TRICARBOXYLIC ACID CYCLE (Krebs cycle) The purpose of the TCA cycle is to complete the oxidation of glucose begun in glycolysis. In the sequence of reactions from citric acid to oxaloacetic acid, pyruvic acid is oxidized to carbon dioxide and water. During this process considerable amounts of energy are released – 93% of the total energy released in glucose oxidation.

moved nitrogen atoms, and by 1932 he had worked out the basic steps involved in what is now known as the urea cycle. Later workers discovered the details of the cycle, but Krebs' original basic scheme was correct.

Krebs is best known, however, for his discovery of the processes involved in the tricarboxylic cycle, by which carbohydrates are aerobically metabolized to carbon dioxide, water and energy. The energy yielded by this pathway is the main source of intracellular energy and therefore of the entire organism. Previous work by Otto Meyerhof and Carl and Gerty Cori had shown that the carbohydrate glycogen is broken down in the liver to lactic acid by a process that does not require oxygen and that yields very little energy. Krebs continued this work (while at Sheffield University) to show how the lactic acid is then metabolized to carbon dioxide, water and energy. As a result of his investigations – performed on pigeon breast muscle – Krebs proposed the self-regenerating biochemical pathway now known as the tricarboxylic acid cycle.

In this cycle the two-carbon acetyl co-enzyme A (acetyl CoA) - derived from lactic acid - combines with the four-carbon oxaloacetic acid to form the six-carbon citric acid, which then undergoes a series of reactions to be reconverted to oxaloacetic acid. This oxaloacetic acid combines with another molecule of acetyl CoA to form citric acid again, and the cycle is repeated. Carbon dioxide, water and hydrogen are produced by the various reactions in the cycle; the hydrogen combines with oxygen, in a complex series of reactions to produce energy and water. The degradation of glucose to carbon dioxide, water and energy occurs in two stages. The first stage – in which acetyl CoA is formed – occurs in the cytoplasm; the second stage, the tricarboxylic acid cycle, takes place in mitochondria.

In addition to carbohydrate metabolism, the tricarboxylic acid cycle is also involved in the degradation of fats and amino acids, and provides substrates for the biosynthesis of other compounds, such as amino acids. Thus the cycle plays a central role in cell metabolism, and Krebs' elucidation of the steps involved in it was therefore a fundamental contribution to biochemistry.

L

Lamarck, Jean Baptiste Pierre Antoine de Monet, Chevalier de (*1744–1829*), was a French naturalist best known for his alternative to Charles Darwin's theory of evolution and the distinction he made between vertebrate and invertebrate animals.

Lamarck was born at Bazantin, Picardy, on 1 August 1744, the eleventh child of a large family of poor aristocrats. This noble background restricted his career and he was expected to join either the army or the Church. The first intention was that he should enter the Church, but when his father died in 1760 he joined the army. After serving in the Seven Years War he left the army in 1766, when his health failed, and eventually went into medicine. He soon became interested, however, in meteorology and botany. He was admitted to the Academy of Sciences in 1778 for his book *Flore française*, written while he was posted in southern France, and attracted the interest of Georges Buffon (1707-1788), the famous French naturalist. With Buffon's assistance he travelled across Europe, having been appointed botanist to King Louis XVI in 1781. He returned in 1785 and three years later took up a botanical appointment at the Jardin du Roi. In 1793 he was made a Professor of Zoology at the Museum of Natural History, in Paris, where he lectured on the "Insecta" and "Vermes" of Linnaeus, which he later called the Invertebrata. He continued his writings, although his sight was failing, with the help of his eldest daughter and Pierre-André Latreille (1762-1833). He died blind and in great poverty, in Paris, on 18 December 1829.

Lamarck's own experiences in both botany and zoology made him realize the need to study living things as a whole, and he coined the word "biology". In 1785 he pointed out the necessity of natural orders in botany by an attempt at the classification of plants. He widely propagated the idea, as Buffon had done before him, that species are not unalterable and that the more complex ones have developed from pre-existent simpler forms.

Lamarck's most important contribution was his detailed investigation of living and fossil invertebrates. At the age of fifty, while lecturing on Linnaeus' classifications, he began the study of invertebrates. So little was known about them at this time that some scientists grouped snakes and crocodiles with insects. Lamarck was the first to distinguish vertebrate from invertebrate animals by the presence of a bony spinal column. He was also the first to establish the crustaceans, arachnids and annelids among the invertebrates.

In studying and classifying fossils Lamarck was led to wonder about the effect of environment on development. In 1809 he published one of his most important essays, *Zoological Philosophy*, which tried to show that various parts of the body developed because they were necessary, or disappeared because of disuse when variations in the environment caused a change in habit. He believed that these body changes are inherited by the offspring, and that if this process continued for a long time, new species would eventually be produced.

Lamarck thought that it ought to be possible to arrange all living things in a branching series showing how some species gradually change into others. Unfortunately he chose poor examples to illustrate his ideas and he did not attempt to show how one species might gradually change into another on the basis of the inheritance of acquired characteristics. One of the well-known examples that constitutes the evidence on which Lamarck based his theory is the giraffe which he assumed, as an antelope-type animal, sought to browse higher and higher on the leaves of the trees on which it feeds, and "stretched" its neck. As a result of this habit continued for a long time in all the individuals of the species, the "antelope's" front limbs and neck gradually grew longer, and it became a giraffe. Another example is that of birds that rest on the water and which, perhaps to chase and find food, spread out their feet when they wish to swim. The skin on their feet becomes accustomed to being stretched and forms a web between the toes. These examples were regarded as rather naïve, even to his contemporaries, which could explain why Lamarck's ideas were not accepted.

A contemporary of Lamarck, Georges Cuvier (1769-1832), proposed his own theory of evolution which although inferior to Lamarck's achieved considerable acclaim. The work of Lamarck received little recognition in his own lifetime and some of his successors, including Darwin, regarded it with ridicule and contempt. There is no doubt, however, that his zoological classifications have aided further study in that field and that he greatly influenced later evolutionists.

Among the many works he produced, one of Lamarck's greatest is the seven-volume book *Natural History of Invertebrates*, produced between 1815 and 1822.

Landsteiner, Karl (*1868-1943*), was an Austrian-born American immunologist who discovered the ABO blood groups, and the M and N factors and Rhesus factor in human blood. For this work he received the 1930 Nobel Prize in Physiology and Medicine.

Landsteiner was born in Vienna, on 14 June 1868, the son of a journalist. He attended the University of Vienna from 1885 to 1891, when he graduated with a doctorate in medicine. He spent the next five years studying at various universities in Europe, including a time with the German chemist Emil Fischer (1852-1919). In 1898 he became a research assistant at the Vienna Pathological Institute and remained there until 1908, when he was appointed Professor of Pathology at the Royal Imperial Wilhelminen Hospital in Vienna. Unsatisfactory working conditions there caused him to leave in 1919, and he went to the RK Hospital in the Hague. He was no happier there, and moved to the United States where he joined the Rockefeller Institute in New York in 1922. He became an American citizen in 1929 and died in New York on 26 June 1943.

While at the Vienna Pathology Institute, Landsteiner published a paper in 1900 which included information on the interagglutination of human blood cells by serum from a different human being. He explained this feature as occurring because of antigen differences in the blood between individuals. In the following year Landsteiner described a technique which enables human blood to be categorized into three groups: A, B and O (and later, AB). His sorting method, which is still used, was to mix suspensions of blood cells with each of the sera, anti-A and anti-B. Landsteiner discovered in this way that serum contains only those antibodies that do not cause agglutination with its own blood cells. It was not until 1907, however, that a blood-match was first carried out and blood transfusions did not become a widespread practice until after 1914 when Richard Lewisohn found that the addition of citrates to blood prevents it from coagulating, enabling it to be preserved.

In 1927 Landsteiner and Philip Levine found that, in addition to antigens A and B, human blood cells contain one or other or both of two heritable antigens, M and N. These are of no importance in transfusions, because human serum does not contain the corresponding antibodies, but being inherited they are of value in resolving paternity disputes.

In 1940, Landsteiner and Levine, together with Wiener, injected blood from a Rhesus monkey into rabbits and guinea pigs. The resulting antibodies agglutinated the Rhesus blood cells because they contain an antigen, named Rh, which is identical or very similar to an antigen present in the Rhesus monkeys. It was shown that the Rh factor is inheritable; those people possessing it are termed Rh positive, and those without it, Rh negative. The connection between this factor and a blood disorder of new-born babies (erythroblastosis foetalis) was revealed. An Rh negative mother pregnant with an Rh positive foetus forms antibodies against the Rh factor. In a subsequent similar pregnancy the oxygen-carrying capacity of the foetus' red cells is impaired and brain damage may result. Diagnostic tests can now enable the necessary preventive measures to be taken.

Landsteiner investigated the Wassermann test (a blood test for syphilis involving adding antigen to detect the presence of antibodies in a patient's blood). Together with Ernest Finger he discovered that the antigen, previously extracted from a syphilitic human being, could be replaced with an extract prepared from ox hearts.

Between 1908 and 1922, Landsteiner researched into poliomyelitis. He injected a preparation of brain and spinal cord tissue, obtained from a polio victim, into a Rhesus monkey, which then developed paralysis. Landsteiner could find no bacteria in the monkey's nervous system and concluded that a virus must be responsible for the disease. He later developed a procedure for the diagnosis of poliomyelitis.

Laveran, Charles Louis Alphonse (*1845-1922*), was a French physician who discovered that the cause of malaria is a protozoon, the first time that a protozoon had been shown to be a cause of disease. For this work and later discoveries of protozoon diseases he was awarded the 1907 Nobel Prize in Physiology and Medicine.

Laveran was born in Paris, on 18 June 1845, the son of an army surgeon. The family moved to Algeria from 1850 to 1855 and then returned to Paris, where he continued his education. He studied medicine in Strasbourg and graduated in 1867. When the Franco-Prussian war broke out he became an army surgeon, and was stationed at Metz from 1870 to 1871. In 1874 he was appointed Professor of Military Medicine at the École du Val-de-Grâce. Between 1878 and 1883 he was posted to Algeria, first to Bône and then Constantine. In 1884 he returned to Val-de-Grâce and served as Professor of Military Hygiene, until 1894, when temporary posts took him to Lille and Nantes. In 1896 he left the army to join the Pasteur Institute in Paris and in 1907 he used the money from his Nobel Prize to open the Laboratory of Tropical Diseases at the Institute. The following year he founded the Société de Pathologie Exotique and was its president until 1920. He died in Paris on 18 May 1922.

While in Algeria, Laveran found malaria rife there and he became interested in the disease, although his early research had concentrated on nerve regeneration. Malaria has affected man for centuries, and at that time was explained by a number of hypotheses, one of the most common being that it was due to bad air, especially over swamps and marshes (*mal aria* are the Italian words for bad air). Scientists were beginning, however, to regard it as a bacterial disease.

It was known that malarial blood contains tiny

black granules which are sometimes located in hyaline cysts inside the red blood cells. In 1880 Laveran examined blood samples from malarial patients and while investigating a cyst, saw flagella pushed out from it, revealing that it was not a granule of pigment (as had been believed), but an amoeba-like organism. Laveran took blood samples from these patients at regular intervals and found that the organisms increased in size until they almost filled the blood cell, when they divided and formed spores. When these spores were liberated from the destroyed blood cell they invaded unaffected blood cells. He noted that the spores were released in each affected red cell at the same time and corresponded with a fresh attack of fever in the patient. The point at which the fever subsided coincided with the invasion of new blood cells. Laveran also found crescent-shaped bodies with black granules lying in the plasma.

Laveran's studies of protozoon diseases included leishmaniasis and trypanosomiasis. His investigations concerning malaria allowed Ronald Ross, after him, to discover that the malarial parasite is transmitted to human beings by the *Anopheles* mosquito and these findings enabled preventive measures to be taken against the disease.

Laveran's publications included *Traité des maladies et épidemies des armées* (*Treatise on Army Sicknesses and Epidemics*, 1875) and *Trypanosomes et trypanosomiasis* (1904).

Leakey, Louis Seymour Bazett (*1903–1972*), was a British archaeologist, anthropologist and palaeontologist who became famous for his discoveries of early hominid fossils in East Africa, indicating that man probably evolved in this part of the world.

Leakey was born in Kabete, Kenya, on 7 August 1903, the son of a British missionary. There were few European settlers in Kenya at that time and he spent his boyhood with the local Kikuyu children, learning their language but receiving little formal schooling. He was sent to Britain when he was 16 years old and entered St John's College, Cambridge, in 1922 to study French and Kikuyu, and later archaeology and anthropology. In 1926 he went to East Africa leading the first of a series of archaeological research expeditions, which continued until 1937. From 1937 until the outbreak of World War II in 1939 he studied and recorded the customs of the Kikuyu people. During the war he was in charge of the African Section at the British Special Branch Headquarters; he was a handwriting expert and remained available as a consultant in this role after the end of the war. During the war he gave

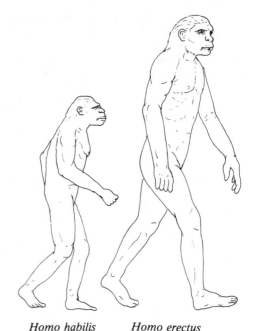

Homo habilis   *Homo erectus*

Among Leakey's most significant finds were skeletal remains of Homo habilis *and* Homo erectus, *early stages in Man's evolution.*

freely of his spare time to the Coryndon Memorial Museum in Nairobi, Kenya, and in 1945 he became its curator. He built up a research centre at the museum and at the same time became one of the founder trustees of the Kenya National Parks and Reserves. He resigned from the museum in 1961 and founded the National Museum Centre for Prehistory and Palaeontology. During the 1960s his health began to fail and he spent less time in the field and more time lecturing and fund-raising. He died in London on 1 October 1972.

Leakey began excavations at Olduvai Gorge, now in Tanzania, in 1931 and it was to become the site of some of his most important finds. During war-time leave he and his wife Mary, an expert on palaeolithic stone implements, discovered a significant Acheulian site at Olorgesailie in the Rift Valley. The Acheulian culture is characterized by stone hand axes and flourished between 1 million and 100,000 years ago. On another occasion the Leakeys found the remains of 20-million-year-old Miocene apes on the island of Rusinga in Lake Victoria. From 1947 they initiated in Nairobi a Pan African Congress on Prehistory, which was a great success and proved to be the first of many.

In 1959 the Leakeys returned to their excavations at Olduvai. In that year they found a skull of *Australopithecus boisei* (Nutcracker Man) and a year later they discovered the remains of *Homo habilis*, established by potassium/argon dating to be 1.7 million years old. A third exciting find was a skull of an Acheulian hand-axe user, *Homo erectus*, which Leakey maintained was an advanced hominid on the direct evolutionary line of *Homo sapiens*, modern man. In 1961 at Fort Ternan, Kenya, he found jawbone fragments of another early primate, *Kenyapithecus wickeri*, believed to be 14 million years old.

Leakey was a man of many talents with firm convictions that man's origins lie in Africa, a view that was totally opposed to contemporary opinion. He discovered sites of major archaeological importance containing vast numbers of bones and artefacts. The status of some of the finds, and Leakey's interpretation of them, is still in dispute, but whatever the eventual outcome he made an unparalleled contribution to knowledge of early man and his contemporaries. He published a large number of scientific papers as well as some books of wider appeal, such as *Stone Age Africa* (1936) and *White African* (1937).

After Louis Leakey's death his work in Africa was continued by his wife and his sons John and Richard. Richard Leakey (1944–) later became a well-known author and broadcaster in his own right.

Lederberg, Joshua (*1925–*). See BEADLE, GEORGE WELLS.

Leeuwenhoek, Anton van (*1632–1723*), was a Dutch microscopist who is famous for the numerous detailed observations he made using his single-lens microscopes. He was not the first of the many well-known early microscopists, being preceded by Marcello Malpighi for example, nor did he make notable innovations to the microscope itself (the forerunner of the modern compound microscope was developed in Leeuwenhoek's lifetime by Robert Hooke, an English physicist and microscopist). But such was the dramatic nature of Leeuwenhoek's discoveries that he became - and remains - world renowned.

Leeuwenhoek was born on 24 October 1632 in Delft, Holland. Relatively little is known of his early life but it seems that he received scant schooling. His stepfather died when Leeuwenhoek was 16 years old and he was apprenticed to a cloth merchant in Amsterdam. He returned to Delft four years later in 1652 and opened a drapery shop. In 1660 he obtained the sinecure of chamberlain to the sheriffs of Delft. Having guaranteed his financial security, Leeuwenhoek devoted much of his time to his hobbies of lens grinding and microscopy. From 1672 to 1723 he

described and illustrated his observations in a total of more than 350 letters to the Royal Society of London, which elected him a Fellow in 1680. Leeuwenhoek continued his work almost until he died, aged 90 years, on 26 August 1723. After his death several of his microscopes were sent to the Royal Society, in accordance with his will.

Leeuwenhoek ground more than 400 lenses, which he mounted in various ways. Most of them were very small (some were about the size of a pinhead) and had magnifying powers of between 50 and about 300 times; but each was meticulously made and the optical excellence of these lenses - combined with Leeuwenhoek's careful observations - undoubtedly helped him to make so many important discoveries. In 1674 he discovered protozoa, which he called "animalicules", and calculated their sizes. He was also probably the first to observe bacteria, when he saw tiny structures in tooth scrapings; the first known drawing of bacteria was made by Leeuwenhoek and appeared in the Royal Society's *Philosophical Transactions* in 1683. He made many other important observations: he was the first to describe spermatozoa (1677) and also studied the structure of the lens in the eye, muscle striations, insects' mouthparts, the fine structure of plants, and discovered parthenogenesis in aphids. And in 1684 he gave the first accurate description of red blood corpuscles, also noticing that they can have different shapes in different animal species.

Leeuwenhoek became world famous during his lifetime and was visited by several reigning monarchs, including Elizabeth I of England, Frederick I of Prussia and Tsar Peter the Great. Many of Leeuwenhoek's observations remained unsurpassed for more than a century - partly because his microscopes were of very high optical quality and partly because he kept secret the details of the techniques he used.

Leishman, William Boog (*1865–1926*), was a British army physician who discovered the protozoon parasite that causes kala-azar, a relatively common and potentially fatal infectious disease endemic to the tropics and subtropics that affects the reticulo-endothelial system (particularly the liver, spleen and bone marrow). The genus of protozoons to which the causative micro-organism belongs is called *Leishmania*, after Leishman. He received many honours for his work, including a knighthood in 1909.

Leishman was born on 6 November 1865 in Glasgow, a son of the Regius Professor of Midwifery at Glasgow University. He was educated at Westminster School, London, then studied medicine at Glasgow University, from which he graduated in 1886. After graduation he obtained a commission in the Royal Army Medical Corps, in which he remained for the rest of his life. He was posted to India from 1890 to 1897, after which he returned to England to the Army Medical School at Netley, Hampshire, where he was soon appointed Assistant Professor of Pathology under Almroth Wright (1861–1947). After Wright resigned, Leishman succeeded him as Professor in 1903; in the same year the Medical School was transferred to London and Leishman moved with it. In 1914 he became a member of the Army Medical Advisory Board, advising the War Office on tropical diseases then, with the outbreak of World War I, he joined the British Expeditionary Force as Advisor in Pathology. After the war ended he became the first Director of Pathology at the War Office in 1919. In 1923 he was appointed Director-General of the Army Medical Service, a position he held until his death on 2 June 1926 in London.

Leishman discovered the protozoon parasite that causes kala-azar in 1900 using his modified form of the Romanowsky stain for protozoa and blood cells (this modified stain is now called Leishman's stain) to examine cells from the spleen of a soldier who had died of kala-azar at Netley. He published his findings in 1903 but in the same year Charles Donovan of the Indian Medical Service independently made the same discovery, as a result of which the causative protozoon was called the Leishman-Donovan body. Other workers later discovered that related species of the kala-azar-causing protozoon were responsible for various other diseases; all such similar protozoons were therefore classified as members of the same genus, named *Leishmania* – the protozoon causing kala-azar being called *Leishmania donovani* – and the diseases they cause were grouped under the term leishmaniasis.

Leishman also assisted Wright in developing an effective antityphoid inoculation, and helped to elucidate the life cycle of the spirochaete (*Spirochaeta duttoni*) which causes African tick fever.

Li, Cho Hao (*1913–   *), is a Chinese-born American biochemist who is best known for his work on the hormones secreted by the pituitary gland.

Li was born in Canton on 21 April 1913 and educated at the University of Nanking, from which he graduated in 1933. He was an Instructor in Chemistry at Nanking University from 1933 to 1935 and then in 1935 he emigrated to the United States, where he took up postgraduate studies at the University of California at Berkeley. After obtaining his PhD in 1938, Li joined the staff of the university, becoming in 1950 Professor of Bio-

chemistry and Professor of Experimental Endocrinology and Director of the Hormone Research Laboratory. In 1955 he was granted United States' citizenship.

Li has spent his entire academic career studying the pituitary gland hormones. In collaboration with various co-workers, he isolated several protein hormones from the pituitary gland, including adreno-corticotrophic hormone (ACTH), which stimulates the adrenal cortex to increase its secretion of corticoids. In 1956 Li and his group showed that ACTH consists of 39 amino acids arranged in a specific order, and that the whole chain of the natural hormone is not necessary for its action. He isolated another pituitary hormone called melanocyte-stimulating hormone (MSH) and found that not only does this hormone produce some effects similar to those produced by ACTH, but also that part of the amino acid chain of MSH is the same as that of ACTH. Li has also studied pituitary growth hormones, finding that they are effective only in the species that produces them – that is, growth hormone from cattle, for example, is ineffective in humans. Continuing this line of research, he discovered in 1966 that human pituitary growth hormone (somatotropin) consists of a chain of 256 amino acids, and in 1970 he succeeded in synthesizing this hormone, thereby setting a record for the largest protein molecule synthesized up to that time.

Linnaeus, Carolus (Carl von Linné) (*1707–1778*), was a Swedish botanist who became famous for introducing the binomial system of biological nomenclature (which is named after him and is universally used today), and for formulating basic principles for classification.

Linnaeus was born on 27 May 1707 in South Råshult, Sweden, the son of a clergyman. He was interested in plants even as a child, but his father sent him to study medicine, first at the University of Lund in 1727 and then at Uppsala University.

In 1730 Linnaeus was appointed Lecturer in Botany at Uppsala and two years later explored Lapland for the Uppsala Academy of Sciences. In 1735 Linnaeus left Sweden for Holland to obtain his MD at the University of Harderwijk. On his return to Sweden in 1738 Linnaeus practised as a physician, with considerable success, and in the following year he married Sara Moraea, a physician's daughter. In 1741 he was appointed Professor of Medicine at Uppsala University but changed this position in 1742 for the Chair of Botany, which he retained for the rest of his life. In 1761 Linnaeus was granted a patent of nobility – antedated to 1757 – by which he was entitled to call himself Carl von Linné. He suffered a stroke

Examples

Kingdom	Plantae	Animalia
Division or Phylum	Spermatophyta	Chordata
Class	Angiospermae	Mammalia
Order	Rosales	Carnivora
Family	Rosaceae	Canidae
Genus	*Rosa*	*Speothos*
Species	*canina* (Dog rose)	*venaticus* (Bush dog)

Linnaeus devised a system of classification that has remained largely unchanged to the present day.

in 1774, which impaired his health, and he died on 10 January 1778 in Uppsala Cathedral, where he was buried.

Linnaeus' best-known work is probably *Systema Naturae*, published in 1735. In this book he introduced a simple yet methodical system of classifying plants according to the number of stamens and pistils in their flowers. This system overshadowed the earlier work of John Ray and was so convenient that it was a long time before it was replaced by a more natural system – despite the fact that Linnaeus himself recognized its artificiality.

Linnaeus made his most important contribution – the introduction of the binomial system of nomenclature by which every species is identified by a generic name and a specific name – in 1753, with the publication of *Species Plantarum*. Even today the starting point in the nomenclature of all flowering plants and ferns is internationally agreed to be the first edition of *Species Plantarum*, together with the fifth edition of *Genera Plantarum* (1754; first edition 1737). In these works he became the first person to formulate the principles for defining genera and species and to adhere to a uniform use of specific names. In 1758 he applied his binomial system to animal classification. With the rapid increase of newly discovered plants and animals that was occurring in the eighteenth century, the value of Linnaeus' system was soon recognized and it had become almost universally adopted by the end of his life. The survival of the system to the present day is probably due to its great flexibility; Linnaeus himself believed that species were immutable and that he was classifying Creation (although he later mo-

dified this viewpoint slightly), but so adaptable was his system that it was able to accommodate modifications that later resulted from the introduction of evolutionary principles to taxonomy.

In addition to his books on classification, Linnaeus wrote many other works, including *Flora Laponica* (1737), the results of his journey to Lapland; *Hortus Cliffortianus* (1738), a description of the plants in the garden of George Clifford, a merchant with whom Linnaeus stayed during much of his time in Holland; and *Flora Suecia* (1745) and *Fauna Suecia* (1746), accounts of his biological observations during his travels in Sweden. After Linnaeus' death, his widow sold his manuscripts and natural history collection to James Edward Smith (1759-1828), the first President of the Linnean Society (founded in 1788), who took them to England. When Smith died the Society purchased Linnaeus' manuscripts and specimens and they are now preserved by the Society in Burlington House, London.

Lister, Joseph (*1827-1912*), was a skilful British surgeon with a great interest in histology and bacteriology. He introduced the concept of antiseptic surgery and was a pioneer, in Britain, of preventive medicine.

Lister was born on 5 April 1827, in Upton, Essex, the son of the British physicist Joseph Jackson Lister (1786-1869). He was educated at various Quaker schools and at University College, London, the only university then open to dissenters. He first studied arts and after graduation took up medicine at University College, where he was taught by the eminent physiologist William Sharpey and graduated in 1852. In 1856 he was a surgeon at the Edinburgh Royal Infirmary as assistant to James Syme, and three years later was appointed Regius Professor of Surgery at the University of Glasgow. In 1861 he took charge of the surgical wards at the Royal Infirmary, Glasgow, and in 1869 became Professor of Clinical Surgery at Edinburgh. Eight years later he took up the Chair in Clinical Surgery at King's College, London. He was knighted in 1883 and was raised to the peerage in 1897. Nearing retirement in 1891 he became Chairman of the newly formed British Institute of Preventive Medicine (later the Lister Institute) and served as President of the Royal Society from 1895 to 1900. He died on 10 February 1912 in Walmer, Kent.

Nearly half the patients who underwent major surgery at that time died as the result of postoperative septic infection. Sepsis was thought to be a kind of combustion caused by exposing moist body tissues to oxygen – an assertion put forward by the German chemist Justus von Liebig in 1839. Great care was therefore taken to keep air from wounds, by means of plasters, collodion or resins. Lister doubted the explanation and these methods; he regarded wound sepsis as a form of decomposition.

In 1865 Louis Pasteur suggested that decay is caused by living organisms in the air, which enter matter and cause it to ferment. Lister immediately saw the connection with wound sepsis. In addition, the previous year he had heard that carbolic acid (phenol) was being used to treat sewage in Carlisle, and that fields irrigated with the final effluent were freed of a parasite that was causing disease in cattle. Lister began to use a solution of carbolic acid for wound cleansing and dressings, and also experimented with operating under a spray of carbolic acid solution. In 1867 he announced to a British Medical Association meeting that his wards in the Glasgow Royal Infirmary had remained clear of sepsis for nine months. At first his new methods met with hostility or indifference, but gradually doctors began to support his antiseptic techniques.

Continuing his studies in histology and bacteriology Lister became interested in Robert Koch's work, carried out between 1876 and 1878, on wound infections. In Germany, Koch was demonstrating that steam was a useful sterilizer for surgical instruments and dressings, and German surgeons were beginning to practise aseptic surgery, keeping wounds free from micro-organisms by using only sterilized instruments and materials. Lister realized that both methods relied on destroying pathogenic micro-organisms, and believed that, in the future, more emphasis would be placed on preventive medicine. He strove for the establishment of an institute of preventive medicine, which he saw opened in 1891.

Lorenz, Konrad Zacharias (*1903–*), is an Austrian zoologist who is generally considered to be the founder of modern ethology. He is best known for his studies of the relationships between instinct and behaviour, particularly in birds, although he has also applied his ideas to aspects of human behaviour, notably aggression. He has received many honours for his work, including the 1973 Nobel Prize in Physiology and Medicine, which he was awarded jointly with Karl von Frisch and Nikolaas Tinbergen.

Lorenz was born in Vienna on 7 November 1903, the son of an orthopaedic surgeon. From an early age he collected and cared for various animals, and he also kept a detailed record of his bird observations. He was educated at the High School in Vienna then in 1922, following his father's wishes, went to the United States to Columbia University and studied medicine. After two years he returned to Austria and continued his medical studies at the University of Vienna, from which he graduated in 1928. In the previous year he had married Margarethe Gebhardt, by whom he later had a son and two daughters. After graduation he studied comparative anatomy as an assistant in the Anatomy Department of Vienna University, where he remained until 1935 – having gained his doctorate in 1933. In 1936 the German Society for Animal Psychology was founded and in the following year Lorenz was appointed Co-Editor-in-Chief of the society's new journal *Zeitschrift für Tierpsychologie*, which became one of the world's leading ethology journals; he held the post for many years. Also in 1937 he became lecturer in Comparative Anatomy and Animal Psychology at Vienna University, remaining there until 1940, when he was appointed Professor and Head of the Department of General Psychology at the Albertus University in Königsberg. From 1942 to 1944 he was a physician in the German army, but was captured in the Soviet Union and spent four years as a prisoner-of-war there. He returned to Austria in 1948 and in the following year was appointed Head of the Institute of Comparative Ethology at Altenberg. In 1951 he established the Comparative Ethology Department in the Max Planck Institute at Buldern, becoming its Co-Director in 1954. He then worked at the Max Planck Institute of Behavioural Physiology in Seewiesen from 1958 to 1973 (as its Director after 1961), when he was appointed Director of the Department for Animal Sociology at the Austrian Academy of Sciences' Institute for Comparative Ethology.

Lorenz made most of his observations and basic discoveries during the late 1930s and early 1940s. From 1935 to 1938 he carried out intensive studies on bird colonies he had established, including jackdaws and greylag geese, and published a series of papers on his observations, which gained him world-wide recognition. In 1935 he described the phenomenon for which he is perhaps best known: imprinting. He discovered that many birds do not instinctively recognize members of their own species but that they do possess an innate ability to acquire this capacity. He observed that during a brief period after hatching a young bird treats the first reasonably large object it sees as representative of its species – the object becomes imprinted. Normally this object is the bird's parent but Lorenz found that it is possible to substitute almost any other reasonably sized object, such as a balloon or a human being, in which case the bird does not respond in the usual manner to other members of its species. There has since been evidence that imprinting may also occur in human children, although this is still a matter of controversy because it is extremely difficult to differentiate between innate and learned responses, especially in man and other higher animals.

After this research, Lorenz collaborated with Nikolaas Tinbergen on further studies of bird behaviour. They showed that the reactions of many birds to birds of prey depend on attitudes or gestures made by the predators and on a particular feature of their shapes – the shortness of their necks, which is common to all birds of prey. Lorenz and Tinbergen found that the sight of any bird with a short neck – or even a dummy bird with this feature – causes other birds to fly away.

On the subject of instinct and behaviour, Lorenz has hypothesized that every instinct builds up a specific type of "desire" in the central nervous system. If there is no appropriate environment that helps to release the behaviour pattern corresponding to the desire, then tension gradually increases, eventually reaching such a level that instincts take control, even when the correct stimulus is lacking. For example, a pregnant ewe acts in a maternal manner towards a new-born lamb, although the ewe herself has not yet given birth.

In his later work Lorenz supplied his ideas to human behaviour, most notably in his book *On Aggression* (1966), in which he argued that aggressive behaviour in human beings has an innate basis but, with a proper understanding of man's instinctual needs, society can be changed to accommodate these needs and so aggression may be diverted into socially useful behaviour.

Ludwig, Karl Friedrich Wilhelm (*1816-1895*), was a German physiologist - one of the great teachers and experimenters in the history of physiology.

Ludwig was born at Witzenhausen, Hesse (now in West Germany) on 29 December 1816. He completed his schooling at Hanau Gymnasium and then went to Marburg University in 1834. He was compelled to leave the university as a result of his political activities, but after studying at Erlangen and at the surgical school in Bamberg, was allowed to return to Marburg to complete his studies. He received his medical degree in 1840, and in 1841 became Professor of Anatomy. He was appointed Associate Professor Extraordinarius at Marburg in 1846 and continued with teaching and research there until 1849 when he moved to Zurich and became Professor of Physiology and Anatomy. Six years later he went to Vienna and served as Professor of Anatomy and Physiology at the Josephinum, the Austrian military medical academy which had been founded the previous year, in 1854. In 1865 he accepted the newly created Chair of Physiology at Leipzig and set out to develop it into an important teaching centre for physiology. He held this post until his death in Leipzig on 23 April 1895.

While studying at Marburg, Ludwig investigated the mechanism of secretion. In 1844 he was studying renal secretion and, on examining the structure of the kidney tubules (glomeruli), he recognized that during the first stage of secretion the surface membrane of the glomeruli acts as a filter. Liquid diffuses through it as a result of the pressure difference on each side of the membrane. Ludwig also devised a system of measuring the level of nitrogen in urine to quantify the rate of protein metabolism in the human body. Continuing his research on secretion, he showed that secretion from the salivary glands is dependent on secretory nerve stimulation and not on blood supply.

Following William Harvey's findings on the circulation of blood it was believed that blood was moved by an unseen vital force. Ludwig was against this idea and in 1847 developed the kymograph (an instrument that continuously records changes in blood pressure and respiration). Ludwig could thus prove that blood is moved by a mechanical force.

In 1856, when studying the effects of certain drugs on the heart, Ludwig discovered that a frog's heart, removed after the death of an animal, could be revived and that organs could be kept alive *in vitro*. This was the first time this operation had been performed successfully and was done by perfusing the coronary arteries under pressure with blood or a salt solution which resembles the composition of the saline medium of the blood.

Ludwig was also the first to discover the depressor and accelerator nerves of the heart, and in 1871, working with Henry Bowditch, an American physiologist, he formulated the "All-or-None" law of cardiac muscle action. This law postulates that when a stimulus is applied to a few fibres of heart muscle, the whole heart muscle contracts to the extent that with increased stimulation there is no further increase in the contraction. The "All-or-None" Law is most evident in cardiac muscle although it can occur elsewhere.

In 1859, in a paper published by his student Sechenov, Ludwig described his invention of the mercurial blood-gas pump, which enabled him to separate gases from a given quantity of blood taken directly in vivo. This invention led to later understanding of the part played by oxygen in the purification of the blood. Ludwig also invented the *stromuhr*, a flowmeter which measures the rate of the flow of blood in the veins.

Ludwig's ingenuity and inventiveness, combined with a good knowledge of physics and chemistry, made him important in the development of modern physiology. The kymograph with its subsequent modifications has become the standard tool for the recording of experimental results, and much of what is now known about the mechanism of cardiac activity is based on his work. Ludwig published a textbook for his students, *Das Lehrbuch der Physiologie* (*A Physiology Textbook*), the first volume in 1852 and the second in 1856, which was the first modern text on physiology.

Lwoff, André Michael (*1902-*), is a French microbiologist who was awarded the 1965 Nobel Prize in Physiology and Medicine for his research into the genetic control of enzyme activity. He shared the prize with his fellow researcher Jacques Lucien Monod and François Jacob.

Lwoff, of Russian–Polish descent, was born in Ainy-le-Château, Allier, on 8 May 1902. He studied natural sciences, graduating in 1921 and taking a post at the Pasteur Institute; in 1927 he received doctorates in medicine and science. During World War II he was an active member of the French Resistance movement, for which his country awarded him the Legion of Honour. From 1959 to 1968 he was Professor of Microbiology at the University of Paris and from 1968 to 1972 he was Head of the Cancer Research Institute at Villejuif.

In his early research carried out in the 1920s, Lwoff demonstrated the co-enzyme nature of vitamins. He also discovered the extranuclear genetic control of some characteristics of protozoa. In the early 1940s the American geneticist George Beadle had done important work that showed that genes are responsible for the production of the enzymes that moderate biochemical processes. Towards the end of the decade Lwoff and his co-workers proved that enzymes produced by some genes regulate the functions of other genes. He worked out the mechanism of lysogeny in bacteria, in which the DNA of a virus become attached to the chromosome (DNA) of a bacterium, behaving almost like a bacterial gene. It is therefore replicated as part of the host's DNA and so multiplies at the same time. But certain agents (such as ultraviolet radiation) can turn the "latent" viral DNA, called the prophage, into a vegetative form which multiplies, destroys its host, and is released to infect other bacteria.

Lyell, Charles (*1797-1875*), was a British geologist who succeeded in turning the opinion of his time away from the theory that the Earth was produced literally along the lines expounded in the Book of Genesis towards the principle of an unlimited, gradual effect of natural forces. His beliefs became known in geology as "Uniformitarianism".

Lyell was born in Kinnordy, Forfarshire, on 14 November 1797, the son of a lawyer and amateur botanist. When he was still a child the family moved away from Scotland and settled in Hampshire. Lyell always had an interest in natural history; he was a keen lepidopterist, and his interest in geology was stimulated by Bakewell's book on the subject. Lyell went to Oxford University to study classics, but also attended lectures given by William Buckland, the Professor of Geology. Buckland was of the opinion that the different strata in rocks result from silt being laid down under water over a long period of time: he was a "Neptunist". Lyell made his first tentative geological observations during family holidays in Britain and from 1818 on the Continent, and he began to believe more fully in the principles of Uniformitarianism. (In fact the geologist James Hutton (1726-1797) had postulated similar theories 50 years earlier, but Lyell formed his conclusions independently; it was only when he later read Hutton's work that he realized that their views were similar.) Lyell continued his education by studying law and was eventually called to the bar in 1822, and started to practise in 1825. In 1823 he became involved in the running of the Geological Society as its Secretary and later as Foreign Secretary; he was twice its President some 15 years later. He also set up the finance for the Lyell Medal and the Lyell Fund. He made a trip to Paris in 1823 and met Georges Cuvier (1769-1832), the eminent French anatomist who had stuck rigidly to the geological theories of "Catastrophism", despite his brilliant understanding in other fields. Lyell also met Alexander von Humboldt (1769-1859), the German naturalist; both men influenced his eventual ideas. In 1831 he became Professor of Geology at King's College, London, and a year later he married the daughter of the geologist Leonard Horner. Lyell was knighted in 1848 and created a baronet in 1864. He died in London on 22 February 1875.

Lyell did not originate much material, but he expounded the theories of Hutton and organized them into popular and coherent form. His masterpiece *The Principles of Geology* was published in three volumes from 1830 to 1833 and was revised regularly until 1875. It laid out evidence to support the theory that the Earth's geological structure evolved slowly through the continuous action of forces still at work today, including the erosive action of the wind and weather. Lyell conceded very little to catastrophism, although modern geologists accept that some "catastrophies" must have occurred - for instance, at the time of the disappearance of the dinosaurs. Lyell classified some geological eras - subdividing the Tertiary into the Eocene, Miocene, Pliocene and Pleistocene – and suggested that some of the oldest rocks may be as much as 240 million years old. People were astonished by such a time scale, even though present-day geologists think that ten times that number may be nearer the probable truth.

The conservative scientists were alarmed by Lyell's theories, but his book was popular and stimulated other geologists to investigate along similar lines. Charles Darwin, a colleague and friend of Lyell's, was deeply impressed, and Lyell in turn eventually embraced the theory of evolution as outlined in Darwin's *Origin of Species* (1859) – it was Lyell and Joseph Hooker who in 1858 presented to the Linnean Society the original papers on natural selection by Darwin and Alfred Wallace. Lyell then went further than Darwin had been prepared to do in an attempt to trace the descent of man, and used archaeological findings as the key to his book *The Geological Evidence of the Antiquity of Man with Remarks on Theories of the Origin of Species by Variation* (1863).

Lysenko, Trofim Denisovich (*1898–1976*), was a Soviet botanist who dominated biology in the Soviet Union from about the mid-1930s to 1965. During this period he was virtual dictator of biology in the Soviet Union and his theories, although largely rejected outside his own country, were officially adopted within the Soviet Union. He actually contributed very little to scientific knowledge and his importance has been attributed to his friendship with the Soviet political leaders Josef Stalin and Nikita Khrushchev, who awarded Lysenko many honours: he was made a Hero of Socialist Labour, and received the Order of Lenin eight times and the Stalin Prize three times.

Lysenko was born on 29 September 1898 in Karlovka in the Russian Ukraine, the son of a peasant, and was educated at the Uman School of Horticulture. After graduating in 1921, he went to the Belaya Tserkov Selection Station then to the Kiev Agricultural Institute to study for his doctorate, which he gained in 1925. He was stationed at the Gandzha (now Kirovabad) Experimental Station from 1925 to 1929, when he became the senior specialist in the Department of Physiology at the Ukrainian All-Union Institute of Selection and Genetics in Odessa. In 1935 he became Scientific Director of this institute and in the following year he was promoted to Director, a post he held until 1938. With the increase of his political influence, Lysenko rose rapidly to the top of the scientific hierarchy, becoming Director of the Institute of Genetics of the USSR Academy of Sciences in 1940. As a result of Khrushchev's

fall from power in 1964, Lysenko's influence diminished considerably and in 1965 he was removed from his post and stripped of all authority. He died on 20 November 1976, his ideas discredited both within the Soviet Union and by the Western world.

Lysenko rose to prominence as a result of his advocating vernalization to increase crop yields. In vernalization – a practice well known since the nineteenth century – seeds are moistened just sufficiently to allow germination to begin then, when the radicles start to emerge, the seeds are cooled to slightly above 0°C, thereby halting further growth. When the seeds are planted in spring, they mature quickly; this is particularly useful in the Soviet Union because large areas of the country have only a very short growing season. Using this method Lysenko achieved considerable increases in crop yields, which gained him substantial political support. A succession of important appointments followed, and by 1935 Lysenko had become a powerful influence in Soviet science.

As Lysenko's influence increased, so he enlarged the scope of his theories, using his authority to remove any opposition. He innovated the doctrine of the phasic development of plants, claiming that all plants develop in recessive phases, each with different requirements. He stated that by altering any stage of development, changes could be caused in successive stages. This doctrine was opposed by Nikolai Vavilov (1887–1942/3), an internationally respected Soviet geneticist, but Lysenko used his political influence to have Vavilov arrested and banished to Siberia, where he died in exile in 1942 or 1943.

Expanding his theories still further, Lysenko defined heredity as the capacity of an organism to require specific conditions for its life and development, and to respond in different ways to various conditions. Moreover, he believed that when an organism is subjected to abnormal environmental conditions, it develops in such a way as to take advantage of these conditions and that the offspring of this organism also tend to develop in the same way as the parent. This idea was, in fact, a restatement of the Lamarckian doctrine of the inheritance of acquired characteristics.

As leader of the Soviet scientific world, Lysenko encouraged the defence of mechanistic views about the nature of heredity and speciation. These views – termed Michurin biology after the prominent Soviet scientist I.V. Michurin – became an integral part of Soviet scientific thought and created an environment conducive to the spread of unverified facts and theories, such as the doctrine of the non-cellular "living" substance and the transformation of viruses into bacteria. To many people, this period represented the dark ages of Soviet science and research in several areas of biology came to a halt.

Although Lysenko's views were imposed on Soviet scientists, his ideas were widely criticized by many European and American scientists and, encouraged by this external support, the struggle to counteract Lysenkoism gained strength.

M

MacArthur, Robert Helmer (*1930-1972*), was a Canadian-born American ecologist who did much to change ecology from a descriptive discipline to a quantitative, predictive science.

MacArthur was born on 7 April 1930 in Toronto, Canada. He studied mathematics at Marlboro College, Vermont, graduating in 1951, and at Brown University, Providence, from which he gained his master's degree in 1953. He then went to Yale University to do his doctorate in mathematics but changed to zoology at the end of his second year and began to study ecology under G. Evelyn Hutchinson, one of the leading American ecologists of the time. MacArthur's studies were interrupted by a two-year period of military service, after which he returned to Yale to complete his doctoral dissertation, which won him the Mercer Award for the best ecology paper of 1957-1958. He then joined the staff of the University of Pennsylvania, first as Assistant Professor of Zoology (from 1958 to 1961) then as Associate Professor of Zoology (1961 to 1964). In 1965 he was appointed Professor of Biology at Princeton University, where he remained until he died of cancer on 1 November 1972, only 42 years old.

In his doctoral thesis, MacArthur studied the relationship between five species of warblers that co-exist in the New England forests; these species (now known as MacArthur's warblers) are ecologically very similar and it was suspected that they violated the competitive exclusion principle. MacArthur discovered, however, that there are subtle differences in the foraging strategies used by each species.

During the remainder of his life, MacArthur devoted himself to investigating population biology. He examined how the diversity and relative abundance of species fluctuate over time and how species evolve - particularly the evolution of communities - and the strategies that co-existing species evolve under the pressures of competition and natural selection. In these studies he attempted to interrelate several important factors: the structure of the environment, the mor-

phology of the species, the economics of species' behaviour and the dynamics of population change. But perhaps his most important contribution was to quantify some of the many factors involved in the ecological relationships between species. For example, complex habitats such as forests support more species of birds than do grasslands, but it was only after MacArthur had devised his index of vegetational complexity (called foliage height diversity) in 1961 that it became possible to translate the observation about bird species' diversity into a definite equation whereby habitat structures can be compared and their bird species' diversity predicted.

McCollum, Elmer Verner (*1879-1967*), was an American biochemist and nutritionist who is best known for his work on vitamins, and for originating the letter system of naming them.

McCollum was born on 3 March 1879 in Fort Scott, Kansas, the fourth child of an initially prosperous farming family. But his father became ill when McCollum was still very young and he had to take a succession of jobs while at school and university to pay for his education and to help to support his parents. McCollum studied at the University of Kansas, graduating in 1903, then gained a postgraduate scholarship to Yale University, from which he obtained his doctorate in 1906. In the following year he joined the faculty of the University of Wisconsin, where he remained for ten years. In 1917 he was appointed Professor of Biochemistry in the School of Hygiene and Public Health at the Johns Hopkins University, a post he held until his retirement in 1944. McCollum died in Baltimore on 15 November 1967.

In his first years at Wisconsin University, McCollum worked on analysing the food and excreta of cattle. He soon decided, however, that it would be much easier to perform this work using a more convenient laboratory animal, and he chose the albino rat. This led to the establishment of the first rat colony for nutrition experiments, and it is largely through McCollum's efforts that albino rats have today become one of the most used animals for research. Investigating the nutritional requirements of his albino rats, McCollum discovered in the early 1910s that growth retardation results from a diet deficient in certain fats and that such deficiencies can be compensated for by providing a specific extract from either butter or eggs. He called this essential component "fat-soluble A", because it dissolves in lipids. This was the start of the alphabetical naming system for vitamins. McCollum then showed that there is another essential dietary component that is not found in lipids but which is water soluble; he called this component "water-soluble B". Initially he thought that the two essential components were single compounds, but he later showed that they are in fact complexes.

McCollum continued his nutritional research at the Johns Hopkins University, where he collaborated in the discovery of vitamin D. He also investigated the way in which sunlight prevents rickets, but it was not shown until later that the anti-rickets effect of sunlight is caused by the conversion of fats in the skin to vitamin D by the ultra-violet component of sunlight. In addition to his work on vitamins, McCollum also researched into the role of minerals in the diet.

Malpighi, Marcello (*1628-1694*), was an Italian physician who discovered, among other things, blood capillaries, and pioneered the use of the microscope in the study of tissues.

Malpighi was born in Crevalcore, Italy, on 10 March 1628. He attended the University of Bologna from 1646 to 1653 and graduated as doctor of medicine and philosophy. He first lectured in Logic at Bologna, and then accepted the Chair in Theoretical Medicine at the University of Pisa in 1656. There he met and befriended the mathematician Giovanni Borelli. Malpighi found that the climate in Pisa did not suit his health and he returned to Bologna after three years, to lecture in theoretical and practical medicine. In 1662 he took up the offer of the Chair in Medicine at the University of Messina, but four years later was back in Bologna. In 1667 the Royal Society invited him to submit his research findings to them and made him an honorary member - the first Italian to be thus elected - and also supervised the printing of his later works. In 1691 Malpighi moved to Rome and retired there as chief physician to Pope Innocent XII. He died in Rome on 30 November 1694.

In Malpighi's time the microscope was a new invention and he became absorbed in using it to study animal and insect tissue, as did Anton van Leeuwenhoek. One of Malpighi's early investigations, in 1661, concerned the lungs of a frog. These organs were previously thought to have been fleshy structures, but Malpighi found them to consist of thin membranes containing fine blood vessels covering vast numbers of small air sacs. This discovery made it easier to explain how air (oxygen) seeps from the lungs to the blood vessels and is carried around the body. Malpighi traced the network of capillaries and found that they provide the means of blood travelling from the small arteries to the small veins. These findings filled the gap in the theory of blood circulation proposed by William Harvey.

Malpighi also investigated the anatomy of insects and found the tracheae, the branching tubes that open to the outside in the abdomen and supply the insect with oxygen for respiration. Turning to the dissection of plants, Malpighi found what he took to be tracheae in the stem - long tubes with rings of thickening. In fact he was looking at young vessels in the xylem. He also discovered the stomata in leaves but had no idea of their function.

Malpighi included the various structures and organs of the human body in his examinations. He indentified the sensory receptors (papillae) of the tongue, which he thought could be nerve endings. He also investigated the spinal cord and nerves and found them to be composed of the same fibres, but did not put forward a correct theory of their function. He proved that bile was uniform in colour, not yellow and black (as had been believed), and also indentified the urinary tubules in the kidney.

Chick embryos also fascinated Malpighi and in his microscope studies he recorded their neural folds and neural tube, the aortic arches, the optic vesicles and feather follicles.

Malpighi was a pioneer in the field of microscopy, and studied such a wide range of material that the curiosity of many scientists was aroused. Their combined efforts laid the foundations for further studies in a number of directions including histology, embryology, and the anatomy of organisms until then too small to observe.

Malthus, Thomas Robert (*1766-1834*), was a British economist who made the first serious study of human population trends, although his views on the future of the human race enraged many thinkers of his day.

Malthus was born near Dorking, Surrey, on or about 14 February 1766. He went to Cambridge University, was ordained in 1788 and in 1796 became a curate in Albury, Surrey. In 1805 he was invited to accept a professorial post at Haileybury College, where he became Professor of History and Political Economy. During this time Malthus produced his major books on economics, *An Inquiry into the Nature and Progress of Rent* (1815) and *Principles of Political Economy* (1820). His work was acknowledged by many foreign academies, and he became a Fellow of the Royal Society in 1819. He died near Bath, Somerset (now Avon), on 23 December 1834.

Malthus's most controversial work was *An Essay on the Principle of Population*, which was published anonymously in 1798. In it he set out his reasons for believing that the human population of the world will increase at such a rate that it will eventually outstrip the Earth's resources. He postulated, that the situation will ultimately become resolved as the numbers are whittled away by starvation and disease, or war. In a later revision of the work Malthus conceded that moral constraints on sexual intercourse and marriage could stabilize population growth.

Malthus's theories brought a storm of protest at the time which only slightly abated with publication of the revised work. Now it is accepted that Malthus was probably correct up to a point. Populations throughout the plant and animal kingdoms also tend to increase faster than the resources to support them until some check builds up sufficiently. After reading Malthus's work, Charles Darwin postulated that the transformation or extinction of species depends on their response (a function of variability) to changing environmental factors.

Mechnikov, Ilya Ilich (*1845-1916*), was a Russian-born French zoologist who discovered phagocytes, amoeba-like blood cells that engulf foreign bodies. For this discovery he was awarded (jointly with Paul Ehrlich) the 1908 Nobel Prize in Physiology and Medicine. His name is sometimes spelled Élie Metchnikoff.

Mechnikov was born on 15 May 1845 in Kharkov, Russia, the son of an officer of the Imperial Guard. He was educated at the University of Kharkov, from which he graduated in 1864. He then travelled to Germany to pursue his studies but returned to Russia in 1867, becoming Professor of Zoology and Comparative Anatomy at the University of Odessa. In 1882 he inherited sufficient money to make him financially independent and moved to Messina in Italy to continue his research. In 1886 he accepted the post of Director of the Bacteriological Institute in Odessa but remained there only a short time, being invited to join the Pasteur Institute where he remained for the rest of his life, becoming Director on Pasteur's death in 1895. Mechnikov died in Paris on 16 July 1916.

Mechnikov first noticed phagocytes while he was in Messina studying the transparent larvae of starfish; he observed that certain cells surrounded and engulfed foreign particles that had entered the bodies of the larvae. He then deliberately introduced bacteria into starfish larvae and fungal spores into water fleas (*Daphnia*) and again observed that special amoeba-like cells moved to where these foreign bodies were and engulfed them. Mechnikov continued this line of research at Odessa and later at the Pasteur Institute, where he demonstrated that phagocytes exist in higher animals. In man about three-quarters of the white blood cells or leucocytes are phagocytic and they form the first line of defence against acute infections, moving to the site of infection and engulf-

ing the invading bacteria. This work opposed the theory of the time, which postulated that leucocytes actually helped the growth of bacteria, but it is now accepted that leucocytes are one of the body's basic defence mechanisms against disease.

In his later years Mechnikov became interested in longevity, and he spent the last decade of his life trying to demonstrate that lactic acid-producing bacteria in the intestine increased a person's life-span.

Medawar, Peter Brian (*1915-*), is a British zoologist who is best known for his important contributions to immunology, for which he shared the 1960 Nobel Prize in Physiology and Medicine with Frank Macfarlane Burnet. He has also received many other honours for his work, including a knighthood in 1965.

Medawar was born on 28 February 1915 in Rio de Janeiro, Brazil. He was educated at Magdalen College, Oxford, from which he graduated in 1939. From 1938 to 1944 and from 1946 to 1947 he was a Fellow of Magdalen College; and from 1944 to 1946 he also held a fellowship at St John's College, Oxford. In 1947 he was appointed Mason Professor of Zoology at Birmingham University and he held this position until 1951, when he became Jodrell Professor of Zoology and Comparative Anatomy at University College, London. Medawar remained at University College until 1962, when he was appointed Director of the National Institute for Medical Research at Mill Hill in London, becoming Director Emeritus in 1975. In 1977 he was appointed Professor of Experimental Medicine at the Royal Institution.

Medawar began his Nobel prize-winning research in the early 1950s. Acting on Burnet's hypothesis that an animal's ability to produce a specific antibody is not inherited, Medawar inoculated mouse embryos of one strain (strain A) with cells from mice of another strain (strain B). He found that the strain A embryos did not produce antibodies against the strain B cells. When the strain A embryos had developed sufficiently to be capable of independent existence, he grafted onto them skin from strain B mice. Again he found that the strain A embryos did not produce antibodies against the strain B tissue. Thus Medawar confirmed Burnet's hypothesis that the ability of an animal to produce a specific antibody develops during the animal's lifetime and is not inherited. This finding suggests that an animal's immune system can be influenced by external factors, which may have significant implications in the field of transplant techniques.

Mellanby, Kenneth (*1908-*), is a British entomologist and ecologist who is best known for his work on the environmental effects of pollution.

Mellanby was born on 26 March 1908 and was educated at the Barnard Castle School. He gained a scholarship to read natural sciences at London University and graduated in 1929. In the following year he became a research worker at the London School of Hygiene and Tropical Medicine, from which he gained his doctorate in 1933, and remained a member of staff there until 1945. During this period he went to East Africa to study the tsetse fly and, while doing his World War II military service, investigated scrub typhus in Burma and New Guinea. In 1945 he was appointed Reader in Medical Entomology at London University, and in 1947 became the Principal of University College Ibadan – Nigeria's first university, which Mellanby played a substantial part in creating. He was then appointed head of the Entomology Department at Rothamsted Experimental Station in 1955, a position he held until 1961, when he founded and became the Director of the Monks Wood Research Station (now called the Institute of Terrestrial Ecology) at Huntingdon in Cambridgeshire. He remained in this post until he officially retired, although he still pursues his research at the Institute. In 1978 he visited Australia to advise the newly established Association for the Protection of Rural Australia, and in 1979 he went to Peru to advise on the ecological effects of the Montaro Transfer Scheme, a plan to divert water from the Montaro River to Lima.

Mellanby's early career was spent in entomological research but his most important contributions are probably his pioneering investigations into the effects of pollution, particularly by pesticides. Shortly after he had established the Monks Wood Research Station, he drew attention to the deleterious effects of pesticides – before Rachel Carson had published her famous book on this theme, *Silent Spring*. Continuing his research, Mellanby undertook a comprehensive study of pesticides, concluding that although these chemicals damage the environment, pests destroy huge amounts of food and other essential materials and must therefore be controlled. Instead of pesticides, however, Mellanby advocated the use of biological control methods, such as introducing animals that feed on pests. He has written several books about entomology, ecology and pollution, and is the editor of *Environmental Pollution*, one of the main research journals in this subject area.

Mendel, Gregor Johann (*1822–1884*), was an Austrian monk who discovered the basic laws of heredity, thereby laying the foundation of modern genetics – although the importance of his work was not recognized until after his death.

Mendel was born Johann Mendel on 22 July 1822 in Heinzendorf, Austria (now Hynčice in Czechoslovakia), the son of a peasant farmer. He studied for two years at the Philosophical Institute in Olmütz (now Olomouc), after which, in 1843, he entered the Augustinian monastery in Brünn, Moravia (now Brno in Czechoslovakia), taking the name Gregor. In 1847 he was ordained a priest. During his religious training, Mendel taught himself a certain amount of science and for a short time he was a teacher of Greek and mathematics at the secondary school in Znaim (now Znojmo) near Brünn. In 1850 he tried to pass an examination to obtain a teaching licence but failed, and in 1851 he was sent by his Abbot to the University of Vienna to study physics, chemistry, mathematics, zoology and botany. Mendel left the university in 1853 and returned to the monastery in Brünn in 1854. He then taught natural science in the local Technical High School until 1868, during which period he again tried, and failed, to gain a teaching certificate that would have enabled him to teach in more advanced institutions. It was also in the period 1854 to 1868 that Mendel performed most of his scientific work on heredity. He was elected Abbot of his monastery at Brünn in 1868, and the administrative duties involved left him little time for further scientific investigations. Mendel remained Abbot at Brünn until his death on 6 January 1884.

Mendel began the experiments that led to his discovery of the basic laws of heredity in 1856. Much of his work was performed on the edible pea (*Pisum* sp.), which he grew in the monastery garden. He carefully self-pollinated and wrapped (to prevent accidental pollination by insects) each individual plant, collected the seeds produced by the plants, and studied the offspring of these seeds. He found that dwarf plants produced only dwarf offspring and that the seeds produced by this second generation also produced only dwarf offspring. With tall plants, however, he found that both tall and dwarf offspring were produced and that only about one-third of the tall plants bred true, from which he concluded that there were two types of tall plants, those that bred true and those that did not. Next he cross-bred dwarf plants with true-breeding tall plants, planted the resulting seeds and then self-pollinated each plant from this second generation. He found that all the offspring in the first generation were tall but that the offspring from the self-pollination of this first generation were a mixture of about one-quarter true-breeding dwarf plants, one-quarter true-breeding tall plants and one-half non-true-breeding tall plants. Mendel also studied other

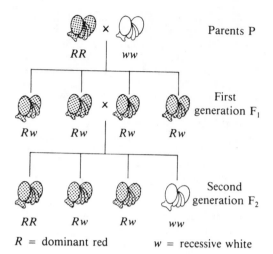

R = dominant red   *w* = recessive white

A   Mendel's law of segregation applied to an initial cross between pea plants with red flowers and pea plants with white flowers. The second generation has red-flowered plants to white-flowered plants in the ratio of 3 : 1.

characteristics in pea plants, such as flower colour, seed shape and flower position, finding that, as with height, simple laws governed the inheritance of these traits. From his findings Mendel concluded that each parent plant contributes a factor that determines a particular trait and that the pairs of factors in the offspring do not give rise to an amalgamation of traits. These conclusions, in turn, led him to formulate his famous law of segregation and law of independent assortment of characters, which are now recognized as two of the fundamental laws of heredity.

Mendel reported his findings to the Brünn Society for the Study of Natural Science in 1865 and in the following year he published *Experiments with Plant Hybrids*, a paper that summarized his results. But the importance of his work was not recognized at the time, even by the eminent botanist Karl Wilhelm von Nägeli, to whom Mendel sent a copy of his paper. It was not until 1900, when his work was rediscovered by Hugo De Vries, Carl Erich Correns and Erich Tschermak von Seysenegg, that Mendel achieved fame – 16 years after his death.

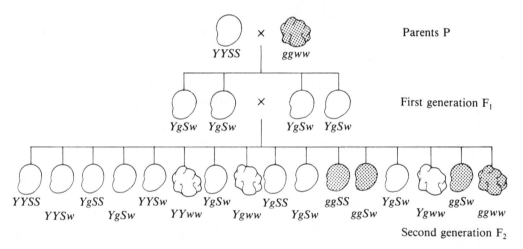

Y = dominant yellow   *S* = dominant smooth   *g* = recessive green   *w* = recessive wrinkled

B   Mendel's law of independent assortment applied to an initial cross between pea plants with smooth yellow seeds and pea plants with green wrinkled seeds. The second generation includes four visibly different types of seeds – yellow smooth, yellow wrinkled, green smooth and green wrinkled in the ratio 9 : 3 : 3 : 1.

Meselson, Matthew Stanley (*1930–*   ), and **Stahl, Franklin William** (*1929–*   ), are American molecular biologists who are best known for their collaborative work that confirmed Francis Crick and James Watson's theory that DNA replication is semi-conservative (i.e. that the daughter cells each receive one strand of DNA from the

original parent cell and one newly replicated strand, in contrast to conservative replication in which one daughter cell would receive both of the parental DNA strands and the other daughter would receive both the newly replicated strands).

Meselson was born on 24 May 1930 in Denver, Colorado. He studied liberal arts at the University of Chicago, gaining his doctorate in 1951, then physical chemistry at the California Institute of Technology, obtaining a second doctorate in 1957. He remained at the California Institute of Technology until 1976 – as Assistant Professor of Chemistry from 1958 to 1960, as Associate Professor of Chemistry from 1958 to 1960, then as Associate Professor and later Professor of Biology. In 1976 he became Cabot Professor of Natural Sciences at Harvard University. Since 1963 he has also been a consultant to the United States Arms Control and Disarmament Agency.

Stahl was born on 8 October 1929 in Boston, Massachusetts. He was educated at Harvard University, from which he graduated in 1951, and at the University of Rochester, from which he gained his doctorate in biology in 1956. He was a Research Fellow in Biology at the California Institute of Technology from 1955 to 1958, when he moved to the University of Missouri, where he was Associate Professor of Zoology from 1958 to 1959 then Associate Professor of the University until 1970. Since 1970 he has been Professor of Biology at the University of Oregon and a Research Associate of the Institute of Molecular Biology.

Meselson and Stahl began their research that demonstrated the semi-conservative nature of DNA replication in 1957. After unsuccessfully experimenting with viruses, they turned their attention to the bacterium *Escherichia coli* (*E. coli*). They grew the bacteria on a culture medium containing nitrogen-15 (a heavy isotope of nitrogen) as the only nitrogen source, so that the nitrogen-15 would become incorporated into the nitrogenous bases of the bacterial DNA. They then transferred the bacteria to a medium containing nitrogen-14 (the normal nitrogen isotope) as the only nitrogen source. After the bacteria had reproduced several times, they were centrifuged to extract their DNA, and the density of the DNA was determined by equilibrium density gradient centrifugation, in which samples of different densities separate into discrete bands; the concentration of DNA in each band can then be determined by ultraviolet absorption spectrography. From these processes Meselson and Stahl obtained three different types of DNA; one containing only nitrogen-14, one containing only nitrogen-15 and a hybrid containing both nitrogen isotopes. On heating, the hybrid separated into two halves, one from the parental DNA and one that had been newly synthesized. These findings demonstrated that the double helix of DNA splits into two strands when the DNA replicates, with each of the single strands acting as a template for the synthesis of a complementary strand; the final result is two DNA molecules, each comprising one strand from the parent molecule and one newly synthesized strand. Thus Meselson and Stahl confirmed the hypothesis of semi-conservative DNA replication, one of the most important concepts in modern molecular biology.

In 1961, working with Sidney Brenner and François Jacob, Meselson and Stahl demonstrated that ribosomes require instructions in order to be able to manufacture proteins, and that ribosomes can make proteins which are different from those normally produced by a particular cell. They also showed that messenger RNA supplies the instructions to the ribosomes.

In addition to their collaborative work, Stahl has researched into the genetics of bacteriophages and has written a book on the mechanism of inheritance; and Meselson has investigated the molecular biology of nucleic acids, the mechanisms of DNA recombination and repair, and the processes of gene control and evolution.

Milstein, César (*1927*-   ), is an Argentinian molecular biologist who has performed important research on the genetics, biosynthesis and chemistry of immunoglobulins (antibodies), developing a technique for preparing chemically pure monoclonal antibodies.

Milstein was born on 8 October 1927 in Bahia Blanca, Argentina. From 1939 to 1944 he was educated at the Collegio Nacional, Bahia Blanca, from which he gained his Bachiller, then in 1945 he went to the University of Buenos Aires, from which he graduated in 1952. He remained at Buenos Aires University until 1963, initially to study for his doctorate (which he obtained in 1957), then as a member of the staff of the Institute of Microbiology. During a period of leave of absence, Milstein worked in the Department of Biochemistry at Cambridge University, from which he gained his second doctorate in 1960. He returned to Cambridge in 1963 as a member of the staff of the Medical Research Council Laboratory of Molecular Biology and later became head (with F. Sanger) of its Protein Chemistry Division.

Milstein and his colleagues were among the first to determine the complete sequence of the short, low molecular weight part of the immunoglobulin molecule (known as the light chain). He then determined the nucleotide sequence of a large portion of the messenger RNA for the light chain and found that there is only one type of messenger RNA for both domains within that chain. The separate domains within the heavy (high molecular weight) and light chains are called constant and variable, and Milstein deduced that although the genes for the constant and variable domains may be separate in the germ line, these genes must have come together in the antibody-producing cells. This finding led Milstein to develop his technique for preparing chemically pure monoclonal antibodies. Working with Köhler in 1975, Milstein succeeded in fusing myeloma cells (which are easily cultured but produce only their own predetermined immunoglobulin) with spleen cells (which cannot be cultured but can produce immunoglobulin against any antigen with which an animal has been injected) to produce hybrid cells that can be cultured and that can produce antibodies against a wide range of antigens. Moreover, by selecting clones Milstein and Köhler obtained cell lines that secreted only one chemically homogenous antibody. This was a revolutionary piece of research, because the permanent cultures derived from one clone can be propagated indefinitely and can therefore provide an unlimited supply of a specific immunoglobulin. The technique was later extended to human cells and can also be used to prepare purified antibodies against impure antigens.

Mitchell, Peter Dennis (*1920–   *), is a British biochemist who has performed important research into the processes involved in the transfer of biological energy. He has received many honours for his work, including the award of the 1978 Nobel Prize in Chemistry.

Mitchell was born on 29 September 1920 in Mitcham, Surrey. He was educated at Queen's College, Taunton, and then at Jesus College, Cambridge, from which he graduated in 1943 and gained his doctorate in 1950. He worked in the Biochemistry Department of Cambridge University from 1943 to 1955, becoming a demonstrator in 1950. In 1955 he was appointed Director of the Chemical Biology Unit in the Department of Zoology at Edinburgh; he was later promoted to Senior Lecturer then, in 1962, to Reader. In the following year he established and became Director of the privately run Glynn Research Institute at Bodmin, Cornwall.

In the early 1960s the way in which the synthesis of ATP (adenosine triphosphate) is linked with the transfer of electrons was still unknown. At the intracellular level, metabolic energy is stored in the form of ATP, produced by phosphorylating the diphosphate ADP (in effect the metabolic energy is stored in ATP's extra chemical bond). The energy needed for this reaction is produced by the transfer of electrons along a chain of proteins attached to the double membrane of mitochondria. In 1961 Mitchell postulated that, simultaneously with this electron transfer, protons are expelled from the outer surface of the inner mitochondrial membrane and are transmitted through the outer membrane by osmosis, thus setting up an ion-concentration gradient (and therefore a potential difference). He further suggested that this potential difference is the form in which the energy needed to convert ADP to ATP is stored. It has since been shown that other cellular processes that require energy involved the mechanism proposed by Mitchell and that the chemical equilibrium in the phosphorylation of ADP to ATP is highly sensitive to the concentration of ions, which is controlled by the mitochondrial membrane. Although greeted with great scepticism at first, Mitchell's theory is now considered to be correct and it has been established as the basic principle in the science of bio-energetics.

Monod, Jacques Lucien (*1910–1976*), was a French biochemist who is best known for his research into the way in which genes regulate intracellular activities. For this research Monod and his co-workers André Lwoff and François Jacob were jointly awarded the 1965 Nobel Prize in Physiology and Medicine.

Monod was born in Paris on 9 February 1910 and was educated at the university there. He graduated in 1931 and carried out research on the origins of life on Earth. He became Assistant Professor of Zoology at the University of Paris in 1934, and gained his doctorate in 1941. He worked for the French Resistance during World War II. From 1945 to 1953 he was laboratory chief at the Pasteur Institute, and it was during this period that he collaborated with Lwoff and Jacob on the work that was to gain them their Nobel Prize. In 1953 Monod became Director of the Department of Cellular Biochemistry at the Pasteur Institute and also a professor in the faculty of sciences at the University of Paris. In 1971 he was appointed Director of the entire Pasteur Institute. Monod died in Cannes on 31 May 1976.

Working on the way in which genes control intracellular metabolism in micro-organisms, Monod and his colleagues postulated the existence of a class of genes (which they called operons) that regulate the activities of the genes that actually control the synthesis of enzymes within the cell. They further hypothesized that the operons suppress the activities of the enzyme-synthesizing genes by affecting the synthesis of messenger RNA (mRNA). This theory has since been proved generally correct for many types of micro-organisms but there is some doubt as to whether or not it applies in more complex plants and animals.

In 1971 Monod published his well-known book *Chance and Necessity*, a wide-ranging biological and philosophical work in which he summoned contemporary biochemical discoveries to support the idea that all forms of life result from random mutation (chance) and Darwinian selection (necessity). In the conclusion to this book, Monod stated his belief that there is no overall plan to human existence and that Mankind must choose its own values in a vast and indifferent universe.

Morgan, Thomas Hunt (*1866–1945*), was an American geneticist and embryologist famous for his pioneering work on the genetics of the fruit fly *Drosophila melanogaster* – now extensively used in genetic research – and for establishing the chromosome theory of heredity. He received many honours for his work, including the 1933 Nobel Prize in Physiology and Medicine.

Morgan was born on 25 September 1866 in Lexington, Kentucky, the son of an American diplomat. He was educated at the State College of Kentucky, graduating in 1886, and then at Johns Hopkins University, from which he gained his PhD in 1890. In the following year he joined the staff of Bryn Mawr College, near Philadelphia, as Associate Professor of Zoology and remained there until 1904, when he became Professor of Experimental Zoology at Columbia University. In 1928 he was appointed Director of the Laboratory of Biological Sciences at the California Institute of Technology, a post he held until his death in Pasadena on 4 December 1945.

Morgan's early work was in the field of embryology, investigating such phenomena as fertilization in nucleated and unnucleated egg fragments, the development of embryos from separated blastomeres, and the effect of salt concentration on the development of unfertilized and fertilized eggs. In about 1907, however, his interest turned to the mechanisms involved in heredity (following the rediscovery of Gregor Mendel's work), and in 1908 he began his famous research on the genetics of *Drosophila* – initially to test Mendel's laws, about which Morgan was sceptical. After breeding several generations of *Drosophila*, Morgan noticed many small phenotypic variations, some of which could not be accounted for by Mendel's law of independent assortment – he discovered, for example, that the *Drosophila* variant now known as white eye is confined almost entirely to males. From his findings he postulated that certain characteristics are sex-linked, that the X-chromosome carries several discrete hereditary units (genes) and that the genes are linearly arranged on chromosomes. Morgan also demonstrated that sex-linked characters are not invariably inherited together, from which he developed the concept of crossing-over and the associated idea that the extent of crossing-over is a measure of the spatial separation of genes on chromosomes. (From these ideas A.H. Sturtevant – one of Morgan's student collaborators – drew up in 1911 the first chromosome map, which showed the positions of five sex-linked genes.) Morgan realized that his findings proved that Mendel's "factors" have a physical basis in chromosomes and revised his earlier scepticism of Mendelian genetics. In 1915, in collaboration with Sturtevant and his other student co-worker A.B. Bridges and Hermann Muller, Morgan published a summary of his work in *The Mechanism of Mendelian Heredity*, which had a profound influence in genetic research and evolutionary theory.

In the following years Morgan and various co-workers continued to elaborate the chromosome theory of heredity. Towards the end of his life, however, he returned to embryological investigations, trying to support with experimental evidence the theoretical links between embryological development and genetic theory. But it is his early work that is the most important, providing one of the cornerstones of modern genetic theory. Moreover, largely as a result of Morgan's experimentation, *Drosophila* became one of the principal experimental animals used for genetic investigations.

Morris, Desmond John (*1928–*), is a British zoologist, well known for his publications and films on animal and human behaviour.

Morris was born on 21 January 1928 and was educated at Birmingham University where he gained a BSc in zoology. He then went to Magdalen College, Oxford, to read for a PhD, working on animal behaviour under Nikolaas Tinbergen (1907–). From 1954 he worked in the Department of Zoology at Oxford before becoming Head of the Granada Television and Film Unit at the Zoological Society in London in 1956. Three years later he was appointed Curator of Mammals at the Zoological Society of London and from 1967 to 1968 served as Director of the Institute of Contemporary Arts in London.

Morris has been a prolific writer, as well as having made several films and presented television programes on social behaviour; many of his works have been produced jointly with his wife Ramona Morris. Probably the best known of his books are *The Naked Ape* (1967), in which he examines the human animal in a brutally objective way, and *The Human Zoo* (1969), which follows on in that he scrutinizes the society that the naked ape has created for itself. Morris compares civilized man with his captive animal counterpart and shows how confined animals seem to demonstrate the same neurotic behaviour patterns as human beings often do in crowded cities. He believes the urban environment of the cities to be the human zoo.

He has done much to popularize sociology and zoology, and is an entertaining presenter of programmes with some social influence.

Morton, William Thomas Green (*1819-1868*), was an American dentist who in 1846 gave the first public demonstration of ether anaesthesia during surgery. Although he was neither the discoverer of the painkilling effects of ether nor the first to use it during a surgical operation, it was largely as a result of his efforts that anaesthesia became quickly and widely adopted by surgeons and dentists.

Little is known about Morton's early years. He was born in Chariton City, Massachusetts, on 9 August 1819, the son of a smallholder and shopkeeper, and is reputed to have graduated from the Baltimore College of Dentistry, although this is uncertain. After a brief period in partnership with Horace Wells, another pioneer in the use of anaesthesia, Morton set up his own dental practice in Boston in 1844 and began investigating ways to deaden pain during dental surgery. After numerous unsuccessful attempts, he consulted the chemist and former physician Charles Jackson (1805-1880), who advised him to try ether as an anaesthetic. (This was not a new idea: Crawford Long (1815-1878) had in 1842 successfully used ether anaesthesia during an operation to remove a tumour from a patient's neck, although he did not publish this work until 1849 – by which time he had been pre-empted by Morton. In addition, Wells used nitrous oxide anaesthesia in a public demonstration – attended and partly arranged by Morton – in 1845, but had failed to convince his spectators of the gas's effectiveness as an anaesthetic.) In 1846 Morton successfully extracted a tooth from a patient under ether and later in the same year staged a public demonstration of ether anaesthesia in an operation (also successful) to remove a facial tumour; this operation was performed at the Massachusetts General Hospital – where Wells had earlier failed in his demonstration. So successful was Morton's demonstration that ether anaesthesia was rapidly adopted by surgeons and dentists in the United States and Europe.

Morton derived no financial benefits from his work. Morton and Jackson had jointly patented the process of ether anaesthesia but Morton attempted to claim sole credit as its discoverer. Jackson strongly contested this claim and Morton spent the rest of his life in costly litigation with him. A large fund was raised for Morton in Britain as an award for his discovery of anaes-thesia but the offer was withdrawn in the face of strong opposition from Jackson. The French Academy of Medicine offered another monetary award to both men jointly, but Morton refused to accept it. Likewise, a bill to award Morton $100,000 in recognition of his work failed to pass in the United States Congress in 1852, 1853 and again in 1854. Meanwhile, official recognition of priority had been accorded to Wells (for discovering nitrous oxide anaesthesia) and Long (for discovering ether anaesthesia). Finally Morton died, bitter and poor, on 15 July 1868 in New York City. Eventually, however, his role in the development of anaesthesia was recognized when he was elected in 1920 to the American Hall of Fame.

Muller, Hermann Joseph (*1890-1967*), was an American geneticist famous for his discovery that genetic mutations can be artificially induced by means of X-rays, for which he was awarded the 1946 Nobel Prize in Physiology and Medicine.

Muller was born on 21 December 1890 in New York City and was educated at Morris High School in the Bronx district of the city. In 1907 he won a scholarship to Columbia University, from which he graduated in 1910. He remained at Columbia to do postgraduate research on genetics – under Thomas Hunt Morgan – and gained his PhD in 1916. Muller then spent three years at the Rice Institute in Houston, Texas, at the invitation of Julian Huxley, followed by a brief period as an Instructor at Columbia University. Then in 1920 he joined the University of Texas, Austin, initially as Associate Professor of Zoology and later as Professor of Zoology. The next 12 years at the University of Texas were the most scientifically productive in Muller's life but eventually the pressure of work, the ending of his marriage to the mathematician Jessie Marie Jacob (whom he married in 1923), and the constraints on his freedom to express his socialist political views all combined to produce a nervous breakdown, and in 1932 Muller left the United States to work at the Kaiser Wilhelm Institute in Berlin. In 1933 he moved to Leningrad to become – at the invitation of Nikolai Vavilov – Senior Geneticist at the Institute of Genetics; the institute was transferred to Moscow in the following year and Muller moved with it. But in the mid-1930s the false ideas of Trofim Lysenko began to dominate Soviet biological research; Muller openly criticized Lysenkoism but so great was Lysenko's political influence that Muller was forced to leave the Soviet Union in 1937. After serving in the Spanish Civil War he worked at the Institute of Animal Genetics in Edinburgh, where in 1939 he met and married Dorothea Kantorowitz, a German refugee. Muller returned to the

United States in 1940. He held various posts at Amherst College, Massachusetts, from 1941 to 1945, when he was appointed Professor of Zoology at Indiana University. He remained there and died on 5 April 1967 in Bloomington, Indiana.

Muller began his research on genetics while working for his doctorate under Morgan, in the course of which he made several important contributions to the understanding of the arrangements and recombinations of genes. During this period he became particularly interested in mutations, and when he began independent research he attempted to find techniques for accelerating mutation rates. In 1919 he found that the mutation rate was increased by heat, and that heat did not always affect both of the chromosomes in a chromosome pair. From this he concluded that mutations involved changes at the molecular or sub-molecular level. Next Muller experimented with X-rays as a means of inducing mutations, and by 1926 he had proved the method successful. This was an important finding because it meant that geneticists could induce mutations when required, rather than having to wait for the considerably slower process of natural mutation, and it also showed that mutations are nothing more than chemical changes.

Muller's research had convinced him that almost all mutations are deleterious. He realized that in the normal course of evolution deleterious mutants die out and the few advantageous ones survive but he also believed that if the mutation rate is too high, the number of imperfect individuals may become too large for the species as a whole to survive. Consequently, he began to concern himself with the social effects of genetic mutations. He campaigned against the needless use of X-rays in diagnosis and treatment, and pressed for safety regulations to ensure that people who were regularly exposed to X-rays were adequately protected. He also opposed nuclear bomb tests, arguing that the radioactive fallout could burden future generations with an excessive number of deleterious mutations. Furthermore, he advocated the establishment of sperm banks, in which the sperm of gifted men could be preserved for use by later generations so that the human gene pool would be improved.

N

Nathans, Daniel (*1928–*), and **Smith, Hamilton Othanel** (*1931–*), are American microbiologists who shared (with Werner Arber, a Swiss microbiologist) the 1978 Nobel Prize in

Physiology and Medicine for their work on restriction enzymes, which are special enzymes that can cleave genes into fragments.

Nathans was born on 30 October 1928 in Wilmington, Delaware. He was educated at the University of Delaware, from which he graduated in 1950, and at Washington University, St Louis, from which he gained his medical degree in 1954. He then worked as a Clinical Associate at the National Cancer Institute until 1957, when he became a resident physician at the Columbia-Presby Medical Center. From 1959 to 1962 he was a guest investigator at the Rockefeller University, New York City, after which he held several positions at the Johns Hopkins University, Baltimore: Assistant Professor then Professor of Microbiology at the School of Medicine there between 1962 and 1976, Director of the Department of Microbiology since 1972 and Boury Professor of Microbiology since 1976.

Smith was born on 23 August 1931 in New York City. He was educated at the University of California, Berkeley, from which he graduated in mathematics in 1952, and at the Johns Hopkins University, from which he obtained his medical degree in 1956. From 1956 to 1957 he was a junior resident physician at Barnes Hospital, then carried out research at the Henry Ford Hospital, Detroit, from 1959 until 1962, when he became a research fellow in microbial genetics at the University of Michigan. Since 1964 he has been at the Johns Hopkins University, as a Research Assistant, Assistant Professor, Associate Professor and, from 1973, Professor of Microbiology at the School of Medicine. He was also Guggenheim Professor there between 1975 and 1976.

Arber discovered restriction enzymes in *Escherichia coli* in the 1960s. These enzymes cleave genes at specific sites on the DNA molecules and thus enable the order of genes on the chromosomes to be determined. The gene fragments can also be used to analyse the chemical structure of genes as well as to create new gene combinations. Smith, working at the Johns Hopkins University independently of Arber, verified Arber's findings and was also able to identify the gene fragments. Smith collaborated with Nathans on some of his work, but Nathans also performed much original research of his own in this field. Using the carcinogenic SV40 virus, he showed in 1971 that it could be cleaved into 11 specific fragments, and in the following year he determined the order of these fragments.

As a result of the work of Nathans, Smith and Arber, it is now possible to determine the chemical formulae of the genes in animal viruses, to map these genes and to study the organization and expression of genes in higher animals.

Needham, Joseph (*1900-*   ), is a British biochemist, science historian and Orientalist whose
most important scientific contribution was in the
field of biochemical embryology. In the later part
of his career his interests turned to the history of
science, particularly the development of science
in China.

Needham was born in London in December
1900, the son of one of the first Harley Street
specialists in anaesthesia. He attended Oundle
School and during the school holidays assisted in
military hospitals, which were greatly under-
staffed due to the influx of casualties from World
War I. From Oundle he went on to study natural
sciences at Gonville and Caius College, Cambridge. On graduation in 1921 he was offered a
place in the research laboratory of Frederick
Gowland Hopkins, and subsequently gained his
doctorate and was elected a Fellow of Gonville
and Caius College. In the same year he married
Dorothy Moyle, a fellow student at Hopkins'
laboratory; she was a talented scientist and her
work on the biochemistry of muscles led to her
election as a Fellow of the Royal Society in 1948
(Needham himself had become a member in
1941).

In 1928 Needham was appointed University
Demonstrator in Biochemistry at Cambridge,
then in 1933 he became Dunn Reader in Biochemistry (also at Cambridge), a post he held until
1966. It was during this latter period that he pro-
gressively reduced his scientific work and became
increasingly devoted to studying Chinese science
and culture. He learned Chinese, and in 1942
accepted an invitation to head the British Scientific Mission to China; he spent the next four
years travelling through the country. From 1946
to 1948 he was head of the Division of Natural
Sciences at the United Nations, after which he
returned to Cambridge. He was elected Master of
Gonville and Caius College in 1966 and held this
post until 1976, when he retired in order to pursue
his Oriental studies at the East Asian History of
Science Library in Cambridge. Needham travelled extensively throughout his career, visiting
and lecturing in numerous universities in the
United States, Europe and Asia.

Needham's principal scientific contributions
were made in the first half of his academic career.
Initially he worked on the biochemistry of embryonic development, trying to discover the processes underlying the development of a fertilized
egg from a mass of undifferentiated cells into a
highly differentiated complex organism. In his
three-volume *Chemical Embryology* (1931) Needham surveyed the morphogenetic changes and the
various attempts to explain them, concluding that
embryonic development is controlled chemically

- in contrast to the traditional vitalistic view of
Otto Driesch and others, which held that some
indefinite principle (called entelechy) caused embryonic changes. The discovery of morphogenetic
hormones that control embryonic development
confirmed Needham's mechanistic view, and he
proceeded - in collaboration with Conrad Wad-
dington (1905-   ) - to hypothesize (before the
discovery of DNA) that only structural chemistry
could fully explain the complex changes that occur
during an organism's development. In *Order and
Life* (1935) Needham foresaw the importance of
organelles, anticipating some of the discoveries
about the microstructure of living cells that later
resulted from electron microscopy.

From about the mid-1930s Needham became
increasingly interested in the history of science,
particularly of Chinese science, and he progres-
sively reduced his scientific investigations in order
to devote himself to a comprehensive study of the
development of Chinese science and culture. The
first volume of *Science and Civilization in China*
was published in 1954 and has since been followed
by several more volumes in this huge synthesis of
history, science and culture in China.

Oparin, Alexandr Ivanovich (*1894-1980*), was a
Soviet biochemist who made important contributions to evolutionary biochemistry, developing
one of the first of the modern theories about the
origin of life on Earth. He received many honours
for his work, particularly from the Soviet Union.

Oparin was born on 3 March 1894 in the small
village of Uglich, north of Moscow, the youngest
of three children. When he was nine years old, his
family moved to Moscow because Uglich had no
secondary school. He studied plant physiology at
Moscow State University, where he was influenced by K.A. Timiryazev, a plant physiologist
who had known Charles Darwin. After graduating in 1917, Oparin researched in biochemistry
under A.N. Bakh, a botanist, then in 1929 became
Professor of Plant Biochemistry at Moscow State
University. In 1935 he helped to found, and began
working at, the Bakh Institute of Biochemistry in
Moscow, which was established in honour of his
former teacher. Oparin became Director of the
Bakh Institute in 1946 and held this post until his
death in April 1980.

Oparin first put forward his ideas about the
origin of life in 1922 at a meeting of the Russian
Botanical Society. His theory contained three
basic premises: that the first organisms arose in

the ancient seas, which contained many already formed organic compounds that the organisms used as nutriment (thus his hypothetical first organisms did not synthesize their own organic nutrients but took them in ready-made from the surrounding water); that there was a constant, virtually limitless supply of external energy in the form of sunlight (thus conditions in which the first forms of life arose did not constitute a closed system and were not limited by the second law of thermodynamics); and that true life was characterized by a high degree of structural and functional organization, an idea that was contrary to the prevailing view that life was basically molecular.

Oparin's theory did not explain how complex molecules could have arisen in the primordial seas, nor how his primitive organisms could reproduce. Later research, however, suggested that a degree of order in the structure of proteins might have occurred as a result of the restrictions imposed on the coupling of amino acids due to their different shapes and distributions of electric charge. Regarding reproduction, later experiments with microscopic coacervate droplets of gelatin and gum arabic demonstrated that these droplets repeatedly grow and reproduce by budding off. Oparin then showed that enzymes function more efficiently inside such synthetic cells than they do in ordinary aqueous solution.

Oparin's theory (which was first published in 1924, although it reached its widest audience after 1936, when he published *The Origin of Life on Earth*) stimulated much research into the origin of life, perhaps the most famous of which is Stanley Miller's attempt in 1953 to reproduce primordial conditions in the laboratory. In his experiment, Miller put sterile water, methane, ammonia and hydrogen (simulating the primordial atmosphere) in a sealed container and subjected the mixture to electrical discharges (simulating lightning). After one week he found that the solution contained simple organic compounds, including amino acids. In addition, C. Ponnamperuma, using slightly different experimental conditions, demonstrated that nucleotides, dinucleotides and ATP can be formed from simple ingredients.

Although best known for his pioneering work on the origins of life, Oparin also researched into enzymology and did much to provide a technical basis for industrial biochemistry in the Soviet Union.

P

Paget, James (*1814–1899*), was a British surgeon, one of the founders of pathology. He is best remembered for describing two conditions named after him: Paget's disease of the nipple, a precancerous disorder, and Paget's disease of the bone, or osteodystrophia deformans. From a fairly humble beginning he rose to be one of the greatest and most respected surgeons of his time.

Paget was born in Great Yarmouth on 11 January 1814. He went to school in Yarmouth, but had to leave at the age of 13 when his father's business ran into hard times. At 16 he became apprenticed to the local surgeon apothecary, Charles Costerton, and in 1834 his elder brother George paid for him to go to St Bartholomew's Hospital in London, where despite the poor standard of teaching at the time, he gained his MRCS in 1836. In his struggle to make up his income, Paget took pupils, worked as a sub-editor on the *Medical Gazette*, reported lectures, reviewed books and translated works. It was not until he became warden of the students' residential college at St Bartholomew's in 1843 that he was able to give up his journalism. He was one of the original 300 Fellows of the Royal College of Surgeons of England in 1843, where he later became Professor of Anatomy and Surgery (1847-1852). At the age of 33 he became Assistant Surgeon at St Bartholomew's Hospital, and four years later in 1851 had his own practice in Cavendish Square. In 1878 he tended the Princess of Wales and his fame spread. He became a rich man, and was appointed Surgeon Extraordinary to Queen Victoria and became a close friend of the Royal Family. During a post-mortem in 1871, Paget contracted a severe infection, through a cut, which left him unable to continue his hospital work, although he did maintain his consulting rooms. He received a baronetcy in 1871 and was a member of the General Medical Council, the Senate of the University of London, and President of the Royal College of Surgeons (1874). He died on 30 December 1899, and his funeral was held at Westminster Abbey.

Paget's original clinical descriptions of the two conditions named after him were so accurate that virtually nothing has needed to be added to them since. Paget's disease of the nipple was described in 1874 and is an eczematous skin eruption that indicates an underlying carcinoma of the breast, although the eruption is not simply an extension of the cancer cells inside the breast. Histologically

Paget cells can be identified and are pathognomonic of the condition.

When Paget described the disease of the bone in 1877, he referred to it as osteitis deformans. This implies an inflammation of the bone, which is not accurate and it is now called osteodystrophia deformans. Paget did, however, accurately describe this idiopathic condition which can affect the bones of the elderly, particularly the femora and tibiae in the legs and the bones of the skull. The bones soften giving rise to deformity of the limbs, which may also fracture easily. If the skull is affected bony changes cause enlargement of the head, and pressure on the VIIIth cranial nerve can cause deafness.

Paracelsus (Philippus Aureolus Theophrastus Bombast von Hohenheim) *(1493-1541)*, was a Swiss physician and chemist whose works did much to overthrow the accepted scientific authorities of his day (such as Galen) and to establish the importance of chemistry in medicine. He adopted the name Paracelsus as a claim to superiority over the Roman physician Celsus, whose works had recently been translated.

Paracelsus was born on or about 10 November 1493 in Einsiedeln, Switzerland, the son of a doctor. On his mother's death, he and his father moved to Villach, Austria, where he attended the Bergschule. This local school specialized in teaching mineralogy to students who would later work in the mines nearby. In 1507 he became, like many of his contemporaries, a wandering scholar. He is said to have obtained a baccalaureate in medicine from the University of Vienna, to have been to the University of Basel and to have studied at several universities in Italy, and may have received a doctorate from Ferrara. He was a military surgeon in Venice in 1521 and then continued his travels as far as Constantinople. He returned to Villach in 1524 and by 1525 had set himself up in medical practice. He was successful enough to be elected Professor of Medicine at Basel from 1527 to 1528. Here he scandalized other academics by lecturing in the vernacular and by his savage attacks on the accepted medical texts. In 1527 he burned the works of Galen and Avicenna in public and the next year was forced to leave Basel. He spent several years travelling once more and then returned to Villach, when he was appointed physician to Duke Ernst of Bavaria, in 1541. He died in Salzburg on 24 September of that year.

Paracelsus substituted the traditional medical theories with an animistic view of nature, believing that all matter possesses its characteristic spirits or life substances, which he called *entia*. He emphasized the importance of the observation of the properties of all things and it was this principle that led him to discover new remedies and means of treatment for many illnesses, some of which he characterized accurately for the first time.

Chemical therapy had been used in the ancient world, although chiefly externally. Paracelsus, however, realized the therapeutic power of chemicals taken internally, although he imposed strict control on their use, dosage and purity. Paracelsus was extremely successful as a doctor. His descriptions of miners' diseases first identified silicosis and tuberculosis as occupational hazards. He also recognized goitre as endemic and related to minerals in drinking water, and originated a medical account of chorea, rather than believing this nervous disease to be caused by possession by spirits. Paracelsus was the first to recognize the congenital form of syphilis, and to distinguish it from the infectious form. He showed that it could be successfully treated with carefully controlled doses of a mercury compound.

Paracelsus' study of alchemy helped to develop it into chemistry. His investigations produced new, non-toxic compounds for medicinal use; he discovered new substances arising from the reaction of metals and described various organic compounds, including ether. He was the first to devise such advanced laboratory techniques as the concentration of alcohol by freezing. Paracelsus also devised a specific nomenclature for substances already known, but not precisely defined. Paracelsian chemicals were introduced into the *London Pharmacopoeia* of 1618, and his attempt to construct a chemical system, grouping chemicals according to their susceptibility to similar processes, was the first of its kind.

Paracelsus' concept of man as a "microcosm" of the natural world led to his theory of an external agency being the source of disease, overturning contemporary views which regarded illness as an imbalance of the four humours (blood, phlegm, choler and spleen) within the body. His ideas encouraged new modes of treatment supplanting, for example, bloodletting, and opened the way for new ideas on the source of infection.

Despite Paracelsus' mystical preoccupations such as astrology and the use of magic seals and amulets, his importance to the development of science is substantial. He can be regarded as a founder of modern medicine, as he was the first to demand that a doctor should master all those arts then divided between barbers, field-surgeons, apothecaries, alchemists and local "wise women". His revolutionary views and vitriolic nature continually involved him in clashes with authority, and his investigations into "forbidden fields" led to frequent accusations against him of sorcery and heresy. Nevertheless, within his works lie the stepping stones between ancient and modern science.

Pasteur, Louis (*1822-1895*), was a French chemist and microbiologist who became world famous for originating the process of pasteurization and for establishing the validity of the germ theory of disease, although he also made many other scientific contributions. Regarded as one of the greatest scientists in history, he received many honours during his lifetime, including the Legion of Honour, France's highest award.

Pasteur was born on 27 December 1822 in Dôle in eastern France, the son of a tanner. While he was still young, his family moved to Arbois, where he attended primary and secondary schools. He was not a particularly good student, but he showed an aptitude for painting and mathematics and his initial ambition was to become a professor of fine arts. He continued his education at the Royal College in Besançon, from which he gained his BA in 1840 and his BSc in 1842. In 1843 Pasteur entered the École Normale Supérieure in Paris, where he began to study chemistry and from which he gained his doctorate in 1847. In the following year he was appointed Professor of Physics at the Dijon Lycée but shortly afterwards, in early 1849, he accepted the post of Professor of Chemistry at the University of Strasbourg. In the same year he married Marie Laurent, the daughter of the university's rector; later they had five children, only two of whom survived beyond childhood. In 1862 Pasteur was elected to the French Academy of Sciences, and in 1863 to a chair at the École Normale Supérieure, a position that was created for him so that he could institute an original teaching programme that related chemistry, physics and geology to the fine arts. Also in 1863 he became Dean of the new science faculty at Lille University, where he initiated the novel concept of evening classes for workmen. Meanwhile, in 1857 he had been appointed Director of Scientific Studies at the École Normale Supérieure. Because of the pressure of his research work, Pasteur resigned from the directorship in 1867 but, with financial assistance from Emperor Napoleon III, a laboratory of physiological chemistry was established for him at the École. Pasteur suffered a stroke in 1868 but, although partly paralysed, continued his work. In 1873 he was made a member of the French Academy of Medicine, and in the following year the French parliament granted him a special monetary award to guarantee his financial security while he pursued his research. In 1882 he was elected to the Academie Française. In 1888 the Pasteur Institute was created in Paris for the purpose of continuing Pasteur's pioneering research into rabies, and he headed this establishment until his death, in Paris, on 28 September 1895.

Pasteur first gained recognition through his early work on the optical activity of stereoisomers. In 1848 he presented a paper to the Paris Academy of Sciences in which he reported that there are two molecular forms of tartaric acid, one that rotates plane polarized light to the right and another (a mirror image of the first) that rotates it to the left. In addition, he showed that one form can be assimilated by living micro-organisms whereas its optical antipode cannot.

Pasteur began his biological investigations – for which he is best known – while at Lille University. After receiving a query from an industrialist about wine- and beermaking, Pasteur started researching into fermentation. Using a microscope he found that properly aged wine contains small spherical globules of yeast cells whereas sour wine contains elongated yeast cells. He also proved that fermentation does not require oxygen, but that it nevertheless involves living micro-organisms and that to produce the correct type of fermentation (alcohol-producing rather than lactic acid-producing) it is necessary to use the correct type of yeast. Pasteur also realized that after wine has formed, it must be gently heated to about 50°C to kill the yeast and thereby prevent souring during the ageing process. Pasteurization – as this heating process is called today – is now widely used in the food-processing industry.

Pasteur then turned his attention to spontaneous generation, a problem that had once again become a matter of controversy, despite Lazzaro Spallanzani's disproof of the theory about a century previously. Pasteur showed that dust in the air contains spores of living organisms which reproduce when introduced into a nutrient broth. Then he boiled the broth in a container with a U-shaped tube that allowed air to reach the broth but trapped dust in the U-bend. He found that the broth remained free of living organisms, thereby again disproving the theory of spontaneous generation. (In the twentieth century, however, the theory yet again became a matter of dispute.)

In the mid-1860s the French silk industry was seriously threatened by a disease that killed silkworms and Pasteur was commissioned by the government to investigate the disease. In 1868 he announced that he had found a minute parasite that infects the silkworms, and recommended that all infected silkworms be destroyed. His advice was followed and the disease eliminated. This stimulated his interest in infectious diseases and, from the results of his previous work on fermentation, spontaneous generation and the silkworm disease, Pasteur developed the germ theory of disease. This theory was probably the most important single medical discovery of all time, because it provided both a practical method of combating disease by disinfection and a theoretical foundation for further research.

Continuing his research into disease, in 1881 Pasteur developed a method for reducing the virulence of certain pathogenic micro-organisms. By heating a preparation of anthrax bacilli he attenuated their virulence but found that they still brought about the full immune response when injected into sheep. Using a similar method, Pasteur then inoculated fowl against chicken cholera. He was thus following the work of Edward Jenner, who first vaccinated against cowpox in 1796. In 1882 Pasteur began what proved to be his most spectacular research: the prevention of rabies. He demonstrated that the causative micro-organism (actually a virus, although their existence was not known at that time) infects the nervous system and then, using the dried tissues of infected animals, he eventually succeeded in obtaining an attenuated form of the virus suitable for the inoculation of human beings. The culmination of this work came on 6 July 1885, when Pasteur used his vaccine to save the life of a young boy who had been bitten by a rabid dog. The success of this experiment brought Pasteur even greater acclaim and led to the establishment of the Pasteur Institute in 1888.

Pavlov, Ivan Petrovitch (*1849-1936*), was a Russian physiologist, best known for his systematic studies of the conditioning of dogs and other animals. For his observations on the gastrointestinal secretion in animals he received the 1904 Nobel Prize in Physiology and Medicine.

Pavlov was born in Ryazan on 24 September 1849. He decided to follow in the footsteps of his father, the local priest, and entered a theological college. In 1870, however, he left the seminary to study chemistry and physiology at the University of St Petersburg (now Leningrad). There he was taught by the Russian chemists Dmitri Mendeleyev (1834-1907) and Alexander Butlerov (1828-1886). He received his medical degree in 1879 from the Imperial Medical Academy, St Petersburg, and his PhD from the Military Academy there in 1883. From 1884 to 1886 he studied cardiovascular and gastrointestinal physiology under Karl Ludwig in Leipzig and Rudolf Heidenhain in Breslau. He researched at the Botkin laboratory in St Petersburg from 1888 to 1890 and in that year was appointed Professor of Physiology at the Imperial Medical Academy, where he remained until he resigned in 1924. He died in Leningrad on 27 February 1936.

Pavlov's first unaided research was on the physiology of the circulatory system, studying cardiac physiology and the regulation of blood pressure. Using experimental animals, he became a surgeon of some distinction, a typical example of his experiments being the dissection of the cardiac nerves of a living dog to show how the nerves that leave the cardiac plexus control heartbeat strength.

During the years from 1890 to 1900, Pavlov investigated the secretory mechanisms of digestion. He developed an operation to prepare an ancillary miniature stomach or pouch, isolated from salivary and pancreatic secretions but with its vagal nerve supply intact. In this way he was able to observe the gastrointestinal secretion of a living animal.

Pavlov then went on to develop the idea of the conditional reflex - the discovery for which he is most famous. Pavlov confined a dog in a soundproof room, in order to ensure that there were no distracting influences such as extraneous sounds and smells. The dog was held in a loose harness so that it could not move about too much. Food was delivered to it by an automatic apparatus operated from outside the room, so that the dog was fed at an appropriate moment without direct interference from the person directing the experiment. The flow of saliva from the dog's parotid gland was collected in a small measuring tube attached to the animal's cheek. The experiment was continued until the dog became used to the artificial situation. Pavlov discovered that if a neutral stimulus, such as a bell, was presented simultaneously with a natural stimulus to salivate (such as the sight of food) and the combination repeated often enough, the sound of the bell alone caused salivation.

Pavlov termed salivation the "unconditioned reflex" and food the "unconditioned stimulus". The sound of the bell is the "conditioned stimulus" and the salivation caused by the bell alone the "conditioned reflex". Many inborn reflexes may be conditioned by Pavlov's method, including responses involving the skeletal muscles (knee-jerking and blinking), as well as responses of the smooth muscles and glands.

A similar approach was developed in Pavlov's work relating to human behaviour and the nervous system, all the time emphasizing the importance of conditioning. He deduced that the inhibitive behaviour of a psychotic person is a means of self-protection. The person shuts out the world and, with it, all damaging stimuli. Following this theory, the treatment of psychiatric patients in Russia involved placing a sick person in completely calm and quiet surroundings.

Pavlov's study of the normal animal in natural conditions enabled him to add greatly to scientific knowledge. He also demonstrated the necessity of providing the right situation for completely objective study and measurement of behaviour, and greatly improved operative and post-operative conditions for animals.

In 1897 Pavlov summarized his findings in his Nobel prize-winning work - *Lectures on the Work of the Principal Digestive Gland.*

Pennycuick, Colin James (*1933-*), is a British biologist who is best known for his extremely detailed studies of flight.

Pennycuick was born in Virginia Water, Surrey, on 11 June 1933, the son of an army officer. He graduated from Merton College, Oxford, in 1956 and obtained his doctorate from Peterhouse College, Cambridge, in 1962. In 1964 he became a lecturer in zoology at Bristol University, with a break between 1971 and 1973 while he was researching at Nairobi University in Kenya.

Pennycuick's research is unusual in that it inter-relates an extremely large number of factors and therefore gives a very detailed account of the various processes involved in flight. In flying vertebrates, for example, he has investigated the mechanics of flapping; the aerodynamic effects of the feet and tail; the physiology of gaseous exchange; heat disposal; the relationship between the size and anatomy of a flying creature and the power it develops; and the frequency of wing beats. In applying the results of his research to bird migration he discovered that many migratory birds have minimal energy reserves and must stop to feed at regular intervals. Therefore the destruction of the intermediate feeding places of these birds could lead to their extinction, even if their summer and winter quarters are conserved. Pennycuick has also hypothesized that migratory birds navigate using the Sun's altitude and its changing position.

Pfeffer, Wilhelm Friedrich Philipp (*1845*-1920), was a German physiological botanist who is best known for his contributions to the study of osmotic pressures, which is important in both biology and chemistry.

Pfeffer was born in Grebenstein, near Kassel, on 9 March 1845, the son of a pharmacist. He went to Göttingen University to study botany and chemistry, and gained his doctorate in 1865. He then went to Marburg University, where he spent several years studying botany and pharmacy. From 1867 to 1870 he studied botany as a private assistant to Nathanael Pringsheim (1823–1894), an algae botanist in Berlin, and then from 1870 to 1871 he worked under the plant physiologist Julius von Sachs (1832–1897) at the University of Würzburg. In 1871 Pfeffer returned to Marburg as

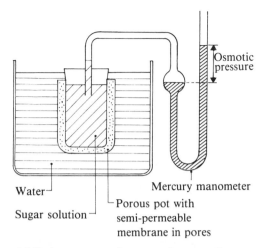

Pfeffer's apparatus for measuring osmotic pressure.

a Privatdozent (an official but unpaid lecturer) and in 1873 he became Extraordinarius at Bonn University, a post he held until 1877, when he was appointed to a professorship at Basel University. In the following year Pfeffer accepted a professorship at Tübingen University, then in 1887 became a professor at Leipzig University. He died on 31 January 1920 in Leipzig.

Pfeffer made the first ever quantitative determinations of osmotic pressure in 1877. The apparatus he used consisted of a semi-permeable container of sugar solution inside immersed in a vessel of water. He connected a mercury-filled manometer to the top of the semi-permeable container to measure the osmotic pressure after the solute and water had reached equilibrium. Using these pressure measurements he also showed that osmotic pressure varies according to the temperature and concentration of the solute. Other scientists later made independent determinations of osmotic pressure and confirmed Pfeffer's results. In addition, Jacobus Van't Hoff established that the osmotic pressure of a solution is analogous to gaseous pressure: a solute (if not dissociated) exerts the same osmotic pressure as the gaseous pressure it would exert if it were a gas occupying the same volume at the same temperature. Pfeffer's work on osmosis led to the modern understanding of osmometry and was of fundamental importance in the study of cell membranes, because semi-permeable membranes surround all cells and play a large part in controlling the internal environment of cells.

In addition to his work on osmosis, Pfeffer also studied respiration, photosynthesis, protein metabolism, and transport in plants. He published more than 100 scientific papers and books, and his three-volume *Handbuch der Pflanzenphysiologie* (translated in 1906 as *Physiology of Plants*) was an important text for many years.

Piaget, Jean (*1896-1980*), was a Swiss psychologist who is famous for his pioneering studies of the development of thought processes, particularly in children. He is generally considered to be one of the most important figures in modern developmental psychology and his work has had a great influence on educational theory and child psychology. He received many international honours for his work, including seven scientific prizes and 25 honorary degrees.

Piaget was born on 9 August 1896 in Neuchâtel, Switzerland. He published his first scientific article (about an albino sparrow) when he was only 10 years old, and by the age of 15 he had gained an international reputation for his work on molluscs. Subsequently he studied at the universities of Neuchâtel, Zurich and Paris, obtaining his doctorate from Neuchâtel in 1918. His interest then turned to psychology and he spent two years at the Sorbonne researching into the reasons why children fail intelligence tests. The results of this research gained him the directorship of the Institut J.J. Rousseau in Geneva in 1921. During his subsequent career Piaget held many academic positions, some of which were concurrent. He was Professor of Philosophy at Neuchâtel from 1926 to 1929; Professor of Child Psychology and History of Scientific Thought at Geneva University from 1929 to 1939; Director of the Institut Universitaire des Sciences de l'Education in Geneva from 1933 to 1971; Professor of Psychology and Sociology at Lausanne University from 1938 to 1951; Professor of Sociology (1938 to 1952) and of Experimental Psychology (1940 to 1971) at Geneva University; Professor of Genetic Psychology at the Sorbonne from 1952 to 1963; and Director of the International Bureau of Education in Geneva from 1929 to 1967. In 1955, with the help of the Rockefeller Foundation and the Swiss National Foundation for Scientific Research, Piaget founded the International Centre of Genetic Epistemology at Geneva University, which he continued to direct after he retired in 1971. He also held several positions with UNESCO at various times during his life. Piaget died in Geneva on 16 September 1980.

Piaget's work on concept formation in children falls into two main phases: an early phase (from 1924 to 1937) in which he established the basic differences between thought processes in children and those in adults, and a late phase (after 1937) in which he carried out detailed investigations of thought development and evolved his theories

about concept formation in children – his best-known work.

In his early work Piaget showed how radically different are the mental processes of children from those of adults: according to his theory – which resembles Sigmund Freud's ideas about the development of the Id, Ego and Superego – children's mental processes are dominated by an egocentric attitude, being influenced mainly by the wishes and inner needs of the child, but as the child develops, his thinking becomes increasingly dominated by the influence of the external environment.

After 1937 Piaget carried out much more rigorous investigations into the origin and development of logical and mathematical concepts in children, and attempted to trace the growth of reasoning capacities from birth to maturity. In developing his famous theory of concept development, Piaget invented a new type of logic (called psycho-logic) in an attempt to apply pure logic to experimental psychology, and as a result of this his writings are highly technical. Stated simply, however, Piaget's theory postulates four main stages in the development of mental processes: sensorimeter, pre-operational, concrete operational and formal operational.

In the sensorimeter stage, which lasts from birth to the age of about two years, infants obtain a basic knowledge of objects by empirical experimentation. Gradually a child forms concepts of objects, and learns that they continue to exist even when out of sight. The pre-operational stage lasts from the age of two years to the age of seven years. In this stage a child learns to imitate and begins to represent concrete objects with words – language starts to develop. From seven to 12 years old a child is in the concrete operational stage; he or she develops the concept of number, begins to classify objects according to their similarities and differences, and can distinguish between past and present. Finally, from 12 onwards, a child is in the formal operational stage, which is characterized by the development of logical thought and mathematical ability; thinking also becomes more flexible – hypotheses are formed and experimented with, for example.

Although it has been criticized for being based on observations of only a small number of subjects, Piaget's work on the development of mental processes is generally considered to be a major achievement and has greatly influenced child psychology and educational theory and practice, particularly the teaching of mathematics.

Porter, Rodney Robert (*1917-*   ), is a British immunologist well known for his contribution to the identification of the structure of antibody molecules. For this work he received the 1972 Nobel Prize in Physiology and Medicine, which he shared with the American Gerald Edelman (1929-).

Porter was born in Liverpool on 8 October 1917 and was educated at Ashton-in-Makerfield Grammar School, and then at Liverpool University, where he gained a BSc in 1939. From 1940 to 1946, including much of World War II, he was in military service. He then returned to Cambridge (gaining his PhD in 1948) and continued his research, aided by Frederick Sanger. In 1949 he was appointed to the staff of the National Institute for Medical Research, a position he held until 1960 when he became Pfizer Professor of Immunology at St Mary's Hospital Medical School, London. From 1967 he was Whitley Professor of Biochemistry at Oxford, and Honorary Director of the Medical Research Council's Immunochemistry Unit.

When Porter started his research after the war, he often referred to Karl Landsteiner's book *The Specificity of Serological Reactions*, and it was from this work that he learnt the technique for preparing certain antibodies. Some aspects of the structural studies of immunoglobins, or antibodies, had been completed, such as those for several human myeloma proteins and some rabbit immunoglobulins. Some work had also been done on the structural basis of the combining specificity of antibodies and in the solution of the genetic origins of antibodies. Porter's major scientific interests have been the structural basis of the biological activities of antibodies - in 1962 he proposed a structure for gamma globulin - and he is now involved in the structure, assembly and activation mechanisms of the components of a substance known as complement. This is a protein normally present in the blood, but which disappears from the serum during most antigen-antibody reactions. Porter is also investigating the way in which immunoglobulins interact with complement components and with cell surfaces.

Purkinje, Jan Evangelista (*1787-1869*), was a Czech histologist and physiologist ·whose pioneering studies were of great importance to our modern knowledge of vision, the functioning of the brain and heart, pharmacology, embryology and histology.

Purkinje was born on 17 December 1787 in Libochovice, Bohemia (now in Czechoslovakia), and was educated there by piarist monks (members of a religious congregation established in 1597 to educate the poor). Before being ordained a priest, however, he went to Prague University to study philosophy but changed to medicine, in which he graduated in 1819 with his famous thesis

on the visual phenomenon now known as the Purkinje effect. After graduating he worked as an assistant in the Department of Physiology at Prague University until 1823, when he was appointed Professor of Physiology and Pathology at the University of Breslau (now Wroclaw in Poland) - perhaps through the influence of the famous German poet Goethe, who had previously befriended Purkinje. At Breslau University Purkinje founded the world's first official physiological institute. In 1850 he returned to Prague University as Professor of Physiology, a post he held until his death on 28 July 1869 (in Prague).

In his famous graduation thesis Purkinje described the visual phenomenon in which, as the light intensity decreases, different coloured objects of equal brightness in high light intensities appear to the eye to be unequally bright - blue objects appear brighter than red objects; this phenomenon is now called the Purkinje effect. In 1832 he was the first to describe what are now known as Purkinje's images: a threefold image of a single object seen by one person reflected in the eye of another person. This effect is caused by the object being reflected by the surface of the cornea and by the anterior and posterior surfaces of the eye lens.

Probably Purkinje's best-known histological work was his discovery in 1837 of large nerve cells with numerous dendrites found in the cortex of the cerebellum; these cells are called Purkinje cells. Two years later he discovered the Purkinje fibres - atypical muscle fibres lying beneath the endocardium that conduct the pacemaker stimulus along the inside walls of the ventricles to every part of the heart. Also in 1839, in describing the contents of animal embryos, Purkinje was the first to use the term protoplasm in the scientific sense.

Purkinje made numerous other important discoveries and observations. In 1823 he recognized that fingerprints can be used as a means of identification. In 1825, while examining birds' eggs, he discovered the germinal vesicle, or nucleus, of unripe ova; this structure is now sometimes called the Purkinje vesicle. He discovered the sweat glands in skin in 1833 and, in 1835, described in detail the structure of the skin. In that year he also described ciliary motion. In 1836 he observed that pancreatic extracts can digest protein, and in 1837 he outlined the principal features of the cell theory - before Theodor Schwann and Matthias Schleiden enunciated this theory in detail. Purkinje also described the effects on the human body of camphor, opium, belladonna and turpentine. And he did much to improve microscopical techniques, being the first to use the microtome, and using glacial acetic acid, potassium dichromate and Canada balsam in the preparation of tissue samples; moreover, he was one of the first to teach microscopy as part of his university course.

In addition to his scientific work, Purkinje also translated the poetry of Goethe and Schiller.

Pye, John David (*1932-*), is a British zoologist who has performed important research in the field of ultrasonic bio-acoustics, particularly in bats.

Pye was born on 14 May 1932 in Mansfield, Nottinghamshire. He was educated at Queen Elizabeth's Grammar School, Aberystweth University (from which he graduated in 1954), and London University (from which he obtained his doctorate in 1961). From 1958 to 1964 he was a zoology research assistant, after which he became a lecturer at King's College, London. In 1970 he was appointed Reader at King's College, then in 1973 he joined the staff of Queen Mary College, London, initially as Professor of Zoology then from 1977 as Head of the Zoology Department.

A surprisingly large number of animals use ultrasound (which has a frequency above about 20 kHz and is inaudible to humans) - bats, the Cetacea (whales, porpoises and dolphins) and many insects, for example. Because of the lack of sufficiently sophisticated detection devices, the phenomenon was not discovered until 1935 (by Pierce, then Professor of Physics at Harvard University), although the first indication that bats use a system other than sight for navigation came with Lazzaro Spallanzani's discovery in 1794 that blinded bats still managed to find food. Even today, with sensitive electronic instruments widely available, biological ultrasound is relatively little studied. Pye is one of the few investigators in this field and has examined the use of ultrasound in many different animals, although he is best known for his work on echolocation in bats. In 1971 he calculated the resonant frequencies of the drops of water in fog and found that these frequencies coincided with the spectrum of frequencies used by bats for echolocation. For this reason, fog absorbs the ultrasound emitted by bats and renders useless their echolocation systems; this is probably the reason why bats avoid flying in fog. Pye also found that ultrasound seems to be important in the social behaviour of rodents and insects which, since many of these creatures are pests, raises the possibility of developing novel control measures.

R

Ramón y Cajal, Santiago (*1852-1934*), was a Spanish histologist whose research revealed that the nervous system is based on units of nerve cells (neurons). For his discovery he shared the 1906 Nobel Prize for Physiology and Medicine with Camillo Golgi.

Ramón y Cajal was born on 1 May 1852, in Petilla de Aragon, Spain, the son of a country doctor. At the insistence of his father he studied medicine at the University of Zaragoza, but he took little interest in the course other than anatomy. He qualified in 1873 and then joined the army medical service, which sent him to Cuba. There he caught malaria and was discharged; he returned to Zaragoza and obtained a doctorate in anatomy in 1877. In 1884 he was appointed Professor of Descriptive Anatomy at the University of Valencia and in 1887 he took up the Histology professorship at the University of Barcelona. From 1892 to 1921 he served at the University of Madrid as Professor of Histology and Pathological Anatomy becoming Director of the new Instituto Nacional de Higiene in 1900. In 1921 he retired from the university to become Director of the Cajal Institute in Madrid, founded in his honour by King Alfonso XIII, and retained this position until he died, in Madrid, on 17 October 1934.

When Ramón y Cajal commenced his research, the path of a nervous impulse was unknown. In his investigations he used potassium dichromate and silver nitrate to stain sections of embryonic tissue, improving on the procedure developed by Golgi.

By this means he demonstrated that the axons of neurons end in the grey matter of the central nervous system and never join the endings of other axons or the cell bodies of other nerve cells. He considered that these findings indicate that the nervous system consists entirely of independent units and is not a network as was previously thought. In 1897 Ramón y Cajal investigated the human cerebral cortex using methylene blue (also used by Paul Ehrlich) as well as Golgi's silver nitrate stain. He described several types of neurons and demonstrated that there were distinct structural patterns in different parts of the cerebral cortex. His findings indicated that structure might well be related to the localization of a particular function to a specific area. In 1903 he found that silver nitrate stained structures within the cell body, which he identified as neurofibrils, and that the cell body itself was concerned with conduction.

During his years at Madrid University, Ramón y Cajal concerned himself with the generation and degeneration of nerve fibres. He demonstrated that when a nerve fibre regenerates it does so by growing from the stump of the fibre still connected with the cell body. In 1913 he developed a gold sublimate to stain nerve structures, which is now valuable in the study of tumours of the central nervous system.

Modern neurology has its foundations in Ramón y Cajal's meticulous work because his investigations are the basis of modern understanding of the part played by the neuron in the nervous function, and of the nervous impulse. He published numerous scientific papers and books, among them the classic *Structure of the Nervous System of Man and other Vertebrates* (1904) and *The Degeneration and Regeneration of the Nervous System* (1913-1914).

Ray, John (*1627-1705*), was a British naturalist whose plant and animal classifications were the first significant attempts to produce a systematic taxonomy based on a variety of structural characteristics, including internal anatomy. He was also the first to use the term species in the modern sense of the word.

Ray was born on 29 November 1627 in the small Essex village of Black Notley. His father was a blacksmith and his mother was an amateur herbalist and medical practitioner. After attending the Grammar School in nearby Braintree, Ray spent two years at Catherine's Hall, Cambridge (now St Catherine's College). He transferred to Trinity College, Cambridge in 1646, and graduated in 1648. He was elected a Fellow of Trinity in the following year and remained at the college for the next 13 years, initially teaching Greek, mathematics and the humanities. In 1650, however, he suffered a serious illness and, while recuperating, spent much time walking through the surrounding countryside; this stimulated his interest in natural history, which thereafter became his main academic pursuit. Ray took holy orders in 1660, but the restoration of Charles II changed the country's religious climate and Ray was obliged to leave Trinity in 1662 because he refused to sign an agreement to the Act of Uniformity, which required from all clergymen a declaration of assent to everything contained in the Prayer Book of Queen Elizabeth I and to conform to the Liturgy of the Church of England. Thus Ray lost his livelihood and for the rest of his life he depended on financial support from his friends, particularly from Francis Willughby, an affluent younger contemporary at Cambridge who shared Ray's interest in natural history. From 1663 to 1666 Ray and Willughby toured Europe to study the flora and fauna and collect specimens. On their return to England, Ray lived at Willughby's home, where they collaborated on publishing the results of their natural history studies. In 1672 Willughby died unexpectedly, but Ray remained at his family home, supported by an annuity left him by Willughby and by his position as tutor to the Willughby children. In 1673 Ray married a governess in the Willughby household. In 1678, however, Willughby's widow forced Ray and his wife to leave, and they returned to Black Notley, where Ray remained for the rest of his life. He died there on 17 January 1705.

Ray's first publication was *Catalogue Plantarum Circa Cantabrigiam Nascentium* (1660; *Catalogue of Plants around Cambridge*), compiled from his observations during his walks while convalescing from illness. The work listed 558 species and was the best attempt then available at cataloguing plants. His first attempt at a genuine classification, however, was a table of plants that he contributed to John Wilkin's book *Essay towards a Real Character* (1668). In 1670 Ray, with Willughby's help, published *Catalogus Plantarum Angliae* (*Catalogue of English Plants*). Ray and Willughby then began work on producing a definitive catalogue and classification of all known plants and animals, with Ray responsible for the botany and Willughby for the zoology. But Willughby died while this work was in its early stages and Ray assumed the task of completing the entire project, since he was a competent zoologist and was familiar with Willughby's material. This task occupied Ray for the rest of his life.

As a tribute to Willughby, Ray published *F. Willughbeii ... Ornithologia* (1676; translated in 1678 as *The Ornithology of F. Willughby*) and *F. Willughbeii ... de Historia Piscium* (1685; *History of Fish*) under Willughby's name, although most of the work was Ray's own. Ray continued his botanical studies and, in *Methodus Plantarum Nova* (1682), developed a clear-cut taxonomic system based on plant physiology, morphology and anatomy. In his system he laid great emphasis on the division of plants into cryptogams (flowerless plants), monocotyledons and dicotyledons, a basic catergorization that is still used today. Within the dicotyledons Ray defined 36 family groupings, many of which are also still used. He also established the species as the fundamental unit of taxonomy, although he mistakenly believed that species are immutable.

The culmination of Ray's work, however, was *Historia Generalis Plantarum*, a monumental three-volume treatise (published between 1686 and 1704) in which he attempted to produce a complete, natural classification of plants. The book covered about 18,600 species (most of which were European) and, in addition to plant classification, it contained much information on the morphology, distribution, habitats and pharmacological uses of individual plant species as well as general aspects of plant life, such as diseases and seed germination. In it he modified his belief in the immutability of species.

Ray also wrote several books on zoology under his own name, notably *Synopsis Methodica Animalium Quadrupedum et Serpentini Generis* (1693; *Synopsis of Quadrupeds*), *Historia Insectorum* (*History of Insects* - published posthumously in 1710) and *Synopsis Methodica Avium et Piscium* (*Synopsis of Birds and Fish*; published posthumously in 1713). In all of these works Ray followed the same format he had used in his *Historia Generalis Plantarum*, giving details of individual species in addition to classification.

Furthermore, Ray also believed that fossils are the petrified remains of dead animals and plants - a concept that, surprisingly, appeared in his theological writings and did not gain general acceptance until the late eighteenth century.

Although it was not possible to devise a natural classification system until Charles Darwin and Alfred Wallace had formulated evolutionary theory, Ray's system approached that ideal far more closely than those of any of his contemporaries and remained the best attempt at classification until superseded by Carolus Linnaeus' taxonomic work in 1735.

Ricketts, Howard Taylor (*1871-1910*), was an American pathologist who discovered the *Rickettsia* (which are named after him), a group of unusual micro-organisms that have both viral and bacterial characteristics. The ten known species in the *Rickettsia* genus are all pathogenic in human beings, causing diseases such as Rocky Mountain spotted fever and forms of typhus.

Ricketts was born on 9 February 1871 in Findlay, Ohio. He was educated at the University of Nebraska, from which he graduated in 1894, and Northwestern University, Chicago, from which he obtained his medical degree in 1897. He then became a junior resident doctor at Cook County Hospital, Chicago, before moving to the Rush Medical College (then affiliated with Chicago University) in 1899 as an instructor in cutaneous pathology. In 1901 Ricketts travelled to Europe, performing laboratory work there. On his return in 1902 he became instructor and later Associate Professor in the pathology department of Chicago University. In 1909 Ricketts went to Mexico City to investigate typhus; while there he became fatally infected with the disease and died on 3 May 1910.

Ricketts began studying Rocky Mountain spotted fever in 1906 and discovered that the disease is transmitted to human beings by the bite of a particular type of tick that inhabits the skins of animals. In 1908 he found the causative micro-organisms in the blood of infected animals and in the bodies and eggs of ticks. This micro-organism is now called *Rickettsia rickettsii*, after its discoverer. In his studies of typhus in Mexico Ricketts demonstrated that this disease is also caused by a type of *Rickettsia* and that the micro-organisms are transmitted to man by the body louse. Before he died from the disease, Ricketts also showed that typhus can be transmitted to monkeys, and that, after recovery, they are immune to further attacks.

Romer, Alfred Sherwood (*1894-1973*), was an American palaeontologist and comparative anatomist who is best known for his influential studies of vertebrate evolution and as the author of several books on the anatomy and evolution of the vertebrates.

Romer was born on 28 December 1894 in White Plains, New York, the son of a journalist. His family moved frequently during his early years, but in 1909 Romer returned to White Plains to live with his grandmother and a more settled phase began. He left high school in 1912 and, because his family was poor, spent a year doing odd jobs to earn money for a college education. In 1913 he entered Amherst College to study history and German literature but his interest soon turned to palaeontology, and he took a course in evolution. He graduated in 1917 after the start of World War I and joined the American Field Service in France; later that year he enlisted in the United States Army, and remained in Europe until 1919. On returning to the United States, he did postgraduate work at Columbia University, from which he gained his doctorate in 1921 with a thesis on comparative myology that is still a classic in its field. He then taught anatomy at the Bellevue Hospital Medical College, New York, until 1923, when he was appointed an Associate Professor in the Department of Geology and Palaeontology at the University of Chicago. He held this post for 11 years, during which period he married Ruth Hibbard, by whom he had three children. In 1934 Romer was appointed Professor of Biology at Harvard University; he also became Director of the Biological Laboratories in 1945 and of the Museum of Comparative Zoology in the following year. He held these three posts until 1965, when he officially retired, although he continued to work and lecture for the rest of his life. Romer died on 5 November 1973 in Cambridge, Massachusetts.

Romer spent almost all of his career investigating vertebrate evolution. Using evidence from palaeontology, comparative anatomy and embryology, he traced the basic structural and functional changes that took place during the evolution of fishes to primitive terrestrial vertebrates and from these to modern vertebrates. In these studies he emphasized the evolutionary significance of the relationship between the form and function of animals and the environment.

One of the most important figures in palaeontology since the 1930s, Romer wrote several well-known books on vertebrates, including *Man and the Vertebrates* (1933), *Vertebrate Palaeontology* (1933), which was widely influential in its field for several decades, and *The Vertebrate Body* (1949), a comprehensive study of comparative vertebrate anatomy which is still a standard textbook today. He also collected an extensive range of fossils from his field trips to South Africa, Argentina and Texas.

Ross, Ronald (*1857-1932*), was a British physician who proved that malaria is transmitted to human beings by the bite of the *Anopheles* mosquito. He also devoted much of his time to public health programmes concerned with the prevention of the disease. For his significant contribution to the battle against malaria, which has plagued man for centuries, he received the 1902 Nobel Prize in Physiology and Medicine.

Ross was born at Almora, India, on 13 May 1857, the son of a British army officer serving there. He was educated in Britain and received his medical training at St Bartholomew's Hospital, London, graduating in 1879. He was unenthusiastic about medicine, his interests at that time being in the arts and mathematics. When he joined the Indian Medical Service in 1881, however, he gradually became absorbed with medical problems. During his first leave in England, from 1888 to 1889, he obtained a Diploma in Public Health and took a course in bacteriology. On retiring from the Indian Medical Service in 1899, he returned to Britain and lectured at the new School for Tropical Medicine in Liverpool, later holding the Chair in Tropical Medicine there. He was knighted in 1911 and a year later moved to London, where he established a consulting practice at King's College Hospital. During World War I he was consultant on malaria to the War Office and when the Ross Institute of Tropical Diseases was opened in his honour, in 1926, he became its first Director. He died in London on 16 September 1932.

While on leave in England in 1894, Ross be-

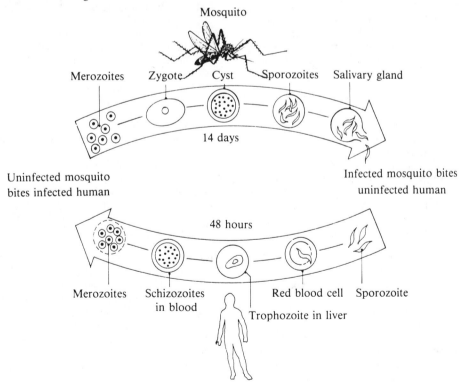

The reproductive cycle of a malarial parasite.

came acquainted with Patrick Manson, who demonstrated that the blood of malarial patients contained pigmented bodies and parasites. (The discovery that malaria was caused by a protozoon in the bloodstream had been made by Charles Laveran in 1883.) Manson's suggestion was that malaria was spread by mosquitoes and Ross returned to India determined to investigate this hypothesis and to identify the mosquito responsible. The shortage in India of literature on the subject delayed the identification of species of mosquitoes and parasites, and Ross was also cut off from the work of others. He missed, for example, Albert King's suggestion that malaria might be transmitted via mosquito bites.

Ross refused to believe the popular idea that malaria was caused by bad air (*mal aria*) or contaminated water and he continued to collect mosquitoes, identifying the various species and dissecting their internal organs. In the stomachs of some insects he found "motile filaments" which, although Ross was unaware of it, were gametes. He thought that the filaments might develop to further stages, and dissected a few mosquitoes that had fed on malarial patients. In August 1897 he discovered in an *Anopheles* mosquito a cyst containing the parasites that had been found by Laveran in the blood of malarial patients. These sporozoites of the malarial parasite remain in the human blood for only an hour after a bite, before invading liver cells, and their subsequent developmental stages are distinct from those in the mosquito. The biting mosquito may suck up various stages of the parasite with the blood, but all are digested except those that produce gametes. After fertilization the zygote bores through the stomach wall of the mosquito and forms an external cyst. Sporozoites are formed in the cyst, which migrate to the mosquito's salivary glands, ready for injection into a victim. Later, using caged birds with bird malaria, Ross was able to show that the "motile filaments" do develop to further stages. The life history of the parasite inside a mosquito was thus revealed and the mode of transmission to the victim was identified as taking place through a mosquito bite.

Roux, Wilhelm (*1850–1924*), was a German anatomist and zoologist who is famous for his work on developmental mechanics in embryology. He founded the first ever journal of experimental embryology and also helped to produce a dictionary of experimental morphology.

Roux was born on 9 June 1850 in Jena (now in East Germany). He attended the Oberrealschule in Meiningen then studied at the universities of Jena – where he was a student of Ernst Haeckel – Berlin and Strasbourg. In 1873 he matriculated

from the medical faculty, and passed his state medical examinations in 1877. After spending several years as an assistant at Franz Hofmann's Institute of Hygiene in Leipzig, Roux moved to the University of Breslau (now Wroclaw in Poland), where he eventually became Director of his own Institute of Embryology. He was Professor of Anatomy at the University of Innsbruck from 1889 to 1895, when he became Director of the Anatomical Institute at the University of Halle, where he remained until his retirement in 1921. Roux died in Halle on 15 September 1924.

Roux's embryological investigations were performed mainly on frogs' eggs. He performed a series of experiments in which he punctured the eggs at the two-cell stage of development (a technique Roux pioneered) and found that they grew into half-embryos; this finding led him to conclude that the fate of the parts had already been determined at the two-cell stage. In the field of embryology Roux also researched into the earliest structures in amphibian development. In 1894 he founded the first journal of experimental embryology; it is still published today and is now called *Roux Archiv für Entwicklungsmechanik*.

Roux also investigated the mechanisms of functional adaptations, examining the physical stresses that cause bones, cartilage and tendons to adapt to malformations and diseases. In addition, he collaborated with two botanists and an anatomist to produce a dictionary of experimental morphology, which provided a valuable compendium of definitions and historical notes in this discipline.

Roux was not the only scientist who performed embryological experiments at that time, but he nevertheless made substantial contributions to the knowledge of embryological development. In his own judgement, however, he grossly overestimated the importance of his work, claiming, for example, that he alone was the first to progress from causal manipulation to a causal analysis of development – an absurd contention because, at the very least, it ignored the work of his contemporaries Oskar Hertwig (1849–1922) and Eduard Pfluger (1829–1910).

Russell, Frederick Stratten (*1897–   *), is a British marine biologist who is best known for his studies of the life histories and distribution of plankton. He received many honours for his work, including a fellowship of the Royal Society of London in 1938, a Gold Medal from the Linnean Society in 1961, and a knighthood in 1965.

Russell was born on 3 November 1897 in Bridport, Dorset, and was educated at Oundle School and then at Gonville and Caius College, Cambridge. His studies were interrupted by World

War I, during which he served with distinction in the Royal Naval Air Service. He graduated in 1922 and then worked for two years for the Egyptian government as Assistant Director of Fisheries Research, after which he returned to Britain and joined the scientific staff of the Marine Biological Association at Plymouth. He remained there for the rest of his working life (although he went on an expedition to the Great Barrier Reef in Australia from 1928 to 1929, and served in Air Staff Intelligence during World War II), becoming its Director in 1945. From 1950 until he retired in 1965 Russell was also a member of the National Oceanographic Council, and from 1962 to 1975 he was Chairman of the Advisory Panel on Biological Research to the Central Electricity Generating Board. He was knighted in 1965.

While working for the Egyptian government, Russell studied the vertical distribution in the sea of the eggs and larvae of marine fish and their migratory movements. Continuing this line of research at the Marine Biological Association, he investigated the different types of behaviour of individual species of fish at various times of the year. He went on to investigate the distribution of *Calanus* (a crustacean copepod) and *Sagitta* (a chaetognath worm). By combining the results of his research, Russell established the value of certain types of plankton as indicators of different types of water in the English Channel and the North Sea. He also offered a partial explanation for the difference in abundance of herring in different areas. In addition, Russell discovered a means of distinguishing between different species of fish shortly after they have hatched, when they are almost identical in appearance. Russell's studies of plankton and of water movements were extremely valuable in providing information on which to base fishing quotas, the accuracy of which is essential to prevent overfishing and the depletion of fish stocks.

Russell also elucidated the life histories of several species of medusa by rearing the hydroids from parent medusae, and he published the two-volume *The Medusae of the British Isles* (1953, 1970).

S

Sabin, Albert Bruce (*1906–*   ), is a Russian-born American virologist who has devoted his long and distinguished career to the development of protective vaccines. He is particularly associated with the oral poliomyelitis vaccine.

Sabin was born on 26 August 1906 in Bialys-

tok, Russia (now in Poland). In 1921 he and his family emigrated to the United States where he attended the New York University from 1926 to 1931, graduating with a medical degree. He then served as House Physician to the Bellevue Hospital in New York from 1932 to 1933. Between 1935 and 1937 he was an Assistant at the Rockefeller Institute and an Associate from 1937. Two years later he was made Associate Professor of Research in Pediatrics at the University of Cincinnati College of Medicine and, after serving as a medical officer in the army during World War II, he became Research Professor of Pediatrics there from 1946 to 1960. He held the position of Distinguished Service Professor from 1960 to 1970 and was President of the Weizmann Institute of Science, Israel, from 1970 to 1972. On his return to the United States he joined the staff of the Medical College of South Carolina, and between 1973 and 1974 he was Expert Consultant to the National Cancer Institute.

Sabin became interested in polio research while working at the Rockefeller Institute. In 1936 he and Peter Olitsky were able to make polio viruses from monkeys grow in tissue cultures from the brain cells of a human embryo that had miscarried. At the same time they were unsuccessful in their attempts to cultivate the virus in other human tissues, which gave weight to the existing theory that the virus attacked nerve cells only. (This theory was disproved in 1949 by Thomas Weller, John Enders and Frederick Robbins.)

Jonas Salk had become engaged in producing an inactive polio vaccine, but Sabin was not convinced that the Salk technique of using dead virus was adequate. He concentrated on developing a live-virus oral vaccine because he felt that the inactive vaccine could be nothing more than a, temporary measure for protection and would require the patient to be re-vaccinated at fairly frequent intervals. Sabin believed that only a living virus could be counted on to produce the necessary antibodies over a long period. Also, the living virus could be taken orally because it would multiply and invade the body of its own accord and would not, like the Salk vaccine, have to be injected. Sabin succeeded in finding virus strains of all three types of polio, each producing its own variety of antibody which is too feeble to produce the disease itself. Sabin's vaccine is known as the live-attenuated vaccine and exerts its effect by inducing a harmless infection of the intestinal tract, thus simulating natural infection without causing any disease. It operates by multiplying in the tissues, giving rise to a mild and invisible infection with subsequent antibody formation and immunity.

The vaccine has the advantage of inducing immunity rapidly, a property that is particularly valuable in the face of an epidemic. When given to a significant proportion of a population, the vaccine induces community protection by rendering the alimentary tract of those vaccinated resistant to re-infection by the polio virus.

It took Sabin many years of patient research but by 1957 he had enough confidence after trying the vaccine out on himself, his family and numerous volunteers, to offer it for field trials to the medical community. They tested it on a massive scale, the tests were successful, and by 1961 the vaccine was available for commercial use.

Today, the "sugar lump" (as it is now known) has become an accepted and easy method of vaccination against polio. Its success can be measured only by the marked decline of the once prevalent disease which killed so many young people or crippled them for life.

Salk, Jonas Edward (*1914–   *), is an American microbiologist who produced the first successful vaccine against the paralytic disease poliomyelitis.

Salk was born in New York, the son of Polish-Jewish immigrants. He graduated in surgery from the College of the City of New York in 1934, and then became a research fellow at the New York University College of Medicine, where he studied the chemistry of proteins. In 1939 he was awarded a doctorate in medicine and during the next three years worked at the Mount Sinai Hospital in New York, before joining the research staff of the Virus Research Unit in the University of Michigan, where he worked on influenza vaccines until 1944. The next two years were spent in consultation regarding the protection of the armed forces from epidemics. In 1946 he became an Assistant Professor in Epidemiology at Michigan and the following year he was invited by the University of Pittsburgh to join a special medical research unit there to carry out a three-year programme on the causes and treatment of virus diseases. The development of the Salk vaccine against poliomyelitis was announced in 1955. He was appointed Director of the Salk Institute for Biological Studies, San Diego, in 1962, and has since been involved with cancer research.

The major obstacle to research on the preparation of vaccines in the 1940s was the difficulty of obtaining sufficient virus. Unlike bacteria, which may be grown in culture, viruses need living cells on which to grow. A breakthrough came when it was found that viruses could be grown in live chick embryos. John Enders improved on this technique with the use of mashed embryonic tissue, supplied with nutrients, and with the addition of penicillin to keep down the growth of bacteria.

Once the method of preparing sufficient quantities of virus was available, Salk set about finding a way of treating the polio virus so that it was unable to cause the disease but was still able to produce an antibody reaction in the human body. He collected samples of spinal cord from many polio victims and grew the virus in the new live-cell culture medium. He studied the reaction of the virus to various chemicals and found that there were three distinct types of virus that cause the disease. Salk experimented with formaldehyde (methanol) to render the virus inactive. By 1952 he had produced a vaccine effective against the three common strains of polio virus in the United States; he tested it on monkeys, which are also susceptible to polio, and found that it worked. Next he tried the vaccine on children who had recovered from polio and were immune to the disease, and he found an increase in the antibody content of their blood. Afterwards, he tried it on his family and children who had not had polio, and again antibodies were formed in the blood.

Salk needed a large-scale clinical trial, however, because a large number of people would need to receive the preventive vaccine if any useful results were to be obtained. The vaccine had to be prepared on a commercial scale and licences were issued to five companies who were instructed in the technique of vaccine production and were responsible for their own quality control, because Salk's laboratory could not cope with the volume of work that testing would involve. In 1955, in a big publicity campaign, some vaccine was prepared without adequate precautions and about two hundred cases of polio, with eleven deaths, resulted from the clinical trials. Salk recommended that the vaccine should be tested by the public health service in future and more stringent control prevented further disasters.

Salk was the first to make use of Enders' method of growing viruses to prepare a vaccine against poliomyelitis. It saved many people from the crippling and often fatal effects of the disease and prompted Albert Sabin to prepare a polio vaccine that can be administered orally rather than by injection.

Schleiden, Matthias Jakob (*1804–1881*), was a German botanist who, with Theodor Schwann, is best known for the establishment of the cell theory.

Schleiden was born on 5 April 1804 in Hamburg and studied law at Heidelberg University from 1824 to 1827. After graduating, he practised as a barrister in Hamburg but soon returned to university, taking courses in botany and medicine at the universities of Göttingen, Berlin and Jena. After graduating in 1831 he was appointed Professor of Botany at Jena, where he remained until he became Professor of Botany at the University of Dorpat, Estonia, in 1862. He returned to Germany to Frankfurt after a short time, however, and from 1864 began teaching privately. Schleiden died in Frankfurt on 23 June 1881.

Although the existence of cells had been known since the seventeenth century (Robert Hooke is generally credited with their discovery in 1665), Schleiden was the first to recognize their importance as the fundamental units of living organisms when, in 1838, he announced that the various parts of plants consist of cells or derivatives of cells. In the following year Schwann published a paper in which he confirmed for animals Schleiden's idea of the basic importance of cells in the organization of organisms. Thus Schleiden and Schwann established the cell theory, a concept that is common knowledge today and which is as fundamental to biology as atomic theory is to the physical sciences.

Schleiden also researched into other aspects of cells. He recognized the importance of the nucleus (which he called the cytoblast) in cell division, although he incorrectly believed that new cells budded off from the nuclear surface. In addition, he noted the active movement of intracellular material in plant tissues, calling this movement protoplasmic streaming. The phenomenon is well known today, although the intracellular material is now called cytoplasm.

Schwann, Theodor (*1810-1882*), was a German physiologist who, with Matthias Schleiden, is credited with formulating the cell theory, one of the most fundamental of all concepts in biology. Schwann also did important work on digestion, fermentation and histology.

Schwann was born on 7 December 1810 in Neuss (now in West Germany). He was educated at the Jesuit college in Cologne then studied medicine at the universities of Bonn, Würzburg and Berlin, graduating from the last in 1834. He spent the next four years - the most scientifically productive period in his life - working as an assistant to the German physiologist Johannes Müller at the Museum of Anatomy in Berlin. In 1839, however, Schwann's work on fermentation attracted so much adverse criticism that he left Germany for Belgium, where he was Professor of Anatomy at the Roman Catholic University in Louvain from 1839 to 1848 then held the same post at the University of Liège until his death in Cologne on 11 January 1882.

In 1834 Schwann began to investigate digestive processes and two years later isolated from the lining of the stomach a chemical responsible for protein digestion, which he called pepsin. This was the first enzyme to be isolated from animal tissue, although Anselme Payan, a French chemist, had isolated an enzyme from malt in 1833. Schwann then studied fermentation and between 1836 and 1837 showed that the fermentation of sugar is a result of the life processes of living yeast cells (he later coined the term metabolism to denote the chemical changes that occur in living tissue). This work on fermentation was later criticized heavily, especially by the German chemists Friedrich Wöhler and Justus von Liebig, and this led to Schwann leaving Germany. It was not until Louis Pasteur's work on fermentation in the 1850s that Schwann was proved correct. Meanwhile, however, Schwann investigated putrefaction in an attempt to disprove the theory of spontaneous generation (which had once again become a matter of debate) repeating, with improved techniques, Lazzaro Spallanzani's earlier experiments. Like Spallanzani, Schwann found no evidence to support the theory, despite which it was still believed by some scientists.

In 1839 Schwann published *Mikroskopische Untersuchungen über die Ueberreinstimmung in der Struktur und dem Wachstum der Tiere und Pflanzen* (translated in 1847 as *Microscopical Researches on the Similarity in the Structure and Growth of Animals and Plants*) in which he formulated the cell theory. In the previous year Matthias Schleiden - whom Schwann knew well - had stated the theory in connection with plants, but it was Schwann who extended the theory to animals and enunciated it in its clearest form.

Schwann and Schleiden are therefore generally credited as co-formulators of the cell theory. Giving numerous examples from many different types of animal tissues, Schwann in his *Microscopical Researches* concluded that all organisms (both animal and plant) consist entirely of cells or of products of cells and that the life of each individual cell is subordinated to that of the whole organism. The cell theory soon became widely accepted and is today recognized as being one of the most important concepts in biology.

Schwann also discovered the cells (now called Schwann cells) that make up the myelin sheath surrounding peripheral nerve axons, and the striated muscle in the upper region of the oesophagus. In addition, he noted that an egg is a single cell that eventually develops into a complex organism - a basic principle in embryology.

Scott, Peter Markham (*1909-   *), is a British ornithologist and artist who is best known for his superb bird paintings, book illustrations and wildlife conservation work, including the foundation of the Wildfowl Trust at Slimbridge, Gloucestershire. He has received numerous honours from many different countries, including several honorary degrees and in 1973, a knighthood.

Scott was born on 14 September 1909, the son of Captain Robert Falcon Scott (1868–1912), the Antarctic explorer. He was educated at Oundle School, from which he went to Trinity College, Cambridge, then to the Munich State Academy and finally to the Royal Academy School, London. In 1936 he represented Britain in the Olympic Games, gaining a bronze medal for the single-handed sailing event. During World War II he served with the Royal Navy, and after the war founded the Wildfowl Trust in 1946. In 1949 he led his first expedition, which was to explore the uncharted Perry River area in the Canadian Arctic, and in 1951 and 1953 he led expeditions to Iceland to mark geese. In addition, Scott has also led ornithological expeditions to Australasia, the Galapagos Islands, the Seychelles and the Antarctic. From 1961 to 1967 he was the first president of the World Wildlife Fund. In 1963 he became Chairman of the Survival Service Commission of the International Union for the Conservation of Nature and Natural Resources, and in 1969 he was made President of the Wildlife Youth Service. He became Chancellor of Birmingham University in 1974.

Scott has done much to promote wildlife conservation, particularly of birds. The Wildfowl Trust contains hundreds of species of birds and attracts thousands of visitors each year. In addition to his conservation work, he has made numerous television appearances and written several books - including *Key to the Wild Fowl of the World* (1949), *Wild Geese and Eskimos* (1951) and *The Eye of the Wind* (1961) - and has illustrated many others, most notably *The Snow Goose*, a novel by Paul Gallico, and *The Swans* (in collaboration with the Wildfowl Trust).

Sharpey-Schafer, Edward Albert (*1850–1935*), was a British physiologist and endocrinologist who discovered the effects of the hormone epinephrine, also known as adrenaline (although the actual hormone was not isolated until five years after his discovery). He received the Royal Medal of the Royal Society in 1902 and its Copley Medal in 1924.

He was born Edward Albert Schäfer in London on 2 June 1850, the son of a merchant. He went to University College, London, in 1871 and graduated in medicine three years later. His Professor of General Anatomy and Physiology was William Sharpey, who deeply impressed him by his skills. Schäfer became Assistant Professor when Sharpey retired in 1874, and eventually became Jodrell

Professor at University College in 1883. In 1876 Schäfer was one of the founder members of the Physiological Society (he wrote a history of the Society in 1927). In 1899 he left University College to take the post of Professor of Physiology at Edinburgh University, which he held until his retirement in 1933. In 1913 he was knighted. He had named one of his sons after his mentor, Sharpey, but after both sons were killed in World War I he affixed Sharpey's name to his own and was thereafter known as Sharpey-Schafer. He died in North Berwick, Scotland, on 29 March 1935.

Sharpey-Schafer's most significant contribution to medical research occurred in 1894. He was working with George Oliver and they discovered that an extract from the central part of an adrenal gland injected into the bloodstream of an animal caused a rise in blood pressure by vasoconstriction. They also noted that the smooth muscles of the animal's bronchi relaxed. These effects were caused by the action of the hormone adrenaline which is produced by the medulla of the adrenal gland; it was later isolated in 1901 by the Japanese-American chemist Jokichi Takamine (1854–1922).

Sharpey-Schafer also suspected that another hormone is produced by the islets of Langerhans in the pancreas. He adopted for it the name insulin (the Latin for island), a name which eventually persisted, although the scientists who isolated it in 1922 at first called it "isletin".

In 1903 Sharpey-Schafer devised the classic position for artificial respiration, the supine position, which was adopted as standard by the Royal Life Saving Society. He was also an ardent supporter and fighter for equal opportunities for women in the world of medicine.

Sherrington, Charles Scott (*1857–1952*), was a British neurologist who is renowned for his research on the physiology of the nervous system, and his laboratories came to be regarded as the best in the world for teaching and research in neurophysiology. For his innovative work on the function of the neuron he was awarded the 1932 Nobel Prize in Physiology and Medicine, which he shared with Edgar Adrian.

Sherrington was born on 27 November 1857 in Islington, London. His father died when he was young, and his mother remarried. Sherrington's stepfather was Dr Caleb Rose, a classical scholar and archaeologist who influenced the young boy and interested him in medicine. He went to Ipswich Grammar School and then entered St Thomas's Hospital, London, in 1876. He interrupted his studies in 1880 to go to Cambridge as a non-collegiate student, where he became a demonstrator in the physiology department and a member of Gonville and Caius College. There he studied under the British physiologist Michael Foster (1836-1907).

In 1881 the International Medical Congress was held in London, and it was there that Sherrington was introduced to and became interested in experimental neurophysiology. He also met Ramón y Cajal whose interests were similar. The following year Sherrington went to Spain as a member of a research team to study a cholera outbreak. He gained his medical degree at Cambridge in 1885 and the next year qualified as a doctor and published his first paper, on the nervous system. In the same year he travelled to Italy to study cholera and then went to Berlin where he visited the pathologist Rudolf Virchow (1821-1902) and Robert Koch. He returned to St Thomas's as a lecturer in physiology and in 1891 was appointed Professor-Superintendent of the Brown Institute, London University's veterinary hospital. He took up the Physiology professorship at Liverpool University in 1895, where he developed many of his original ideas on practical teaching. In 1913 he became Professor of Physiology at Oxford, a position he retained, although with interruptions, until 1935. During World War I he was heavily involved in government committees on the study of industrial fatigue and for three months he worked incognito as a labourer in a munitions factory. The observations he made there did much to improve safety for factory workers. He was elected President of the Royal Society in 1920 and was knighted two years later. Sherrington was also a poet and philosopher, and published his writings. He was made President of the British Association in 1922. He died in Eastbourne on 4 March 1952.

One of Sherrington's important findings, published in 1894, was that the nerve supply to muscles contains between 25 and 50 per cent sensory fibres, as well as motor fibres concerned with stimulating muscle contraction. The sensory fibres carry sensation to the brain so that it can determine, for example, the degree of tension in the muscles. His discovery helped to explain some of the disorders of the nervous system in which there is a deterioration in muscular co-ordination.

Sherrington then went on to study reflex actions and formulated theories of the way in which antagonistic muscles co-ordinate behaviour. He showed that reflex actions do not occur independently, as a result of reflex arcs, but in a movement integrated with the movement of other muscles (i.e. when one set of muscles is activated, the opposing set is inhibited). This theory of reciprocal innervation is known as Sherrington's law.

Sherrington divided the sense organs into three groups: interoceptive, characterized by taste receptors; exteroceptive, such as receptors that detect sound, smell, light and touch; and proprioceptive, which involve the function of the synapse (Sherrington's word) and which respond to events inside the body. In 1906 he investigated the scratch reflex of a dog using an "electric flea" and found that the reflex stimulated 19 muscles to beat rhythmically five times a second, and brought into action a further 17 muscles which kept the dog upright. The exteroceptive sensors initiated the order to scratch, and the proprioceptors initiated the muscles to keep the animal upright. Sherrington then removed the cerebrum of the dog and cut the epidermal tactile receptors and found that the proprioceptors still worked, against gravity, and activated the muscles to keep the dog upright.

Sherrington also plotted the motor areas of the cerebral cortex of the brain and identified the regions that govern movement and sensation in particular parts of the body. He experimented on the brain of a live gorilla, which caused an observer to comment that he did not know whether to admire most the skill or the courage of the experimenter.

In 1893, while Sherrington was in charge of the Brown Institute, he investigated diphtheria antitoxins. While experimenting for the first time on a horse (used to produce the antitoxin), an urgent message reached him that a young relative was desperately ill with diphtheria. He bled the horse, prepared the antitoxin, and on reaching the boy found that he had only a few hours to live. He injected the child with the antitoxin, and the boy recovered. It was the first use of diphtheria antitoxin in Britain.

Sherrington carried out significant work in the development of antitoxins, particularly those for cholera and diphtheria. In addition his observations of the nervous function in animals, described in *The Integrative Action of the Nervous System* (1906), greatly influenced modern neurophysiology, particularly brain surgery and the treatment of nervous disorders.

Simpson, George Gaylord (*1902-*), is an American palaeontologist who has studied the evolution of mammals and applied population genetics to the subject and to analyse the migrations of animals between continents.

Simpson was born on 16 June 1902 in Chicago, Illinois, the son of a lawyer. He attended the University of Colorado and after graduation went to Yale University, where he gained his PhD in 1926 with a thesis on Mesozoic mammals. A year later he took a post in New York City at the

American Museum of Natural History, where he remained for 32 years, continuing his palaeontological research and becoming curator in 1942. He took a professorial appointment at Columbia University in 1945, and from 1959 to 1970 he was Alexander Agassiz Professor of Vertebrate Palaeontology at the Museum of Comparative Zoology, Harvard. He went to Tucson in 1967 to take up an appointment as Professor of Geosciences at the University of Arizona.

Simpson's chief work in the 1930s concerned early mammals of the Mesozoic, Palaeocene and Eocene, which entailed many extensive field trips throughout the Americas and to Asia to study fossil remains. This led him to consider the taxonomy of mammals, and in the 1940s he began applying genetics to mammalian evolution and classification. Much of his work was summarized in a series of textbooks, including *Tempo and Mode in Evolution* (1944), *The Meaning of Evolution* (1949), *The Major Features of Evolution* (1953) and *The Principles of Animal Taxonomy* (1961), which were influential in establishing the neo-Darwinian theory of evolution.

Simpson, James Young (*1811-1870*), was a British obstetrician and one of the founders of gynaecology, who pioneered the use of chloroform as an anaesthetic.

Simpson was born at Bathgate near Linlithgow, Scotland, on 7 June 1811, the son of a village baker. He was a brilliant pupil at school and at the age of only 14 he went to Edinburgh University to study medicine, and graduated in 1832 to become assistant to one of the university professors on the merit of his exceptional thesis. He became Professor of Midwifery in 1840 at the age of 29, and seven years later his skill as an obstetrician was acknowledged when he was requested to attend Queen Victoria during her stays in Scotland. By this time he had a thriving private practice and was making pioneering advances in modern gynaecology; he was eventually appointed physician to Queen Victoria. He was made a baronet in 1866, and died in London on 6 May 1870.

Although Simpson made great advances in gynaecology, his most famous work was in the field of anaesthesia. In 1846 the American dentist William Morton had successfully extracted a tooth painlessly by using ether as an anaesthetic. Simpson was impressed and began experimenting himself, but he was not particularly successful with ether, although he did use it on a patient in childbirth in early 1847. He then heard of the work of the French physiologist Jean Flourens (1794-1867), who was experimenting with chloroform on animals, and of the successful use of chloroform in surgery by Robert Liston at University College Hospital, London. In November 1847 Simpson introduced the use of chloroform in his practice, particularly to relieve the pain of childbirth. He described his cases in *Account of a New Anaesthetic Agent* (1847). This caused a storm of opposition from Calvinists, who regarded labour pains as God-given and heretic to relieve. It was not until Royal intervention in 1853 that the controversies died down. Queen Victoria, who never pretended that pregnancy and childbirth were anything but loathsome, accepted the use of chloroform during the birth of Prince Leopold, her seventh child. She described the new drug as "miraculous" and her praises of Simpson knew no bounds. Thus criticism of his techniques abated, and they were soon universally adopted.

Skinner, Burrhus Frederic (*1904-*), is an American psychologist who is famous for his staunch advocacy of behaviourism, which attempts to explain human behaviour solely in terms of observable responses to external stimuli. He is also well known for his controversial ideas about the relationship between individuals and society, for inventing the Skinner box and the teaching machine, and for developing programmed learning.

Skinner was born on 20 March 1904 in Susquehanna, Pennsylvania, and was educated at Harvard University. After obtaining his doctorate in 1931 he remained at the university as an instructor until 1936, when he moved to the University of Minnesota, Minneapolis - initially as an instructor, then as assistant professor from 1937 to 1939. During World War II he was an associate professor in a research programme for the United States Office of Scientific Research and Development. In 1945, after the war, he was appointed Professor of Psychology at Indiana University, Bloomington, then in 1948 he returned to Harvard as Professor of Psychology, becoming Edgar Pierce Professor of Psychology there in 1958.

Skinner's best-known research work concerns operant conditioning which, in general, involves influencing voluntary behaviour patterns by means of rewards or punishments or a combination of both. In his research, Skinner takes a firm behaviouristic standpoint, believing that behaviour can be studied properly only by objective experimentation and observation of reactions to definable stimuli, and that all subjective phenomena should be discounted. Although many psychologists consider Skinner's ideas to be rather extreme, he has succeeded in bringing a considerable degree of methodological rigidity to psychological experimentation.

In the field of operant conditioning, Skinner conducted many highly original experiments, mainly using pigeons. For example, during World War II he trained pigeons to pilot bombs and torpedoes, although the pigeons were never actually used as missile guides; and later, at Harvard, he taught pigeons to play table tennis. In the course of his work on training animals he developed the Skinner box which, in its basic form, comprises a box with a lever-operated food delivery device inside; when the experimental animal presses the lever, a pellet of food is delivered. More sophisticated versions of the Skinner box have since been developed and have proved extremely useful in studying the behaviour of a wide variety of animals.

The step-by-step training of experimental animals led Skinner to develop teaching machines and the associated concept of programmed learning. Similar in many respects to the Skinner box, a teaching machine presents information to a student at a pace determined by the student himself, then tests the student on the material previously presented; correct answers are "rewarded," thereby reinforcing learning.

Skinner first gained public attention, however, with his invention in the mid-1940s of the Air-Crib, a large, air-conditioned, soundproof box intended to serve as a mechanical baby minder and designed to provide the optimum environment for child growth during the first two years of life. But Skinner aroused the greatest controversy with *Walden Two* (1948), a fictional description of a modern utopia, and *Beyond Freedom and Dignity* (1971), a non-fiction work in which, using the results of modern psychological research to support his case, Skinner presents his ideas for the improvement of society. The central theme in both of these books is essentially the same: an ideal society can be attained and maintained only if human behaviour is modified – by means of such techniques as conditioning – to fit society instead of society adapting to the needs of individuals.

Smith, Hamilton Othanel (*1931–*). See
NATHANS, DANIEL.

Spallanzani, Lazzaro (*1729-1799*), was an Italian physiologist who is famous for disproving Needham's theory of spontaneous generation. In his later years Spallanzani became widely renowned for his biological investigations and received many academic honours, including a fellowship of the Royal Society of London in 1768.

Spallanzani was born on 12 January 1729, the son of a distinguished lawyer. He attended the local school until he was 15, when he went to the Jesuit college at Reggio. He was invited to join the Jesuit order, but declined. He then studied law at the University of Bologna where, under the influence of his cousin Laura Bassi, who was the Professor of Physics and Mathematics, Spallanzani became interested in science and broadened his education to include mathematics, chemistry, natural history and French. In 1754, after obtaining his doctorate, he was appointed Professor of Logic, Metaphysics and Greek at Reggio College. Three years later he was ordained a priest, but performed his priestly duties irregularly and devoted himself almost entirely to his scientific studies – which were greatly facilitated by the moral protection and financial assistance provided by the Church. Spallanzani was Professor of Physics at Modena University from 1760 to 1769, when he became Professor of Natural History at the University of Pavia, a position he held for the rest of his life. In his later years Spallanzani travelled widely in order to further his scientific investigations. He died in Pavia on 11 February 1799.

Spallanzani is best known for finally disproving the theory of spontaneous generation. Francesco Redi's experiments on fly maggots in 1668 proved that complex animals do not arise spontaneously, but until Spallanzani's investigations, it was still generally believed that simple forms of life were generated spontaneously. After performing hundreds of experiments in which he boiled infusions of vegetable matter in hermetically sealed flasks, Spallanzani reported in 1765 that microorganisms do not arise spontaneously.

Spallanzani also investigated many other biological problems, such as the physiology of blood circulation. In 1771, while examining the vascular network in a chick embryo, he discovered the existence of vascular connections between arteries and veins – the first time this connection had been observed in a warm-blooded animal. He also studied the effects of growth on the circulation in chick embryos and tadpoles; the influence of gravity and the effects of wounds on various parts of the vascular system; and changes that occur in the circulation of dying animals. In addition, Spallanzani showed that the arterial pulse is caused by sideways pressure on the expansile artery walls from heart beats transmitted by the bloodstream.

Spallanzani also studied digestion and, after administering food samples in perforated containers to a wide variety of animals then recovering the containers and examining them, concluded that the fundamental factor in digestion is the solvent property of gastric juice – a term first used by him. In his investigations of reproduction, he showed that the clasp reflex in amphibians persists after the male has been severely mutilated or even decapitated. (The clasp reflex is an automatic action on the part of the male in which he tightly holds the female during mating.) And in 1765 he performed an artificial insemination of a dog. Spallanzani's other biological investigations included the resuscitation of rotifers; the regeneration of decapitated snails' heads; the migration of swallows and eels; the flight of bats; and the electric discharge of torpedo-fish. In his later years Spallanzani studied respiration, proving that tissues use oxygen and give off carbon dioxide.

In addition to his biological work, Spallanzani also studied various problems in physics, chemistry, geology and meteorology, as well as pioneering the science of vulcanology.

Spemann, Hans (*1869-1941*), was a German embryologist who discovered the phenomenon now called embryonic induction - the influence exerted by various regions of an embryo that controls the subsequent development of cells into specific organs and tissues. For this outstanding achievement he was awarded the 1935 Nobel Prize in Physiology and Medicine. In carrying out his embryological research, Spemann also pioneered techniques of microsurgery.

Spemann was born on 27 June 1869 in Stuttgart, the eldest of the four children of a bookseller. He attended school at the Eberhard-Ludwigs-Gymnasium, after which he was obliged to do a year of military service with the Kassel Hussars. When his military service ended, Spemann went to Heidelberg University to study medicine, but soon abandoned it in order to study zoology. On his graduation in 1894 he went to Würzburg University to study for his doctorate, and in 1898 was appointed Lecturer in Zoology there. Spemann remained at Würzburg until 1908, when he was appointed to the Chair of Zoology at Rostock University. From 1914 to 1919 he was Director of the Kaiser Wilhelm Institute of Biology in Berlin-Dahlem, after which he became Professor of Zoology at the University of Freiburg-im-Breisgau, a position he held until his retirement in 1935. Spemann died in Freiburg on 12 September 1941.

Spemann's Nobel prize-winning research was carried out on newt embryos. Previous workers had already shown that, as a newt embryo develops, an outgrowth of its brain comes into contact with the ectoderm and that this outgrowth develops into the retina of the eye while the area of ectoderm it has come into contact with develops into the lens. By carefully destroying the outgrowths at an early stage in their development, Spemann found that neither the retina nor the lens subsequently develop. This finding led him to the conclusion that the stimulus causing ectoderm to develop into lens tissue comes from the brain outgrowth. In his next series of experiments, Spemann - using delicate microsurgical techniques that he himself had developed - removed the piece of ectoderm that would normally become the lens and replaced it with a piece of ectoderm from elsewhere in the embryo. He found that, regardless of its site of origin, the transplanted ectoderm develops into a lens if it is in contact with the developing retina.

Spemann continued his line of research by investigating the effect of ligaturing embryos into halves. Embryos at an early stage of development either died or developed into a whole embryo; there were no half embryos formed. Similar results were obtained using embryos in the blastula stage (when the embryo is a hollow ball of cells), but when performed after gastrulation and invagination, ligaturing resulted in half embryos. It seemed, therefore, that as the embryo developed, the fates of different parts became determined. Spemann next began to search for the cause of specific aspects of embryonic development. Working with Otto Mangold, he transplanted various embryonic parts to other areas of the embryo and to different embryos. They discovered that any part of the ectoderm that comes into contact with the mesoderm during gastrulation eventually develops into the central nervous system. By transplanting mesoderm from the dorsal lip region of one embryo into an intact second embryo, Spemann managed to induce the development of a second central nervous system. Thus Spemann and Mangold demonstrated that one area of embryonic tissue influences the development of neighbouring tissues. Spemann named these influential regions organizers.

To investigate whether or not there was any predetermination within embryos, Spemann next conducted a series of experiments in which he exchanged tissue between newt's and frog's embryos. He found that embryonic tissue from newts always gives rise to newt organs, even when transplanted into a frog embryo, and that frog tissue always develops into frog organs in a newt embryo. Thus Spemann demonstrated that embryonic tissue responds to induction from foreign tissue but has the potential to develop only into the organs of the species from which it originated and is therefore predetermined to some extent.

Stahl, Franklin William (*1929-   *). See MESELSON, MATTHEW STANLEY.

Starling, Ernest Henry (*1866-1927*), was a British physiologist, remembered for his work on the heart, his studies of body functions and on hormones (which he first named).

Starling was born in London on 17 April 1866; his father was a barrister who worked in India, and whom he rarely saw. He was educated at King's College, London, from 1880 to 1882, and then at Guy's Hospital. He gained his medical degree there in 1889, having spent a summer in Heidelberg in 1885 working in the laboratories of the German physiologist Willy Kühne, and was a demonstrator at Guy's in 1887. In 1889 he was appointed a lecturer in physiology at Guy's and retained the position until 1899. During that period he was a part-time researcher at University College, London, in 1890, where he got to know William Bayliss, with whom he was to work a few years later. In 1892 he went to Breslau where he spent some time in the laboratories of Rudolf Heidenhain. From 1899 to 1923 he was Professor of Physiology at University College. World War I interrupted this appointment and in 1914 he became Director of Research at the Royal Army Medical Corps College, where he investigated antidotes to poisonous gases. From 1917 to 1919 he served as Chairman of the Royal Society's Food Committee and as scientific adviser to the Ministry of Food. He retired from University College in 1922 and became a Research Professor of the Royal Society. He died while on a Caribbean cruise, in Kingston, Jamaica, on 2 May 1927.

Starling spent several years studying the conditions that cause fluids to leave blood vessels and enter the tissues. In 1896 he demonstrated the Starling equilibrium – the balance between hydrostatic pressure, causing fluids to flow out of the capillary membrane, and osmotic pressure, causing the fluids to be absorbed from the tissues into the capillary. The most important plasma protein in this fluid exchange, which helps to generate intravascular pressure, was found to be albumin.

When he started working at University College with Bayliss, Starling researched the nervous mechanisms that control the activities of the organs of the chest and abdomen, and together they discovered the peristaltic wave in the intestine. Their most important discovery, however, was in 1902, when they found the hormone secretin. This substance is found in the epithelial cells of the duodenum and excites the pancreas to secrete its digestive juices when acid chyme passes from the stomach into the duodenum – hence the name "secretin". It was the first time that a specific chemical substance had been seen to act as a stimulus for an organ at a distance from its site of origin. Starling and Bayliss coined the word "hormone" in 1905 to characterize secretin and other similar substances produced internally and carried in the bloodstream to other parts of the body where they affect the function of organs.

Starling is probably best known for his work on the heart and on circulation. In 1918 he devised a heart-lung preparation by which the heart was isolated from all the other organs except the lungs, and attached only by the pulmonary blood vessels. The blood circulation in the heart was recorded by manometers. In this experiment Starling demonstrated the mechanism by which the heart is able to increase automatically the energy of each contraction in proportion to the mechanical demand made upon it and how it can adapt its work to the needs of the body independently of the nervous system. This mechanism, which Starling called the Law of the Heart, states that the more the heart is filled during diastole (relaxation), the greater is the following systole (contraction), i.e. that the one is directly proportional to the other. This mechanism enables the heart to adjust the strength of its beat to variations in bloodflow without changing its rate. If a heart is impaired, it has to dilate more to achieve the same amount of work as it did when undamaged. Constant dilation of the heart is therefore used as a primary indication that it is damaged. This physiological phenomenon is not a feature exclusive to cardiac muscle but occurs in all contractile tissues whether heart, skeletal or plain muscle, although in the heart the function is more immediately vital.

In 1924 Starling succeeded in maintaining the mammalian kidney in isolation from the body, and found that substances lost in the excretory filtrate, such as carbonates, glucose and chlorides, are reabsorbed in the lower parts of the glomeruli.

Steele, Edward John (*1948-   *), is an Australian immunologist whose research into the inheritance of immunity has lent a certain amount of support to the Lamarckian theory of the inheritance of acquired characteristics, thus challenging modern theories of heredity and evolution.

Steele was born in Darwin on 27 October 1948 and educated at the University of Adelaide, South Australia, from which he graduated in molecular biology in 1971 and gained his doctorate in 1975. In 1976 he began his post-doctoral work at the John Curtin School of Medical Research, Canberra, studying naturally occurring auto-immune disease. He moved to Canada in 1977 and continued his research at the Ontario Cancer Institute. In 1978 he became interested in evolutionary theory, and early in 1980 he moved to the Clinical Research Centre of the Medical Research Council at Harrow, Middlesex.

The modern neo-Darwinistic theory of evolution is a synthesis of Darwin's idea of survival of the fittest by means of natural selection, and Mendelian genetics: according to neo-Darwinism chance, in the form of genetic mutations, plays an important role in evolution; and competition for limited resources - natural selection - eventually kills off the "bad" mutations. These ideas are in direct opposition to Jean Lamarck's theory of the inheritance of acquired characteristics, according to which various parts of the body develop or disappear as necessitated by changes in habits resulting from environmental changes. Lamarck, however, believed that these acquired changes could be passed on to subsequent generations and that, if continued for a long time, a new species would eventually develop. Steele, working with Reginald Gorczynski, found that mice which have been made immune to certain antigens can pass on this acquired immunity to first and second generations of their offspring. This finding suggests that although Lamarck's original ideas are too unsophisticated to be correct, in a subtler, more refined form they may make a valuable contribution towards a better understanding of evolutionary processes.

Stephan, Peter (*1943–*), is a doctor of homeopathic medicine, known for his work in the field of therapeutic immunology.

Stephan was born in Middlesborough, Yorkshire (now Cleveland), on 18 September 1943, the son of Ernest Stephan, a pioneer of cell therapy and the first person to introduce the method into British medical practice (in 1952). Peter Stephan was brought up by his mother and educated at Wallace Tutors, London. He then worked with his father, learning about cell therapy. His father died in 1964, leaving his son the Harley Street clinic at the age of only 21. He studied homeopathic medicine and graduated in 1970. He is now Director of the International Society for Therapeutic Immunology.

The cells that make up the organs and systems of the human body are continually dying and are replaced by healthy cells. But as the body ages, its cells become less healthy and the replacement cells are also inferior; there is also an increase in poorer cells in someone who is ill. The concept of cell therapy is that by injecting healthy cells into the body, the general state of health of the body as a whole can be improved.

In 1931 Paul Niehans made the first successful transfer of healthy cellular material from an animal to a human being by injection as a method of treatment. He injected whole cells, calling the technique cell replacement therapy. But cells are antigens and when "foreign" cells are injected the body's immune system produces antibodies, a reaction that may cause discomfort to the patient

for a few days. Dyckerhoff discovered that a cell's condition is governed by its constituent RNA and that it is necessary only to inject RNA. Also an RNA injection causes no antigen-antibody reaction because RNA is organ-specific not species-specific; for instance, animal kidney RNA is the same as human kidney RNA. Jean Thomas developed a third type of treatment that involves the injection of tissue-specific antisera. An antiserum is an antibody, and its introduction either enlivens sluggish cells or kills them; this treatment is called serocytology.

Stephan's treatment involves injecting an organ-specific RNA to boost the cellular RNA and then injecting tissue-specific antisera. These antisera travel to the "sick" cells and kill them while at the same time they stimulate the body's immune system, and the healthy cells become active and reproduce.

Stephan's recent work has been concerned with the substance that is formed prior to the production of the antibody from which he prepares his sera. This substance seems to have beneficial effects which may be used therapeutically. In 1981 he developed Omnigen, a total cellular extract and serum for treating premature cellular degeneration.

Steptoe, Patrick (*1913–*). See EDWARDS, ROBERT.

Stopes, Marie Charlotte Carmichael (*1880–1958*), was an early British advocate of birth control who, in 1921, founded the first instructional clinic for contraception in Britain.

Marie Stopes was born on 15 October 1880 in Edinburgh. Her mother was a feminist and one of the first woman members of Edinburgh University; her father was a brewing engineer from Essex. She read botany at University College, London, graduating in 1902, then went to the University of Munich, from which she gained her doctorate in 1904. She was awarded her DSc from London University in 1905, when only 25 years old, and then taught at the University of Manchester - the first woman to be appointed to the science staff there. For several years she continued her palaeobotanical research into fossil plants and primitive cycads and became one of the foremost investigators in her field. In 1911 she married Reginald Ruggles Gates, a Canadian botanist, and left Manchester University. But the marriage was not consummated and was annulled in 1916.

The breakdown of her marriage stimulated Marie Stopes' interest in the subject of sexual intercourse, personal relationships and marriage, and in 1918 she published *Married Love*, the

underlying theme of which is that women should be able to enjoy sexual intercourse on the basis of equality with men; in the book she also referred briefly to contraceptive methods. This topic was extremely controversial in Britain at that time and she had great difficulty in finding a publisher. And after it was published, *Married Love* met with considerable opposition: for example, C.P. Blacker (later to help in the creation of the International Planned Parenthood Foundation) said that the book was "responsible for printing instructions to girls of initially dubious virtues as to how to adopt the profession of more or less open prostitution". Nevertheless, Marie Stopes received many requests for more information and advice about contraception from women who had read her book, so later in the same year she wrote and published *Wise Parenthood*, in which she attempted to answer the queries she had received.

Also in 1918 Marie Stopes married for the second time; her husband was Humphrey Verdon Roe, the co-founder of the A.V. Roe aircraft company. Roe supported Marie Stopes' ideas and he sponsored her birth control clinic, the first one in Britain, which opened in 1921 in Marlborough Road, Holloway, London. This event re-aroused vehement opposition, especially from the Roman Catholic Church, and Marie Stopes spent the next few years both promoting and defending the idea of contraception. In 1934 she published another book *Birth Control Today*, in which she voiced her disapproval of abortion as a means of population control, describing women who sought abortions as "a danger to the human race". She continued to champion the cause of birth control in her later years, travelling to many different countries to do so. She died on 2 October 1958 near Dorking, Surrey, having brought about a considerable change in general attitudes towards a more widespread acceptance of contraception, a trend that continued after her death - although even today the subject still arouses controversy and opposition, particularly from certain religious groups.

Stokes, William (*1804-1878*). See CHEYNE, JOHN.

Sutherland, Earl Wilbur (*1915-1974*), was an American biochemist who was awarded the 1971 Nobel Prize in Physiology and Medicine for his work with cyclic adenosine monophosphate (cyclic AMP), the chemical substance that moderates the action of hormones.

Sutherland was born in Burlingame, Kansas, on 19 November 1915. He graduated from Washburn College, Topeka, in 1937 and received his MD from Washington University Medical School, St Louis, in 1942. After serving as an army officer during World War II he took an appointment at Washington University to do research on hormones under Carl and Gerty Cori. In 1953 he became Director of the Department of Medicine at Western Reserve (now Case Western Reserve) University in Cleveland. Ten years later he was appointed Professor of Physiology at Vanderbilt University, Nashville, and from 1973 until his death he was a member of the faculty of the University of Miami Medical School. He died in Miami on 9 March 1974.

Sutherland began working with hormones at Washington under the Coris and then spent the 1950s doing research on his own - other workers took little interest in his studies. At that time it was thought that hormones, carried in the bloodstream, activated their target organs directly. Sutherland showed that the key to the process - the activating agent of the organ concerned - is cyclic adenosine 3′,5′-monophosphate (cyclic AMP). The arrival of a hormone increases the organ's cellular level of cyclic AMP, which in turn triggers or inhibits the cellular activity.

Cyclic AMP is present in every animal cell and therefore affects "everything from memory to toes", as Sutherland himself said, so the implications of his discovery were enormous. The 1971 Nobel Prize committee commented that it is rare for such a discovery to be credited to only one person. By the end of the 1960s Sutherland was no longer alone in his research; hundreds of scientists throughout the world were keen to do research on the newly discovered substance.

Sutton-Pringle, John William (*1912-*   ), is a British zoologist who is best known for his substantial contribution to our knowledge of insect flight.

Sutton-Pringle was born on 22 July 1912 and was educated at Winchester College and King's College, Cambridge. After graduation he was appointed Demonstrator in Zoology at Cambridge in 1937, a post he held for two years. From 1938 to 1945 he was a Fellow of King's College Cambridge. In 1945 he was appointed to a lectureship at Cambridge, and became a Fellow of Peterhouse College in the same year. He was a Reader in Experimental Cytology from 1959 to 1961, when he became Emeritus Fellow at Peterhouse. In 1977 he was elected President of the Society for Experimental Biology.

Sutton-Pringle helped to establish much of our present knowledge of the anatomical mechanisms involved in insect flight. Most insects have two hindwings and two forewings, and in many species each hindwing is linked to its anterior forewing, thus enabling each pair of wings to act in unison. Not all species use both pairs of wings

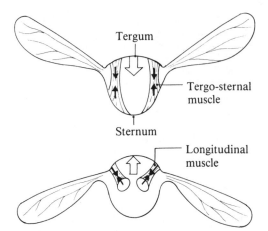

Sutton-Pringle showed that the rapid wing-beats necessary for flight in insects are achieved by alternate actions of the tergo-sternal and longitudinal muscles.

for flight, however; in the housefly, for example, the hindwings are reduced in size and serve as balancing organs during flight.

Insect flight is achieved by simple up and down movements of the wings. In aphids, for example, these wing movements are brought about by the contractions of two separate sets of muscles: contraction of the longitudinal muscles results in depression of the wings; contraction of the dorso-ventral muscles causes elevation of the wings. When moving through the air, the anterior edge of the wings remains rigid while the posterior edge bends. On the downward stroke, the posterior edge is displaced upwards, and on the upward stroke the posterior edge is displaced downwards. This, in turn, causes the development of a localized region of high pressure air behind the insect, which propels the insect forwards. The faster the rate of wing beats, the greater the displacement of the posterior wing edges, the greater the pressure exerted on the insect from behind, and therefore the faster the insect flies.

Swammerdam, Jan (*1637-1680*), was a Dutch naturalist who investigated many aspects of biology but who is probably best known for his outstanding microscope observations, his detailed and accurate anatomical descriptions, and his studies of insects. He is considered by many to be a founder of both comparative anatomy and entomology.

Swammerdam was born in Amsterdam on 12 February 1637. He was the son of an apothecary whose hobby was a museum of curiosities, a hobby that stimulated the younger Swammerdam's interest in natural history, particularly in insects. He graduated with a medical degree from Leyden (now Leiden) University in 1667 but never practised as a physician, preferring to pursue his interest in natural history. Subsequently his father, who wanted his son to become a priest, withdrew his financial support – despite which the younger Swammerdam continued his biological studies, although he suffered severe privations and became chronically ill, both physically and mentally. In 1673 Swammerdam came under the influence of the religious zealot Antoinette Bourignon and became increasingly embroiled in religious controversy until he died, only 43 years old, in Amsterdam on 15 February 1680.

Swammerdam made many important contributions to biological knowledge but most of his studies were of insects. He accurately described and illustrated the life cycles and anatomies of many species, including bees, mayflies and dragonflies. In mayflies and dragonflies the change from the last nymph stage to the winged adult is outwardly the most striking, but Swammerdam showed that rudimentary wings occur in the aquatic nymphs some time before the final moult. He also showed that caterpillars develop wings and adult-type legs shortly before pupating. From his observations of their metamorphic development Swammerdam classified insects into four major groups, three of which are still used in a modified form in modern insect classification. In addition, he disproved many false beliefs about insects – for example, that their bodies are structureless, fluid-filled cavities without fully formed internal organs.

Swammerdam also studied vertebrates, about which he provided a substantial body of new knowledge, most of which was correct. He showed that the lungs of newly born mammals sink in water when the lungs are taken from the animals before breathing has started but that lungs taken from young animals whose respiration has been established float. He also erroneously believed, however, that the movements of the chest in mammals are unrelated to inhalation and exhalation but are associated with transferring air from the lungs to the heart. Swammerdam demonstrated that muscles removed from a frog could be stimulated to contract and that when muscle (including heart muscle) contracts it does not increase in volume. Furthermore, he anticipated the discovery of the role of oxygen in respiration by postulating that air contained a volatile element that could pass from the lungs to the heart (contributing to the respiration operation of the heart) and then to the muscles, providing the energy for muscle contraction. Investigating the anatomy of the frog, he observed that the frog's egg passes through a stage when it consists of four joined globules (now known to be the second cleavage of the fertilized egg). He was also probably the first to discover red blood corpuscles when he observed oval particles in frog's blood in 1658.

In his work on human and mammalian anatomy, Swammerdam discovered valves in the lymphatic system; these valves are now called Swammerdam valves. He also investigated the human reproductive system and was one of the first to show that female mammals produce eggs, analogous to birds' eggs. In addition he perfected a technique for injecting dyes into dissected cadavers in order to display anatomical details.

Swammerdam's work – particularly his insect studies – had a profound impact on scientific thinking, although his manuscripts were not published in full until 1737, when Hermann Boerhaave published *Biblia naturae* (*Bible of Nature*), a two-volume Latin translation of Swammerdam's Dutch text that included illustrations engraved from Swammerdam's own drawings. The work is one of the finest collections of biological observations ever published and, even today, many of Swammerdam's illustrations remain unsurpassed.

T

Tansley, Arthur George (*1871–1955*), was a British botanist who was a pioneer in the science of plant ecology. He helped to promote the subject through his teaching, and by writing and editing textbooks and journals (including contributing to and editing the first major book on the vegetation of the British Isles). He was also instrumental in the formation of organizations devoted to the study of ecology and the protection of wildlife. Tansley's contributions to botany were recognized by the award of several honours, including a fellowship of the Royal Society of London in 1915, the Gold Medal of the Linnean Society in 1941 and a knighthood in 1950.

Tansley was born in London on 15 August 1871. He was educated at Highgate School from 1886 to early 1889 (and later commented on the inadequacy of the science teaching of that time), after which he attended science classes at University College, London, where he received his first instruction in botany from Francis Oliver. In 1890 he went to Trinity College Cambridge, graduating in 1894. He combined his last year of study with a teaching post at University College and, after graduation, returned there as an assistant to Oliver and Demonstrator in Botany, a position

he held until 1906. Between 1900 and 1901 Tansley visited Ceylon (now Sri Lanka), the Malay peninsula and Egypt to study their flora. On his return, he found that there was no suitable journal in which to publish his findings, so he founded *The New Phytologist* in 1902, remaining its editor for 30 years. In 1907 he was appointed University Lecturer in Botany at Cambridge University.

After World War I, however, his interest turned temporarily towards psychology, and in 1923 he resigned his lectureship in order to study under Sigmund Freud in Austria. Tansley returned to Britain the following year, and in 1927 was appointed Sherardian Professor of Botany at Oxford University, a position that carried with it a fellowship at Magdalen College. He remained at Oxford until his retirement in 1939. Tansley continued to be active after retiring. He was Chairman of the Nature Conservancy from 1949 to 1953 and President of the Council for the Promotion of Field Studies (now called the Field Studies Council) from 1947 to 1953, having played a large part in the establishment of these organizations.

Most of Tansley's work concerned British plants and plant communities. He co-ordinated a large project (which lasted from 1903 to 1907) to map the vegetation of the British Isles; the surveys that were completed are still models of vegetation mapping technique. The scientists involved in this project published their findings in *Types of British Vegetation* (1911), of which Tansley was the editor and major contributor. Although this book was a masterly summary of British flora, Tansley and the other scientists felt that a wider approach to plant ecology was needed, so on 12 April 1913 the group founded the British Ecological Society, with Tansley as its president. The society founded the *Journal of Ecology*, which Tansley edited from 1916 to 1938.

While Professor of Botany at Oxford, Tansley enlarged and rewrote *Types of British Vegetation*. The new work, *The British Islands and their Vegetation* (1939), was Tansley's greatest single achievement. In it he showed how vegetation is affected by soil, climate, the presence of wild and domesticated animals, previous land management and contemporary human activities. He also reviewed all known accounts of British flora and then linked the two themes, thereby demonstrating which factors are important in influencing the various types of vegetation. In 1949 he published *Britain's Green Mantle*, a shorter and more popular version.

Tansley also helped to promote the study of plant ecology through his teaching; by writing several practical guides, such as *Practical Plant Ecology* (1923); and by campaigning for the establishment formation of ecological organizations.

Tatum, Edward Lawrie (*1909–1975*). See BEADLE, GEORGE WELLS.

Temin, Howard Martin (*1934–   *), is an American virologist concerned with cancer research. For his work on the genetic inheritance of viral elements he received the 1975 Nobel Prize in Physiology and Medicine, which he shared with David Baltimore (1938–   ) and Renato Dulbecco (1914–   ).

Temin was born in Philadelphia on 10 December 1934 and educated at Swarthmore College, Pennsylvania, where he gained a BA in 1955. He then obtained his PhD at the California Institute of Technology, Pasadena, in 1959 for a thesis on animal virology. During the following year he was a post-doctoral fellow there. Between 1960 and 1964 he became Assistant Professor of Oncology at the University of Wisconsin, and then Associate Professor from 1964 to 1969. He was appointed Professor of Oncology at Wisconsin in 1969 and Professor of Cancer Research in 1971. Since 1974 he has been Professor of Viral Oncology and Cell Biology at Wisconsin.

In the early attempts at organ transplants in the human body, the patient did not live long after the operation because the transplanted organ was rejected by the recipient's body as foreign tissue. Peter Medawar experimented with mice and found that if the intended recipient was injected at the embryo stage with cells from the future donor, its body did not reject the transplant, but accepted the foreign cells as its own. He also found that this acquired immunological tolerance can be handed down to a second generation. Following on Medawar's experiments, Macfarlane Burnet found that the ability of the human body to produce antibodies is not learnt through a process of evolution but he suggested that the genes of the antibody-producing cells contain a region which is continually mutating, with each mutation leading to the production of a new antibody variant.

Temin's prize-winning research was on a virus that has a mechanism which incorporates its material into mammalian genes. He discovered that beneficial mutations outside the germ line are naturally selected and that the mechanism adds genetic information from outside into the germ line.

It has been suggested since that this inheritance might operate in the blood cells, the gut lining and perhaps in the nervous system, from where it enters the germ line. Experimental evidence suggests that acquired characteristics can be passed on through genes, in agreement with Lamarck. For instance, the incidence of chemically induced brain tumours has been found to be very high in the offspring of affected parents.

Theiler, Max (*1899–1972*), was a South African-born American microbiologist who developed an effective vaccine against yellow fever, an achievement that gained him the 1951 Nobel Prize in Physiology and Medicine. He also researched into various other diseases, including Weil's disease and poliomyelitis.

Theiler was born on 30 January 1899 in Pretoria, South Africa, the son of a Swiss-born veterinary surgeon. After doing his preliminary medical training at Rhodes University College and the University of Cape Town, Theiler went to Britain and completed his training at St Thomas's Hospital and the London School of Hygiene and Tropical Medicine, from which he received his medical degree in 1922. After graduating, Theiler went to the United States and joined the Department of Tropical Medicine at Harvard University Medical School. In 1930 he moved to the Rockefeller Institute for Medical Research (now Rockefeller University), New York City, becoming Director of the Virus Laboratory there in 1950. In the same year he was also made a Director of the Division of Medicine and Public Health. Theiler was appointed Professor of Epidemiology and Microbiology at Yale University in 1964 and held this post until he retired in 1967. He died on 11 August 1972 in New Haven, Connecticut.

By the time Theiler began his research into yellow fever, Walter Reed (1851–1902), an American army doctor, had proved in 1900 that the disease is carried by the *Aëdes aegypti* mosquito, and Stokes, Bauer and Hudson had discovered that the causative agent is a virus. Furthermore it had been established that certain mammals can act as reservoirs of infection and that *Aedes aegypti* is not the only species of mosquito that can transmit yellow fever.

Theiler's early work on the disease – carried out at Harvard – demonstrated that common albino mice are susceptible to yellow fever, and that when they are infected, the virus undergoes certain changes. Continuing his research at the Rockefeller Institute, he found that when the mice are given intracerebral injections of yellow fever virus they develop encephalomyelitis but, unlike monkeys and human beings, do not develop heart, liver or kidney disorders. He passed the virus through the brains of several mice in order to produce a fully mouse-adapted strain of the virus, which he then injected subcutaneously into monkeys and human volunteers. Theiler found that this mouse-adapted strain produced full, active immunity in monkeys but still affected the kidneys in humans. But when he combined the mouse-adapted viral strain with serum from the blood of people who had recovered from yellow fever and injected the mixture into humans, he found that it produced immunity without affecting the kidneys; he had succeeded in producing a safe vaccine against yellow fever.

This method of making the vaccine is not suitable for large-scale production, however, because human serum containing antibodies against yellow fever is difficult to obtain. Theiler therefore began working on a method of producing yellow fever vaccine that did not require human serum, and in 1937 he developed vaccine 17-D still the main form of protection against yellow fever. In 1931 E.W. Goodpasture developed a method of culturing viruses by injecting them into chick embryos. Theiler made vaccine 17-D by combining Goodpasture's technique with his own method of making mouse-adapted viral strain. He passed yellow fever virus successively through 200 mice then cultured the virus in 100 chick embryos; this yielded a mutant form of the virus that caused only mild symptoms when injected into humans yet gave complete immunity against yellow fever.

In addition to his work on yellow fever, Theiler also investigated Weil's disease, amoebic dysentery and poliomyelitis. He hypothesized that the poliomyelitis virus is widespread in the intestines, where it is harmless, and that symptoms are produced only in the rare instances where the virus enters the central nervous system.

Theophrastus (*c. 372-c. 287* BC), was an ancient Greek thinker who wrote on a wide range of subjects - science, philosophy, law, literature, music and poetry, for example - but who is best known as the father of botany.

Theophrastus was born in *c.* 372 BC in Eresus on the Greek island of Lesbos. He studied under Plato at the Academy in Athens, where Aristotle was also working, and then under Aristotle after he had left the Academy in 348 BC. When Aristotle returned to Athens and founded the Lyceum in 335 BC, Theophrastus became his chief assistant, eventually succeeding him as head of the Lyceum in 323 BC, when Aristotle again left Athens. Enrolment at the Lyceum reached its peak under Theophrastus, and he employed the pupils, many of whom came from distant parts of Greece, to make botanical observations near their homes. He remained head of the Lyceum until his death in *c.* 287 BC.

Theophrastus was a prolific writer: more than 200 books are attributed to him but most are known only by their titles. The most important of his surviving works are those on botany. In these books he covered most aspects of the subject - descriptions of plants, classification, plant distribution, propagation, germination and cultivation. He described and discussed more than 500 species and varieties of plants from lands bordering the Atlantic and Mediterranean and from India, referring in his descriptions to information from people who had been on Alexander the Great's campaigns and so had first-hand knowledge of foreign flora. On the basis of his collection of information about a wide range of flora, Theophrastus classified plants into trees, shrubs, undershrubs and herbs. In his detailed study of flowers, he noted that some flowers bear petals whereas others do not, and observed the different relative positions of the petals and ovary. He also distinguished between two major groups of flowering plants - dicotyledons and monocotyledons in modern terms - and between flowering plants and cone-bearing trees - angiosperms and gymnosperms. In his work on propagation and germination, Theophrastus described the various ways in which specific plants and trees can grow - from seeds, from roots, from pieces torn off, from a branch or twig, or from a small piece of cleft wood. He also accurately described the germination of seeds.

Theophrastus provided an excellent foundation for the science of botany - his writings are comprehensive and are generally very accurate, even by modern standards, although he was not infallible - for example, like all other pre-seventeenth-century scientists Theophrastus believed in spontaneous generation. But he usually substantiated statements with observed facts, thus helping to establish a sound method of scientific investigation.

Thompson, D'Arcy Wentworth (1860-1948), was a British biologist and classical scholar who is best known for his book *On Growth and Form*, first published in 1917. He also studied fisheries and oceanography and published several works on classical science.

Thompson was born on 2 May 1860 in Edinburgh; his father was an authority on ancient Greece. He was educated at the Edinburgh Academy, Edinburgh University and Trinity College, Cambridge. In the late 1870s, while studying medicine at Edinburgh University, he came under the influence of Charles Thomson (1830-1882) - the university's Professor of Natural History who had recently returned from the Challenger Expedition for the exploration of the ocean depths - and became interested in biology and oceanography. In 1884 Thompson was appointed Professor of Biology at University College, Dundee, then became Senior Professor of Natural History at St Andrews University in 1917 – a post he held for the remainder of his career. Concerned about conservation, in 1896 and 1897 Thompson went on expeditions to the Pribilof Islands as a member of the British–American commission on fur-seal hunting in the Bering Sea. He was also one of the British representatives on the International Council for the Exploration of the Sea and a member of the Fishery Board of Scotland. Thompson died on 21 June 1948 in St Andrews.

Thompson's principal contribution to biology was his highly influential *On Growth and Form* (1917), in which he interpreted the structure and growth of organisms in terms of the physical forces to which every individual is subjected throughout its life. He also hypothesized that the evolution of one species into another results mainly from major transformations involving the entire organism – a view contrary to the traditional Darwinistic theory of species arising as a result of numerous minor alterations in the body parts over several generations. In the 1942 revised edition of his book, however, Thompson admitted that his evolutionary theory did not adequately account for the cumulative effect of successive small modifications.

In addition to his theoretical work on growth, form and evolution, Thompson wrote many papers on fisheries and oceanography. He also published works on classical natural history, notably *A Glossary of Greek Birds* (1895) and an edition of Aristotle's *Historia Animalium* (1910).

Tinbergen, Nikolaas (*1907–*   ), is a Dutch-born British ethologist who studied many animals in their natural environments but is best known for his investigations into the courtship behaviour of sticklebacks and the social behaviour of gulls. He did much to revitalize the science of ethology for which, among many other honours, he shared the 1973 Nobel Prize in Physiology and Medicine with Konrad Lorenz (with whom he worked on several research projects) and Karl von Frisch.

Tinbergen was born on 15 April 1907 in The Hague and was educated at Leiden University, from which he gained his doctorate in 1932. During 1931 and 1932 he went with a scientific expedition to the Arctic and on his return became a lecturer at Leiden University. Except for a period of military service during World War II, Tinbergen remained at Leiden – becoming Professor of Experimental Zoology in 1947 – until 1949, when he was appointed Professor of Zoology at Oxford University. He established a school of animal behaviour studies at Oxford and remained at the university until he retired in 1974.

One of Tinbergen's best-known studies was of the three-spined stickleback, described in *The Study of Instinct* (1951). During the spring mating season the male stickleback marks out its individual territory and attacks any other male sticklebacks that enter its domain. If a female stickleback enters his territory, however, the male does not attack but courts her instead. Tinbergen showed that the aggressive behaviour of the male is stimulated by the red coloration on the underside of other males (this red patch develops on the underbelly of males during the mating season but does not appear on females). Tinbergen also demonstrated that the courtship dance of the male is stimulated by the sight of the swollen belly of a female that is ready to lay eggs. If the female responds to the male's zig-zag courtship dance, she follows him to the nest that he has already prepared. The female enters the nest first and is followed by the male who pokes her under the tail with his snout, causing her to release eggs and to emit a chemical that stimulates the male to ejaculate sperm into the water.

In *The Herring Gull's World* (1953) Tinbergen described the social behaviour of gulls, again emphasizing the importance of stimulus-response processes in territorial behaviour. Defence of territory is particularly important for birds such as herring gulls, which nest in large, densely populated colonies. Although these gulls possess a large vocabulary of warning calls, Tinbergen's findings suggest that gestures are equally, if not more important in warning off other gulls. For example, he found that when two male herring gulls meet at territorial boundaries, one or both of the gulls tugs at the grass with his beak, rather than immediately fighting. Another similar behaviour pattern – the choking gesture – is performed by male and female gulls to warn off invaders: again, rather than fight, the gulls lower their heads, open their mouths and appear to choke. Tinbergen hypothesized that these gestures are normal behaviour patterns (grass-pulling, for example, occurs during nest-building) that have become adapted to denote aggression – and are recognized as aggressive by other birds – in order to prevent fighting and the possible injury or death that could result.

Tinbergen investigated other aspects of animal behaviour, such as the importance of learning in the feeding behaviour of oystercatchers, and also studied human behaviour particularly aggression, which he believes is an inherited instinct that developed when humans changed from being predominantly herbivorous to being hunting carnivores.

Tradescant, John (*1570–1638*), and **Tradescant, John** (*1608–1662*), father and son, were English horticulturalists and pioneers in the collection and cultivation of plants. Linnaeus named the flowering plant genus *Tradescantia* (the spiderworts) after them.

Tradescant senior is generally considered to be the earliest collector of plants and other natural history objects. In 1604 he became gardener to the Earl of Salisbury who, in 1610, sent him to Belgium to collect plants; the Brussels strawberry was one of the plants that he brought back. The following year he went to France, visiting Rouen and the Apothecary Garden in Paris, and in 1618 went to Russia with an official party sent by James I. Two years later Tradescant accompanied another official expedition – this time one against the North African Barbary pirates – and brought back to England gutta-percha, mazer wood and various fruits and seeds. Between 1625 and 1628 he was employed by the Duke of Buckingham and during this period joined an expedition to La Rochelle, France. Later, when he became gardener to Charles I, Tradescant set up his own garden and museum in Lambeth, London, which he stocked from his private collection of plants and other natural history specimens. In 1624 he published a catalogue of 750 plants grown in his garden; the only known copy of this catalogue is now in the library of Magdalen College, Oxford.

The younger Tradescant, sharing his father's enthusiasm for plants, became a member of the Company of Master Gardeners of London when only 26 years old. Three years later, in 1637, he went to Virginia, America, to collect plants and shells for his father's museum. After his father's death in 1638, the younger Tradescant succeeded him as gardener to Charles I, and went on several plant-collecting expeditions, adding to his father's collection. He published two lists of plants in the collection – in 1634 and 1656, the latter incorporating his father's specimens – most of which were unknown in England before 1600.

The younger Tradescant died on 22 April 1662 in Lambeth. His collection was eventually incorporated with that of Elias Ashmole (1617-1692) who, in turn, gave it to Oxford University in 1683, thereby founding the Ashmolean Museum.

Twort, Frederick William (*1877-1950*), was a British bacteriologist, the original discoverer of bacteriophages (often called phages), the relatively large viruses that attack and destroy bacteria. He also researched into Johne's disease, a chronic intestinal infection of cattle. The only major honour that Twort received for his work was his election as a Fellow of the Royal Society in 1929.

Twort was born on 22 October 1877 in Camberley, Surrey, the son of a physician. He studied

medicine at St Thomas's Hospital, London, obtaining his degree in 1900. He then spent a year as Assistant Superintendent of the Clinical Laboratory at St Thomas's before becoming Assistant Bacteriologist at the London Hospital in 1902. In 1909 Twort was appointed Superintendent of the Brown Institute, a pathology research centre. He remained there (except for a period of war service during World War I) until he retired 35 years later, having also been made Professor of Bacteriology at the University of London in 1919. He died in Camberley on 20 March 1950.

Twort is probably best known for his discovery in 1915 of what is now called a bacteriophage. While working with cultures of *Staphylococcus aureus* (the bacterium that causes the common boil), he noticed that colonies of these bacteria were being destroyed. Twort isolated the substance that produced this effect and found that it was transmitted indefinitely to subsequent generations of the bacterium. He then suggested that the substance was a virus, a prediction that was later proved correct. He was unable to continue his work, however, and his discovery aroused little interest at the time. Two years later, in 1917, the same discovery was made independently by a Canadian bacteriologist, Félix d'Hérelle, who named the active substance bacteriophage. Again, bacteriophages were virtually ignored and it was not until the 1950s, with the work of Heinz Fraenkel-Conrat and others, that their importance was recognized. Since then bacteriophages have been widely used in microbiology, mainly for studying bacterial genetics and cellular control mechanisms.

Twort was also the first to culture the causative bacillus of Johne's disease, and showed that a specific substance is essential for the growth of this bacillus. In addition, he discovered that vitamin K is needed by growing leprosy bacteria, which opened a new field of research into the nutritional requirements of micro-organisms.

Van Leeuwenhoek, Anton (*1632-1723*). See LEEUWENHOEK, ANTON VAN.

Vesalius, Andreas (*1514-1564*), was a Belgian physician who was a founder of modern anatomy.

Vesalius was born in Brussels on 13 December 1514, to a family of physicians from Wesel (the derivation of Vesalius), in Germany. His father was the royal pharmacist to Charles V of Germany, and from an early age Vesalius showed an inclination to follow in the family tradition, by dissecting dead birds and mice. He was educated at the University of Louvain and then studied medicine in Paris. After a period as a military surgeon, he moved to Padua where he gained his medical degree in 1537, and was then appointed lecturer in surgery and anatomy. At Padua he published his famous book *De humani corporis fabrica* (1543) which met with vigorous opposition and led to bitter controversy. In a fit of despondency, he gave up anatomy and resigned his chair at Padua. He became court physician to Charles V, and later to his son Philip II of Spain. On his way back from a pilgrimage to Jerusalem, on 15 October 1564, he died in a shipwreck off the island of Zante (now called Zakinthos) near Greece.

Vesalius was taught anatomy in the Galenist tradition. The Greek physician had never dissected a human body – all Galen's accounts of the human anatomy were based on his research of the Barbary ape – although he was regarded as infallible and was venerated until the Renaissance: Vesalius was therefore taught principles of anatomy that had not been questioned for 1,300 years.

The artists of Vesalius' time encouraged the study of anatomy because they wanted accurate representations of the human body. The greatest of these were Leonardo da Vinci (1452-1519), Albrecht Dürer (1471-1528) and Michelangelo (1475-1564). Da Vinci, who made more than 750 anatomical drawings, paved the way for Vesalius. Vesalius became dissatisfied with the instruction he had received and resolved to make his own observations, which disagreed with Galen. For instance, he disproved that men had a rib less than women – a belief that had been widely held until then. He also believed, contrary to Aristotle's theory of the heart being the centre of the mind and emotion, that the brain and the nervous system are the centre.

Between 1539 and 1542 Vesalius prepared his masterpiece, a book that employed talented artists to provide the illustrations. The finished work, published in 1543 in Basel, is one of the great books of the sixteenth century. The quality of anatomical depiction introduced a new standard into all illustrated works and especially into medical books. The text, divided into seven sections, is of great importance in expressing the need to introduce scientific method into the study of anatomy. The *De humani corporis fabrica* did for anatomy what Copernicus' book did for astronomy (they were both published in the same year). Vesalius upset the authority of Galen and

his book, the first real textbook of anatomy, marks the beginning of biology as a science.

von Baer, Karl Ernest Ritter (*1792-1876*), was an Estonian embryologist famous for his discovery of the mammalian ovum, and who made a significant contribution to the systematic study of the development of animals.

Von Baer was born on 29 February 1792, at Piep, in Estonia, on his father's estate. The size of the family – he was one of ten children – forced his parents to send him to live with his paternal uncle and aunt, although his father was a wealthy landholder and district official. On his return home at the age of seven, he was privately tutored until 1807, when he attended a school for members of the nobility for three years. He then went to the University of Dorpat, the local university, where he was taught by Karl Burdach (1776-1847), the Professor of Physiology there who had a great influence on his life. He graduated with a medical degree in 1814 and went to Vienna for a year. During the following year he spent some time studying comparative anatomy at the University of Würzburg, where he met Ignaz Döllinger (1770-1841), who was the Professor of Anatomy (and father of the well-known Catholic theologian). Döllinger first introduced him to embryology. In 1817, at the invitation of his old teacher, Burdach, he joined him at the University of Königsberg, where he taught zoology, anatomy and anthropology. Two years later he was appointed Assistant Professor of Zoology. In 1820 he married Auguste Medem, and later had

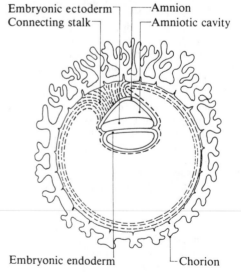

Embryonic ectoderm — Amnion
Connecting stalk — Amniotic cavity

Embryonic endoderm — Chorion

Von Baer pioneered embryology and was the first to distinguish between the ectoderm and endoderm in a developing mammalian embryo.

six children. He became restless at Königsberg, and in 1834 moved to St Petersburg (now Leningrad), where he took up the appointment of Librarian of the Foreign Division, at the Academy of Sciences. In 1837 he led the first of many expeditions into Novaya Zemlya, in Arctic Russia, where he was the first naturalist to collect plant and animal specimens. He later led expeditions to Lappland, the Caucasian and the Caspian Seas. In 1846 he became the Professor of Comparative Anatomy and Physiology at the Medico-Chirurgical Academy in St Petersburg. He retired from the Academy in 1862 but remained working for them until 1867, as an honorary member. He died on 28 November 1876 at Dorpat, in Estonia (now Tartu, in Estonian S.S.R.).

At Würzburg, Döllinger had suggested that von Baer study the blastoderm of chick embryos removed from the yolk, but the cost of a sufficient number of eggs for observation and someone to look after the incubator was too high and he left the investigation to his more affluent friend, Christian Pander (1794–1865). Von Baer carried on Pander's research and applied it to all vertebrates. In 1817 Pander had described the formation of three layers in the vertebrate embryo - the ectoderm, endoderm and mesoderm. Von Baer developed a theory regarding these germ layers in which he conceived that the goal of early development is the formation of these three layers, out of which all later organs are formed. At the same time he proposed the "law of corresponding stages", which contradicted the popular belief that vertebrate embryos develop in stages similar to adults of other species. Instead, he suggested that the younger the embryos of various species are, the stronger is the resemblance between them. He demonstrated this fact by deliberately leaving off the labels of embryo species and saying: "I am quite unable to say to what class they belong. They may be lizards, or small birds, or very young mammalia, so complete is the similarity in the mode of formation of the head and trunk in these animals. The extremities are still absent, but even if they existed, in the earliest stage of the development we should learn nothing, because all arise from the same fundamental form." From this demonstration he formed his concept of epigenesis, that an embryo develops from simple to complex, from a homogenous to a heterogeneous stage.

In 1827, von Baer published the news of his most significant discovery - the mammalian ovum. William Harvey before him had tried to find it, dissecting a deer, but had searched for it in the uterus. Von Baer found the egg inside the Graafian follicle in the ovary of a bitch belonging to Burdach, which had been offered for the ex-

periment. Von Baer's publication stated that "every animal which springs from the coition of male and female is developed from an ovum, and none from a simple formative liquid".

In his observations of the embryo, von Baer discovered the extraembryonic membranes - the chorion, amnion and allantois - and described their functions. He also identified for the first time the notochord, a gelatinous, cylindrical cord which passes along the body of the embryo of vertebrates. In the lower vertebrates it forms the entire back skeleton, whereas in the higher ones the backbone and skull are developed around it. He revealed the neural folds, and suggested that they were the beginnings of the nervous system, and described the five primary brain vesicles.

On his expeditions, von Baer made a significant geological discovery concerning the forces that cause a particular formation on riverbanks in Russia. His study of fishes, made at the same time, in his *Development of Fishes* (1835) stimulated the development of scientific and economic interest in fisheries in Russia.

Von Baer collected skull specimens for his lectures on physical anthropology, the measurements of which he recorded. In 1859, the same year that Darwin published *The Origin of Species*, he published independently a work that suggested that human skulls might have originated from one type.

Von Baer's publication *De Ovi Mammalium et Hominis Genesi* (*On the Mammalian Egg and the Origin of Man*, 1827), and his *Über Entwicklunggeschichte der Thiere* (*On the Development of Animals*, Vol. 1., 1828, Vol. 2., 1837) paved the way for modern embryology and gave a basis for new and scientific interpretation of embryology and biology.

Von Frisch, Karl (*1886–   *), is an Austrian-born German ethologist who is best known for his studies of bees, particularly for his interpretation of their dances as a means of communicating the location of a food source to other bees. He was awarded many honours for his research into animal behaviour, including the 1973 Nobel Prize for Physiology and Medicine (shared with Konrad Lorenz and Nikolaas Tinbergen).

Von Frisch was born on 20 November 1886 in Vienna, Austria. He was educated at the Schottengymnasium in Vienna then at the universities of Vienna and Munich, gaining his doctorate from Munich in 1910. In the same year he became a research assistant there, and then lecturer in zoology and comparative anatomy in 1912. From 1921 to 1923 he was Professor and Director of the Zoological Institution at the University of Rostock, then held the same post at the University of

Breslau. He returned to the University of Munich in 1925 and established a Zoological Institution there. But the Institution was destroyed during World War II, and so Von Frisch moved to the University of Graz in 1946. He returned again to Munich in 1950, however, and remained there until his retirement in 1958.

Von Frisch's most renowned work concerned communication among honey-bees. By marking bees and following their movements in special observation hives, he found that foraging bees that had returned from a food source often perform a dance, either a relatively simple round dance when the food is within 100 metres of the hive, or a more complex waggle dance when the food is farther away. He also found that bees dance only when they have encountered a rich food source, and concluded that these dances are a means of communicating information to other bees about food sources. In the round dance, the returned forager moves round and round in a tight circle on the honeycomb. Other bees cluster round and touch the dancing bee with their an-

tennae, thereby detecting the scent of the feeding place (bees' scent organs are located on their antennae). According to Von Frisch, the round dance tells the bees only that there is food within about 100 metres of the hive; it does not give the exact location. If the food is more than 100 metres away, the returned forager performs the waggle dance, in which the bee moves through a figure of eight, its abdomen waggling vigorously during the straight cross-piece of the figure of eight. Von Frisch claims that the waggle dance conveys both the distance of the food from the hive and the direction of the food relative to the hive: the distance is proportional to the time taken to complete one circuit of the dance, and the direction of the food in relation to the sun is indicated by the angle between the vertical (the dance is performed on a vertical honeycomb) and the cross-piece of the figure of eight.

Von Frisch published his findings in 1943, but doubt has since been thrown on his interpretation of the significance of the dances. Other researchers have found that bees emit various sounds, some of which seem to relate to the location of food. This does not imply that bees do not dance; they do, but their dances may not be the means by which they communicate.

In addition to his studies of bees' dances, Von Frisch also researched into the visual and chemical sense of bees and fishes. In 1910 he began an investigation which demonstrated that fishes can distinguish between differences in brightness and colour (the subject of his PhD thesis). And in 1919 he showed that bees can be trained to discriminate between various tastes and odours.

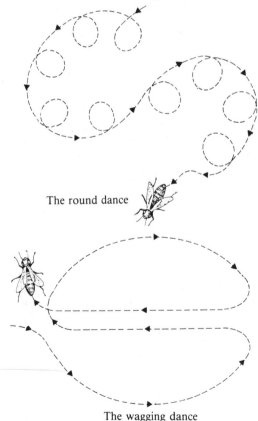

The round dance

The wagging dance

Von Frisch interpreted the meanings of the "dances" performed on the vertical honeycomb by returning foraging bees.

W

Wallace, Alfred Russel (*1823–1913*), was a British naturalist who is best known for proposing a theory of evolution by natural selection independently of Charles Darwin.

Wallace was born in Usk, in Wales, on 8 January 1823. After a rudimentary education (he left school when he was 14 years old), he joined an elder brother in a surveying business. In 1844, however, he became a teacher at the Collegiate School, Leicester, where he met Henry Bates, who interested him in entomology. Together they planned a collecting trip to the Amazon, and arrived in South America in 1848; Bates remained there for 11 years but Wallace returned to England in 1852. Unfortunately, the ship sank on the return voyage and although Wallace survived, all his specimens were lost, the only remaining ones being those previously sent to England. In 1853 he published an account of his experiences in South America in *A Narrative of Travels on the Amazon and Rio Negro*.

From 1842 to 1862 Wallace explored the Malay Peninsula and the East Indies, from which he collected more than 125,000 specimens. During this expedition he observed the marked differences that exist between the Australian and Asian faunas and later, when writing about this phenomenon, drew a hypothetical line that separates the areas in which each of these two distinct faunas exist. This line, now called the Wallace line, follows a deep-water channel that runs between the larger islands of Borneo and Celebes and the smaller ones of Bali and Lombok. In 1855, while in Borneo, he wrote *On the Law Which Has Regulated the Introduction of New Species*, in which he put forward the idea that every species had come into existence coincidentally, both in time and place, with a pre-existing, closely allied species. He also believed that the Australian fauna was less highly developed than the Asian fauna, the survival of the Australian fauna being due to the separation of Australia and its nearby islands from the Asian continent before the more advanced Asian fauna had developed. These ideas then led Wallace to the same conclusion that Charles Darwin had reached (although had not published at that time) – the idea that species evolve by natural selection. Then, while suffering from malaria, in 1858, Wallace wrote an essay outlining his ideas on evolution and sent it to Darwin, who was surprised to find that Wallace's ideas were the same as his own. The findings of the two men were combined in a paper read before the Linnean Society on 1 July 1858. Wallace's section, entitled *On the Tendency of Varieties to Depart Indefinitely from the Original Type*, described how animals fight to survive, the rate of their reproduction and their dependence on supplies of suitable food. In the conclusion to his section Wallace wrote "those that prolong their existence can only be the most perfect in health and vigour; ... the weakest and least perfectly organised must always succumb". He described his work more fully in *The Malay Archipelago*, published in 1869; Darwin's *The Origin of Species* had appeared in 1859.

Wallace continued to gather evidence to support the theory of evolution and in 1870, while on an expedition to Borneo and the Molucca islands, published *Contributions to the Theory of Natural Selection*. In this work he diverged from Darwin's views: both thought that Mankind had evolved to its present physical form by natural selection but, in keeping with his spiritualistic beliefs, Wallace was of the opinion that man's higher mental

capabilities had arisen from some "metabiological" agency. Wallace also differed from Darwin about the origins of the brightly coloured plumage of male birds and the relative drabness of female birds; Wallace believed that it was merely natural selection that had led to the development of dull, protectively coloured plumage in females, rather than subscribing to Darwin's idea that females are attracted by brightly coloured plumage in males.

Wallace also studied mimicry in the swallowtail butterfly and wrote a pioneering work on zoogeography, *Geographical Distribution of Animals* (1876). In addition he spent much time promoting socialism by, for example, campaigning for women's suffrage and land nationalization.

Public recognition of Wallace's important work on evolution came late in his life; he was elected a Fellow of the Royal Society in 1893 and received the Order of Merit in 1910. He died in Broadstone, Dorset, on 7 November 1913.

Warburg, Otto Heinrich (*1883-1970*), was a German biochemist who made several important discoveries about metabolic processes, particularly intracellular respiration and photosynthesis, and pioneered the use of physicochemical methods for investigating the biochemistry of cells. Probably his most important contribution was his outstanding work on respiratory enzymes, for which he was awarded the 1931 Nobel Prize in Physiology and Medicine.

Warburg was born on 8 October 1883 in Freiburg-im-Breisgau, the son of a physics professor at the University of Berlin. He studied chemistry under Emil Fischer (1852-1919) at the University of Berlin, obtaining his doctorate in 1906, and then read medicine at the University of Heidelberg, gaining his medical degree in 1911. In 1913 he went to the Kaiser Wilhelm (later Max Planck) Institute for Cell Physiology in Berlin–Dahlem, becoming a professor there in 1918 and its Director in 1931 (having served in the Prussian Horse Guards during World War I). In 1941 Warburg, being part-Jewish, was removed from his post but such was his international prestige and so important was his research that he was soon reinstated and he remained the Director of the institute for the rest of his life. In 1944 he was nominated for a second Nobel Prize but was not allowed to accept the award, because Germans were forbidden to do so under Adolf Hitler's regime. Warburg died in West Berlin on 1 August 1970.

One of Warburg's chief interests was intracellular respiration, and in the early 1920s he devised a method for determining the uptake of oxygen by living tissue using a manometer. Continuing this general line of research, he began to investigate oxidation-reduction reactions involved in intracellular respiration. Warburg and the German chemist Heinrich Wieland (1877–1957) held opposite views about the mechanism of the reaction:

$$AH_2 + B \xrightarrow{\text{catalyst}} A + BH_2$$

(hydrogen donor) (hydrogen acceptor) (oxidized) (reduced)

Warburg believed that the hydrogen acceptor had to be activated and made capable for accepting hydrogen, whereas Wieland thought that the hydrogen donor was activated and made to yield its hydrogen to a hydrogen carrier. Warburg demonstrated that his proposed mechanism was possible and postulated that, in living cells, an iron-containing enzyme activated oxygen (the hydrogen acceptor) and rendered it capable of accepting the hydrogen. He noted that animal charcoal, produced by heating blood, catalyses the oxidation of many organic compounds – oxygen being consumed in the process – whereas vegetable charcoal produced by heating sucrose does not behave in this way. From this finding Warburg concluded that the difference in the behaviour of the two types of charcoal was due to the presence of iron in the blood. He discovered that charcoal systems and living cells behave in similar ways in some respects: in each case, the uptake of oxygen is inhibited by the presence of cyanide or hydrogen sulphide, both of which combine with heavy metals and inhibit respiration. He also showed that, in the dark, carbon monoxide inhibits the respiration of yeast but does not do so in the light. He was aware that heavy metals form complexes with carbon monoxide and that the iron complex is dissociated by light, which provided further evidence for the existence of an iron-containing respiratory enzyme. Warburg then investigated the efficiency of light in overcoming the carbon monoxide inhibition of respiration, finding that the light's efficiency depended on its wavelength. And by plotting the wavelength against the light's efficiency, he determined the photochemical absorption spectrum of the respiratory enzyme, which proved to be a haemoprotein (a protein with an iron-containing group) similar to haemoglobin; he called it iron oxygenase. It was for this work that Warburg was awarded a Nobel Prize in 1931.

Meanwhile, the British biologist David Keilin (1887–1963) had discovered cytochromes (the hydrogen carriers in intracellular respiration whose existence had been postulated by Wieland) and cytochrome oxidase, believed to be identical to Warburg's iron oxygenase. Therefore both Wieland and Warburg had been correct in their views about the mechanisms involved in intracellular respiration; they had merely been investigating different stages in this extremely complex pathway.

Warburg also studied co-enzymes and he and his collaborators isolated NADP (nicotinamide adenine dinucleotide phosphate) in 1935 and FAD (flavine adenine dinucleotide) in 1938, both of which are important in respiration.

Working on photosynthesis Warburg showed that, given suitable conditions, it can take place with almost total thermodynamic efficiency – that is, virtually 100 per cent of the light energy can be converted to chemical energy. Later he discovered the mechanism of the conversion of light energy to chemical energy that occurs in photosynthesis. In addition, he studied cancer and was the first to discover that malignant cells require less oxygen than do normal cells. This finding was unique at the time, and even today, remains one of the relatively few facts that applies to all types of cancer.

Warming, Johannes Eugenius Bülow (*1841–1924*), was a Danish botanist whose pioneering studies of the relationships between plants and their natural environments established plant ecology as a new discipline within botany.

Warming was born on 3 November 1841 on the island of Mandø, Denmark. He studied at the University of Copenhagen but, while still a student, spent the years 1863 to 1866 at Lagoa Santa, Brazil, assisting the Danish zoologist P. W. Lund in a project involving the excavation of fossils. During this expedition, Warming undertook a thorough study of tropical vegetation, the results of which took 25 years to publish fully, although a summary (*Lagoa Santa, a Contribution to Biological Phytogeography*) appeared in 1892. After his return from Brazil, Warming studied for a year at Munich University under Karl von Nägeli (1817–1891) and then spent another year at Bonn University under J. L. von Hanstein. In 1871 Warming gained his doctorate from the University of Copenhagen and he taught botany there from 1873 to 1882, when he became Professor of Botany at the Royal Institute of Technology in Stockholm, Sweden. He went on an expedition to Greenland in 1884 and to Norway in 1885, after which he returned to Copenhagen to become Professor of Botany at the university and Director of the Botanical Gardens, positions he held until his retirement in 1911. His last major expedition, which lasted from 1890 to 1892, was to the West Indies and Venezuela. Warming died in Copenhagen on 2 April 1924.

Warming's most important contribution to botany was in the area of plant ecology. Ernst Haeckel coined the term "ecology" in 1866 and it was introduced into botany by Reiter in 1885, but it was Warming who provided the foundation for the study of plant ecology. He investigated the relationships between plants and various environmental conditions, such as light, temperature and rainfall, and attempted to classify types of plant communities (he defined a plant community as a group of several species that is subject to the same environmental conditions, which he called ecological factors). Warming set out the results of his work in *Plantesamfund* (1895), in which he not only provided a theoretical basis for the study of plant ecology but also formulated a programme for future research into the subject, including the investigation of factors responsible for the congregation of plants into communities, and of the evolutionary and environmental pressures that lead to the development of particular habits and habitats in each plant species. *Plantesamfund* was translated into several languages, including English (as *Oecology of Plants* in 1909), and had a tremendous impact in stimulating research into plant ecology.

Warming also investigated a wide range of other areas in botany – including tropical, temperate and arctic flora (about which he provided a vast amount of data), purple bacteria, flower ovules, and the classification of flowering plants.

Watson, James Dewey (*1928–*). See CRICK, FRANCIS HARRY COMPTON.

Weismann, August Friedrich Leopold (*1834–1914*), was a German zoologist who is best known for his germ-plasm theory of heredity and for his opposition to Jean Lamarck's doctrine of the inheritance of acquired characteristics. Weismann was one of the founders of the science of genetics, and many of the ideas he put forward on the subject are essentially correct, including his germ-plasm theory. For his outstanding contribution towards elucidating the mechanism of inheritance, Weismann received many honours, including a medal awarded by the Linnean Society of London at the Darwin–Wallace celebration in 1908 and the Darwin Medal, which was awarded at the anniversary meeting of the Royal Society of London.

Weismann was born on 17 January 1834 in Frankfurt am Main, Germany, the son of a classics professor at the Gymnasium there. In 1852 he went to the University of Göttingen to study medicine and graduated in 1856, after which he briefly held several positions, including those of a doctor in the Baden army (Baden was then an autonomous Grand Duchy) and private physi-

cian to Archduke Stephen of Austria. In 1860 Weismann visited Freiburg-im-Breisgau, which impressed him so much that he felt he would like to live there. In the following year a brief period studying under Karl Leuckart (1822–1898) in Giessen reawakened Weismann's childhood interest in natural history, and in 1863 he joined the University of Freiburg's medical faculty as a teacher of zoology and comparative anatomy. He persuaded the university to build a zoological institute and museum, and he became its first director. Weismann remained at the University of Freiburg until his retirement in 1912. During his later years, he travelled extensively and became famous for his lectures on heredity and evolution. He was extremely patriotic and renounced all the British honours awarded him when World War I broke out. He died in Freiburg on 5 November 1914.

In his early years at Freiburg, Weismann studied insect metamorphosis and the sex cells of hydrozoa. In the mid-1860s, however, his eyesight began to deteriorate and he was unable to perform the microscope work necessary for this research. After a rest his eyesight improved and he resumed his earlier work, but the improvement was only temporary and by the mid-1880s he was forced to abandon the observational part of his work and to concentrate on theory.

Although an admirer of Charles Darwin, Weismann began by questioning pangenesis (Darwin's theory that every cell of the body contributes minute particles – gemmules – to the germ cells and therefore participates in the transmission of inherited characteristics) and then proceeded to attack the Lamarckian theory of the inheritance of acquired characteristics. Weismann's early work on hydrozoan sex cells led him to postulate that every living organism contains a special hereditary substance, the germ plasm, which controls the development of every part of the organism and is transmitted from one generation to the next in an unbroken line of descent. Furthermore, he realized that repeated mixing of the germ plasm at fertilization would lead to a progressive increase in the amount of hereditary material, and therefore predicted that there must be a type of nuclear division at which each daughter cell receives only half of the original germ plasm. This prediction was proved correct by the cytological work of Oskar Hertwig (1849–1922) and others, which then led Weismann to propose that the germ plasm was situated in what were later called the chromosomes of the egg nucleus.

Weismann's germ-plasm theory is still basically true today, although we now use the terms chromosomes, genes and DNA to refer to the hereditary material Weismann called germ plasm.

In one important respect, however, Weismann was not completely correct: he believed that the germ plasm cannot be altered by the action of the environment and that variations among individuals arise from different combinations and permutations of the germ plasm. Although different combinations of the hereditary material do give rise to individual variations, the genetic material can be modified by environmental influences – as later demonstrated by Hugo De Vries and Hermann Muller.

Wells, Horace (*1815-1848*), was an American dentist who discovered nitrous oxide anaesthesia and, in 1844, was the first to use the gas in dentistry – although ether anaesthesia had previously been used in other surgical operations.

Wells was born in Hartford, Vermont, on 21 January 1815. He was educated at private institutions in Massachusetts and New Hampshire then, at the age of 19, began to study dentistry in Boston. He subsequently set up a dental practice in Hartford, Connecticut, initially in partnership with William Morton – who later pioneered the use of ether as an anaesthetic – and with John Riggs (1810-1885) as one of his students. In late 1844, while watching an exhibition of the effects of laughing gas (nitrous oxide) staged by a travelling show, Wells observed that the gas induced anaesthesia – an effect also noticed previously by Crawford Long (1815-1878), another pioneer of anaesthesia. Wells then arranged to have one of his wisdom teeth extracted by Riggs while the showman administered nitrous oxide. Having felt no pain during this operation, he subsequently used nitrous oxide anaesthesia to perform painless extractions on his patients.

In January 1845 Wells went to Boston where, with the help of Morton (then no longer his partner), the chemist Charles Jackson (1805-1880) and the surgeon John Warren (1778-1856), he arranged to demonstrate a painless tooth extraction using nitrous oxide anaesthesia to students at the Massachusetts General Hospital. During the demonstration, however, the patient cried out and, although the patient later claimed to have felt no pain, the audience believed that the demonstration had failed. After this débâcle Wells gave up his dental practice and became a travelling salesman, selling canaries and then showerbaths in Connecticut. In 1846 Morton gave a successful demonstration of ether anaesthesia in the same operating theatre that Wells had used, and in the following year Wells went to Paris to try to establish his priority in using anaesthesia. At about this time he also began experimenting on himself with nitrous oxide, ether and various other intoxicating chemicals; as a result he be-

came addicted to chloroform and mentally unstable. In 1848, having returned to the United States, he was imprisoned in New York City for throwing acid in the face of a prostitute and, while in his prison cell, committed suicide on 24 January of that year. Ironically, during his imprisonment the Paris Medical Society accepted Wells' claim to priority in the discovery of anaesthesia.

White, Gilbert (*1720-1793*), was a British naturalist and clergyman who is remembered chiefly for his book *The Natural History and Antiquities of Selborne* (1789), a classic work in which White vividly records his acute observations of the flora and fauna in the area of Selborne (now in Hampshire).

White was born on 18 July 1720 in Selborne and, after attending schools in Farnham and Basingstoke, went to Oriel College, Oxford, in 1740. He graduated in 1743, was elected a Fellow of his college in 1744 and obtained a master's degree in 1746. Although many of his associates believed him capable of a successful academic career, White chose to become a clergyman and took deacon's orders in 1747, subsequently becoming a curate in his uncle's parish of Swarraton, near Selborne. White was ordained a priest in 1750 and, after refusing several positions, eventually accepted a post at Moreton Pinkney, Northamptonshire, where his living was paid by Oriel College. But he was strongly attracted to the countryside of his birthplace, so he left the care of the Moreton Pinkney parish to a curate and returned to the family home in Selborne. White subsequently held curacies in several parishes in the neighbourhood but continued to live in Selborne itself until his death on 26 June 1793.

After his return to Selborne, White spent much of his time studying the wildlife in the area. He kept a diary of his observations and also wrote of his findings to his two naturalist friends Thomas Pennant and Daines Barrington. These letters, which cover a period of about 20 years, form the basis of *The Natural History of Selborne*. Elegantly written, it is characterized by acute observations of a wide variety of natural history subjects, as well as descriptions of rural life in eighteenth-century England. The book is more than merely a record, however, it also contains White's theories and speculations and several important discoveries, such as the migration of swallows, the recognition of three distinct species of British leaf warblers, and the identification of the harvest mouse and the noctule bat as British species. On its publication in 1789, *The Natural History of Selborne* was widely praised by leading naturalists; it also has great popular appeal and has been reprinted many times.

White also wrote *Calendar of Flora and the Garden* (1765), an account of observations he made in his garden in 1751, and *Naturalist's Journal* (begun in 1768), a similar but more sophisticated work.

Wigglesworth, Vincent Brian (*1899–*), is a British entomologist whose research covered many areas of insect physiology but who is best known for his investigations into the role of hormones in growth and metamorphosis. He received many honours for his contributions towards an understanding of insect physiology, including the Royal Medal of the Royal Society of London in 1955 and a knighthood in 1964.

Wigglesworth was born on 17 April 1899 in Kirkham, Lancashire, the son of a doctor. He was educated at Repton then won a scholarship to Caius College, Cambridge. From 1917 to 1918 he served in France in the Royal Field Artillery before resuming his university education and graduating in physiology and biochemistry. He did two years' research under Frederick Gowland Hopkins, during part of which time he worked with J.B.S. Haldane, and then qualified in medicine at St Thomas's Hospital, London. In 1926 he was appointed Lecturer in Medical Entomology at the London School of Hygiene and Tropical Medicine, and then Reader in Entomology at London University from 1936 to 1944. Wigglesworth became Director of the Agricultural Research Council Unit of Insect Physiology at Cambridge in 1943 and remained there until he retired in 1967. During his directorship, he also held the post of Quick Professor of Biology at Cambridge from 1952 to 1966.

Wigglesworth's work on insect metamorphosis was carried out mainly on the bloodsucking insect *Rhodnius prolixus*, which was brought from South America by E. Brumpt (1877–1951) and proved suitable for experimentation. In 1917 it had been demonstrated that the hormone responsible for growth and moulting is secreted only when the insect's brain is present; decapitated insects live but do not moult. By transplanting various parts of the brain into decapitated *Rhodnius* specimens, Wigglesworth proved that this hormone (which he called moulting hormone) is produced in the region of the brain containing the neurosecretory cells. In addition, he showed that another hormone – one that prevents the development of adult characteristics until the insect larva is fully grown – is also produced in the head. He then demonstrated that this second hormone (which he called juvenile hormone) is secreted by the corpus allatum, an endocrine gland near the brain. Wigglesworth investigated the effects of the two hormones and found that insect larvae

exposed to juvenile hormone grow but remain in the larval form; that adult insects exposed to moulting hormone moult again and, when also exposed to juvenile hormone, some of their organs partly regress to the larval forms. He also found that juvenile hormone is necessary for normal reproduction in many insects.

Although best known for his work on insect growth and metamorphosis, Wigglesworth also investigated many other aspects of insect anatomy and physiology, including the mechanisms involved in hatching; the mode of action of adhesive organs in walking; the role of the outer waxy layer on insects' bodies in preventing water loss; the respiration of insect eggs; insect sense organs and their use in orientation; and the functions of insect blood cells. His book *The Principles of Insect Physiology* (1939) has been reprinted in several editions as the standard general text on insect physiology.

Withering, William (*1741–1799*), was a British physician, botanist and mineralogist, best known for his work on the drug digitalis (from the foxglove plant), which he initially used as a diuretic to treat dropsy (oedema).

Withering was born on 17 March 1741 in Wellington, Shropshire, where his father was an apothecary. He went to the Edinburgh Medical School and graduated in 1766, taking the post of physician at Stafford Infirmary for the next nine years. In 1775 Erasmus Darwin suggested that Withering should take over a practice in Birmingham that had belonged to William Small (1734–1775), founder of the Lunar Society, who had just died. Withering did so, and also became a member of the Lunar Society where he met Matthew Boulton, Joseph Priestley and other contemporary scientists. His practice in Birmingham did well and he became physician at Birmingham General Hospital. He contracted tuberculosis and retired in 1783; he was elected a Fellow of the Royal Society a year later. He publicly expressed his sympathies with the French Revolution, and in 1791 his house was attacked by a mob (as was Priestley's). He visited Portugal for a year between 1792 and 1793, and died in Birmingham on 6 October 1799.

In 1785 Withering published *Account of the Foxglove*, which detailed the controlled use of the drug digitalis for the treatment of dropsy. The drug was made from the leaves of *Digitalis purpurea*. He had begun studying digitalis in 1775, after noting its use in traditional herbal remedies. He worked out precise dosages of dried foxglove leaves. He also suggested the possible use of the drug in the treatment of heart disease, and he was of course correct because digitalis increases the heart's output without increasing the heart rate, thus clearing the interstitial fluid that is responsible for dropsy. Digitalis, in the form of digoxin, is still one of the most widely used drugs for treating heart failure.

Withering also made a name for himself in the field of botany after the publication of his *Botanical Arrangement* (1776), which was based on Linnaeus and became a standard work, and his activities in geology are remembered through the mineral ore witherite (barium carbonate), which was named after him.

Wolff, Kaspar Friedrich (*1733–1794*), was a German surgeon and physiologist who has become regarded as the father of embryology, although his findings were largely ignored for more than 50 years.

Wolff, was born in Berlin on 18 January 1733 and he studied at Halle and the Berlin Medical School, from which he graduated in 1759. He was an army surgeon during the Seven Years War (1756–1763), and then lectured in pathology in Berlin. Despite the success of his lectures he was not offered a professorship, and so in 1766 he accepted an invitation from Catherine II of Russia to take the post of Academician for Anatomy and Physiology in St Petersburg (now Leningrad). He remained there until his death on 22 February 1794.

Wolff produced his revolutionary work *Theoria generationis* in 1759. Until that time it was generally believed that each living organism develops from an exact miniature of the adult within the seed or sperm – the so-called preformation or homunculus theory. Wolff introduced the idea that cells which are initially unspecialized later differentiate to produce the separate organs and systems of the plant or animal body with their distinct types of tissues. In fact Wolff's view that plants and animals are composed of cells was still a subject of controversy. His name is also associated with, among other parts of the anatomy, the Wolffian body, a structure in an animal embryo that eventually develops into the kidney.

Wilkins, Maurice Hugh Frederick (*1916–*).
See CRICK, FRANCIS HARRY COMPTON.

Woodger, Joseph Henry (*1894–*), is a British biologist who is known principally for his theoretical work on the underlying philosophical basis of scientific methodology in biology, especially for his attempt to provide biology with a strict and logical foundation on which observations, theories and methods could be based.

Woodger was born on 2 May 1894 in Great Yarmouth, Norfolk, and was educated at Felsted

School then University College, London (where he studied under J.P. Hill, one of the leading British zoologists of the time). Woodger enrolled in the army in 1915 and then after World War I spent a brief period in Baghdad. He returned to London in 1919 and began investigating newly discovered cell organelles, including Golgi bodies and mitochondria. In 1924 he was appointed Reader in Biology at the Middlesex Hospital Medical School in London, and became a professor there in 1947. He retired in 1959.

Woodger's transition from practical work to the theoretical and philosophical aspects of biology dated from his appointment to the readership in biology. Confronted for the first time with having to teach, he found no textbooks that gave an adequate grounding in the fundamental scientific principles involved in biology and medicine, so he wrote one – *Elementary Morphology and Physiology* (1924). He became increasingly concerned with the problems of methodology and interpretation in biological experimentation and with the need for "a critical sorting of fundamental concepts to promote a strictness of thought equal to the strictness of investigation required in the new biology".

There was at that time no generally accepted (biological) theory of organism, only a host of facts and conflicting ideas ranging from total mechanism to vitalism. The new biology required a causal description for each vital process and as a means of understanding how such processes as nutrition, development and behaviour are related to the life of a particular organism or species.

Woodger began by teaching himself philosophy, with particular reference to A.N. Whitehead and Whitehead and Russell's *Principia Mathematica*. He developed the idea that one of the characteristics of a living system is the organization of its substance, and that this order is of a hierarchical nature. Thus the components of an organism can be classified on a scale of increasing size and complexity: molecular, macromolecular, cell components, cells, tissues, organs and organisms. Each class exhibits specifically new modes of behaviour, which cannot be interpreted as being merely additive phenomena from the previous class.

Woodger's major work, *Biological Principles: a critical study* (1929), examines the fundamental requirements of theories in biology. He was able to show how to resolve many of the apparent antitheses in biology (such as those between structure and function, preformation and development, and mechanism and vitalism). He also made the first attempt to put embryological ideas on a logistic basis by analysing at length, and in strict logical form, the process of cell division. He demonstrated that living matter shows not only spatial hierarchical order but also divisional hierarchies (each cell or group of cells has a parent cell), and that many difficulties in biological theory arose originally through the abstraction from time – that is, viewing an organism as a series of spatially ordered components only. He summarized many of these ideas in his book *The Technique of Theory Construction* (1939).

Wright, Almroth Edward (*1861–1947*), was a British bacteriologist who did pioneering work in the field of immunology, notably in the development of a vaccine against typhoid fever. He received numerous honours for his work, including a knighthood in 1906.

Wright was born on 10 August 1861 in Middleton Tyas, a small village near Richmond in Yorkshire. His father was an Irish Presbyterian clergyman who, between 1863 and 1885, held ministries in Dresden, Boulogne and Belfast, and Wright received his early education from his parents and private tutors. While his family was in Belfast, however, he attended the Royal Academic Institution and then in 1878 entered Trinity College Dublin, from which he graduated in modern literature in 1882 and in medicine in the following year. Subsequently he studied – on a travelling scholarship – pathological anatomy at the universities of Leipzig and Marburg and physiological chemistry at Strasbourg University. He then went to Australia, where he was a demonstrator of physiology at Sydney University from 1889 to 1891. After his return to England, Wright worked for a short time in the laboratories of the College of Physicians and Surgeons in London until, in 1892, he was appointed Professor of Pathology at the Army Medical School in Netley, Hampshire. It was while he held this post that he developed a vaccine against typhoid, but he disagreed with the army authorities over the use of his vaccine and he resigned his professorship in 1902. In the same year he became Professor of Pathology at St Mary's Hospital in London and held this post until he retired in 1946; in 1908 he also became responsible for the Department of Therapeutic Inoculation (later called the Institute of Pathological Research) at St Mary's. In 1911 Wright went to South Africa, where he introduced prophylactic inoculation against pneumonia for the workers in the Rand gold mines. On returning to England, he was appointed Director of the Department of Bacteriology of the newly founded Medical Research Committee (later Council) at the Hampstead Laboratory, London. During World War I he served in France as a temporary Colonel in the Army Medical Service, afterwards returning full-time to his professorship at St

Mary's Hospital. Wright died at his home in Farnham Common on 30 April 1947.

Wright first began bacteriological research while he was Professor at the Army Medical School, and by 1896 he had succeeded in developing an effective anti-typhoid vaccine, which he prepared from killed typhoid bacilli. Preliminary trials of the vaccine on troops of the Indian Army proved its effectiveness and the vaccine was subsequently used successfully among the British soldiers in the Boer War. In addition to this important development, Wright established a new discipline within medicine, that of therapeutic immunization by vaccination, which was aimed at treating microbial diseases rather than preventing them. He proved that the human bloodstream contains bacteriatrophins (opsonins) in the serum and that these substances can destroy bacteria by phagocytosis. He researched into wound infections, his work in this area leading to the use of salt solution as an osmotic agent to draw lymph into wounds, thereby accelerating their closure. And he also originated vaccines against enteric tuberculosis and pneumonia.

Y

Young, John Zachary (*1907–   *), is a British zoologist whose discovery of and subsequent work on the giant nerve fibres in squids contributed greatly to knowledge of nerve structure and function. He also did research on the central nervous system of octopuses, demonstrating that memory stores are located in the brain. Young is probably most widely known, however, for his zoological textbooks, *The Life of Vertebrates* (1950) and *The Life of Mammals* (1957). As a result of his work, he received many honorary university degrees, and in 1967 was awarded the Royal Medal of the Royal Society of London.

Young was born on 18 March 1907 in Bristol and was educated at Wells House, Malvern Wells, and at Marlborough College, Wiltshire. He graduated from Magdalen College, Oxford, in 1928 then went to Naples as a Biological Scholar. After his return to England, Young was elected a Fellow of Magdalen College in 1931 and remained there until 1945, when he became Professor of Anatomy at University College, London – the first non-medical scientist in Britain to hold a professorship in anatomy. In the same year he was also made a Fellow of the Royal Society. He remained at University College until he retired in 1974.

Young began his work on the nerves in squids

before World War II. He discovered that certain of their nerve fibres are exceptionally thick – up to 1 mm in diameter (about 100 times the diameter of mammalian neurons) – and are covered with a relatively thin myelin sheath (unlike mammalian nerve fibres, which have thick sheaths), properties that make them easy to experiment on. For example, almost all the intracellular contents can be extracted without destroying the fibre's ability to conduct nerve impulses, and electrodes can easily be inserted into the fibres because of their large diameter. Moreover, extracting the contents of the giant fibres is still the only way of obtaining intracellular nerve material uncontaminated by the myelin sheath or other cells. Young's work on the giant nerve fibres in squids has been invaluable, not only because of his own findings, but also because these fibres are extremely useful for experimentation and have been used by many other researchers in their investigations of nerves.

During the war, Young set up a unit at Oxford to study nerve regeneration in mammals and, with Peter Medawar and others, devised a method of rejoining small severed nerves by using intracellular plasma as a "glue". Young also researched into the rates of neuron growth and the factors that determine neuron size.

After the war Young turned his attention to the central nervous system, using octopuses as research animals. Working with Brian Boycott, he showed that octopuses can learn to discriminate between different orientations of the same object – when presented with horizontal and vertical rectangles, for example, the octopuses attacked one but avoided the other. He also demonstrated (this time working with M.J. Wells) that octopuses can learn to recognize objects by touch. In addition, Young proved that the memory stores are located in the brain and proposed a model to explain the processes involved in memory.

Glossary

accelerator nerve A nerve that conducts impulses to the heart. On stimulation of the cardiac sympathetic nerves, the rate and strength of the heartbeat increases.

acetylcholine (ACh) A nerve transmitter chemical. When a nerve impulse arrives at the end of a nerve cell (*neuron*), it stimulates the release of ACh which chemically transmits the impulse across the *synapse* to the next nerve cell.

action potential The characteristic momentary electric potential across a nerve cell membrane during the passage of a nerve impulse.

actin A protein that occurs in muscles. See *myosin*.

acoustics The science and study of sound, its generation, properties and reception (detection).

adenosine diphosphate (ADP) A nucleotide *co-enzyme* found in living organisms, essentially involved in the conversion of energy (either light energy in *photosynthesis* or energy derived from metabolic processes) into a more available form – that of ATP.

adenosine triphosphate (ATP) A nucleotide *co-enzyme* that occurs in all organisms. It is derived from ADP and is the principal energy source for biochemical reactions. Energy is provided by a combination of *enzyme* action and the subsequent transfer of a phosphate group from ATP to a substance.

ADP See *adenosine diphosphate*.

adrenocorticotrophic hormone (ACTH) A *hormone* that stimulates the adrenal cortex to release its hormones. ACTH is released into the bloodstream from the anterior lobe of the pituitary gland at the base of the brain.

aerobic Describing an atmosphere of free (gaseous or dissolved) oxygen. An aerobic organism requires such an atmosphere for respiration and life.

afferent nerve A nerve that carries impulses towards the central nervous system (i.e., the spinal cord or brain).

albinism A pigment-free condition found in animals and plants caused by a lack of a *melanin*-synthesizing *enzyme*. Albino animals are characterized by white fur or hair, pink skin and pupils, and a high sensitivity to the Sun's radiation.

alkali A solution of a metal hydroxide, especially a hydroxide of an alkali metal such as potassium or sodium. The presence of an alkali may be detected by using a chemical indicator such as litmus (which turns blue in the presence of an alkali). Alkalis produce hydroxyl (OH$^-$) ions in solution and the term is often extended to other compounds, such as bicarbonates, (hydrogen carbonates) that give an alkaline reaction in solution.

alkyl Any of a series of hydrocarbon radicals such as methyl (CH_3-), ethyl (C_2H_5-), and so on.

alkylation A chemical process by which an *alkyl* group is incorporated into a compound, replacing a hydrogen atom.

allantois A bladder in the embryo of reptiles, birds and mammals, which grows outside the embryo into the wall of the yolk-sac of reptiles and birds and under the *chorion* of mammals. In mammals, blood vessels in the allantois carry blood to the *placenta*; in reptiles and birds the blood vessels permit respiration. As they develop, the vessels become the umbilical vein and arteries.

allele (or allelomorph) A pair of *genes*, located at the same sites (loci) on paired *chromosomes*, that determine specific characteristics. Alleles are denoted by a double-letter symbol, a capital letter indicating a *dominant* gene and a lower case letter indicating a *recessive* gene (e.g., Bb).

alpha chain A particular secondary structure of the polypeptide chain (of a protein) brought about by hydrogen bonding between adjacent *peptide* units. Alpha chains occur, for example, in the *haemoglobin* molecule.

amino acid Any of a series of organic acids that contain one or more amino groups (-NH_2). There are more than 100 different amino acids, of which about 20 (called the alpha amino acids) are found – joined by *peptide* linkages – in proteins. The alpha amino acids have the general formula $RCHNH_2COOH$, where R is an *alkyl* group. In higher animals, *essential* amino acids have to be supplied by the diet (because they cannot be synthesized by the liver, as can *non-essential* amino acids).

amnion The innermost embryonic membrane in reptiles, birds and mammals. In human beings, for example, the amnion suspends the foetus in fluid until about the eighth week, when it becomes incorporated into the *chorion* to form the amniochorionic sac.

anaerobic Describing an atmosphere lacking any free (gaseous or dissolved) oxygen. An anaerobic organism can live in such an atmosphere, obtaining its oxygen from the chemical breakdown of oxygen compounds.

anaesthesia The diminution or absence of sensation or awareness in the whole body (general anaesthesia) or in part of the body (local anaesthesia). It may result from a disorder or can be induced artificially using drugs. General anaesthesia is achieved by blocking nervous impulses in the brain; local anaesthesia affects the sodium-potassium ion interchange across specific nerve cell membranes when an impulse attempts to pass.

angiogram An X-ray photograph in which blood vessels are made visible by injecting them with a radiopaque substance (such as an iodine compound).

angiosperm A flowering plant, a member of a sub-division of the Spermatophyta. In contrast to a *gymnosperm*, an angiosperm has a covered seed carried in an enclosed megasporophyll; the female gametophyte develops inside the megaspore. Also the *xylem* in the stem of an angiosperm usually has vessels (whereas that in a gymnosperm usually does not). The angiosperm group includes the *monocotyledon* and *dicotyledon* classes.

anisotropic (or aelotropic) Describing a substance that has different physical properties in different directions. Some crystals, for example, have different refractive indices in different directions.

antagonistic Describing a pair of muscles that act in opposition to each other so that when one contracts, the other relaxes (e.g., the biceps and triceps muscles of the upper arm).

antibiotic A chemical substance, often used as a drug in medical treatment, that kills or prevents the growth of micro-organisms such as *bacteria*. Antibiotics are produced by fungi or bacteria, or they may be chemically synthesized. Antibiotic therapy blocks a chemical reaction that is essential to a bacterial parasite; penicillin, for example, obstructs the development of a protective cell wall in some pathogenic bacteria.

antibody A protein formed by plasma cells in the spleen or lymph nodes whose production is stimulated by the presence of an *antigen* (a parasite or other "foreign" substance). Antibodies circulate in the body's fluids and combine chemically with the specific antigen that stimulated their formation. *Immunity* to disease can be induced (e.g., by *vaccination*) by injecting specific antigens into the body and thus stimulating the formation of the required antibodies.

antigen A substance that gains access to the body and in so doing stimulates the formation of *antibodies*. Many antigens are, like antibodies, proteins; others (such as pollen) are not themselves proteins but act by modifying existing proteins which then behave as antigens and stimulate the defensive response; often this mechanism is the cause of an allergy.

antiseptic Any chemical substance that prevents the growth of or destroys (pathogenic) micro-organisms.

antiserum Serum extracted from the blood of human beings or other animals that have been infected by a *pathogen* (such as a virus or bacterium) contains *antibodies* against a specific *antigen* and may be used in treatment. Many antisera have been superseded by *antibiotic* therapy, although sera are still used to treat some poisons and bacterial diseases.

antitoxin A naturally produced *antibody* that neutralizes specific *toxins* produced by *bacteria* (such as those released by tetanus and diphtheria bacteria). Antitoxins derived from the serum from infected human beings or other animals may be used as immunizing *vaccines*.

aqueous humour A transparent watery solution containing trace salts and albumin that is contained between and nourishes the cornea and lens of the vertebrate eye.

ATP See *adenosine triphosphate*.

attenuation In biology and medicine, the reduction in the virulence of a pathogenic micro-organism by culturing it in unfavourable conditions, by drying or heating it, or by subjecting it to chemical treatment. Attenuated *viruses*, for example, are used in *vaccines*.

audiometer An instrument for testing hearing at various frequencies and loudness levels.

autophagy A process in which a cell synthesizes substances and then metabolizes and absorbs them for its own sustenance.

axon A long nerve fibre (usually covered by a *myelin* sheath) that conducts impulses away from a nerve cell body. Most axons end in ganglia, effector organs or *synapses*.

axoplasm The *cytoplasm* of an *axon*, containing the *neurofibrils* of the nerve fibre.

bacillus A rod-shaped bacterium. See *bacteria*.

bacteria A group of uni- or multicellular micro-organisms that exist in colonies of the same species. They contain no *chlorophyll* and therefore cannot photosynthesize, although in other respects they are similar to plants. They are microscopic and classified mainly by their distinctive shapes: a coccus is spherical (irregular clusters are staphylococci, chains of cocci are streptococci), a spirillium is spiral, a spirochaete forms a flexible spiral, and a bacillus has a rod-like shape. Bacteria may be non-motile (atrichous) or move by means of motile filaments. They reproduce asexually by binary fission (sometimes extremely rapidly). Some process food from inorganic sources, but most feed off organic matter as parasites or saprophytes, and most are *aerobic*.

bacteriophage A virus that infects or parasitizes *bacteria*. It has a polyhedral head containing DNA and an elongated hollow tail of protein. It attaches its tail to the cell wall of a bacterium and produces *enzymes* that break through the wall. The phage then modifies the bacterial cell's metabolism, resulting in the production of more bacteriophages which are released when the host cell disintegrates.

bacteriotropin (or opsonin) A substance in blood serum that helps to make *bacteria* more vulnerable to *leucocytes*, which can then engulf and destroy them.

base In molecular biology, one of the nitrogen-containing compounds that (together with a phosphate group and deoxyribose or ribose) form *nucleotides*, the constituents of DNA and RNA. In DNA the bases are adenine and guanine (purine compounds), and cytosine and thymine (pyrimidine compounds); RNA has the same bases except it contains the pyrimidine uracil instead of thymine.

behaviourism A theory that regards animal behaviour as a consequence determined by conditioned responses (both nervous and hormonal).

beta chain A particular secondary structure of the polypeptide chain (of a protein) which makes it adopt the shape of a pleated sheet. See also *alpha chain*.

bile A digestive juice secreted by the liver and stored in the gall bladder which emulsifies fats and facilitates their digestion. It also stimulates the secretion of digestive *enzymes* and aids the absorption of fat-soluble *vitamins*.

biosynthesis (or anabolism) The natural formation of more complex biochemical compounds from less complex molecules (as in the synthesis of proteins from *amino acids*). This building-up process requires energy, stored in compounds such as *adenosine triphosphate* (ATP) which are formed during catabolism, the opposite of biosynthesis.

blastocyst A developmental stage in a mammalian embryo following cleavage, when the embryo consists of a thin outer layer of cells (*trophoblast*) enclosing a central mass of cells.

blastoderm A sheet of cells that grows on the surface of a fertilized ovum. In mammals it forms a disc of cells that eventually develops into the embryo between the amniotic cavity and the yolk sac. The *endoderm*, *mesoderm* and *ectoderm* also develop from the blastoderm.

blastula A stage in the embryonic development of lower animals that corresponds to the *blastocyst* in mammals.

blood groups A method of categorizing blood types. The most commonly used classification of human blood is the A, B, AB and O group system, which depends on the presence or absence of one or two *antigens* (in the blood cells) and one or two agglutins (in the serum).

carbohydrate Any of a large group of biologically important organic compounds composed only of carbon, hydrogen and oxygen, with the general formula $C_n(H_2O)_n$. There are three main types of carbohydrates: monosaccharides (or simple sugars), which contain between three and nine carbon atoms, e.g., glucose, fructose and dextrose; disaccharides (also sugars), which consist of two monosaccharides linked together e.g., sucrose (normal table sugar) consists of a molecule of glucose linked to a molecule of fructose; and polysaccharides, which consist of three or more (up to about 1,000) monosaccharides linked together, e.g., starch and cellulose.

carcinogenesis The production of cancer, or a carcinoma.

catalyst A substance that brings about or accelerates a chemical reaction while remaining unchanged at the end of it; the phenomenon is called catalysis. An *enzyme* is a type of catalyst in biochemical reactions.

catastrophism A theory that regards the variations in fossils from different geological strata as having resulted from a series of natural catastrophies that gave rise to new species.

cell theory A theory (proposed by Schleiden and Schwann in 1838–1839) which regards all living things as being composed of cells and that their replication and growth result from cell division.

centrifugation A method of separating substances suspended in a liquid using the force of gravity induced by spinning a sample at high speed.

centrosome An area of *cytoplasm*, near the nucleus of a cell, which contains the centriole.

chemotherapy The treatment of an infection or other disorder using drugs.

chlorophyll A green pigment that occurs in all green plants, contained in the *chloroplasts* (except in blue-green algae). Chlorophyll absorbs light during *photosynthesis* and is involved in the transformation of light energy into chemical energy (stored as ATP) which the plant uses to manufacture carbohydrates (and oxygen). Of the four known chlorophylls, a, b, c and d, only chlorophyll-a is found in all green plants.

chloroplast A small subcellular pigment-containing body found in photosynthetic plants (except *bacteria* and blue-green algae). In addition to *chlorophyll*, chloroplasts contain other pigments such as carotene and xanthophyll.

chordate Any animal that belongs to the phylum Chordata, which at some developmental stage has a *notochord*. Vertebrates constitute a sub-phylum of the chordates.

chorion The outer layer of the embryonic membrane formed from the *trophoblast* and the *mesoderm*. In its early stages it forms the outer cell wall of the *blastocyst* and later gives rise to the chorionic villi, which are eventually involved in the formation of the *placenta*.

chromatin A nucleoprotein found in *chromosomes* and thought to be the molecular substance of heredity. It is readily stained by basic dyes and is therefore easily identified and studied under the microscope.

chromosome A body that exists in the *nucleus* of a cell, made up mainly of nucleoproteins and bearing the *genes* which constitute the hereditary material. Each species has a constant number of chromosomes; human beings, for example, have 23 pairs of chromosomes in each cell (except in gametes), whereas the fruit fly has only four pairs. *Gametes* (eggs and sperm) have half the normal number of chromosomes, so that union of gametes produces a fertilized ovum with the full comple-ment of chromosomes, half derived from the mother and half from the father. See also *allele*.

chromosome map A description of the position of *genes* along a *chromosome*.

clone A cell (which may develop into a whole organism) descended from another cell by asexual reproduction and theoretically having a genetic make-up identical to that of the original cell.

coacervate A collection of particles in an emulsion that can be reversed into droplets of liquid before they flocculate.

coccus Any spherical bacterium (see *bacteria*).

codon The sequence of three *nucleotides* that code for a specific *amino acid* in (or at the termination of) a polypeptide chain, especially in DNA or *messenger RNA*.

co-enzyme An organic compound that activates some *enzymes* to catalyse biochemical reactions. It is weakly attached to the enzyme and may be chemically changed in the reaction, during which it may act as a carrier. It is regenerated by further reactions.

competitive exclusion principle A principle of natural selection (in evolution) whereby similar species are forced to specialize ever more minutely so as not to overlap with each other in a particular niche; if they do not specialize adequately, they die and become extinct.

complement A protein substance in blood serum which reacts with almost all *antibody-antigen*

systems, lysing (breaking down) the antigen from the antibody and disappearing in the process.

complex In chemistry, a compound whose molecules involve co-ordination (or complex) bonds, often between a transition element and organic groupings.

complex In psychoanalysis, an association of mental factors in the unconscious which relate to an emotional experience involving something unacceptable to the individual, often affecting the individual's behaviour.

compound A substance consisting of two or more elements in chemical combination; it is made up of molecules. Unlike a mixture, a compound can be separated into its components only by chemical means.

conditioned reflex A (behavioural) reflex acquired by repetitive training and conditioning with an originally neutral stimulus.

conditioned stimulus An originally neutral stimulus applied in conditioning experiments which evokes a trained or conditioned response. In Pavlov's classical experiments with dogs, the neutral stimulus (the sound of a bell) originally evoked no salivation reflex; but after being presented for a time with an *unconditioned stimulus* (food), it became the conditioned stimulus which evoked the conditioned response.

corpuscle In biology, a free-floating or fixed cell or body such as a blood cell or the enclosed end of a sensory nerve.

cortex The outer layer of an organ or plant. For example, the cerebral cortex constitutes the outer nerve cells of the brain.

corticoid (or corticosteroid) Any of various steroid substances (mainly *hormones*) secreted by the adrenal cortex, or a synthetic substance closely resembling them.

crossing-over The interchange between chromatids of one or more pairs of allelic *genes* on homologous *chromosomes* which results in an overall recombination of genetic material. It occurs during the *meiosis* that characterizes *gamete* formation.

cyst A sac containing fluid or solid matter which forms or causes a swelling. In animals, cysts commonly occur in the skin or organs (such as the ovary) and may result from an obstruction (in a duct) or from a cell disorder.

cytoblast The *nucleus* of a cell.

cytochrome Any of a group of protein compounds containing incorporated iron, as in *haemoglobin*. Cytochromes are found in all *aerobic* plant and animal tissues, where they have an important role in oxidation-reduction reactions.

cytoplasm The viscous fluid inside a cell, including particles such as the *Golgi apparatus* and *mitochondria* but excluding the *nucleus*. The cytoplasm and the nucleus together form the *protoplasm* of a cell.

dark reaction A series of reactions in *photosynthesis* (which do not require light) in which carbon dioxide is incorporated into three-carbon sugar phosphate molecules; it depends on the *light reaction* (which does require light).

deamination The removal of an amino ($-NH_2$) group from an organic compound. In mammals, for example, deaminizing *enzymes* in the liver and kidneys oxidize *amino acids* (and the ammonia formed is converted into urea by the liver).

degradation The breaking down of compounds into simpler molecules; e.g., the action of enzymes brings about the degradation of proteins to amino acids.

dendrite One of the many branched protoplasmic projections of a nerve cell (*neuron*). Dendrites carry impulses into the nerve cell body and connect via *synapses* to *axons* of other nerve cells.

depressor nerve A nerve which, when stimulated induces reflex vasodilation and thus slows the heartbeat (resulting in a fall in blood pressure).

dialysis A method of separating dissolved colloids from non-colloids (crystalloids) using a semi-permeable membrane, which does not allow the passage of colloids. It is the main working principle of a kidney machine for removing waste products from blood.

diastole A period of relaxation in the rhythm of the heartbeat when the fibres of the heart muscle lengthen and the ventricles dilate and fill with blood.

dicotyledon Any member of the larger of the two subdivisions of the *angiosperms* (the other being the *monocotyledons*). Dicotyledon plants are characterized by having two seed-leaves (cotyledons), flower parts arranged in fours or fives (or multiples thereof), net-veined leaves, and vascular bundles in the stem arranged in a ring.

differentiation The transformation of cells (or tissues) of a uniform type into cells (tissues) that have distinct and specialized structures and functions.

diffusion The tendency of the molecules of a gas or mixture of gases to mix uniformly and spread to occupy evenly the whole of any vessel containing them. Molecules or ions of a dissolved substance (the solute) also tend to diffuse through the solvent to produce a solution of uniform concentration.

diphosphate A chemical compound containing two phosphate groups, as in *adenosine diphosphate* (ADP).

DNA (deoxyribonucleic acid) A naturally occurring compound found in the *chromosomes* of plant and animal cells which carries genetic information (and therefore functions as the biochemical basis for heredity). Its molecule consists of two long chains of *nucleotides* linked at regular intervals like the rungs of a ladder; the whole "ladder" is twisted into a double helix. Each nucleotide is composed of the sugar deoxyribose, a phosphate group and one of four nitrogenous *bases*. DNA stores the genetic code in the sequential arrangement of these bases; each linear sequence of three bases constitutes the code for one *amino acid* (see *codon*).

dominant Describing a *gene* that is expressed physically whether it is present as both or as only one of the pair that make up an *allele*. See also *recessive*.

echolocation In zoology, a method by which an animal locates an object by means of echoes reflected from it of high-pitched sounds emitted by the animal. Mammals that use echolocation include various species of bats and dolphins.

ectoderm The outer layer of cells in an embryo and all the tissues that it gives rise to.

efferent nerve A nerve that conducts impulses away from the central nervous system (brain and spinal cord). Most efferent nerves are *motor nerves* and run to effector organs.

ego The part of an individual's personality that recognizes reality and maintains the balance between primitive, instinctive wishes (the *id*), the restraint exercised by the conscience (the *superego*) and reality.

electroencephalograph (EEG) An instrument that records the electrical activity in the brain (brain waves). Electrodes attached to the surface of the scalp monitor changing electric potentials in the cerebral cortex and the signals are amplified and displayed on a cathode-ray oscilloscope or recorded on a multi-trace chart recorder.

electrolyte A substance that in the molten state or dissolved in a solvent consists of ions and can conduct an electric current. Typical electrolytes include acids, bases (in the chemical sense) and salts; their solutions are also termed electrolytes.

electron acceptor A chemical compound that can accept an electron and is reduced in doing so; it can therefore take part in oxidation-reduction reactions.

element A substance that is made up of atoms of the same atomic number; it cannot be converted chemically into any simpler substance.

endocytosis The ingestion of material by a cell, including *phagocytosis* and *pinocytosis*.

Phagocytosis is the engulfment and ingestion by a white blood cell of *bacteria* or other foreign particles; pinocytosis involves the absorption and ingestion by a cell of surrounding fluid by the folding-in of the cell membrane to form a vesicle which (eventually) releases some of its contents into the cell's *cytoplasm.*

endoderm The innermost of the three germ layers of an embryo.

endoplasmic reticulum A complex network of tubes in the *cytoplasm* of a cell, which are covered with membranes that are thought to control the exchange of matter in and out of the tubes; rough-surfaced tubes carry *ribosomes* and smooth-surfaced ones do not.

endoscope An instrument for making an internal examination of a body cavity. It consists of a tube with an optical system and a light source and is inserted into a natural opening or a small surgical incision. It may also have room for a catheter through which to introduce or remove various substances.

endplate A mass of motor nerve endings that penetrate a muscle fibre.

enteric Describing something concerning the intestinal tract.

enzyme Any of a large number of protein substances produced by living organisms that catalyse chemical reactions involved in various biological processes (see *catalyst*). Most enzymes are intracellular, although many occur in the digestive tract (where they act on and break down the components of food into simpler chemical substances). Enzymes act by combining temporarily with a substrate and many are specific to only one reaction; some require activation by a *co-enzyme.*

enzyme induction The stimulation of enzyme formation by the presence of its *substrate* or a derivative of the substrate.

epithelium A close-knit network of cells in tissues that line the surfaces of the body's cavities and tubes. It may be a single layer of cells or consist of several layers of flattened, cuboidal or columnar cells, often with a secretory function.

ethology The scientific study of animal behaviour and habits in a normal environment.

eugenics The study and manipulation of genetic qualities in the human population.

excitation In physiology, the stimulation of a sense receptor or nerve. In chemistry, the injection of energy into an atom (which may be part of a radical or molecule) which raises it or one of its components to a higher energy level.

exocytosis The ejection from a cell of undigested remnants of material.

exteroceptive Describing receptors that receive stimuli from outside the body, such as those of the ear and the eye.

fat Any of a large class of organic compounds (collectively called *lipids*) that consist of esters of glycerol with various fatty acids. Fats, oils (excluding mineral oils, which are *hydrocarbons*) and waxes are chemically similar. They are used as storage materials by animals and plants and are an essential part of the human diet. Most are digested in the intestine by the hydrolytic action of *enzymes* such as lipase. Stored fats can be quickly converted into fuel for energy.

fermentation A slow decomposition process brought about in organic substances by micro-organisms (e.g., *yeast* and *bacteria*) as a result of *enzyme* action. A common example is the alcoholic fermentation resulting from the action of zymase (an enzyme produced by yeast) on sugars, producing alcohol and carbon dioxide.

food chain A scheme that shows the interdependence of organisms in an ecosystem; each organism in the chain is the source of food of at least the next member of the chain.

gamete A sexually differentiated mature reproductive cell - in animals, typically a *spermatozoon* (male gamete) or an *ovum* (female gamete). The fusion of their two nuclei in fertilization results in a *zygote* which develops into an embryo.

gamma globulin One of a group of proteins or *immunoglobulins* in the blood that act as *antibodies* to specific infections. Gamma globulins extracted from the blood of a patient who has recovered from an infection may be used as *vaccines* to stimulate artificial immunity in others.

gastrula A stage in embryonic development following the *blastula* stage in which *gastrulation* occurs.

gastrulation Cell movements during embryonic development (after cleavage) in which cells move to the positions in which they eventually give rise to the organs of the growing embryo.

gemmule In early genetic theory, minute particles thought to consist of miniature copies of all parts of the body carried in the blood to the *gametes* and from which their larger forms eventually developed. In modern usage, a gemmule is a bud formed on a sponge that may break free and develop into a new animal.

gene A basic unit of heredity being part of a *chromosome.* Genes that occur as *alleles* control particular hereditary characteristics, each allelic partner occupying the same site on a pair of chromosomes (and one or both of which may be *dominant* or *recessive*).

gene pool All the genes found in a single interbreeding population of a plant or animal.

genetic engineering The artificial manipulation of the nucleic acids DNA or RNA to produce new, modified species of plants or, possibly, animals.

genetics The study of heredity and species variation in organisms.

genotype The genetic make-up of an organism as opposed to its physical characteristics (see *phenotype*).

germ plasm theory In early genetics, the theory that of the two tissue types in multicellular animals (somatoplasm in body cells and germ plasm in reproductive cells), only the integrity of germ plasm is necessary for the inheritance of characteristics.

glycolysis The transformation of glucose, by enzyme action, into *lactic acid* or pyruvic acid. This process usually occurs during the preliminary stages of *fermentation* and tissue respiration and provides energy for short-term bursts of activity.

Golgi apparatus (or body) A scattered structure of smooth double-membraned vesicles found in the *cytoplasm* of cells which may have secretory and/or transport roles in *metabolism*.

gymnosperm Any plant of a sub-division of the Spermatophyta distinguished from the other sub-division (the *angiosperms*) by having ovules relatively unprotected on the surface of the megasporophylls, which usually take the form of cones. Also (unlike angiosperms) very few gymnosperms have vessels in the *xylem* of their stems.

haemoglobin The red respiratory pigment in red blood cells, consisting of a protein containing iron (see *haemoprotein*).

haemoprotein A protein containing an iron-porphyrin group. The green plant pigment *chlorophyll* and the red blood pigment *haemoglobin* are both haemoproteins.

hermaphroditism A condition in which both male and female reproductive organs are present in the same organism.

heterozygous Describing a pair of allelic *genes* in which one is different from the other. See also *allele*; *homozygous*; *zygote*.

homeopathy A non-orthodox form of medical treatment in which very small doses of drugs that cause the symptoms of an illness are administered to treat it.

hominid Man and his man-like ape predecessors, which together constitute the family Hominidae.

homozygous Describing a pair of identical allelic *genes*. See also *allele*; *heterozygous*; *zygote*.

hormone Any of a group of substances present in plants (phytohormones) and animals which play essential roles in growth, development, function and behaviour. In animals, hormones are released from endocrine (ductless) glands into the bloodstream and take effect on more or less specific target organs or tissues.

hydrocarbon An organic compound consisting only of hydrogen and carbon.

hydrogen carrier A compound that accepts hydrogen ions in biochemical reactions and is therefore important in oxidation-reduction reactions such as the intracellular use of oxygen.

id One of the three aspects of personality (as used by Freud) and representing the primitive, instinctive aspect but which is constantly seeking expression but which is repressed by the *ego* (acknowledgement of reality) and the *superego* (social conditioning).

immunity An organism's resistance to infection. Immunity may be natural (as a result of the presence of natural *antibodies*) or acquired (as a result of *antigens* introduced by an infection, *immunization* or *vaccination*). Active immunity is induced by the introduction of antigens, and passive immunity is conferred by the introduction of antibodies from another organism.

immunization The technique of artificially conferring *immunity* to a disease by the introduction into the body of "live" *antigens*, usually given in repeated small doses.

immunoglobulin Any globulin (a protein) that acts as an *antibody*.

immunosuppressive Describing any drug that serves to suppress the body's natural immune response to an *antigen*.

imprinting A process of learning that takes place in the highly impressionable period soon after birth in which a pattern is set for the recognition of and reaction to particular objects (each with a particular function).

impulse In nerves, the electrical signal that is transmitted along a nerve fibre which has been sufficiently stimulated.

industrial melanism Dark or highly pigmented colouring in a "variety" of a species that evolves in a region with high atmospheric pollution.

inoculation The injection of micro-organisms, toxin or infected material (i.e., *antigens*) to stimulate *immunity* to a particular infection. See also *vaccination*.

insemination The introduction, by natural or artificial means, of sperm into the female reproductive tract (or the transfer of a fertilized ovum from one female to another).

intelligence quotient (IQ) An intelligence rating ascertained through answers to a test, which are expressed as a score and placed on an index of scores. Formerly, IQ was defined as (mental age/calendar age) $\times$ 100

interoceptive Describing a receptor that receives

stimuli that originate within the body.

invagination The formation of an inner pocket within a layer of cells by part of the layer pushing inwards to form a cavity that remains open to the original surface. See also *endocytosis*.

in vitro Describing the experimental observation of an organism (or part of an organism) in an artificial environment.

in vivo Describing the experimental observation of a biological process in an organism (or part of it) in its natural environment.

ion An electrically charged atom or group of atoms. Positively charged ions (cations), such as Na^+ and $(NH_4)^+$, have fewer electrons than are needed for the atom or group of atoms to be electrically neutral; negatively charged ions (anions), such as Cl^- and OH^-, have more.

isomerism The existence of two or more different substances that have the same chemical compositions but different arrangements of their atoms.

isotopes Species of the same chemical element (i.e., having the same atomic number) that differ in their mass numbers (and therefore in the number of neutrons in their atomic nucleus). An element's isotopes have identical chemical and physical properties, except those determined by the mass of the atom.

kymograph A recording produced by an instrument that detects variations such as small muscular contractions or slight changes in arterial blood pressure.

lactic acid An organic acid, chemical formula $CH_3CH(OH)COOH$ (hydroxypropanoic acid), which exists as three *stereoisomers*. It is formed in the body during *glycolysis* (the breakdown of glucose derived from glycogen), and occurs in sour milk (derived from lactose) and other foods where it is produced by the action of micro-organisms.

laparoscope A type of *endoscope* used for abdominal investigations.

leucocyte A white blood cell (with no *haemoglobin*) which serves chiefly to destroy foreign cells, such as pathogenic micro-organisms. There are three main types: granulocytes (neutrophils, basophils and eosinophils), lymphocytes and monocytes. They are produced in the bone marrow, although lymphocytes are also produced in the lymph nodes, thymus and spleen, and monocytes are formed in the cell walls of blood vessels and various organs.

Leyden jar An early form of condenser consisting of a glass jar with an interior and exterior coating of metal foil, used to store static electricity.

light reaction The part of the *photosynthesis* process in green plants that requires sunlight (as opposed to the *dark reaction*, which does not). During the light reaction light energy is used to generate ATP (by the *phosphorylation* of ADP), which is necessary for the dark reaction.

linkage group All the *genes* on a given *chromosome*; the genes are more or less linked to each other and, as a result, tend to be inherited together.

lipid Any of a group of diverse organic compounds that are *esters* of *fatty acids*. Typically, they are oily or greasy and insoluble in water (but soluble in organic solvents). Simple lipids – fatty-acid esters of glycerol – include oils, fats and waxes; they occur as a stored energy source in plants and animals.

luteinization The development of an ovum in a ruptured Graafian follicle within the ovary, initiated by oestrogen which in turn is activated by luteinizing *hormone*.

lysogeny The presence of non-virulent or temperate *bacteriophages* in a bacterium that do not lyse it (damage the outer cell membrane). The phage does not replicate after entering the bacterial cell, although its DNA combines with that of the bacterium and is reproduced with it every time the bacterium multiplies. The basic characteristics of the host bacterium remain unchanged.

lysosome A small double-membraned vesicle that occurs in the *cytoplasm* of certain animal (tissue) cells. Lysosomes contain various digestive *enzymes* or cell nutrients.

manometer A device for measuring liquid or gaseous pressure, consisting classically of a glass U-tube containing a liquid (such as mercury).

mast cell A granular cell common in fatty tissue that secretes heparin and histamine. It plays an important part in stimulating the coagulation of blood when the tissue is injured.

medium In bacteriology, an environment in which micro-organisms can be cultured. Common mediums include agar, broth and gelatin, often with added salts and trace elements.

meiosis Two successive special cell divisions of a diploid (paired-*chromosome*) cell to form four haploid (unpaired-chromosome) daughter cells such as *gametes*. See also *mitosis*.

melanin A dark brown pigment present as granules in cells, responsible for the yellow, brown or black colour of, for example, skin and hair.

melanocyte A cell that produces *melanin*.

membrane potential The potential difference that exists across a membrane or cell wall, such as that across the wall of a nerve cell (*neuron*).

mesoderm The central layer of embryonic cells between the *ectoderm* and the *endoderm*.

messenger RNA (mRNA) A single-stranded nucleic acid (made up of *nucleotides*) found in *ribosomes*, *mitochondria* and nucleoli of cells that carries coded information for building chains of *amino acids* into polypeptides. See *ribonucleic acid*.

metabolism The chemical processes that take place in an organism and result in the breakdown of large or complex organic molecules into simpler ones (catabolism) with the release of energy or result in the building-up of larger organic molecules from simpler ones (anabolism) and the storage of energy. These processes are usually moderated by *enzymes*.

micro-organism A (usually unicellular) organism that is too small to be seen with the naked eye. Common micro-organisms include *bacteria*, *viruses*, various fungi and protozoa; some are pathogenic (disease-causing).

microsome A minute particle occurring in the cytoplasm of a cell composed of vesicles with attached *ribosomes* which are thought to derive from the *endoplasmic reticulum*. Microsomes are also thought to give rise to *mitochondria*.

microtome A device for cutting extremely thin slices of tissue for microscopic examination. The tissue is embedded in wax or a synthetic resin (or is frozen) for ease of handling.

mimicry The similarity in behaviour or appearance of one animal to another as a form of protection; it is commonest among insects. In Batesian mimicry, a harmless animal is protected by its similarity in appearance to a toxic or distasteful animal. In Müllerian mimicry, the similarity in appearance between two or more equally dangerous species gives them mutual protection.

mitochondrion A microscopic double-membraned body that occurs in the *cytoplasm* of nearly every type of cell (except *bacteria* and blue-green algae). The inner membrane is folded into cristae which carry oxidative *enzymes* and some DNA. Mitochondria are the sites of much of the *metabolism* necessary for the production of ATP (including the citric acid cycle); they are also involved in the metabolism of lipids and *protein synthesis*.

mitosis The normal process of cell division in which the (paired) *chromosomes* duplicate at the beginning of the process and each of the two daughter cells formed has pairs consisting of one original and one new (replicated) chromosome. See also *meiosis*.

molecular biology The study of the chemical and physical properties of molecules that occur in living organisms.

monoclonal Describing genetically identical cells produced from one *clone*.

monocotyledon Any member of the smaller of the two subdivisions of the *angiosperms* (the other being the *dicotyledons*). Monocotyledon plants are characterized by having a single seed-leaf (cotyledon), flower parts arranged in threes (or multiples thereof), parallel-veined leaves, and closed vascular bundles arranged randomly in the stem tissue.

morphogenesis The development of forms and structures in an organism.

morphology The study of form and structure in an organism.

motor nerve A nerve (in the peripheral nervous system) that carries impulses from the central nervous system (brain and spinal cord) to an effector organ.

mutant A *gene*, organism or population that has undergone a change in character because of *mutation*.

mutation A spontaneous or artificially induced qualitative or quantitative change in a *gene* or *chromosome*. A mutation to a gene in a *gamete* is inherited and expressed in the next generation. Evolution occurs by *natural selection* of random mutations (although most mutations are harmful, often leading to the death of the organism concerned).

myelin A fatty substance that forms a sheath around the nerve fibres of vertebrates.

myeloma A malignant or non-malignant tumour that forms in bone-marrow cells.

myofibril One of many minute fibrils that together make up a fibre of smooth or striped muscle, running along the length of the muscle.

myosin A protein made up of a chain of polypeptides that forms filaments in smooth (or striped) muscle fibrils. During muscle contraction it combines with *actin* (another muscle protein, contained in thinner filaments) to form actomyosin; the actin filaments are pulled into the myosin filaments, which shortens the *myofibrils*.

natural selection The preservation of favourable and rejection of unfavourable variations within a species, such variations resulting from *mutations* (of *genes* or *chromosomes*). It is the principal process of evolution; variants with favourable mutations survive and therefore tend to leave more offspring, whereas variations with unfavourable or harmful mutations tend to die out (leaving fewer progeny).

neural fold One of two longitudinal (ectodermal) ridges along the dorsal surface of a vertebrate embryo. The ridges fuse to form the *neural tube*.

neural tube A tube in a vertebrate embryo formed by the fusion of the *neural folds*. It has a prominent bulge at the anterior end, which eventually develops into the brain; the rest of the tube gives rise to the spinal cord and the nerves of the peripheral nervous system.

neurofibril One of the many fibrils in the cytoplasm of a *neuron*, which extend into its *axon* and *dendrites*.

neuron A nerve cell, the structural unit of the nervous system of animals. Each neuron is composed of a cell body (perikaryon) containing *cytoplasm* (which encloses a *nucleus*) and an *axon* and *dendrites*. Impulses pass from neuron to neuron across a *synapse* between the axon of one nerve cell and the dendrites of an adjacent cell.

neurosecretory cell A nerve cell that secretes a chemical substance, such as a *hormone*.

neurosis A collective term for several mental disorders that result from psychological disturbances, rather than from a physiological illness. A neurotic patient is trying to resolve an unconscious conflict, which may manifest itself as, for example, hysteria, hypochondriasis or hyperanxiety.

neurotransmitter A chemical compound, such as adrenaline or *acetylcholine* (ACh), that is secreted by nerve fibre endings and, on diffusing across a *synapse* from the *axon* of a *neuron* to the *dendrites* of an adjacent one, transmit and perpetuate a nervous impulse.

notochord A skeletal rod of connective tissue that occurs in the embryos of *chordates*. It lies dorsally along the length of the embryo and is eventually replaced by the vertebral column and skull.

nucleated Describing a cell that has a *nucleus*.

nucleic acid One of many large organic molecules made up of long chains of *nucleotides* which occur in cells, particularly in their nuclei. Deoxyribonucleic acid (DNA) and ribonucleic acid (RNA) are the most important nucleic acids and are responsible for transmitting hereditary characters. The genetic code that controls *protein synthesis* is stored in triplet sequences (*codons*) of three nitrogenous *bases* along the DNA and RNA strands.

nucleotide A compound composed of a pentose sugar (such as ribose), a phosphate group and nitrogenous purine or pyrimidine *bases*; it is a structural unit of a *nucleic acid* molecule, and may also form part of a *co-enzyme*.

nucleus In biology, the central vital body of a plant or animal cell. Each nucleus is surrounded by a membrane and contains mainly *nucleoprotein* and *DNA* in the form of *chromosomes*. The nucleus is therefore essential to cell reproduction and the control of the whole cell's *metabolism*.

ontogeny The history of an individual's development and growth.

operant conditioning The conditioning of an individual's response (to a stimulus) by means of a reward so that the individual eventually behaves so as to be rewarded (see *conditioned reflex*).

optic vessel One of two bulges on each side of the anterior expansion of the *neural tube* in a vertebrate embryo from which arise the essential nervous structures of the eyes.

optical isomer (or enantiomorph) One of a pair of compounds whose chemical composition is similar but whose molecular structures are mirror images of each other. The presence of an asymmetric (usually carbon) atom makes each isomer optically active (i.e., its crystals or solutions rotate the plane of polarized light); the direction of rotation is different (left or right, denoted by *d* or *l*) for each isomer.

organelle Any sub-cellular structure with a specialized function, such as *mitochondria*, *lysosomes* or the *Golgi apparatus*.

organizers Cells in embryonic tissue that induce the morphological development of tissues in other parts of it.

organ of Golgi An elongated structure that occurs at the junction of a muscle and a tendon, which responds to *proprioceptive* stimuli.

osmosis The movement of any substance across a differentially permeable membrane down a chemical gradient from a solution of high concentration to one of lower concentration; eventually the molecular distribution of the two solutions is equalized. Osmosis occurs in all cells and sub-cellular organelles that are surrounded by membranes.

osmotic pressure The pressure that must be applied to a solution so that it no longer takes up pure solvent (usually water) across a membrane that is permeable to solvent but not to solute (the dissolved substance).

ovum An unfertilized egg-cell (a female *gamete*) which, in sexual reproduction develops into a new individual after fertilization (with a male gamete to form a *zygote*).

oxidation Any reaction in which oxygen is combined with another substance, hydrogen is removed from it, or in which an atom or group of atoms lose electrons.

oxygenation The combination of (gaseous or dissolved) oxygen with a substance, such as with the blood in the lungs during respiration.

oxyhaemoglobin *Haemoglobin* carrying oxygen. The *oxygenation* of haemoglobin takes place in the lungs (where the oxygen pressure is relatively high) and oxyhaemoglobin carries the oxygen in the bloodstream to the tissues (where the oxygen is released).

paedomorphosis The persistence of embryonic or juvenile characteristics into an adult form.

pangenesis An erroneous theory that stated that bodies in *gemmules* transported by the blood to a parent's reproductive cells represented invisible (but exact) copies of the rest of the organism. After fertilization and combination with the other parent's gemmules these bodies were supposed to develop and grow into the "adult" forms.

papilla A small growth from the surface of a tissue, such as the papillae on the surface of the tongue.

parthenogenesis Unisexual reproduction by multiplication of an *ovum*, in which an ovum develops into a new individual without being fertilized by a male *gamete*. The ovum is usually diploid (with paired *chromosomes*), and the offspring is usually identical to the parent.

pasteurization A method of treating a liquid, such as milk or wine, in which it is heated (to 62-65°C for 30 minutes or to 72°C for 15 seconds) and then quickly cooled. The heat kills micro-organisms that do not form spores (such as *Salmonella* bacteria).

pathogen Any disease-causing micro-organism.

peptide Any organic compound whose molecules are made up of *amino acids* joined by a peptide linkage ($-NH-CO-$) between the carboxyl group ($-COOH$) of one acid and the amino group ($-NH_2$) of the other. A long chain formed in this way is called a polypeptide. *Proteins* consist of one or more polypeptide chains cross-linked in various ways.

perfusion The *in vitro*-induced passage of blood or a nutrient fluid through the blood vessels of an organism to keep it supplied with oxygen and nutrients.

peristalsis A directional involuntary muscular contraction that occurs in body tubes, especially those of the alimentary canal, to move fluid or semi-fluid contents. The rhythmic contraction is produced by smooth muscle fibres and controlled by autonomic nerves.

phagocyte A white blood cell that ingests foreign substances, such as *bacteria* and dead cells or tissue. Those that remove debris are called macrophages; bacteria are ingested by microphages.

phagocytosis The process by which *phagocytes* surround foreign particles (by an amoeboid movement), engulf and digest them. See also *endocytosis*.

phenotype The total characteristics (physical and behavioural) displayed by an organism, excluding its genetic make-up (see *genotype*).

phloem Connective tissue that occurs in vascular plants which carries processed foods (such as sugars, minerals and proteins). It is characterized by the presence of sieve-tubes, parenchyma and companion cells.

phosphorylation The chemical addition of a phosphate group to a (organic) molecule. One of the most important biochemical phosphorylations is the addition of phosphate to ADP to form the energy-rich ATP. Phosphorylation involving light (as in *photosynthesis*) is termed photophosphorylation.

photosynthesis A process in which green plants transform light energy into chemical energy and manufacture *carbohydrates* and oxygen from a combination of water and carbon dioxide. The reactions take place within *chlorophyll*-containing *chloroplasts* and the energy is stored as ATP, formed by the *phosphorylation* of ADP. Photosynthesis takes place in stages (see *light reaction; dark reaction*).

phylogeny The history of the development of a species or other group of organisms.

pinocytosis The ingestion of the contents of a vesicle by a cell (see *endocytosis*).

placenta In mammals (excluding egg-laying monotremes) a flattened structure in the uterus that allows interaction between the blood circulation of the mother and the developing foetus to permit respiration and nutrition. It is formed by fusion of the *allantois* and *chorion* with the wall of the uterus. In plants, the placenta is the (fleshy) part of the wall of the carpel to which ovules become attached.

plane-polarized light Light in which the electric and magnetic vibrations of the waves are restricted to a single plane, the plane of the magnetic vibration being at right angles to that of the electric one.

plankton A colony of plants and animals that live near the surface of the sea or fresh water. It is a vital food source for larger organisms.

plasma The liquid (non-cellular) component of blood and lymph in which blood cells and platelets are suspended. It consists of water containing various dissolved substances, such as proteins, sugars and gases.

plasmolysis In a plant cell, the shrinkage of the cell contents away from the cell wall as a result of *osmosis* in which water diffuses out of the cell.

pluteus In echinoderms, an advanced larval stage characterized by bilateral symmetry.

polar body In *meiosis*, any of three (haploid) egg nuclei that develop from a secondary oocyte (the fourth nucleus is the *ovum*); the three polar bodies degenerate.

polysaccharide A carbohydrate consisting of

large molecules made up of many smaller units. See *carbohydrate*.

population genetics The study of the genetic make-up of a population, involving an analysis of the stability or fluctuation of various gene frequencies in an interbreeding group.

pre-operational Describing a stage of human development between the ages of two and seven years in which a child learns to imitate and acquires language to describe concrete objects.

prophage The DNA of a non-virulent *bacteriophage* that has become linked with the bacterial host's DNA and which is replicated with it. See *lysogeny*.

prophylaxis Preventive medical treatment.

proprioceptive Describing receptors (such as those in muscles) that respond to internal stimuli.

protein Any one of a group of complex nitrogen-containing organic compounds present in plants and animals and essential to the formation, repair and regeneration of tissues and as a source of energy. A protein molecule is composed of thousands of *amino acids* combined in one or more polypeptide chains. The arrangement of amino acids, which determine the properties of the protein, is itself ultimately determined by the sequence of *nucleotides* in DNA. Many proteins include other components (as well as amino acids), such as fats (lipoproteins) and carbohydrates (glycoproteins).

protein synthesis The building-up of a *protein*, one *amino acid* at a time, which takes place at the *ribosome* of a cell. It involves the production of *transfer RNA* (which has complementary bases to those of *messenger RNA*) to determine the correct order of amino acids.

protoplasm The contents of a living cell. It consists of the *nucleus* and *cytoplasm* bounded by a membrane (the cell wall) which mediates the passage of substances into and out of the cell.

protozoon A member of the sub-kingdom or phylum Protozoa, which includes the simplest and smallest organisms in the animal kingdom. Most are unicellular, and many reproduce asexually by some sort of fission or budding process; many live as parasites on other animals.

psychoanalysis A technique used to treat mental disorders (such as *neuroses*) by bringing unconscious problems into the patient's conscious mind.

psychotic Describing a severe mental disturbance or a person suffering from it, in which the individual loses touch with reality and suffers from delusions, hallucinations or mental confusion.

pulmonary circulation The movement of de-oxygenated blood from the right ventricle of the heart through the pulmonary arteries to the lungs, where it is oxygenated. The oxygenated blood is then transported by the pulmonary veins to the left atrium for circulation (via the left ventricle) round the body.

putrefaction The breakdown of organic matter, particularly by *bacteria* or fungi. The decomposition of *proteins*, especially, gives rise to bad-smelling amines and poisonous substances such as ptomaines and hydrogen sulphide.

quartan fever A type of fluctuating malarial fever that peaks every fourth day.

radioactive fallout Airborne radioactive material resulting from a natural phenomenon or from a man-made occurrence, such as the explosion of a nuclear bomb.

radioimmunoassay A technique that involves the radioactive labelling (using a radioactive isotope) of *antigens*, whose movements can then be followed using a radiation detector.

radiotherapy The use of ionizing radiation in medical treatment, particularly X-rays or radioactive isotopes.

recessive Describing a *gene* or genetic character that is the converse of *dominant*. A recessive gene has no phenotypic expression unless it is *homozygous*.

reciprocal innervation The reciprocal action of paired sets of nerves that have opposite effects on the same organ.

reduction A chemical reaction in which a substance gains hydrogen, loses oxygen, or gains electrons.

reflex action An involuntary response to a stimulus.

reflex arc The route of nervous impulses from the point of stimulation, along *sensory nerve* fibres to the central nervous system, and back along *motor nerve* fibres to the effector organ or muscle.

rejection In medicine, the destruction of transplanted tissues or organs by the immune system of the host.

replication A process that results in the exact duplication of a biochemical molecule. In the replication of DNA, for example, the two helical strands part and by complementary base-pairing a new strand is built onto each old half, to form two identical double-stranded DNA molecules.

repressor substance A substance produced by a DNA regulator *gene*. When the repressor is inactivated by an inducer, the DNA structural genes are freed for the synthesis of *messenger RNA*.

resting potential The potential difference across a nerve or muscle membrane in the absence of a stimulus.

reticulo-endothelial system A group of cells that exist in continual contact with the blood and lymph, i.e., in the bone marrow, spleen, liver and lymph nodes. They ingest bacteria, other foreign particles and dead tissue, and aid tissue repair.

Rhesus factor A substance present in the blood of most people, who are termed Rhesus positive (Rh^+); people lacking the factor are Rhesus negative (Rh^-). Rh^- people do not possess *antibodies* specific to the Rhesus *antigen*, but can acquire them by blood transfusion.

ribonucleic acid (RNA) A cellular substance found mainly in *microsomes, mitochondria* and nucleoli. It has long molecules, usually consisting of a single chain of *nucleotides* formed from the sugar ribose, a phosphate group, and one of the four nitrogenous bases that occur in DNA (except for thymine, which is replaced by uracil). RNA has an important function in *protein synthesis; messenger RNA* (mRNA) carries the coded information from the *chromosome* (DNA) to the *ribosomes,* where protein is manufactured. Ribosomes are composed mainly of RNA, as are many *viruses.*

ribosome A minute granular particle composed of protein and RNA and present in the *cytoplasm* of plant and animal cells. Often associated with *endoplasmic reticulum,* ribosomes occur singly or in clusters (called polyribosomes). They play an important part in *protein synthesis.*

RNA See *ribonucleic acid.*

Schwann cell In vertebrates, the neurilemma cell of myelinated peripheral nerve fibres, important in the manufacture of *myelin.* On myelin-coated fibres a Schwann cell occurs between each pair of adjacent nodes.

self-pollination The pollination of a plant by itself, whether intra- or interfloral.

sensori-motor phase The first stage in human mental development from birth to about two years of age in which reflex actions lead to an awareness of the permanence of objects.

sensory nerve An afferent nerve of the peripheral nervous system, made up of sensory *neurons,* which carries impulses to the central nervous system.

sepsis The invasion of tissue by pathogenic micro-organisms and their products. Sepsis involving bacteria throughout the bloodstream is commonly termed blood poisoning.

sodium pump A hypothetical mechanism that maintains the asymmetry of the ionic (concentration) balance across a nerve cell membrane, reflected in the cell's *resting potential.*

sodium theory A theory which proposes that the excitation of a nerve results from momentary changes in the selective permeability of a nerve cell membrane, which admits sodium and chloride ions into the cell and allows potassium ions to diffuse out. The ion movements briefly reverse the polarization of the membrane, resulting in an *action potential* which constitutes the nerve impulse.

somatic cell Any cell in an organism, excluding the reproductive cells.

speciation The formation and development of species.

spermatozoon or **sperm** A male germ cell (*gamete*). It possesses a flat oval head (containing the nucleus), a middle piece (containing *mitochondria*), and a long tail of cytoplasm; it moves using a whip-like motion of the tail. At fertilization, the nucleus of the sperm fuses with that of an *ovum* to form a *zygote.*

spirillium A bacterium with a spiral shape (see *bacteria*).

spirochaete A bacterium with a flexible spiral shape (see *bacteria*).

spontaneous generation (abiogenesis) A concept, now discredited, which proposed that living matter can originate from non-living matter.

spore A (usually) unicellular reproductive cell in *bacteria,* plants and some *protozoa.* Often spores are released in enormous numbers to ensure that at least some of them survive. Bacterial spores are extremely hardy and can survive prolonged exposure to extreme temperatures.

sporozoite A *protozoon* of the class Sporozoa, such as the malarial parasite *Plasmodium.*

staining The selective pigmentation of microscopic objects and tissues so that they or their structure may be more easily seen.

staphylococcus A bacterium that takes the form of irregular clusters of spherical cocci (see *bacteria*).

stereoisomer One of two (or more) isomers that have the same molecular structure but which differ in the spatial arrangement of their atoms.

stone The common name for a calculus, a hard accretion of organic or inorganic salts that precipitate and grow in the kidneys, urinary tract or gall bladder. Calculi are often associated with, or cause, infection in the organs concerned.

streptococcus A bacterium that takes the form of a chain of spherical cocci (see *bacteria*).

subarachnoid Describing the fluid-filled region between the arachnoid membrane and the pia mater membrane which surround the brain and spinal cord.

substrate In biochemistry, a substance on which an *enzyme* acts.

sugar A mono- or disaccharide, characterized by a sweet taste, crystalline form and solubility in water, and grouped according to its number of carbon atoms (e.g., a pentose has five carbon atoms, a hexose has six). The sugar glucose is a key substance in the metabolism of plants and animals; ordinary cane or beet sugar is sucrose. See *carbohydrate*.

superego The part of an individual's personality that includes self-criticism (and therefore conscience), and which enforces the rules for social behaviour. See also *id; ego*.

synapse The point of contact between two nerve cells (*neurons*). Impulses are usually transmitted across the synaptic gap by *nerve transmitter* chemicals.

syndrome A collection of various symptoms that together characterize a particular condition or disorder.

systole A phase in the cycle of heart muscle action in which it contracts, emptying the ventricles (into the arterial system) and allowing the atria to fill.

tertian fever A type of fluctuating malarial fever that peaks every third day.

thermocouple An instrument that measures temperature by making use of thermoelectricity. It incorporates two wires of different metals joined at their ends. One junction is maintained at a constant (low) temperature; the temperature is measured at the other ("hot") junction in terms of the electric current generated in the circuit.

thermodynamics The study of the laws that govern heat as a form of energy and its transformation and conservation.

tolerance The ability (of an organism) to sustain the effects of a drug or poison without harm. Tolerance can be acquired, and built up, by repeated small doses of the drug or poison.

toxicity A measure of the poisonous nature of a substance.

toxin A poison (often a protein), usually produced by *bacteria*. Bacterial toxins are classified as endotoxins, which affect only local tissues, or as exotoxins, which are released into the bloodstream and can cause damage far from their site of origin.

transfer RNA (tRNA) A relatively small molecule of *ribonucleic acid*, the function of which is to carry *amino acids* to *ribosomes* where *protein synthesis* occurs. Each amino acid is borne by a different tRNA molecule. tRNA is complementary to *messenger RNA* (mRNA).

transformation In genetics, the substitution of one section of *DNA* by another. It requires at least two cross-overs (or breaks) in the *DNA* and is a source of genetic variation.

transpiration The evaporation of water vapour from plants, mostly through the stomata and sometimes the cuticle. The movement of water within the plant transports mineral salts via the *xylem* to the leaves, where transpiration also helps to cool the plant.

tricarboxylic acid cycle (Krebs' cycle) The final stages in the biochemical breakdown of *carbohydrates*, whose oxidation releases energy, which take the form of a succession of *enzyme*-catalysed reactions.

tripeptide A sequence of three *amino acids*, often occurring in the biochemical synthesis or breakdown of *proteins*.

trophoblast Epithelial cells that surround all the structures of a placental embryo, forming the outer layer of the *chorion* and the embryonic side of the *placenta*.

trypanosome A protozoon of the genus *Trypanosoma*, many of which are parasitic on insects which transmit them as *pathogens* to human beings. Sleeping sickness (trypanosomiasis) is caused by a trypanosome carried by the tsetse fly.

ultrasound Sound waves at a frequency beyond the range of normal human hearing (more than 20KHz). Bats, cetaceans and some insects emit ultrasound.

unconditioned reflex A behavioural reflex or response that is natural and not acquired by training or conditioning (see *conditioned reflex*).

unconditioned stimulus A natural stimulus unassociated with behavioural training; it evokes a natural or unconditioned reflex or response (see *conditioned stimulus*).

uniformitarianism A theory concerning the evolution of the Earth that acknowledges the constant character and continual action of natural forces (such as erosion) that shape its surface features.

urea cycle (Krebs-Henseleit cycle) A succession of reactions in which nitrogen (in the form of ammonia) is metabolized to produce urea.

vaccination *Inoculation* with a killed or attenuated virus or bacterium to confer resistance by stimulating the immune response to it (i.e., the production of the appropriate *antibodies*).

vaccine A suspension of killed or attenuated pathogenic micro-organisms (such as viruses or bacteria) used for the treatment or prevention of an infectious disease.

vacuole A fluid-filled vesicle that occurs in the *cytoplasm* of cells.

vascular Describing the systems that conduct fluids in plants (*xylem* and *phloem*) and animals (the blood and lymph systems).

vasoconstriction The constriction of vessels especially blood vessels.

vector A carrier (often an insect) of a *pathogenic* micro-organism, which may be parasitic on the vector and transmitted to other animals through the vector's bite.

vernalization A technique for controlling the flowering times of plants, particularly crop plants (cereals) that are normally sown in winter. It involves moistening the seed so that it just germinates and exposing the seedling's radicles for a few weeks to temperatures just above freezing. The plant then behaves like a spring-sown plant and crops relatively early in the summer of the same year, with obvious economic advantages.

vesicle A small fluid-filled bladder or blister.

vestigial Describing a partial, diminished or redundant structure in an organism.

virus A parasitic micro-organism (often *pathogenic* that consists of a strand of *nucleic acid* covered with a protein or lipoprotein layer. Viruses that parasitize animals contain DNA or RNA; those that live on plants contain RNA only; and most *bacteriophages* contain DNA only. Viruses infect cells by injecting their nucleic acid into them, where it activates further synthesis of virus cells. They may be spread by *vectors*; in air, soil or water; or by physical contact with an infected organism.

vitalism A now discredited belief that the life, development and functions of organisms result from a vital force that only living organisms possess.

vitamin An accessory food factor, one of a group of organic substances (excluding fats, carbohydrates, proteins and minerals) that play an important part in the development, metabolic processes amd health of the body. Most vitamins cannot be synthesized in the body and must be obtained from the diet; exceptions include vitamin A (formed from the plant pigment carotene), vitamin D (manufactured by a process involving the action of ultraviolet light on the skin) and vitamin K (which is synthesized by intestinal bacteria).

white blood cell See *leucocyte*.

X-ray diffraction A method of determining the structure of molecules, particularly those of crystals, by analysing the way in which their atoms diffract a beam of X-rays.

xylem The vascular tissue in a plant that carries water and dissolved substances (such as minerals) from the roots and throughout the plant. Primary xylem develops by differentiation from the procambium and is divided into protoxylem (produced before its surrounding area becomes elongated) and metaxylem (formed after elongation); secondary xylem develops from the cambium. Xylem tissue is composed of basic cells (tracheids), vessels, fibres and undifferentiated tissue (parenchyma). The woody stems of mature plants consist mainly of xylem.

yeast Any of the many species of unicellular fungi of the class Ascomycetes of the division Ascomycota. Yeasts reproduce asexually by alternation of (diploid and haploid) generations, which results in a spore-forming *zygote*. Yeasts contain *enzymes* which are exploited commercially (in brewing and baking, for example) because of their ability to initiate *fermentation* (e.g., of sugars to produce alcohol). They are also a dietary source of protein and vitamin B.

zygote A fertilized *ovum* formed by the union of male and female *gametes*. It contains paired *chromosomes*, half of each pair being derived from each of the gametes.

Index

The index entry in **bold** type will direct you to the main text entry in which the information you require is given.

157